◇ "南京师范大学研究生课程案例库"建设项目经费资助

法律英语翻译案例教程

A Case Coursebook for Legal English Translation

董晓波　主编

清华大学出版社
北京交通大学出版社
·北京·

内容简介

本书从语言学、法学及翻译学三维角度对法律英语翻译进行较为全面、系统的诠释，立足于高素质专门化翻译人才之培养创新，着重于专业化与学术化之高度结合，理论与实践相得益彰，策略与技巧有机融合，内容丰富、系统，视野宽阔，素材新颖、典型、应有尽有。

本书主要供高等院校英语专业（经贸、法律、翻译等方向）本科生和研究生，法律专业的本科生、研究生，以及英语教师、法律英语研究人员作为教材或参考书使用。

本书封面贴有清华大学出版社防伪标签，无标签者不得销售。
版权所有，侵权必究。侵权举报电话：010-62782989　13501256678　13801310933

图书在版编目（CIP）数据

法律英语翻译案例教程／董晓波主编. —北京：北京交通大学出版社：清华大学出版社，2015.7（2018.8 重印）
ISBN 978-7-5121-2312-0

Ⅰ.①法… Ⅱ.①董… Ⅲ.①法律-英语-翻译-教材 Ⅳ.①H315.9

中国版本图书馆 CIP 数据核字（2015）第 153079 号

策划编辑：王晓春
责任编辑：王晓春　　特邀编辑：孙晴霞
出版发行：清 华 大 学 出 版 社　　邮编：100084　　电话：010-62776969　　http://www.tup.com.cn
　　　　　北京交通大学出版社　　邮编：100044　　电话：010-51686414　　http://www.bjtup.com.cn
印　刷　者：北京时代华都印刷有限公司
经　　　销：全国新华书店
开　　　本：185 mm×260 mm　　印张：20.75　　字数：518 千字
版　　　次：2015 年 7 月第 1 版　　2018 年 8 月第 2 次印刷
书　　　号：ISBN 978-7-5121-2312-0/H·432
定　　　价：42.00 元

本书如有质量问题，请向北京交通大学出版社质监组反映。对您的意见和批评，我们表示欢迎和感谢。
投诉电话：010-51686043，51686008；传真：010-62225406；E-mail：press@bjtu.edu.cn。

前言

随着我国加入世贸组织和世界经济一体化进程的不断加快,国际交流合作日益增多,涉外法务活动空前频繁,法律翻译的重要性日益凸显。为了适应时代需求,培养高层次、应用型专门人才,国务院学位委员会 2007 年 1 月通过了翻译硕士专业学位。为了适应翻译硕士专业学位案例教学的需要,本教材以真实的翻译案例为基础,从语言学、法学及翻译学三维角度对法律英语翻译进行较为全面、系统的诠释。其中每个案例设计由三部分组成:① 译例研究,汉译英、英译汉全面展开,目的掌握重点难点词汇、翻译要点;② 技能拓展,详细讲解各类翻译技巧,介绍专业化法律知识,术语积累;③ 练习,对词汇、篇章进行强化训练。为了方便自学,所有练习均在书后附有参考答案。

实践能力原则是案例教学的第一原则,实践能力是案例教学的出发点和立足点,案例教学注重培养学生的思维能力、分析能力、判断能力,以及运用所学到的知识处理复杂问题的能力。案例教学为理论与实践的整合提供了一条独特的路径,在理论与实践的沟壑之间架设了一道桥梁。本教材的特点就是以案例为媒介、以问题为起点,结合翻译理论及其技巧点拨,着重专业化与学术化之高度结合,理论与实践相得益彰。

作为"南京师范大学研究生课程案例库"建设项目的研究成果,本书的许多内容在南京师范大学翻译硕士专业学位"法律文本翻译"的课堂上讲授过,取得了良好的效果。现将内容整理、完善成书,以飨读者。在整个写作过程中,作者力求完美,但是限于水平和资料等原因,不乏偏颇和疏漏之处,恳请广大同仁和读者不吝指正,以便将来进一步充实与完善。此外,感谢研究生黄戈、汪梦竹、蒋歌、周嘉慧、苏菲菲、李慧等同学帮助搜集资料、整理书稿。

董晓波

2015 年 6 月

目录 Contents

Unit One　Legal System　法律制度 ·· 1

  Section I　译例研究 ·· 1
    Passage One　Introduction to the U.S. Legal System ················ 1
    Passage Two　社会主义法系 ·· 6
  Section II　技能拓展 ·· 9
    翻译技巧　法律术语的特点及翻译 ····································· 9
    法律宝典　法律体系及其分类 ··· 10
  Section III　巩固练习 ·· 13

Unit Two　Constitutional Law and Constitutionalism　宪法与宪政 ········· 16

  Section I　译例研究 ·· 16
    Passage One　The Constitution of the United States of America ····· 16
    Passage Two　中华人民共和国宪法 ·································· 22
  Section II　技能拓展 ··· 30
    翻译技巧　shall 的使用和翻译 ······································· 30
    法律宝典　宪法历史与发展 ·· 32
  Section III　巩固练习 ·· 34

Unit Three　The Legal Profession　法律职业 ······························ 37

  Section I　译例研究 ·· 37
    Passage One　The Bar ··· 37
    Passage Two　法律职业中的妇女和少数民族 ························· 43
  Section II　技能拓展 ··· 49
    翻译技巧　法律文本翻译的步骤和要点 ······························· 49
    法律宝典　Lawyer 是"律师"？ ······································ 51
  Section III　巩固练习 ·· 53

Unit Four　Administrative Law　行政法 ·································· 55

  Section I　译例研究 ·· 55
    Passage One　Introduction to Administrative Law ················· 55

I

Passage Two　行政法的概念和基本原则 ………………………………… 60
　　Section II　技能拓展 …………………………………………………………… 64
　　　翻译技巧　法律文本翻译中的转换 ……………………………………… 64
　　　法律宝典　行政法的过去与现在 ………………………………………… 68
　　Section III　巩固练习 ………………………………………………………… 72

Unit Five　Civil Law　民法 …………………………………………………… 74

　　Section I　译例研究 …………………………………………………………… 74
　　　Passage One　The Institutes of Justinian …………………………………… 74
　　　Passage Two　民法法系 …………………………………………………… 80
　　Section II　技能拓展 …………………………………………………………… 84
　　　翻译技巧　法律文本翻译中的增补和省略 ……………………………… 84
　　　法律宝典　民法 …………………………………………………………… 88
　　Section III　巩固练习 ………………………………………………………… 92

Unit Six　Criminal Law　刑法 ………………………………………………… 94

　　Section I　译例研究 …………………………………………………………… 94
　　　Passage One　The Legal Definition of Crime ……………………………… 94
　　　Passage Two　我国刑法中的正当防卫 …………………………………… 99
　　Section II　技能拓展 ………………………………………………………… 102
　　　翻译技巧　法律文本程式化、固定结构的翻译 ………………………… 102
　　　法律宝典　正当防卫 ……………………………………………………… 105
　　Section III　巩固练习 ………………………………………………………… 109

Unit Seven　Contract Law　合同法 …………………………………………… 112

　　Section I　译例研究 ………………………………………………………… 112
　　　Passage One　Introduction to Contract Law ……………………………… 112
　　　Passage Two　中华人民共和国合同法 …………………………………… 117
　　Section II　技能拓展 ………………………………………………………… 123
　　　翻译技巧　英语贸易合同汉译技巧的探讨 ……………………………… 123
　　　法律宝典　合同法的形成和发展 ………………………………………… 127
　　Section III　巩固练习 ………………………………………………………… 131

Unit Eight　The Law of Property　财产法 …………………………………… 133

　　Section I　译例研究 ………………………………………………………… 133
　　　Passage One　Real Property Law ………………………………………… 133
　　　Passage Two　中华人民共和国民法通则 ………………………………… 139
　　Section II　技能拓展 ………………………………………………………… 146
　　　翻译技巧　法律英语词汇的特点及其翻译 ……………………………… 146
　　　法律宝典　两大法系财产法的差异 ……………………………………… 150

Section III　巩固练习 ··· 153

Unit Nine　The Intellectual Law　知识产权法 ······························· 155

　　Section I　译例研究 ··· 155
　　　　Passage One　Copyright Protection ·· 155
　　　　Passage Two　中华人民共和国专利法 ······································· 161
　　Section II　技能拓展 ·· 166
　　　　翻译技巧　法律语言的语言特征 ··· 166
　　　　法律宝典　知识产权分类与保护 ··· 170
　　Section III　巩固练习 ··· 173

Unit Ten　Law of Succession　继承法 ·· 175

　　Section I　译例研究 ··· 175
　　　　Passage One　Last Will of Michael Joseph Jackson ······················ 175
　　　　Passage Two　中华人民共和国继承法 ······································ 182
　　Section II　技能拓展 ·· 187
　　　　翻译技巧　法律翻译的基本原则 ··· 187
　　　　法律宝典　继承法基础知识 ··· 194
　　Section III　巩固练习 ··· 197

Unit Eleven　Commercial Law　商法 ··· 199

　　Section I　译例研究 ··· 199
　　　　Passage One　Convention on Combating Bribery of Foreign Public Officials in
　　　　　　　　　　International Business Transactions ··························· 199
　　　　Passage Two　个体工商户、个人合伙与法人 ····························· 204
　　Section II　技能拓展 ·· 211
　　　　翻译技巧　国际商法的语言特点及翻译 ···································· 211
　　　　法律宝典　国际商法基础知识 ·· 215
　　Section III　巩固练习 ··· 219

Unit Twelve　Securities Law　证券法 ·· 221

　　Section I　译例研究 ··· 221
　　　　Passage One　Registration of Securities and Taking Effect of Registration
　　　　　　　　　　Statement ·· 221
　　　　Passage Two　证券发行 ··· 227
　　Section II　技能拓展 ·· 232
　　　　翻译技巧　信用证英语的语言特点及翻译 ································· 232
　　　　法律宝典　金融证券基础知识 ·· 238
　　Section III　巩固练习 ··· 243

III

Unit Thirteen　Public Law　国际公法 ······ 245

Section I　译例研究 ······ 245
Passage One　The Rio Declaration on Environment and Development ······ 245
Passage Two　公民权利和政治权利国际公约 ······ 249
Section II　技能拓展 ······ 253
翻译技巧　被动语态在法律英语中的运用及翻译 ······ 253
法律宝典　国际法基础知识 ······ 257
Section III　巩固练习 ······ 260

Unit Fourteen　Arbitration　仲裁 ······ 264

Section I　译例研究 ······ 264
Passage One　Convention on the Recognition and Enforcement of Foreign Arbitral Awards ······ 264
Passage Two　中华人民共和国仲裁法 ······ 268
Section II　技能拓展 ······ 273
翻译技巧　论法律专业术语的特殊性及其英译技巧 ······ 273
法律宝典　仲裁基础知识 ······ 276
Section III　巩固练习 ······ 279

Unit Fifteen　The World Trade Organization　世界贸易组织 ······ 282

Section I　译例研究 ······ 282
Passage One　Marrakesh Agreement Establishing the World Trade Organization ······ 282
Passage Two　中华人民共和国加入议定书 ······ 286
Section II　技能拓展 ······ 291
翻译技巧　法律文本翻译中模糊词语的处理 ······ 291
法律宝典　世界贸易组织基础知识 ······ 294
Section III　巩固练习 ······ 297

Keys ······ 300

References　参考文献 ······ 321

Unit One

Legal System
法 律 制 度

Section I 译例研究

>> **Passage One**
Introduction to the U.S. Legal System

  The U.S. Constitution which became binding on the U.S. people in 1788 is the origin of U.S. legal system. The federal Constitution comprises seven articles and twenty-seven amendments. Articles I, II and III set forth the basic structure of the U.S. government. Article I defines congressional lawmaking powers. Article II sets forth the presidential executive powers, and Article III establishes federal judicial powers. The first ten amendments to the U.S. Constitution, known as the Bill of Right, enumerate certain individual liberties that must be protected against government infringement. The rest of the Constitution contains miscellaneous other provisions, many of which are intended to maintain a dual system of government in which the federal government shares sovereignty with the states.

  The U.S. Constitution is the highest law in the land and the foundation on which all U.S. law has been built. It effectively built the dual system of government in which the federal government shares sovereignty with the states. Under the Constitution, both the federal government and each state government are divided into executive, legislative, and judicial branches and then form a system of separated power, check and balance among the branches.

Sources and Hierarchy of Law

The Constitution

  The federal Constitution establishes a system of the federal government and defines the boundaries of authority granted to the government. The U.S. Constitution is the preeminent source of law in U.S. legal system, and all other rules, whether created by the state or federal government, must comply with its requirements. The federal courts have sole authority to interpret the Constitution and to evaluate the federal constitutionality of federal or state laws.

International Treaties

Treaties entered into by the United States are also considered the supreme law of the land pursuant to the U.S. Constitution, as are federal laws. In the case of a conflict between a treaty and a federal statute, the one that is later in time or more specific will typically control. Treaties are often implemented by federal statutes.

Federal Statutes

Federal Statutes are created by the legislative branch of the federal government. Statutes can be used to raise revenue, define crimes, create administrative agencies, and generally determine public policy. Federal Statutes are published first in Slip Law, then in the Statutes at Large, and subsequently in the United States Code.

Agency Rules and Executive Orders

Administrative agencies are usually created by legislative action and operate under the control of the executive branch. Federal administrative bodies issue rules and regulations of a quasi-legislative character; valid federal regulations have the force of law and pre-empt state laws and rules.

Rules and regulations may be issued only under statutory authority granted by Congress. The President also has broad power to issue executive orders. An executive order is a directive from the President to other officials in the executive branch. Proposed and final rules, executive orders, and other executive branch notices are published daily in the Federal Register. No person may be subject to any rule that is required to be published in the Federal Register and is not so published. Federal regulations are published in the Code of Federal Regulations. The federal courts have sole authority to review agency rules and actions to ensure that they are legal under the substantive federal statute.

Judicial Opinions

The United States is a common law country. Every U.S. state has a legal system based on the common law, except Louisiana. Common law has no statutory basis; judges establish common law by applying previous decisions (precedents) to present cases. Although typically affected by statutory authority, broad areas of the law, most notably relating to property, contracts, and torts, are traditionally part of the common law. These areas of the law are mostly within the jurisdiction of the states, and thus state courts are the primary source of common law. Federal common law is relatively narrow in scope, being limited primarily to clearly federal issues that have not been addressed by a statute.

State Constitutions and Statutes

State constitutions are the supreme law within the state. Although a state constitution may grant greater rights than those secured by the federal Constitution, it cannot provide lesser rights than the federal Constitution does. State statutes must conform to the respective state's constitution. All state constitutions and legislation can be pre-empted by federal legislation or the federal Constitution.

Municipal charters, ordinances, rules, and regulations apply only to local issues; either state or federal law typically can pre-empt them.

▶ 词汇提示

set forth　陈述，阐明
enumerate　*v.* 列举
miscellaneous　*adj.* 各种各样的
hierarchy　*n.* 层级，位阶
preeminent　*adj.* 卓越的，超群的
comply with　遵守，按……行事
pursuant　*adj.* 依照的，依据的
in the case of　在……情况下
Slip Law　议案单行法
Statutes at Large　法规大全
United States Code　美国法典
pre-empt　*v.* 优先于
Federal Register　联邦公报，联邦日志
subject to　受制于
Code of Federal Regulations　美国联邦法规
agency rules　机构法规
substantive　*adj.* 实体的
Louisiana　路易斯安那州
supreme law　最高法
conform to　符合，遵照
municipal charters　市政宪章

▶ 法律术语

article　*n.* 条款，规约
amendment　*n.* 修正，修正案
judicial　*adj.* 司法的，法律的
Bill of Rights　人权法案
infringement　*n.* 违反法规，侵犯权利
provision　*n.* 规定，条款
dual system　双轨制
authority　*n.* 权力
statute　*n.* 法令，法规，条例，成文法
implement　*v.* 实施，履行

constitutionality　*n.* 符合宪法
legislative action　立法行为
issue　*v.* 颁布
quasi-legislative　*adj.* 准立法的
review　*v.* 复查，复审
common law　普通法系
precedent　*n.* 判例，惯例
tort　*n.* 侵权行为
jurisdiction　*n.* 管辖权
ordinance　*n.* 条例，法令，法规

要点解析

1.《人权法案》（Bill of Rights），是指美国《1787年宪法》通过后首批10条宪法修正案。它是应数个州的要求，于1789年9月25日由国会通过10条修正案并交由各州批准。从1791年12月15日这些修正案得到批准起，开始生效。因其主要内容是弥补宪法在人民权利等方面的不足，故被后人称为《人权法案》。

2. 单行法（Slip Law），是指一些单行条例。一般英美法系采用的判例法就主要是单行法的模式，这与大陆法系制定法典的做法是相对的。单行法是和一般法相对应的称谓。一般法规定的是比较综合的法律问题，而单行法是对一般法中规定的某个特别法律事项进行的特别规定。

3.《美国法典》（United States Code），美国任何一部法律的产生首先由美国国会议员提出法案，当这个法案获得国会通过后，将被提交给美国总统给予批准，一旦该法案被总统批准（有可能被否决）就成为法律（Act）。一部法律通过后，国会众议院就把该法律的内容公布在《美国法典》上。

4. Under the constitution, both the federal government and each state government are divided into executive, legislative, and judicial branches and then form a system of separated power, check and balance among the branches.

本句采用增译法，明确了是在"联邦和州之间、在各个不同部门之间"构筑起了法律制度，将前半句的 the federal government and each state government 和后半句中的 among the branches 统一起来，意思完整，表达清晰。

5. Treaties entered into by the United States are also considered the supreme law of the land pursuant to the U.S. Constitution, as are federal laws.

理解本句子的要点在于明确句子主干，即：Treaties are considered the supreme law of the land. 然后，再把定语等一个个加上去，将 pursuant to the U.S. Constitution 置于句首，表示来源；entered into by the United States 修饰条约；而 as are federal laws 的意思即 as federal laws are the supreme law of the land，因此可以译为"相当于联邦法律"。

6. Federal common law is relatively narrow in scope, being limited primarily to clearly federal issues that have not been addressed by a statute.

"being limited to..."是一个非谓语动词词组，进一步解释联邦普通法范围狭窄的原因。

 参考译文

美国法律体制简介

美国的法律体制根源于1788年生效的联邦宪法，该宪法有七款条文和二十七条修正案。宪法第一、二、三条规定美国政府的基本结构，其中第一条确立国会的立法权，第二条确立总统的行政权，第三条确立联邦司法权；宪法的前十条修正案被称为权利法案，列举特定为防止政府侵犯人权而应加以保护的个人权利；宪法的其余部分主要是为保持联邦政府和州共享主权的双轨制政府体制而设的各项规定。

联邦宪法是美国最高位阶的法律，是制定美国国内其他法律的基础。它有效地确立了联邦政府和州共享主权的双轨政府体制，而且将联邦政府及各州政府分为行政、立法和司法三部门，从而在联邦和州之间、在各个不同部门之间构筑起彼此权利独立、相互制衡的法律体制。

美国法律的渊源及位阶

宪法

联邦宪法构建了联邦政府体系，并确定授予联邦政府权限的范围。联邦宪法是美国法律最重要的渊源，无论是州或是联邦政府所制定的任何法律法规，与联邦宪法冲突的都归于无效。联邦法院是唯一有权解释宪法并审查联邦法律或州法律合宪性的权威机构。

国际条约

依照美国宪法，美国参加的条约也被认为是全国最高位阶的法律，相当于联邦法律。在条约与联邦立法相冲突的情形下，适用时间在后或者有特别规定的一方。但条约通常需通过联邦立法确认才能实施。

联邦法规

联邦法规是由联邦政府立法部门制定的，旨在提高税收、定义犯罪行为、设立行政机构，并通常用于决定公共政策。联邦法规颁布的形式主要有议案单行法、法规大全和美国法典三种。

联邦机构的规章和行政命令

行政机构通常是通过立法行为设立并在行政部门的管理下运作的。联邦行政机构颁布具有准立法性质的规章，生效的联邦规章具有法律效力，并对州法律和法规具有优先性。

联邦行政机构仅可依国会授予的法定权力而颁布法规和规章。总统也拥有广泛的权力发布行政命令，行政命令是总统对行政部门其他公务员的指示。试行的及最终的法规、行政命令及其他行政部门的通知每日公布在联邦日志上。任何法规如被要求在联邦日志上公布而未根据要求进行公布的，将不对任何人产生约束力。联邦法规以联邦政府行政法规汇编的形式颁布。联邦法院是唯一有权审查机构法规及政府机构行为并根据实体联邦法律来确保这一机构法规及政府行为具有合法性的法院。

法院判例

美国是普通法国家。除路易斯安那州属大陆法系外，美国的其他州都属普通法系。普通法没有成文法基础，法官通过将判例适用到当前的案件形成普通法。虽然受到成文法的影响，

但主要与财产、合同及侵权相关的大量法律领域,一直是普通法的传统组成部分。这些法律领域大多在州的管辖权范围内,因此州法院是普通法的主要来源。联邦普通法在范围上相对狭窄,主要限于成文法调整范围外明确由联邦解决的问题。

州宪法和制定法

州宪法是州一级的最高位阶的法律,州宪法授予的权利只可能多于联邦宪法所保护的权利。州的法规必须符合各州的宪法。联邦宪法或联邦法律对所有州宪法和法律具有优先性。市政宪章、法令、法规和规章仅适用于地方问题,无论州法律还是联邦法律都对其具有优先性。

Passage Two
社会主义法系

社会主义的法独自构成一个法系,与其他法系迥异。那些过去属罗马日耳曼法系的社会主义国家,至今仍保存着罗马日耳曼法系的某些特征。但是除这些相似点之外,也确实存在如此这般的区别;因此至少在今天,把社会主义的法看作是独立于罗马日耳曼法系的一个不同的法系(社会主义的法学家是十分坚持这一看法的),看来是恰当的。

社会主义法的独到之处,因该法具有的革命性尤为明显。与罗马日耳曼法一定程度静止的特征相反,社会主义法学家们公开宣告的雄心壮志是推翻旧社会,从而为连国家与法的概念本身也将消亡的社会新秩序创造条件。社会主义法律规则的唯一渊源在于表达人民意志的立法者,他们是严格地受共产党领导的。但法学不是建立新秩序的主要依靠对象。根据马克思列宁主义这一科学的真理,法是严格从属于创立新的经济基础这一任务的。遵循马克思列宁主义的教导,一切生产资料都集体化了。因此,同马克思以前的时期比较起来公民之间可能发生私法关系的范围大为缩小了;如今,私法既如强弩之末,一切也就都成了公法。这一新概念把资产阶级各国法学家看作是法律规则的一整套规则,从法的王国中排除出去了。

社会主义法系起源于苏维埃社会主义共和国联盟。那里,上述概念占绝对优势;自1917年革命以来,一套新法也已形成。但在分类上,必须把欧、亚社会主义共和国或人民共和国的法列入不同于苏维埃法的类别。虽然这些法律都属社会主义法系,但在欧洲一类中反映出原属罗马日耳曼法特征的残余较多,而在亚洲一类中,则以下探索是有用的,即上述新概念是怎样在实践中同社会主义时期以前统治各该社会的远东文明原则调和起来的。

▶ 词汇提示

法系 legal family
迥异 distinct from
罗马日耳曼 Romano-Germanic
法学家 jurist
公开宣告的 proclaimed
推翻 overturn

人民意志　popular will
共产党　Communist Party
法学　legal science
依靠　count upon
马克思列宁主义　Marxism-Leninism
从属于　subordinate to
生产资料　means of production
集体化　collectivize
私法　private law
资产阶级　bourgeois
苏维埃社会主义共和国联盟　Union of Soviet Socialist Republics
调和　reconcile

要点解析

1. 社会主义法律规则的唯一渊源在于表达人民意志的立法者，他们是严格地受共产党领导的。

此句中"在于"可用 lie with 来表达，"人民意志"指的是群众的意愿，故译为 popular will 较妥。

2. 与罗马日耳曼法一定程度静止的特征相反，社会主义法学家们公开宣告的雄心壮志是推翻旧社会，从而为连国家与法的概念本身也将消亡的社会新秩序创造条件。

此句翻译要点为"与……相反"，"一定程度静止"，"推翻旧社会"以及最后一句长句。前三个词组可分别译为 in opposition to，somewhat static 和 overturn society。而最后一句需要调整语序，首先要明确是"为……创造条件"，然后再用一个定语从句修饰是怎样的一个"社会新秩序"，即译为 create the conditions of a new social order in which the very concepts of state and law will disappear。

3. 根据马克思列宁主义这一科学的真理，法是严格地从属于创立新的经济基础这一任务的。

"马克思列宁主义这一科学的真理"，"科学真理"是马克思列宁主义的一个属性，在翻译时可用破折号表示科学真理作为插入语来修饰马克思列宁主义，即"Marxism-Leninism — a scientific truth — "。

4. 遵循马克思列宁主义的教导，一切生产资料都集体化了。

本句的翻译难点在于对"遵循"的把握，事实上，对于马克思列宁主义教导的遵循，是以实际践行体现出来的，因此，可译为 in execution of its teachings。

5. 强弩之末。汉译英中常常会遇到含义丰富的成语，首先要理解成语的意思，然后再着手将其适用的意义翻译出来。"强弩之末"，即强弩所发的箭，已达射程的尽头。比喻强大的力量已经衰弱，起不了什么作用。在文中，指私法的统治地位已经渐渐削弱，故译成 lost its preeminence 较合适。

6. 社会主义法系起源于苏维埃社会主义共和国联盟。那里，上述概念占绝对优势；1917

年革命以来，一套新法也已形成。

本句的翻译难点在于如何将这些零散的信息串起来，整合成一个完整的英语长句。仔细分析后可以发现，这两句都是在描述社会主义法系这一主题，因此可以将其作为主语，然后把其余信息以从句形式添加上去，即："The family of socialist laws originated in the Union of Soviet Socialist Republics where these ideas prevailed and a new law developed since the 1917 Revolution."

 参考译文

Family of Socialist Laws

The socialist laws make up a separate family, distinct from the other legal families. Those socialist countries which formerly belonged to the Romano-Germanic family have preserved some of the characteristics of Romano-Germanic law. But apart from these points of similarity, there do exist such differences that it seems proper to consider the socialist laws as detached from the Romano-Germanic family — the socialist jurists most decidedly do — and as constituting a distinct legal family, at least at the present time.

The originality of socialist laws is particularly evident because of the revolutionary nature attributed to them, in opposition to the somewhat static character of Romano-Germanic laws, the proclaimed ambition of socialist jurists is to overturn society and create the conditions of a new social order in which the very concepts of state and law will disappear. The sole source of Socialist rules of law lies with legislators who express popular will, narrowly guided by the Communist Party. However, legal science is not principally counted upon to create the new order; law according to Marxism-Leninism — a scientific truth — is strictly subordinate to the task of creating a new economic structure. In execution of its teachings, all means of production have been collectivized. As a result, the field of possible private law relationships between citizens is extraordinarily limited compared to the pre-Marxist period; private law has lost its preeminence — all has now become public law. This new concept subtracts from the realm of law a whole series of rules which jurists of the bourgeois countries would consider legal rules.

The family of socialist laws originated in the Union of Soviet Socialist Republics where these ideas prevailed and a new law developed since the 1917 Revolution. However, the laws of the socialist or people's republics of Europe and Asia must be classed as groups distinct from Soviet law. These laws belong to the socialist family, but in the first group a greater persistence of characteristics properly Romano-Germanic is detected, while in the second it is useful to enquire how these new concepts are reconciled in practice with the principles of Far Eastern civilization which governed those societies before the Socialist era.

Section II 技能拓展

翻译技巧

法律术语的特点及翻译

所谓法律术语就是用来准确表达特有法律概念的专门用语。法律术语的来源有多种途径，有的从常用词汇转化而来，有的从古代的法律沿用至今，也有的是从外国法律文件中移植而来，还有的是在法律事务实践中创造出来的。根据其用法的不同，法律术语一般又可分为两类：

一类是专门用于法律事务领域的法律术语（legal term of art）。它们专用于法律范畴。这类专用法律术语为数不多，且都有特定的确切的含义和适用范围，但它们不能被其他词汇取代，也不能随意引申。从事法律工作的专业人士必须掌握这类法律术语。例如：tort（侵权），omission（不作为），review（审查案件，复审）。另一类表示特定的法律概念，因为随着应用范围的扩大和全民词汇发生密切联系而经常互相交换与影响，结果由原来只有法律工作者知晓的术语扩展到全民词汇领域中。例如：law（法律），lawyer（律师），debt（债务），murder（谋杀），crime（罪行），prison（监狱），court（法庭）。

法律术语一般有以下特征。

1. 词义具有明显的专业性

法律术语是法律制度中核心的部分，是在长时间使用过程中逐渐析出并固定下来的。一个术语可能表示一种法律概念（如民法的"物""法人""无行为能力人"等），也可能表示一种法律制度（如"consideration 约因""estoppel 禁止翻供"等），甚至会链接特定的历史背景（如 sealed contract），其含义不能单单从其构成的字词去理解。

2. 词义具有排他性

一般而言，法律术语形成后，便有了特定的使用群体，含义相对固定，形成了形式上的确定性。即使一些形成时不很准确的术语，如果其内涵已经为人们熟知，也不宜再随意改动。也就是说，法律术语的词义必须单一而固定。任何人在任何情况下必须对其有同一解释。在英语中，negligence（过失）不能用 mistake 来代替；uncompleted murder（谋杀未遂）不能用 failure in murder 来代替。在汉语中，"故意"不能用"存心""特意"来代替，"犯罪嫌疑人"不能用"犯罪可疑人"来代替。

3. 词义具有保守和权威性

法律术语词义还具有保守和权威性的特点。相对于普通语言而言，其词义相对稳定、精确，变动较小，这是为了减少法律适用上的任意性，实现社会正义。法律英语术语中大量古体词从古英语和中古英语时期沿袭而来，其来源由两部分组成，有些来自于法语、拉丁语和少量希腊语等外来词语，如 suit, testimony……另外一些来源于古英语，如由 here-, there-和

where-组成的复合词（hereunder=under it, thereof=of that, wherefore=for the reasons mentioned above）用来表示确定的含义。法律汉语术语的古体词例如"刑罚""自首"等主要是文言词语，这些文言词语所表示的事物经过历史的过程在现实社会中依然存在，它们作为人类的法律文化具有继承性。

在对法律术语进行翻译时，首先要研究所要翻译的源语言法律术语的含义。译者在对所涉及的法律体系进行比较之后，必须在目标语言法律体系中寻找具有相同内容的术语，即必须在目标法律语言中发现源语言法律术语的对应词。如果由于法律体系的不相关性，译者找不到可以接受的对应词，可以使用下列解决办法：

- 使用源语言术语最初的或转录的译本（original transcribed version）；
- 使用解释（paraphrase）；
- 创造一个新语（neologism），即使用目标语言中并不构成现有目标语言术语一部分的一个新术语，必要的话再附上解释性脚注。

具体翻译方法

1. 改变词义范围（Lexical Expansion or Narrowness）

有时因为某个汉语功能对等词的必要特征与英语源术语的必要特征不同，该汉语功能对等词便不能用来翻译源术语，译者在这种情况下可以采用扩充词义的方法限定或扩大该功能对等词的意义以弥补术语之间的不一致。扩充词义有两种情况：如果译入语中某个功能对等词的意义比源术语的意义宽泛，译者可以确定或缩小该功能对等词的意义范围；而对于意义比源术语较窄的功能对等词，译者则可以通过扩充词义扩大它的含义。这样做可以使译入语的概念与源语中的概念相对应。

例如，在翻译 barrister 和 solicitor 时，译者就碰到这样的问题：汉语中"律师"的含义比这两个英语术语的含义范围大。有些字典把它们分别译为"专门律师、大律师"和"初级律师"，实际上就是采用了缩小功能对等词意义的方法。

2. 释义（Paraphrase）

释义是指舍弃源语中的具体形象，直接用译入语将其意图内涵表达出来。在翻译一些具有鲜明国家或民族特色的法律术语时，如果直译不能使译入语读者明白，加注又使译文冗长烦琐时，就可采用释义法。它既可使法律译本简练，又不损害对源语信息的表达，是解决缺少确切对等词的一个有效方法。使用别的法律制度中已有的术语直译对等词，在法律领域很常见。

例如，把 Queen's Counsel (Q. C.)译为"（女皇）御用大律师"，把 Chancery Division 译为"衡平法法院；大法官法庭"就使用了直译对等词。

 **法律宝典**

法律体系及其分类

法律体系是比较法中用来对各种法律进行划分的概念，意指具有相同或相近传统、原则、制度和特征等要素的一类法律制度的总和。

世界上的法系主要可以分为英美法系、欧陆法系、斯堪的那维亚法系、中华法系、社会主义法系、伊斯兰法系、印度教法系等。其中英美法系和欧陆法系一般被认为是当今世界最重要的两大法律体系，但这两大法律体系在当今也多有交流与融合之处。

英美法系

"英美法系"，又称"普通法系"（Common Law System），是一种由英格兰古代开始发展而成的法律体系。以英国为首的，以及所有现在或以前曾经是英国殖民地、属土，或英联邦国家，如加拿大、澳大利亚、新西兰、新加坡、马来西亚、印度、巴基斯坦等地，均采用这种法系。香港在主权移交予中华人民共和国以前，一直紧随英国的法制，而主权移交后，根据《香港基本法》规定，继续使用普通法系。

这种法系由公元1066年英王威廉一世（William I，又称 William the Conqueror）带领诺曼人征服英格兰（史称诺曼征服）开始慢慢在12及13世纪成形。当时英格兰王室为加强司法审判权，派出法官巡回各地审判案件。当时有很多法律问题，都没有白纸黑字的法例规范，因此法官都是根据当地的社会风俗、习惯、道德观念和一般常理来作出判决，其中基督教圣经的教训对当时英格兰社会的道德观念也有着重要的影响。当这些判例一个又一个地累积起来，加上当时的法官习惯上都会尊重和跟随以前法官（尤其是较高级法庭的法官）判案的原则，于是过了几百年，累积起来的判例便形成了适用于全国的法律。尤其是在印刷术开始普及之后，许多重要的判例都由律师用文字记录下来，然后印刷出版，每当律师接手办理新的案件时，都会翻查以往出版的判例作为依据，法官审每一件案件时也越来越详细地解释他判案的理由，并分析以前的判例作为支持他判案的理据。到了大约15世纪，这种无须经过立法机关立法而成的"法律"慢慢确立，所以普通法又叫不成文法。有些法律学者甚至认为，从理论层面来看，这种慢慢累积而来的"法律"就好像公义、道德这些观念一样，在一切制度还未确立以前，其实已经存在于每个人的良知里，法官的职责就像把这些法律原则"找出来"一样，而不是"创立"法律。

大陆法系

"大陆法系"（Civil Law System）一词中的"大陆"两字指欧洲大陆，故又可称为"欧陆法系"。这个法系现时主要由欧洲大陆的国家（如法国、意大利、德国、荷兰、葡萄牙等）及其他受上列国家影响的国家或地区（如日本、澳门）采用。欧陆法系在英文中一般称为 civil law system，主要历史渊源是古时罗马帝国的法律，其后在欧洲中世纪的后期（即文艺复兴以前，约12世纪至15世纪），罗马法在欧洲大陆又再度受到重视。到了18世纪，欧洲大陆的许多国家都颁布了法典，尝试列出各种法律分支的规范。

混合法系

也有一些地方的法系，同时带有普通法系和欧陆法系的一点特色，例如苏格兰由于历史原因，虽然属于英国的一部分，但是在法律体系上，也受到欧陆法系很深的影响，在有些法律范畴中，显出欧陆法系的特色多于普通法系。比较重要的混合法系有美国路易斯安那州、加拿大魁北克省、南非等。

美国虽然是普通法系国家，但是为了配合近数十年来经济和科技的迅速发展，也要积极编写法典配合，而并非单依靠案例来发展法律。这种趋势在世界各国都是越来越普遍。

术语积累

法律体系　legal system
普通法　Common Law
民法　Civil Law
社会主义法　Socialist Law
欧洲大陆法　European Continental Law
宗教法　Religious Law
伊斯兰法　Islamic Law
教会法　Canon Law
衡平法　equity
成文法　written law
制定法　statutory law
判例法　case law
立法机构　legislature
立法性的法规　legislative enactments
司法先例　judicial precedents
遵从前例　stare decisis
国法大全　Corpus Juris Civilis
审判法庭　Court of Justice
司法官，审判员　judiciary
公诉制度　public prosecution
分散制　decentralization
有约束力的解释　binding interpretation
牛津条例　Provisions of Oxford
特定履行　specific performance
本案令状　writ upon the case
巡回法官　itinerant judges
最高法院　Supreme Court
衡平法院　Court of Chancery
司法系统　Judicial System
上诉法院　appellate court
国家机器　state apparatus
管辖权　jurisdiction
强制实施　put teeth in(into)
正式法律　the official law
法理学　jurisprudence
公法　public law

私法　private law
欧洲大陆　continental Europe
法律概念　legal concept
立法实证主义　legislative positivism

Section III　巩固练习

词汇与短语

1. set forth
2. pre-empt
3. quasi-legislative
4. enumerate
5. legislative action
6. pursuant
7. substantive
8. implement
9. judicial
10. Bill of Right
11. 普通法
12. 民法
13. 遵从前例
14. 衡平法
15. 最高法院
16. 判例法
17. 从属于
18. 私法
19. 法学
20. 先例，惯例

句子与段落

1. 有时候法律被称作实体的或程序的。
2. 实体法界定权利，程序法则确立保护权利并使其生效的程序。
3. 把已判决的案例作为法的一个渊源，这种概念常被称为普通法系，它有别于欧洲大陆的大陆法系。
4. 大陆法系国家把它们的法律编成了法典，因此这些国家的法的渊源在成文法规里而不在案例里。
5. 法律不仅是一套行为规则，也是一种明确责任并促进社会正义的手段。
6. The tax law fits in well with the concept of law as a command from the superior to the inferior.
7. Public law affects the public generally, while private law deals with the relationship between individuals in an organized society.
8. Laws can be classified according to their sources into constitutions, legislation, judicial decisions and administrative rules and regulations.
9. In America, decided cases are also a source of law. This contrasts with countries in continental

Europe, where the main source of law is in the statutes.

10. Of the three major legal traditions in the modern Western world the Romano-Germanic legal tradition is the oldest, the most influential and the most widely distributed.

11. 在美国，普通法的影响一直是主要的。因为大多数移民来自英国，他们自然遵循他们祖国的法律和习惯。但在路易斯安那州，大陆法对其法律制度有影响，得克萨斯州和加利福尼亚州在一定程度上也是如此，因为这些州是由法国和西班牙人创建的。然而，美国各州相当一部分法律是成文法，成文法正变得日益重要。判例法，也即普通法，仍是法的一个重要的渊源，因为在产生争议之前把所有法律都变成成文法典是极其困难的。

12. 依照宪法，美国签订的条约根据美国宪法也需同联邦法令一样尊重最高法律。在条约和联邦法令冲突的情形下，迟颁布的或更具体的法规有效。美国作为一方签订的条约可以在美国条约服务署找到。大部分的法令、条约及其他国际法规都是由国务院发布，还包括联合国条约集。条约通常由联邦法贯彻实行。

13. 联邦行政机构发布规章制度是一个准立法行为；有效的联邦规章有法律效力并且优于州法律法规。规章制度只能在国会赋予的法定职权内颁布。总统也有广泛的权力发布行政命令。行政命令是行政机构中总统对其他官员的指示。

14. 美国是普通法系国家，每个州依据普通法有一个法律体系，除了路易斯安那（其依据的是法国民法典）。普通法系没有成文法的基础，法官通过在断案中适用从前的案例（先例）来建立普通法系。尽管明显地受到成文法权威的影响，但大多数法律，特别是关于财产、合同及侵权的法律仍旧是普通法系的传统部分。

15. 美国最高法院和大多数上诉法院的判决录都能在各自法院的官方汇编中找到。这些至少从1887年开始，到今日为止的判决也可以在一个非官方的汇编体系—国家报告体系中找到。

16. The U.S. court system, as part of the federal system of government, is characterized by dual hierarchies: there are both state and federal courts. Each state has its own system of courts, composed of civil and criminal trial courts, sometimes intermediate courts of appeal, and a state supreme court.

17. English law began as tribal law, chiefly based on Saxon Custom. The tribal meeting was the place of justice. Later the shire courts or moots, the hundred court（百户法庭）, the franchise courts settled disputes. The law was enforced by a system called "frankpledge".

18. After the Norman Conquest, a strong central government was run by the King, advised by the Curia Regis, which was legislature, administration and judiciary all rolled into one. A common law was established by the "general eyre"（常设巡回法庭）, a system of sending out members of the King's Council to tour the shires and check administration, collect taxes and try cases. A process of upholding good local customs and refusing to uphold bad ones established the common law.

19. The terms "common law", law found in court decisions, and statutory law, law based on legislative enactments, are used to indicate the general sources of law within a society with a common law legal system. Although the common law of the United States originated in

the customs and practices of the people in England, today in the United States the term "common law" generally refers to the case law that results from court decisions.

20. The term "statutory law" generally refers to the laws that have been formally adopted by legislative bodies. In the United States, legislative bodies include the U.S. Congress, the state legislatures, and local city councils or commissions. Administrative rules and regulations are also generally classified as statutory laws. Finally, while the laws and regulations of municipal bodies are sometimes referred to more specifically as ordinances, they are also a type of statutory law.

Unit Two

Constitutional Law and Constitutionalism
宪法与宪政

Section I 译例研究

Passage One
The Constitution of the United States of America

U.S. Constitution: Preamble

We the People of the United States, in order to form a more perfect union, establish justice, insure domestic tranquility, provide for the common defense, promote the general welfare, and secure the blessings of liberty to ourselves and our posterity, do ordain and establish this Constitution for the United States of America.

Article I

Section 1. All legislative powers herein granted shall be vested in a Congress of the United States, which shall consist of a Senate and House of Representatives.

Section 2. The House of Representatives shall be composed of members chosen every second year by the people of the several states, and the electors in each state shall have the qualifications requisite for electors of the most numerous branch of the state legislature.

No person shall be a Representative who shall not have attained to the age of twenty five years, and been seven years a citizen of the United States, and who shall not, when elected, be an inhabitant of that state in which he shall be chosen.

Representatives and direct taxes shall be apportioned among the several states which may be included within this union, according to their respective numbers, which shall be determined by adding to the whole number of free persons, including those bound to service for a term of years, and excluding Indians not taxed, three fifths of all other persons. The actual Enumeration shall be made within three years after the first meeting of the Congress of the United States, and within every subsequent term of ten years, in such manner as they shall by law direct. The number of Representatives shall not exceed one for every thirty thousand, but each state shall have at least one Representative; and until such enumeration shall be made, the state of New Hampshire shall be entitled to chuse three, Massachusetts eight, Rhode Island and Providence Plantations one, Connecticut five, New York six, New Jersey four, Pennsylvania eight, Delaware one, Maryland six, Virginia ten, North Carolina five, South Carolina five, and Georgia three.

When vacancies happen in the Representation from any state, the executive authority thereof shall issue writs of election to fill such vacancies.

The House of Representatives shall choose their speaker and other officers; and shall have the sole power of impeachment.

Section 3. The Senate of the United States shall be composed of two Senators from each state, chosen by the legislature thereof, for six years; and each Senator shall have one vote. Immediately after they shall be assembled in consequence of the first election, they shall be divided as equally as may be into three classes. The seats of the Senators of the first class shall be vacated at the expiration of the second year, of the second class at the expiration of the fourth year, and the third class at the expiration of the sixth year, so that one third may be chosen every second year; and if vacancies happen by resignation, or otherwise, during the recess of the legislature of any state, the executive thereof may make temporary appointments until the next meeting of the legislature, which shall then fill such vacancies.

No person shall be a Senator who shall not have attained to the age of thirty years, and been nine years a citizen of the United States and who shall not, when elected, be an inhabitant of that state for which he shall be chosen.

The Vice President of the United States shall be President of the Senate, but shall have no vote, unless they be equally divided.

The Senate shall choose their other officers, and also a President pro tempore, in the absence of the Vice President, or when he shall exercise the office of President of the United States.

The Senate shall have the sole power to try all impeachments. When sitting for that purpose, they shall be on oath or affirmation. When the President of the United States is tried, the Chief Justice shall preside. And no person shall be convicted without the concurrence of two thirds of the members present.

Judgment in cases of impeachment shall not extend further than to removal from office, and disqualification to hold and enjoy any office of honor, trust or profit under the United States, but the party convicted shall nevertheless be liable and subject to indictment, trial, judgment and punishment, according to law.

Section 4. The times, places and manner of holding elections for Senators and Representatives, shall be prescribed in each state by the legislature thereof; but the Congress may at any time by law make or alter such regulations, except as to the places of choosing Senators.

The Congress shall assemble at least once in every year, and such meeting shall be on the first Monday in December, unless they shall by law appoint a different day.

Section 5. Each House shall be the judge of the elections, returns and qualifications of its own members, and a majority of each shall constitute a quorum to do business; but a smaller number may adjourn from day to day, and may be authorized to compel the attendance of absent members, in such manner, and under such penalties as each House may provide.

Each House may determine the rules of its proceedings, punish its members for disorderly behavior, and, with the concurrence of two thirds, expel a member.

Each House shall keep a journal of its proceedings, and from time to time publish the same, excepting such parts as may in their judgment require secrecy; and the yeas and nays of the members of either House on any question shall, at the desire of one fifth of those present, be entered on the journal.

Neither House, during the session of Congress, shall, without the consent of the other, adjourn for more than three days, nor to any other place than that in which the two Houses shall be sitting.

Section 6. The Senators and Representatives shall receive a compensation for their services, to be ascertained by law, and paid out of the treasury of the United States. They shall in all cases, except treason, felony and breach of the peace, be privileged from arrest during their attendance at the session of their respective Houses, and in going to and returning from the same; and for any speech or debate in either House, they shall not be questioned in any other place.

No Senator or Representative shall, during the time for which he was elected, be appointed to any civil office under the authority of the United States, which shall have been created, or the emoluments whereof shall have been increased during such time: and no person holding any office under the United States, shall be a member of either House during his continuance in office.

词汇提示

preamble   *n.* 序言，序文
posterity   *n.* 子孙，后代
congress   *n.* 国会
senate   *n.* 议会
House of Representatives   众议院
qualification   *n.* 资格，条件
requisite   *adj.* 必备的，需要的
elector   *n.* 选举人
attain to   *v.* 达到
direct tax   *n.* 直接税
apportion   *v.* 分配，分摊
free person   自由人
bound to   *v.* 束缚于

Unit Two Constitutional Law and Constitutionalism 宪法与宪政

enumeration　*n.* 计算，人口清查
chuse　*v.* 选择（古语中等于 choose）
New Hampshire　新罕布什尔
Massachusetts　马萨诸塞
Rhode Island　罗得岛
Providence Plantations　普罗维登斯垦殖区
Connecticut　康涅狄格
Delaware　特拉华
Maryland　马里兰
in consequence of　由于……的缘故
vacate　*vi.* 空出
expiration　*n.* 届期
resignation　*n.* 辞职
recess　*n.* 休会
president pro tempore　参议员临时议长
oath　*n.* 誓言
Chief Justice　首席大法官
preside　*v.* 担任主席
prescribed　*adj.* 规定的
assemble　*v.* 集合
yea　*n.* 赞成
nay　*n.* 反对
emolument　*n.* 薪水，报酬

▶ 法律术语

ordain　*v.* 颁布命令
herein　*adv.* 于此，在这方面
vest in　*vt.* 归属于
be entitled to　有权
vacancy　空缺，缺额
executive authority　行政长官
thereof　*adv.* 由此，关于
writ of election　选举令
impeachment　*n.* 弹劾
exercise　*vt.* 行使权力
try　*v.* 审判
convict　*v.* 定罪
concurrence　*n.* 赞同

indictment　　*n.* 公诉，公诉书
return　　*n.* 选举结果报告
quorum　　*n.* 法定人数
adjourn　　*vt.* 休会
proceeding　　*n.* 议事规则
at the desire of　　应……的请求
session　　*n.* 开会，开庭
sitting　　*n.* 入席
be ascertained by law　　经法律确认
treasury　　*n.* 国库
treason　　*n.* 叛国罪
felony　　*n.* 重罪
breach of the peace　　妨害治安
in office　　执政，在位

▶ 要点解析

1. All legislative powers herein granted shall be vested in a Congress of the United States, which shall consist of a Senate and House of Representatives.

本句要注意 shall 的程式化语言结构，在本节的翻译技巧中将重点解析。另外，本句中的 herein granted 指的就是宪法所赋予的，因此可以译为"本宪法所规定的"。

2. in order to form a more perfect Union, establish Justice, insure domestic Tranquility, provide for the common defense, promote the general welfare, and secure the blessings of liberty to ourselves and our posterity

翻译此组短语的要点在于选择合适的词语进行动宾搭配，使用精简的语句表达原文意义，因此可将其分别译为"组织一个更完善的联邦"，"树立正义"，"保障国内的安宁"，"建立共同的国防"，"增进全民福利"，"确保我们自己及我们后代能安享自由带来的幸福"。

3. electors of the most numerous branch of the state legislature

这里的难点在于理解 the most numerous branch。从字面来看，是指"数目最大的分支"，将此意义放到法律语境以及此处所说的州议会的上下文来看，应该是指"州议会中人数最多之一的院"，数目最多指的是人数最多，而分支指的是议会下面的院。

4. No person shall be a Representative who shall not have attained to the age of twenty five years, and been seven years a citizen of the United States, and who shall not, when elected, be an inhabitant of that state in which he shall be chosen.

此句运用双重否定来规定成为众议员的条件，因此其译文结构最好译为"凡……未满/并非……，均不得……"。

5. The Vice President of the United States shall be President of the Senate, but shall have no vote, unless they be equally divided.

本句的翻译难点在于最后一小句，即 unless they be equally divided。要翻译好这个句子，

Unit Two　Constitutional Law and Constitutionalism　宪法与宪政

首先要理解 they 和 be divided 到底指的是什么意思。从上文的 vote 来看，本句应与副总统的投票权有关，这样，我们可以推断出，they 指的是投票的票数，而 be equally divided 指的是票数平分，票数相等。因此，这一句在调整语序后应译为"合众国副总统应为参议院议长，除非在投票票数相等时，议长无投票权。"

6. Each House shall be the judge of the elections, returns and qualifications of its own members, and a majority of each shall constitute a quorum to do business; but a smaller number may adjourn from day to day, and may be authorized to compel the attendance of absent members, in such manner, and under such penalties as each House may provide.

本句中要特别注意一下短语 Each House，a majority of，quorum to do business 及 adjourn from day to day 的翻译。首先，Each House 指的是国会下面的参议院和众议院，因此，可译为"参众两院"；同样的，a majority of 也应明确化翻译，译为"过半数"；quorum to do business 不能按字面理解为"做生意的人数"，而是"议事的法定人数"；最后，adjourn from day to day 指的是"一天推一天地延期开会"。

7. The Senators and Representatives shall receive a compensation for their services, to be ascertained by law, and paid out of the treasury of the United States.

本句应译为："参议员与众议员应因其服务而获报酬，报酬的多少由法律定之，并由合众国国库支付。"需要特别注意的是"报酬的多少"这一增译译法。

参考译文

美 国 宪 法

序言

我们美利坚合众国的人民，为了组织一个更完善的联邦，树立正义，保障国内的安宁，建立共同的国防，增进全民福利和确保我们自己及我们后代能安享自由带来的幸福，乃为美利坚合众国制定和确立这一部宪法。

第一条

第一款　本宪法所规定的立法权，全属合众国的国会，国会由一个参议院和一个众议院组成。

第二款　众议院应由各州人民每两年选举一次之议员组成，各州选举人应具有该州州议会中人数最多之一院的选举人所需之资格。凡年龄未满二十五岁，或取得合众国公民资格未满七年，或于某州当选而并非该州居民者，均不得任众议员。众议员人数及直接税税额，应按联邦所辖各州的人口数目比例分配，此项人口数目的计算法，应在全体自由人民——包括订有契约的短期仆役，但不包括未被课税的印第安人——数目之外，再加上所有其他人口之五分之三。实际人口调查，应于合众国国会第一次会议后三年内举行，并于其后每十年举行一次，其调查方法另以法律规定之。众议员的数目，不得超过每三万人口有众议员一人，但每州至少应有众议员一人；在举行人口调查以前，各州得按照下列数目选举众议员：新罕布什尔三人、马萨诸塞八人、罗德岛及普罗维登斯垦殖区一人、康涅狄格五人、纽约州六人、新泽西四人、宾夕法尼亚八人、特拉华一人、马里兰六人、弗吉尼亚十人、北卡罗来纳五人、南卡罗来纳五人、佐治亚三人。任何一州的众议员有缺额时,该州的行政长官应颁布选举令,选出众议员以补充缺额。众议院应选举议长及其他官员;只有众议院具有提出弹劾案的权力。

第三款 合众国的参议院由每州的州议会选举两名参议员组成,参议员的任期为六年,每名参议员有一票表决权。参议员于第一次选举后举行会议之时,应立即尽量均等地分成三组。第一组参议员的任期,到第二年年终时届满,第二组到第四年年终时届满,第三组到第六年年终时届满,俾使每两年有三分之一的参议员改选;如果在某州州议会休会期间,有参议员因辞职或其他原因出缺,该州的行政长官得任命临时参议员,等到州议会下次集会时,再予选举补缺。凡年龄未满三十岁,或取得合众国公民资格未满九年,或于某州当选而并非该州居民者,均不得任参议员。合众国副总统应为参议院议长,除非在投票票数相等时,议长无投票权。参议院应选举该院的其他官员,在副总统缺席或执行合众国总统职务时,还应选举临时议长。所有弹劾案,只有参议院有权审理。在开庭审理弹劾案时,参议员们均应宣誓或申明。如受审者为合众国总统,则应由最高法院首席大法官担任主席;未得出席参议员的三分之二人数的同意,任何人不得被判有罪。弹劾案的判决,不得超过免职及取消其担任合众国政府任何有荣誉、有责任或有俸给职位之资格;但被判处者仍须服从另据法律所作之控诉、审讯、判决及惩罚。

第四款 各州州议会应规定本州参议员及众议员之选举时间、地点及程序;但国会可以随时以法律制定或变更此种规定,唯有选举议员的地点不在此例。国会应至少每年集会一次,开会日期应为十二月的第一个星期一,除非他们通过法律来指定另一个日期。

第五款 参众两院应各自审查本院的选举、选举结果报告和本院议员的资格,每院议员过半数即构成可以议事的法定人数;不足法定人数时,可以一天推一天地延期开会,并有权依照各议院所规定的程序和罚则,强迫缺席的议员出席。参众两院可各自规定本院的议事规则,处罚本院扰乱秩序的议员,并且得以三分之二的同意,开除本院的议员。参众两院应各自保存一份议事记录,并经常公布,各院认为应保守秘密之部分除外;两院议员对于每一问题之赞成或反对,如有五分之一出席议员请求,则应记载于议事记录内。在国会开会期间,任一议院未得别院同意,不得休会三日以上,亦不得迁往非两院开会的其他地点。

第六款 参议员与众议员应因其服务而获报酬,报酬的多少由法律定之,并由合众国国库支付。两院议员除犯叛国罪、重罪以及扰乱治安罪外,在出席各院会议及往返各院途中,有不受逮捕之特权;两院议员在议院内所发表之演说及辩论,在其他场合不受质询。参议员或众议员不得在其当选任期内担任合众国政府任何新添设的职位,或在其任期内支取因新职位而增添的俸给;在合众国政府供职的人,不得在其任职期间担任国会议员。

Passage Two
中华人民共和国宪法

第二章 公民的基本权利和义务

第三十三条 凡具有中华人民共和国国籍的人都是中华人民共和国公民。

中华人民共和国公民在法律面前一律平等。

国家尊重和保障人权。

任何公民享有宪法和法律规定的权利，同时必须履行宪法和法律规定的义务。

第三十四条 中华人民共和国年满十八周岁的公民，不分民族、种族、性别、职业、家庭出身、宗教信仰、教育程度、财产状况、居住期限，都有选举权和被选举权；但是依照法律被剥夺政治权利的人除外。

第三十五条 中华人民共和国公民有言论、出版、集会、结社、游行、示威的自由。

第三十六条 中华人民共和国公民有宗教信仰自由。

任何国家机关、社会团体和个人不得强制公民信仰宗教或者不信仰宗教，不得歧视信仰宗教的公民和不信仰宗教的公民。

国家保护正常的宗教活动。任何人不得利用宗教进行破坏社会秩序、损害公民身体健康、妨碍国家教育制度的活动。

宗教团体和宗教事务不受外国势力的支配。

第三十七条 中华人民共和国公民的人身自由不受侵犯。

任何公民，非经人民检察院批准或者决定或者人民法院决定，并由公安机关执行，不受逮捕。

禁止非法拘禁和以其他方法非法剥夺或者限制公民的人身自由，禁止非法搜查公民的身体。

第三十八条 中华人民共和国公民的人格尊严不受侵犯。禁止用任何方法对公民进行侮辱、诽谤和诬告陷害。

第三十九条 中华人民共和国公民的住宅不受侵犯。禁止非法搜查或者非法侵入公民的住宅。

第四十条 中华人民共和国公民的通信自由和通信秘密受法律的保护。除因国家安全或者追查刑事犯罪的需要，由公安机关或者检察机关依照法律规定的程序对通信进行检查外，任何组织或者个人不得以任何理由侵犯公民的通信自由和通信秘密。

第四十一条 中华人民共和国公民对于任何国家机关和国家工作人员，有提出批评和建议的权利；对于任何国家机关和国家工作人员的违法失职行为，有向有关国家机关提出申诉、控告或者检举的权利，但是不得捏造或者歪曲事实进行诬告陷害。

对于公民的申诉、控告或者检举，有关国家机关必须查清事实，负责处理。任何人不得压制和打击报复。

由于国家机关和国家工作人员侵犯公民权利而受到损失的人，有依照法律规定取得赔偿的权利。

第四十二条 中华人民共和国公民有劳动的权利和义务。

国家通过各种途径，创造劳动就业条件，加强劳动保护，改善劳动条件，并在发展生产的基础上，提高劳动报酬和福利待遇。

劳动是一切有劳动能力的公民的光荣职责。国有企业和城乡集体经济组织的劳动者都应当以国家主人翁的态度对待自己的劳动。国家提倡社会主义劳动竞赛，奖励劳动模范和先进工作者。国家提倡公民从事义务劳动。

国家对就业前的公民进行必要的劳动就业训练。

第四十三条 中华人民共和国劳动者有休息的权利。

国家发展劳动者休息和休养的设施，规定职工的工作时间和休假制度。

第四十四条　国家依照法律规定实行企业事业组织的职工和国家机关工作人员的退休制度。退休人员的生活受到国家和社会的保障。

第四十五条　中华人民共和国公民在年老、疾病或者丧失劳动能力的情况下，有从国家和社会获得物质帮助的权利。国家发展为公民享受这些权利所需要的社会保险、社会救济和医疗卫生事业。

国家和社会保障残废军人的生活，抚恤烈士家属，优待军人家属。

国家和社会帮助安排盲、聋、哑和其他有残疾的公民的劳动、生活和教育。

第四十六条　中华人民共和国公民有受教育的权利和义务。

国家培养青年、少年、儿童在品德、智力、体质等方面全面发展。

第四十七条　中华人民共和国公民有进行科学研究、文学艺术创作和其他文化活动的自由。国家对于从事教育、科学、技术、文学、艺术和其他文化事业的公民的有益于人民的创造性工作，给以鼓励和帮助。

第四十八条　中华人民共和国妇女在政治、经济、文化、社会和家庭生活等各方面享有同男子平等的权利。

国家保护妇女的权利和利益，实行男女同工同酬，培养和选拔妇女干部。

第四十九条　婚姻、家庭、母亲和儿童受国家的保护。

夫妻双方有实行计划生育的义务。

父母有抚养教育未成年子女的义务，成年子女有赡养扶助父母的义务。

禁止破坏婚姻自由，禁止虐待老人、妇女和儿童。

第五十条　中华人民共和国保护华侨的正当的权利和利益，保护归侨和侨眷的合法权利和利益。

第五十一条　中华人民共和国公民在行使自由和权利的时候，不得损害国家的、社会的、集体的利益和其他公民的合法的自由和权利。

第五十二条　中华人民共和国公民有维护国家统一和全国各民族团结的义务。

第五十三条　中华人民共和国公民必须遵守宪法和法律，保守国家秘密，爱护公共财产，遵守劳动纪律，遵守公共秩序，尊重社会公德。

第五十四条　中华人民共和国公民有维护祖国的安全、荣誉和利益的义务，不得有危害祖国的安全、荣誉和利益的行为。

第五十五条　保卫祖国、抵抗侵略是中华人民共和国每一个公民的神圣职责。

依照法律服兵役和参加民兵组织是中华人民共和国公民的光荣义务。

第五十六条　中华人民共和国公民有依照法律纳税的义务。

词汇提示

通信　correspondence
退休制度　system of retirement
事业组织　undertaking
烈士　martyr
优待　give preferential treatment

全面的　all-round
同工同酬　equal pay for equal work
干部　cadre
华侨　Chinese nationals residing abroad
归侨　returned overseas Chinese
侵略　aggression
服兵役　perform military service
依照　in accordance with

▶ 法律术语

国籍　nationality
公民　citizen
权利　right
义务　duty
居住期限　length of residence
被选举　stand for election
剥夺　deprive
集会　assembly
结社　association
游行　procession
示威　demonstration
国家机关　state organ
社会团体　public organization
强制　compel
破坏　disrupt
损害　impair
妨碍　interfere
宗教团体　religious body
外国势力　foreign domination
检察院　procuratorate
公安机关　public security organ
拘禁　detention
人格尊严　personal dignity
侮辱　insult
诽谤　libel
诬告　false charge
陷害　frame-up
侵入　intrusion

侵犯　infringe
检查/审查　censor
国家工作人员　functionary
失职　dereliction
捏造　fabrication
歪曲　distortion
压制　suppress
打击报复　retaliate
公民权利　civil rights
报酬　remuneration
有劳动能力的　able-bodied
国有企业　state enterprises
集体经济　economic collective
劳动竞赛　labour emulation
休养　recuperation
保险　insurance
救济　relief
医疗卫生事业　medical and health services
军人　military personnel
计划生育　family planning
未成年　minor
成年　come of age
虐待　maltreatment
正当的　legitimate
遵守　abide by/ observe
社会公德　social ethics
职责　obligation
民兵组织　militia
纳税　pay taxes

▶ 要点解析

1. 任何公民享有宪法和法律规定的权利，同时必须履行宪法和法律规定的义务。

翻译此句时注意，由于不管是权利还是义务都是由宪法和法律规定的，因此可以将两者合并起来，译为："Every citizen enjoys the rights and at the same time must perform the duties prescribed by the Constitution and the law."

2. 任何国家机关、社会团体和个人不得强制公民信仰宗教或者不信仰宗教，不得歧视信仰宗教的公民和不信仰宗教的公民。

"任何……都不得……"的句子在法律文本中非常常见，通常将其译为"No...may..."，因此此句可译为："No state organ, public organization or individual may compel citizens to believe in, or not to believe in, any religion; nor may they discriminate against citizens who believe in, or do not believe in, any religion."

3. 禁止非法拘禁和以其他方法非法剥夺或者限制公民的人身自由，禁止非法搜查公民的身体。

这一条文是典型的表达禁止性的程式化语言结构，在英语中可以用"be prohibited/not allowed; be not obliged/permitted; shall/may/must not +v."来表达，因此，本句可以译为："Unlawful deprivation or restriction of citizens' freedom of person by detention or other means is prohibited; and unlawful search of the person of citizens is prohibited."

4. 国有企业和城乡集体经济组织的劳动者都应当以国家主人翁的态度对待自己的劳动。

在翻译时应注意，"以国家主人翁的态度对待自己的劳动"即在劳动实践时劳动者所持的态度应与其所处地位相符，因此，可译为"perform their tasks with an attitude consonant with their status as masters of the country"。

5. 中华人民共和国公民有维护国家统一和全国各民族团结的义务。

这是表达义务性的程式化语言结构，通常用"It is the duty..."来表达，因此，本句可译为："It is the duty of citizens of the People's Republic of China to safeguard the unity of the country and the unity of all its nationalities."

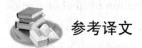
参考译文

CONSTITUTION OF THE PEOPLE'S REPUBLIC OF CHINA

CHAPTER II   THE FUNDAMENTAL RIGHTS AND DUTIES OF CITIZENS

Article 33. All persons holding the nationality of the People's Republic of China are citizens of the People's Republic of China. All citizens of the People's Republic of China are equal before the law. State respects and safeguards human rights. Every citizen enjoys the rights and at the same time must perform the duties prescribed by the Constitution and the law.

Article 34. All citizens of the People's Republic of China who have reached the age of 18 have the right to vote and stand for election, regardless of nationality, race, sex, occupation, family background, religious belief, education, property status, or length of residence, except persons deprived of political rights according to law.

Article 35. Citizens of the People's Republic of China enjoy freedom of speech, of the press, of assembly, of association, of procession and of demonstration.

Article 36. Citizens of the People's Republic of China enjoy freedom of religious belief. No state organ, public organization or individual may compel citizens to believe in, or not to believe in, any religion; nor may they discriminate against citizens who believe in, or do not believe in, any religion. The state protects normal religious activities. No one may make use of religion to engage in activities that disrupt public order, impair the health of citizens or interfere with the educational system of the state. Religious bodies and religious affairs are not subject to any foreign domination.

Article 37. The freedom of person of citizens of the People's Republic of China is inviolable. No citizen may be arrested except with the approval or by decision of a people's procuratorate or by decision of a people's court, and arrests must be made by a public security organ. Unlawful deprivation or restriction of citizens' freedom of person by detention or other means is prohibited; and unlawful search of the person of citizens is prohibited.

Article 38. The personal dignity of citizens of the People's Republic of China is inviolable. Insult, libel, false charge or frame-up directed against citizens by any means is prohibited.

Article 39. The home of citizens of the People's Republic of China is inviolable. Unlawful search of, or intrusion into, a citizen's home is prohibited.

Article 40. The freedom and privacy of correspondence of citizens of the People's Republic of China are protected by law. No organization or individual may, on any ground, infringe upon the freedom and privacy of citizens' correspondence except in cases where, to meet the needs of state security or of investigation into criminal offences, public security or procuratorial organs are permitted to censor correspondence in accordance with procedures prescribed by law.

Article 41. Citizens of the People's Republic of China have the right to criticize and make suggestions to any state organ or functionary. Citizens have the right to make to relevant state organs complaints and charges against, or exposures of, violation of the law or dereliction of duty by any state organ or functionary; but fabrication or distortion of facts with the intention of libel or frame-up is prohibited. In case of complaints, charges or exposures made by citizens, the state organ concerned must deal with them in a responsible manner after ascertaining the facts. No one may suppress such complaints, charges and exposures, or retaliate against the citizens making them. Citizens who have suffered losses through infringement of their civil rights by any state organ or functionary have the right to compensation in accordance with the law.

Article 42. Citizens of the People's Republic of China have the right as well as the duty to work. Using various channels, the state creates conditions for employment, strengthens labour protection, improves working conditions and, on the basis of expanded production, increases remuneration for work and social benefits. Work is the glorious duty of every able-bodied citizen. All working people in state enterprises and in urban and rural economic collectives should perform their tasks with an attitude consonant with their status as masters of the country. The state promotes socialist labour emulation, and commends and rewards model and advanced workers. The state encourages citizens to take part in voluntary labour. The state provides necessary vocational training to citizens before they are employed.

Article 43. Working people in the People's Republic of China have the right to rest. The state expands facilities for rest and recuperation of working people, and prescribes working hours and vacations for workers and staff.

Article 44. The state prescribes by law the system of retirement for workers and staff in enterprises and undertakings and for functionaries of organs of state. The livelihood of retired personnel is ensured by the state and society.

Article 45. Citizens of the People's Republic of China have the right to material assistance from the state and society when they are old, ill or disabled. The state develops the social insurance, social relief and medical and health services that are required to enable citizens to enjoy this right. The state and society ensure the livelihood of disabled members of the armed forces, provide pensions to the families of martyrs and give preferential treatment to the families of military personnel. The state and society help make arrangements for the work, livelihood and education of the blind, deaf-mute and other handicapped citizens.

Article 46. Citizens of the People's Republic of China have the duty as well as the right to receive education. The state promotes the all-round moral, intellectual and physical development of children and young people.

Article 47. Citizens of the People's Republic of China have the freedom to engage in scientific research, literary and artistic creation and other cultural pursuits. The state encourages and assists creative endeavours conducive to the interests of the people made by citizens engaged in education, science, technology, literature, art and other cultural work.

Article 48. Women in the People's Republic of China enjoy equal rights with men in all spheres of life, political, economic, cultural and social, and family life. The state protects the rights and interests of women, applies the principle of equal pay for equal work for men and women alike and trains and selects cadres from among women.

Article 49. Marriage, the family, and mother and child are protected by the state. Both husband and wife have the duty to practise family planning. Parents have the duty to rear and educate their minor children, and children who have come of age have the duty to support and assist their parents. Violation of the freedom of marriage is prohibited. Maltreatment of old people, women and children is prohibited.

Article 50. The People's Republic of China protects the legitimate rights and interests of Chinese nationals residing abroad and protects the lawful rights and interests of returned overseas Chinese and of the family members of Chinese nationals residing abroad.

Article 51. The exercise by citizens of the People's Republic of China of their freedoms and rights may not infringe upon the interests of the state, of society and of the collective, or upon the lawful freedoms and rights of other citizens.

Article 52. It is the duty of citizens of the People's Republic of China to safeguard the unity of the country and the unity of all its nationalities.

Article 53. Citizens of the People's Republic of China must abide by the constitution and the law, keep state secrets, protect public property and observe labour discipline and public order and respect social ethics.

Article 54. It is the duty of citizens of the People's Republic of China to safeguard the security, honour and interests of the motherland; they must not commit acts detrimental to the security, honour and interests of the motherland.

Article 55. It is the sacred obligation of every citizen of the People's Republic of China to defend the motherland and resist aggression. It is the honourable duty of citizens of the People's Republic of China to perform military service and join the militia in accordance with the law.

Article 56. It is the duty of citizens of the People's Republic of China to pay taxes in accordance with the law.

Section II 技能拓展

 翻译技巧

shall 的使用和翻译

在法律英语中，情态动词主要用来表达当事人的权利和义务及其范围和程度。法律语言的社会功能，使得法律英语动词使用的语气、语态和时态与普通英语有所区别。

由于法律、法规代表统治阶级的意志，表现司法主体对司法客体的行为制约，它通常要求司法客体"必须""可以""应该"或"不许""不能""不得"做什么，用词通常带命令语气。因此，法律的这种强制性，使得祈使语句在法律英语中很普遍，所以 shall, may, must, should 的使用频率很高。例如：

① A party may suspend the performance of his obligation.

一方当事人可以中止履行义务。

② Nothing in this article shall prejudice any right of recourse as between the carrier and the actual carrier.

本条规定不得妨碍承运人和实际承运人之间的任何追索权。

在普通英语中 shall 是典型的表示未来的情态动词，传统语法规定 shall 只能用于第一人称，否则用 will 会更合适。在美国英语中一般不用 shall 表示将来，几乎已被废弃，所以表示将来的唯一情态动词只能用 will。在法律英语中 shall 并不表示将来，而有着与普通英语完全不同的含义。Frederick Bowers（1989）认为 shall 被广泛运用于法律英语的真正原因是 shall 被看作是具有法律权威特征的一种象征。

Longman Dictionary of Contemporary English 中 shall 的解释为：fml (used esp. in official writing to show a promise, command, or law)。在具体翻译中，一般肯定形式应译为"应当"，否定形式应译为"不得"。例如：

The reward shall be fixed with a view to encouraging salvage operations, taking into full account the following criteria: the reward shall not exceed the value of the ship and other property salved.

确定救助报酬，应当体现对救助作业的鼓励，并综合考虑下列各项因素：救助报酬不得超过船舶和其他财产的获救价值。

虽然在法律英语中，情态动词 shall 通常表述各项具体的规定与要求，带有指令性和强制性，充分体现了法律文件的权威性和约束性。中文通常译为"应当"，但在具体行文中，还是应该根据上下文来界定 shall 的含义。

以下是 shall 在法律英语翻译中常见的几种处理方法。

1. 表示某种命令或某种法律义务，相当于普通英语中的 must，通常翻译为"必须"

例如：① All the activities of a joint venture shall comply with the provisions of the law, decrees and pertinent regulations of the People's Republic of China.

合营企业的一切活动必须遵守中华人民共和国的法律、法令和有关的条例规定。

分析：这里所用的 shall 并不表示对将来事件的预测，而是设定了企业的活动必须遵守法律规定的义务。使整个句子更具法律权威性。

② Under California law, someone who qualifies as a sex offender shall register with the chief of police or sheriff within a special time.

依据加利福尼亚州法律，一个被指控为性骚扰的人必须在特定的时间到警察局长或地方法官那里去登记。

2. 表示法律上的正式"宣告""宣布"

例如：

① *The Contract Law of the People's Republic of China* shall take effect on Oct. 1, 1999.

《中华人民共和国合同法》将于1999年10月1日生效。

② This Act shall be known as The Penal Code of California.

这部法律被正式宣布为加利福尼亚州的刑法典。

3. 用于表述合同条款，表述一定要做到的事，表示"一定会"(promise to）或"将会"(will or to be to)

例如：The Publisher shall pay the Author in advance, which shall be a charge of all sums to the Author under this Agreement.

出版商应当预付作者稿酬，这笔稿酬是按合同规定的总稿酬中的一部分。（这里 shall 为合同中的一方设定了给付报酬的义务。句中的第一个 shall 指"一定会"；第二个 shall 是指一种"承诺"或一种正式"声明"，但没有"命令"的含义。）

当然，shall 在法律英语中的含义并不一定就限于以上三种情况。李克兴（2007）归纳了 shall 不译的两种情况：

（1）其对象为广大民众的表示概括性的立法性文本；

（2）在法律和普通合同文本中，当 shall 之后所跟的动词本身就能表示权利、义务或责任以及主句的基本结构为 shall+be+predicative（表语）时。例如：

① All Hong Kong residents shall be equal before law.

香港居民在法律面前一律平等。

② The homes and other premises of Hong Kong residents shall be inviolable. Arbitrary or unlawful search of, or in intrusion into, a resident's home or other premises shall be prohibited.

香港居民的住宅和其他房屋不受侵犯。禁止任意或非法搜查、侵入居民的住宅和其他房屋。

③ The (arbitration) board shall have such jurisdiction and powers as are conferred on it by this or any other Ordinance.

仲裁处具备本条例或任何其他条例授予的管辖权及权力。

④ If the Buyers fail to provide such letter of credit in the Seller's favour as prescribed above, the seller shall have the option of reselling the contracted goods for the account of the Buyers or delaying any shipment and/or canceling any others at any time on the Buyer's account and risk.

如果买方未能向卖方提供上述规定的这种信用证，卖方有权选择把合同规定的买方账上的货物转售或随时推迟付运和（或）撤销任何订单，损失和风险由买方承担。

⑤ The landlord shall not be in any way responsible to the Tennant for any damages caused to be said premises or the contents thereof arising as a result of the negligence of any other tenant of the said building.

由于该大厦其他任何住户的过失而产生的对该楼宇或其里面的东西的任何损坏，业主对租户不负任何责任。

shall 与 should 在法律文本中具有以下区别。

shall 在合同文件中是使用频率最高的词，在合同文件中 shall 表示强制性承担法律或合同所规定的义务，在表达"应该"或"必须"做某事时，应用 shall，而不能用 must，或 should，但有时可用 will，力度比 shall 弱。Should 在法律文件中往往作 if 解，只表示"如果"之意。例如：

The board meeting shall be called and presided over by the Chairman. Should the Chairman be absent, the vice Chairman shall, in principle, call and preside over the board meeting .

董事会会议应由董事长召集、主持；如董事长缺席，原则上应由副董事长召集、主持。

同样，在汉译英中，在翻译像"应""应该""必须""非……不可"之类的，表示法律上可以强制执行的义务的时候，应该用"shall"来翻译。例如：

① 承运人应在开航前和开航当时克尽职责使船舶适航。

The carrier shall, before and at the beginning of the voyage, exercise due diligence to make the ship seaworthy.

② 货物由承运人接收或者装船后，应托运人的要求，承运人应当签发提单。

When the goods have been taken over by the carrier or have been loaded on board, the carrier shall, on demand of the shipper, issue to the shipper a bill of loading.

法律宝典

宪法历史与发展

宪法一词来源于拉丁文 constitutio，本是组织、确立的意思。古罗马帝国用它来表示皇帝的"诏令""谕旨"，以区别于市民会议通过的法律文件。欧洲封建时代用它表示在日常立法中对国家制度基本原则的确认，含有组织法的意思。英国在中世纪建立了代议制度，确立了国王没有得到议会同意就不得征税和进行其他立法的原则。后来代议制度普及于欧美各国，人们就把规定代议制度的法律称为宪法，指确认立宪政体的法律。

"宪""宪令""宪法"等词在中国古代典籍中与"法"同义，日本古代"宪"也指法令、制度，都与现代"宪法"一词含义不同。19世纪60年代明治维新时期，随着西方立宪政治概念的传入，日本才有相当于欧美的宪法概念出现。1898年，中国戊戌变法时，以康有为为首的维新派要求清廷制定宪法，实行君主立宪。1908年清政府颁布《钦定宪法大纲》，从此"宪法"一词在中国就成为国家根本法的专用词。

从理论上讲，宪法的效力高于本国其他法律和法规。但在现实里，宪法并不是在所有国家中都具有权威性。为保证宪法的权威性，需要相应的一套体系来确保宪法没有被违背。这套体系被称为宪法审查制度。在现代民主国家，由于宪法审查制度的实施，一条法规如果和宪法相抵触，就不能得以应用。而在非民主国家，宪法的最高效力经常不能得到有效的维护，以至于宪法成为一纸空文。使一条和宪法抵触的法规不能得以应用的方法有多种，根据宪法审查制度的不同，可以事先审查，也可以事后审查。奥地利的法律学家凯尔孙（Hans Kelsen）最先提出。法律和法规以及宪法构成一个金字塔。宪法位于塔顶，拥有最高权威；法律由立法机关通过，其效力仅次于宪法；法规是由行政机关颁布，它的效力最低，因此位于金字塔底。因此一条法规不能违背高于它的法律和宪法，否则它可能被撤销。同样，一条法律不能和宪法相抵触，否则它能被撤销。

现代概念中宪法是公民与国家的契约，它在国家的法律体系中有最高的地位，因此它是国家的根本法，拥有最高的法律效力。宪法规定的事项主要有国家政治架构，政府组成与职能，权力制衡模式和公民的权利等。有些国家的宪法还规定了公民的义务，但大多宪法学者认为，宪法规定公民的义务，不仅没有必要，而且难以实行。

有人认为，宪法最为重要的意义在于它是一部权利宣言书。《美国宪法》是这一表述的最好的注解。但对权利的列举式规范并非宪法的绝对要件，美国宪法在订立之初并无权利条款，法国第五共和的宪法也未列明权利条款，但这都无损于它们是有效宪法规范的事实。

宪法可以是成文的，也可以没有明文规定，随着历史的发展，习惯形成的。例如《英国宪法》，便不是一部单一的法律，而是由包括《大宪章》、《英国权利法案》、大量《国会法案》（Act of Parliament）和相关法律，再加上很多习惯、判例累积组成。

术语积累

政体　form of government
条款　article
正式批准　ratify
授予，赋予　vest
不成文宪法　unwritten constitution
不可抗力　force majeure
不可侵犯性　inviolability
成文宪法　written constitution
达到法定年龄　come of age
地方各级人民代表大会　local people's congresses at different levels
地方各级人民法院　local people's courts at different levels
地方各级人民检察院　local people's procuratorates at different levels
地方各级人民政府　local people's governments at different levels
限制解释　restrictive interpretation
宪法的解释　interpretation of constitution

宪法修正案　constitution amendment
依照法律的规定　as prescribed by law
有法律约束力　legally binding
有条件解释　conditional interpretation
有效期间　time of effect; term of validity
与法律相抵触的行为　act going against the law
作为或不作为　act or omission
司法解释　judicial interpretation
司法审查　judicial review
无效，失效　null and void
依法取缔　outlaw
权利法案　Bill of Rights
合法地位　legal status
合法权益　the lawful rights and interests
合法行为　lawful acts

Section III　巩固练习

词汇与短语

1. 禁止
2. 侵犯
3. 职责
4. 正当的
5. 游行
6. 示威
7. 公民权利
8. 国家机关
9. 社会团体
10. 依照
11. prescribed
12. vest in
13. writ of election
14. impeachment
15. quorum
16. exercise
17. adjourn
18. be entitled to
19. at the desire of
20. attain to

句子与段落

1. 中华人民共和国公民有劳动的权利和义务。
2. 国家发展劳动者休息和休养的设施，规定职工的工作时间和休假制度。

Unit Two Constitutional Law and Constitutionalism 宪法与宪政

3. 国家保护妇女的权利和利益，实行男女同工同酬，培养和选拔妇女干部。
4. 禁止破坏婚姻自由，禁止虐待老人、妇女和儿童。
5. 保卫祖国、抵抗侵略是中华人民共和国每一个公民的神圣职责。
6. All legislative powers herein granted shall be vested in a Congress of the United States, which shall consist of a Senate and House of Representatives.
7. The Vice President of the United States shall be President of the Senate, but shall have no vote, unless they be equally divided.
8. The Congress shall assemble at least once in every year, and such meeting shall be on the first Monday in December, unless they shall by law appoint a different day.
9. Each House may determine the rules of its proceedings, punish its members for disorderly behavior, and, with the concurrence of two thirds, expel a member.
10. Neither House, during the session of Congress, shall, without the consent of the other, adjourn for more than three days, nor to any other place than that in which the two Houses shall be sitting.
11. 中华人民共和国年满十八周岁的公民，不分民族、种族、性别、职业、家庭出身、宗教信仰、教育程度、财产状况、居住期限，都有选举权和被选举权；但是依照法律被剥夺政治权利的人除外。
12. 中华人民共和国公民的通信自由和通信秘密受法律的保护。除因国家安全或者追查刑事犯罪的需要，由公安机关或者检察机关依照法律规定的程序对通信进行检查外，任何组织或者个人不得以任何理由侵犯公民的通信自由和通信秘密。
13. 劳动是一切有劳动能力的公民的光荣职责。国有企业和城乡集体经济组织的劳动者都应当以国家主人翁的态度对待自己的劳动。国家提倡社会主义劳动竞赛，奖励劳动模范和先进工作者。国家提倡公民从事义务劳动。
14. 中华人民共和国公民在年老、疾病或者丧失劳动能力的情况下，有从国家和社会获得物质帮助的权利。国家发展为公民享受这些权利所需要的社会保险、社会救济和医疗卫生事业。国家和社会保障残废军人的生活，抚恤烈士家属，优待军人家属。
15. 中华人民共和国公民有进行科学研究、文学艺术创作和其他文化活动的自由。国家对于从事教育、科学、技术、文学、艺术和其他文化事业的公民的有益于人民的创造性工作，给以鼓励和帮助。
16. We the People of the United States, in order to form a more perfect union, establish justice, insure domestic tranquility, provide for the common defense, promote the general welfare, and secure the blessings of liberty to ourselves and our posterity, do ordain and establish this Constitution for the United States of America.
17. No person shall be a Representative who shall not have attained to the age of twenty five years, and been seven years a citizen of the United States, and who shall not, when elected, be an inhabitant of that state in which he shall be chosen.
18. The Senate shall have the sole power to try all impeachments. When sitting for that purpose, they shall be on oath or affirmation. When the President of the United States is tried, the Chief Justice shall preside. And no person shall be convicted without the concurrence of

two thirds of the members present.

19. Judgment in cases of impeachment shall not extend further than to removal from office, and disqualification to hold and enjoy any office of honor, trust or profit under the United States, but the party convicted shall nevertheless be liable and subject to indictment, trial, judgment and punishment, according to law.

20. The Senators and Representatives shall receive a compensation for their services, to be ascertained by law, and paid out of the treasury of the United States. They shall in all cases, except treason, felony and breach of the peace, be privileged from arrest during their attendance at the session of their respective Houses, and in going to and returning from the same; and for any speech or debate in either House, they shall not be questioned in any other place.

Unit Three

The Legal Profession
法 律 职 业

Section I 译例研究

▶ Passage One
The Bar

    The regulation of the legal profession primarily the concern of the states, each of which has its own requirements for admission to practice. Most require three years of college and a law degree. Each state administers its own examination to applicants for its bar. Almost all states make use of the Multistate Bar Exam, a day-long multiple-choice test, to which the state adds a day-long essay examination emphasizing its own law. A substantial fraction of all applicants succeed on the first try, and many of those who fail pass on a later attempt. In all, over forty thousand persons succeed in passing these examinations each year and, after an inquiry into their character, are admitted to the bar in their respective states. No apprenticeship is required either before or after admission. The rules for admission to practice before the federal courts vary with the court, but generally those entitled to practice before the highest court of a state may be admitted before the federal courts upon compliance with minor formalities.

    A lawyer's practice is usually confined to a single community for, although a lawyer may travel to represent clients, one is only permitted to practice in a state where one has been admitted. It is customary to retain local counsel for matters in other jurisdictions. However, one who moves to another state can usually be admitted without examination if one has practiced in a state where one has been admitted for some time, often five years.

    A lawyer may not only practice law, but is permitted to engage in any activity that is open to other citizens. It is not uncommon for the practicing lawyer to serve on boards of directors of corporate clients, to engage in business, and to participate actively in public affairs. A lawyer remains a member of the bar even after becoming a judge, an employee of the government or of a private business concern, or a law teacher, and may return to private practice from these other activities. A relatively small number of lawyers give up practice for responsible executive positions in commerce and industry. The mobility as well as the sense of public responsibility in the profession is evidenced by the career of Harlan Fiske Stone, who was, at various times, a successful New York lawyer, a professor and dean of the Columbia School of Law, Attorney General of the United States, and Chief Justice of the United States.

There is no formal division among lawyers according to function. The distinction between barristers and solicitors found in England did not take root in the United States, and there is no branch of the profession that has a special or exclusive right to appear in court, nor is there a branch that specializes in the preparation of legal instruments. The American lawyer's domain includes advocacy, counseling, and drafting. Furthermore, within the sphere broadly defined as the "practice of law" the domain is exclusive and not open to others. In the field of advocacy, the rules are fairly clear; any individual may represent himself or herself in Court but, with the exception of a few inferior Courts, only a lawyer may represent another in Court. No lawyers are, however, authorized to represent others in formal proceedings of a judicial nature before some administrative agencies. The lines of demarcation are less clear in the areas of counselling and drafting of legal instruments, as for example between the practice of law and that of accounting in the held of federal income taxation. However, the strict approach of most American courts is indicated by a decision of New York's highest Court that a lawyer admitted to practice in a foreign country but not in New York, is prohibited from giving legal advice to clients in New York, even though the advice is limited to the law of the foreign country where the lawyer is admitted. A foreign lawyer may, however, be admitted to the bar of one of the states and may, even without being admitted, advise an American lawyer as a Consultant on foreign law.

House Counsel

Of the lawyers who are not in private practice, many are employed by private business concerns, such as industrial corporations, insurance companies, and banks, usually as house (or corporate) counsel in the concern's legal department. The growth of corporations, the complexity of business, and the multitude of problems posed by government regulation make it desirable for such firms to have in their employ persons with legal training who, at the same time, are intimately familiar with the particular problems and conditions of the firm. In large corporations the legal department may number one hundred or more. The general counsel, who heads the office, is usually an officer of the company and may serve on important policy making committees and perhaps even on the board of directors. House counsels remain members of the bar and are entitled to appear in court, though an outside lawyer is often retained for litigation. However, it is the house counsel's skill with the employer's problems; house counsel is ideally situated to practice preventive law and may also be called upon to advise the company on its broader obligation to the public and the nation.

Unit Three   The Legal Profession   法律职业

Lawyers in Government

A parallel development has taken place in government and out of twenty lawyers who are not in private practice are employees of the federal, state, country, and municipal governments, exclusive of the judiciary. Those entering public service are often recent law graduates who find government salaries sufficiently attractive at this stage of their careers and seek the training that such service may offer as a prelude to private practice. Limitations on top salaries, however, discourage some from continuing with the government. Most government lawyers serve by appointment in the legal departments of a variety of federal and state agencies and local entities. The United States Department of Justice alone employs nearly eight thousand, and the Law Department of City of New York about six hundred. Others are engaged as public prosecutors, federal prosecutors, the United States attorneys and their assistants, are appointed by the President and are subordinate to the Attorney General of the United States. State prosecutors, sometimes known as district attorneys, are commonly elected by each country and, together with their assistants, are not under the control of the state attorney general. Though the participation of lawyers in government has declined recently, for two centuries lawyers make up roughly half of the Congress of the United States and of the state governors. These figures bear out the comment of Chief Justice Stone that, "No tradition of our profession is more cherished by lawyers than that of its leadership in public affairs."

词汇提示

fraction   *n.* 小部分
character   *n.* 品格
compliance with   遵循
be confined to   限制于
engage in   从事
mobility   *n.* 流动性
take root in   生根，扎根
specialize in   专门研究
be authorized to   经授权的
customary   *adj.* 习惯的，通常的
demarcation   *n.* 分界，界限
multitude   *n.* 多数
serve on   担任……职位
number   *v.* 总数达到
preventive   *adj.* 预防的
parallel   *adj.* 类似的
prelude   *n.* 前奏，序曲
be subordinate to   从属于
bear out   证明

法律术语

bar　*n.* 律师
legal profession　法律职业
practice　*n.* 实践，惯例
admission　*n.* 准入
Multistate Bar Exam　跨州律师考试
apprenticeship　*n.* 学徒期
formality　*n.* 手续
client　*n.* 委托人
counsel　*n.* 法律顾问
jurisdiction　*n.* 管辖区
boards of directors　董事会
business concern　企业
Attorney General　司法部长
Chief Justice　首席法官
barrister　*n.* 出庭律师
solicitor　*n.* 律师，法务官
legal instrument　法律文书
advocacy　*n.* 辩护
draft　*v.* 起草
practice of law　律师实务
proceeding　*n.* 程序
house counsel　企业法律顾问
general counsel　总顾问
committee　*n.* 委员会
litigation　*n.* 诉讼
municipal　*adj.* 市政的
judiciary　*n.* 司法部
entity　*n.* 实体
prosecutor　*n.* 检察官
attorney　*n.* 律师，代理人
assistant　*n.* 助理

要点解析

1. The bar　原指法庭中将公众与法官、律师及其他诉讼参与人分隔开来的一种隔板，后来才用于通指法律职业或律师职业。Bar Association 一词通译为律师协会。

2. Harlan Fiske Stone 哈兰·菲斯克·斯通（1872—1946）从哥伦比亚大学法学院毕业之后，曾一度同时教学和作律师。1910 年至 1923 年，他担任哥伦比亚大学法学院院长。1924 年，他被任命为司法部长（总检察长，U.S. Attorney General）。1925 年，他被任命为联邦最高法院法官，并于 1941 年接替查尔斯·伊万斯·休斯（Charles Evans Hughes）担任最高法院首席大法官（Chief Justice）。

3. barrister and solicitor, 英国的开业律师分为两种：诉讼律师和非诉律师。前者又译为大律师或出庭律师，有资格出席法庭审判并代理诉讼；后者又译为律师或诉状律师或事务律师，只能担任案件的诉讼准备工作和从事非诉讼律师业务。

4. house counsel 指受雇于某公司企业而非独立开业的律师。也可称为 corporate counsel, 公司或团体法律顾问。

5. …seek the training that such service may offer as a prelude to private practice…

寻求这种工作可以提供的锻炼作为私人开业的前奏。（美国检察人员的平均工作年限仅为 4～5 年，其原因之一就是到检察机关工作的法学院毕业生在积累了一定的审判经验之后便转去私人开业了。）

6. Attorney General 大写通常译为司法部部长，小写则是州司法局局长或州检察长。

7. No tradition of our profession is more cherished by lawyers than that of its leadership in public affairs.

在我们职业传统中，律师无疑最钟爱担任公共事务的领导。

参考译文

律 师 职 业

对法律职业的管理主要是各州需要考虑的问题，每个州对其执业准入都有自己的要求。大多数州都要求（未来执业者）有 3 年以上的大学本科教育以及获得法学学位。每个州都自行对申请进入法律职业的申请者举行书面考试。但是几乎所有的州都会使用"跨州律师考试"——这是一个持续一天的多项选择考试。各州再加上一天针对本周法律命题的写作考试。全部申请者中只有很少一部分能在第一次考试中通过，很多没有通过的人在后来的考试中得以通过。总的来说，每年大约有 4 万人能成功地通过这些考试，再经过对他们的品格考核后，这些人被录取到各自所在州的法律职业界。在录取前、录取后均无作学徒的要求。关于联邦法院执业的准入规则，各法院在这方面的规定不尽一致，但是一般来讲，那些有资格在州最高法院执业的人在办完一些小手续后便可能被获准在联邦法院执业。

律师的执业范围通常会被限制在一个地区，因为他只是在其被准入的州获得了执业资格，尽管该律师可以作为其当事人的代理人到不同地区办理案件。为处理在别的管辖区内的法律问题而聘请当地的律师是很平常的事。但是，一个律师迁居到另一州往往可以不参加考试便可获准执业，条件是如果他已在先前被获准执业的州执业了一段时间，通常是 5 年。

律师不仅可以从事律师职业，还可以从事任何向其他公众开放的活动。执业律师可以在其委托人的公司董事会担任董事，经商或者积极参与公众事务，这已十分普遍。即使律师作了法官，成了政府雇员或是私企雇员，或者作了法学教师，该律师仍然是律师界的一员，而且也可以从其他活动中重新回来作执业律师。相对人数较少的一些律师会因为在工商界担任要职而放弃执业。这一职业所具有的流动性和公众义务感在哈兰·菲斯克·斯通职业生涯中得到验证。在不同的时期,斯通曾是纽约一位出色的律师,曾经担任过哥伦比亚法学院教授、院长,后被任命为美国司法部长(总检察长)、联邦首席大法官。

　　律师按照其功能没有正式的区分。英国历史上形成的出庭律师和事务律师的区别没有在美国扎根,也就是说在美国,律师这一职业没有区分为一些律师是享有特殊的或排他的权利而出庭辩护,另一些律师是专长于起草法律文书。美国律师的执业领域不仅包括出庭辩护,而且包括提供法律咨询及起草法律文书。而且,在人们宽泛界定的"律师实务"的范围内,律师从业的领域是具有排他性的,也不向外公开。在辩护这一领域,规则是十分清楚的,任何个人在法庭上都可以代理他(她)自己,但是须将低等法院除外,因为在这里只有律师才可以在法庭上代理他人。不过,非律师也被授权在具有司法性质的行政机关正式程序中为他人作代理。在法律咨询和起草法律文书方面,界限难以划清,就好比联邦收入所得税领域中"律师实务"与"会计实务"难以划清一样。然而,大多数美国法院的严格规定是根据纽约最高法院的一项决定作出的。该规定指出:在外国而非纽约取得执业资格的律师,禁止向纽约的委托人提供法律建议,即便所提供的建议仅限于外国法。但是,外国律师可以被某一州的律师界所认可,即便是未经认可,也可以作为一名顾问就外国法向美国律师提供咨询意见。

公司法律顾问

　　在非私人执业律师中,许多人受雇于私人企业,例如工业公司、保险公司、银行,他们通常在公司内法律部门中担任法律顾问。随着公司的成长、企业的复杂化,由政府规章所引起的大量问题使得这样的企业非常迫切地希望在他们雇用的人中有受过法律培训的员工,这些人同时对企业的特定问题与情况非常熟悉。在大公司,法律部的人数可能达到100人或更多。总顾问,既是办公室的领导,通常也是公司成员,他服务于企业大决策委员会,可能是企业董事会的成员。公司法律顾问仍然是律师界的成员并享有出庭辩护的权利,尽管通常聘请外面的律师参与诉讼。然而,公司法律顾问作为一名咨询员所拥有的才能而非辩护本身才是其价值不菲的资本。不断接触企业的各种法律问题,使得公司顾问成为理想的预防法律纠纷出现的行家,而且也会被常常邀请就公司对其公众和国家所负义务提供咨询。

政府律师

　　政府部门中的律师业得到了相应的发展,20名律师中的2名律师现在是联邦、州、县、镇政府的雇员,这里面不包括法官。那些加入到公共服务队伍中去的律师通常是最近才毕业的法科生,他们发现在其事业的这个阶段,政府的薪水还是十分诱人的,而且可以寻求到锻炼,这样的经历可以成为其私人执业的前奏。但是,最高薪水的限制挫伤了一些律师继续在政府工作的积极性。(政府律师中的)大多数被任命到联邦和州政府机构及当地实体中的法律部门任职。联邦检察官,即(受雇于)美国的律师及其助手,是由总统任命的,隶属于美国司法部长。州检察官,有时称为地区律师,通常是由每个县选举产生并且不隶属于州司法局局长。尽管参与政府管理的律师数量近年来有所下降,但200年来(政府律师的人数)已达到美国国会人数的大约一半、州长人数的一半。这些数字证明了首席大法官斯通的评论:"在我们职业传统中,律师无疑最钟爱担任公共事务的领导。"

Passage Two
法律职业中的妇女和少数民族

美国当代法律职业主要形成于 19 世纪 70 年代至 20 世纪 50 年代之间,而且已发展为一个自我限定和自我规制的职业。通过地方、州和全国律师协会的发展,通过职业道德规范、纪律规则程序的颁行,以及对法学院入学条件的界定与紧控,法律职业得以控制律师来源并限制对该职业的接近与进入。直到 20 世纪 60 年代,法律职业中绝大多数且占绝对优势的人都是男性白人;而在该职业等级系统的高层次上的人都是"瓦斯普"(WASP,即白种、盎格鲁撒克逊、新教徒人)。实际上,"在我们历史的大部分时期内,律师一词都意味着'男性白人'。在 19 世纪 70 年代以前,律师协会中没有一名妇女,而黑人亦寥寥无几。"1872 年,迈拉·布莱德韦尔由于伊利诺伊州拒绝了她担任律师的申请而提起诉讼。合众国最高法院对她说:"妇女的最高使命就是履行作为妻子和母亲的崇高且慈祥的职责。"

当代法律职业的状况如何?发生了什么变化?根据巴巴拉·柯伦最近的研究,在 1951 年至 1984 年间,法律职业在规模、年龄和性别分配等方面开始发生变化。法律职业的人数日益增多且日益年轻化,其中女性人数也在增长。律师人数从 1951 年的 221 605 人上升为 1984 年的 649 000 人,几乎增加了 200%。法律工作者的平均年龄也从 46 岁下降到 39 岁。1951 年,女性律师仅占法律职业人员总数的 2.5%;到 1984 年,妇女在法律工作者中所占的比例已上升为 12.8%。

理查德·艾贝尔在评论这些变化对律师协会的影响时指出:这些变化的一个可能的意义在于"极少数年长的男性白人控制着律师协会,而这会深深地影响到包括有相当数量的女性和少数民族成员在内的大量年轻律师的生活"。由于年轻一代的律师在今后 10 年至 20 年内不可能占据掌权的位置以及该组织管理上那突出的老年统治特征,所以在统治者和被统治者之间的不同利益、风格和人数分布就很可能生成相当紧张的关系。

例如,看一下妇女在大律师事务所的分布情况便可发现,女律师占律师事务所律师总数的 30.4%,而仅占其合伙人的 5%。正像罗纳德·切斯特所指出的那样,现在妇女大量地进入法律职业并不一定导致妇女将获得诸如高级合伙人、终身教授、重要法官以及高级政府官员等"有权力的职位"。在更多的妇女占据这种有权力的职位之前,她们不可能影响到"法律职业的运转方式和职业进步中所使用的标准"。

詹姆斯·怀特在第一份关于在传统上由男人统治的法律职业中妇女待遇问题的全国性研究报告中指出,男女律师的工资差别反映出法律职业中广泛存在歧视现象。"结论很明确,男律师的收入远远高于女律师。"虽然近几年来法学院毕业生所面临的男女工资差别并不像过去那么大,但是女律师们仍然要面对那微妙和公开的性别歧视待遇和态度。

法院中妇女问题的纽约专门调研组在 22 个月的调查之后得出如下结论:针对女诉讼人、女律师和女法院雇员的性别偏见是一个广泛存在的问题。在这一点上,妇女必须容忍冷漠、歧视和敌对的氛围。在法庭上,法官经常提出一些令人尴尬的问题,如"你丈夫对你在这工作有何想法?"或者,法官以一种蔑视且非职业化的方式对待女律师,称呼她们为"小姐""小姑娘""蜜甜心"或"律师娘"。这种性别歧视和非职业化行为不仅降低了女律师的威信,影响了女律师的工作,而且破坏了律师制度的统一性。

尽管各种关于司法行为的州委员会已经对那些在法庭上表现出性别歧视、大声呵斥与非职业化行为的法官做出了纪律处分，但是要改变性别歧视态度及其文化背景则远非处分几个违纪者所能实现的。

与法律职业中妇女那有限的增长相比，黑人和其他少数民族在法律职业中的增长就更为有限了。根据1980年的统计，所有少数民族律师的人数仅占全国律师总数的4.8%。1981年，在全国574 810名律师中，黑人律师仅占1.7%。在几乎所有关于法律职业构成的研究或讨论中，亚裔人甚至往往不被作为统计研究的对象，或者不被认定为一个少数民族的亚群体。

少数民族律师进入大律师事务所的机会如何？换言之，大律师事务所在受到有关种族主义和崇尚社会名流的批评之后，在雇人实践中有何反映？1982年，根据对200个最大的律师事务所中的150个所做的调查，25个律师事务所中没有黑人律师；86个律师事务所中没有拉美裔律师。1984年，《国家法律学报》对100个最大的律师事务所中的92个进行了调查，发现黑人律师仅占其律师总数的1.5%；拉美裔律师仅占0.65%；但女律师的比例却上升为20.19%。全国黑人律师协会主席丹尼斯·阿切尔指出，"那是种族主义或老哥们关系网或者无论你称其什么……那些在大律师事务所掌管雇用权的律师就是不雇黑人。"

然而，大律师事务所雇用少数民族律师的百分比尚不足以说明全部问题。获准进入有名气的律师事务所合伙人级别的少数民族律师的比例更低。1982年的《全国法律学报》调查发现：在106个律师事务所中没有黑人合伙人；在133个律师事务所中没有拉美裔合伙人。大门可能已经敞开，但是少数民族仍处于权力、名气和报酬较低的位置。

尽管"老哥们关系网"已受到广泛的批评，但是保持这种关系的组织力量依然存在。那些认识候选人而且其评价很受其他机构的同行欢迎和重视的高级合伙人、法官、教授几乎都是男性白人。那种更容易承认与自己同性别或同种族的人或者最适于被视为自己的门徒的人的智力与创造学识之非凡能力的倾向是完全自然的。但是，这种观点反映了错误地把一种价值观作为"自然"条件的危险。

再者，如果参与有关该问题的公众讨论是一种迹象的话，那么大律师事务所未必意识到那些关于妇女和少数民族律师的统计数字是个重要问题。1985年，美国律师协会举行了一系列关于妇女和少数民族律师问题的听证会。在被邀请的400家律师事务所中，只有两家出席了听证会。那些律师事务所对未能出席所给出的解释包括：听证会时间不方便，以及由于其事务所没有或几乎没有雇用少数民族律师，所以相信它们对听证会做不出什么贡献。

▶ 词汇提示

自我规制的　self-regulating
职业道德规范　ethics codes
最高使命　paramount destiny
组织管理　governance
分布　allocation
占（比例）　account for
大量地进入　influx
由男人统治的　male dominated

公开的 overt
性别歧视的 sexist
冷漠 condescension
敌对 hostility
称呼 address
破坏 undermine
少数民族 minority
统计 census
亚群体 subgroup
崇尚社会名流的 elitism
拉美裔 Hispanics
老哥们 good-old-boy
门徒 protege

▶ 法律术语

颁行 promulgation
新教徒 Protestant
最高法院 Supreme Court
老年统治 gerontocratic
人数分布 demography
律师事务所 law firm
高级合伙人 senior partnership
终身教授 tenured professorial position
高级政府官员 upper level government job
专门调研组 Task Force
诉讼人 litigant
律师娘 lawyeretee
处分 reprimand
国家法律学报 National Law Journal
全国黑人律师协会 Black National Bar Association
美国律师协会 American Bar Association
听证会 hearing

▶ 要点提示

1. 由于年轻一代的律师在今后10年至20年内不可能占据掌权的位置以及该组织管理上那突出的老年统治特征，所以在统治者和被统治者之间的不同利益、风格和人数分布就很可能生成相当紧张的关系。

本句的翻译重点在于"占据掌权的位置","老年统治特征"和"生成紧张的关系"。第一个,占据掌权的位置也就是说要从不掌权到掌权是一个上升的过程,因此用带有上升意义的 ascend 较妥,因此译为 ascend to positions of power;"老年统治特征"是一个专有名词,gerontocratic character;而最后一个"生成紧张关系"要注意"紧张关系"其实就是"紧张"的意思,不必译出 relationship。因此,这句话可译为:"Since the younger generation of lawyers will not ascend to positions of power for another decade or two, given the strongly gerontocratic character of professional governance, the divergence of interests, styles, and demography between rulers and ruled is likely to generate considerable tension."

2. 现在妇女大量地进入法律职业并不一定导致妇女将获得诸如高级合伙人、终身教授、重要法官以及高级政府官员等"有权力的职位"。

本句中术语较多,如"高级合伙人""终身教授""高级政府官员"等,另外还应注意"并不一定导致……"的翻译,指的是 A 与 B 的关系并非直接的因果关系。综上所述,本句可译为:"The present influx of women into the profession has not necessarily resulted in women gaining access to 'power positions' such as senior partnerships, tenured professorial positions, important judgeships, and upper level government jobs."

3. 这种性别歧视和非职业化行为不仅降低了女律师的威信,影响了女律师的工作,而且破坏了律师制度的统一性。

翻译本句中要注意,中文中的"降低威信"实质上就是指破坏了一个人的威信,因此不宜用 reduce 或者 minimize 来译,而用 undermine 更为贴切。整句译为:"This kind of sexist and unprofessional behavior not only undermines the authority and effectiveness of women lawyers, but also undermines the integrity of the legal system."

4. 换言之。

英文中有不少表达方法可以表示"换言之"的意思,如:in other words, to put it in another way,或者 to pose this another way 等。

5. 美国律师协会,The American Bar Association (ABA) 是美国律师的全国性组织,建立于 1878 年,目的是推动法律科学,提高律师素质,完善司法管理,促进立法与裁判的统一性,并加强成员之间的社会交流。自愿性组织,工作出色的律师都可参加。设有代表机构,协会的工作由代表机构的主管委员会及其他委员会监督、指导。下设许多分部,每一分部负责法律的一个领域或法律事务的一个分支。注重保持律师职业行为的准则及提高法学教育水平,支持有助于完善司法管理与实现立法统一的措施。

参考译文

Women and Minorities in the Profession

The American contemporary legal profession was largely constructed between the 1870's and the 1950's and has developed as a self-defining, self-regulating profession. Through the development of local, state, and national bar associations, the promulgation of ethics codes, disciplinary rules and procedures, and the definition and tightening of the entrance requirements to law schools, the legal profession was able to control the supply of lawyers and limit access and entry into the profession. Until the 1960's, the legal profession was overwhelmingly and predominantly white, male, and in the higher echelons of the professional hierarchy, solidly "WASP" (White, Anglo-Saxon, Protestant). In fact, "for much of our history, lawyer meant 'White male'. Not a single woman was admitted to the bar before the 1870's, and precious few blacks. " In 1872, Myra Bradwell, in her challenge to the State of Illinois' denial of her application to become a member of the bar, was told by the Supreme Court of the United States that the "paramount destiny and mission of woman are to fulfill the noble and benign offices of wife and mother. "

What does the contemporary legal profession look like? What changes have occurred? According to Barbara Curran's recent study, in the period between 1951-1984, changes in size, age and sex distribution began to occur. The profession is growing in numbers, becoming younger, and increasing in the numbers of women in the profession. The number of lawyers grew from 221,605 lawyers in 1951 to 649,000 lawyers in 1984, and increase of almost 200%. The median age has shifted from 46 years to 39 years. In 1951, the percentage of women lawyers was only 2.5%. By 1984, the percentage of women in the profession had grown to 12.8%.

In terms of impact on the organized bar, Richard Abel has suggested that one possible significance of these changes is that "a very small cohort of elderly white men are governing associations that deeply affect the lives of a very large younger cohort with significant female and minority membership. Since the younger generation of lawyers will not ascend to positions of power for another decade or two, given the strongly gerontocratic character of professional governance, the divergence of interests, styles, and demography between rulers and ruled is likely to generate considerable tension. "

For example, looking at the presence and allocation of women in the large firms reveals that while women associates may account for 30.4% of law firm associates, women account for only 5% of the partners. As Ronald Chester has pointed out, the present influx of women into the profession has not necessarily resulted in women gaining access to "power positions" such as senior partnerships, tenured professorial positions, important judgeships, and upper level government jobs. Until more women hold such power positions, they will not be able to affect "the way the legal profession is run and the criteria it uses for professional advancement".

James White, in the first national study which looked at the treatment of women in this traditionally male dominated profession, indicated that there was widespread discrimination which was reflected in the pay scales of male and female lawyers. "The conclusion is clear: the males make a lot more money than the females. " Although the sex differential in terms of salaries may be becoming less substantial for more recent law school graduates, women still face the problem of subtle and overt sexist treatment and attitudes.

After a 22-month investigation, the New York Task Force on Women in the Courts concluded that gender bias against women litigants, attorneys, and court employees was a pervasive problem in which women must endure a climate of condescension, indifference and hostility. In court, judges have asked embarrassing questions, "What does your husband think about you working here?"; or have treated women lawyers in a condescending and unprofessional manner, addressing them as "young lady", "little girl", "honey", or "lawyeretee". This kind of sexist and unprofessional behavior not only undermines the authority and effectiveness of women lawyers, but also undermines the integrity of the legal system.

Although various state commissions on judicial conduct have disciplined judges who have exhibited sexist, blatant and unprofessional behavior on the bench, changes in sexual attitudes and cultural conditioning will require more than formal reprimands of the few individuals who are singled out for disciplinary action.

Compared to the limited gains by women in the profession, the gains for blacks and other minorities are even more limited. According to the 1980 census, the total minority lawyer population was only 4.8% of all lawyers. In 1981, out of a total lawyer population of 574,810 lawyers, black lawyers accounted for only 1.7%. Asians are often not even a focus of statistical studies or identified as a minority subgroup in virtually all of the studies or discussions of the composition of the profession.

In terms of access to the big law firms, how are minority lawyers doing? Or to pose this another way, how are the law firms doing in terms of responding to criticisms of elitism and racism in their hiring practices? Based on a survey of 151 of the 200 largest firms, a 1982 National Law Journal survey revealed that there were no black lawyers at 25 firms, while 86 had no Hispanics. A 1984 National Law Journal survey of 92 of the nation's 100 largest law firms revealed that blacks represented only 1.5% and Hispanics only 0.65% of the lawyers employed by those firms while the percentage of women had risen to 20.1%. Dennis Archer, president of the Black National Bar Association stated, "It's racism or the good-old-boy network or whatever you want to call it… The lawyers who hire in big firms aren't hiring blacks."

Yet the percentage of minority lawyers hired at the big firms may not tell the whole story. The number of minorities allowed to enter the prestigious partner ranks was even lower. The 1982 National Law Journal survey found that there were no black partners in 106 firms and no Hispanic partners in 133. While the doors may be opening, minorities continue to be relegated to lower positions of power, prestige and economic rewards.

Although the criticisms about the "Old Boy Network" are voiced by many, the institutional forces which maintain it are still present: the professors, judges and senior partners who know the candidates, and whose judgment is sought out and given credence by their counterparts in other institutions, are overwhelmingly white and male. The tendency to recognize intellectual power and unusual capacity for creative scholarship more easily in persons of one's own sex and race and in persons who can be viewed most comfortably as one's proteges is perfectly natural. However, this view reflects the danger of mistaking a value for a "natural" condition.

Furthermore, if participation in public forums on the issue is an indication, the big firms may not necessarily perceive the dismal statistics on minorities and women in the firms as a major problem. In 1985, the American Bar Association (ABA) held a series of public hearings on problems of minorities in the legal profession. Out of 400 law firms invited, only two participated in the hearings.

Some of the explanations offered for this lack of response included the inconvenience of timing of the hearings and the belief that since the firms employed few or no minorities, they had little to contribute.

Section II 技能拓展

 翻译技巧

法律文本翻译的步骤和要点

在翻译文本过程中如何把握住英汉法律语言的主旨至关重要,法律文本的翻译应在尽可能简洁的语句中清楚地表达法律文本的本来意思。法律文本译文的准确是法律文本翻译的根本,而翻译失真则是法律文本翻译的大患。例如我国《中外合资经营企业法实施条例》第五十条规定:"合营企业所需的机器设备……在同等条件下,应优先在中国购买。"本条条文却被译成"…a joint venture should give first priority to Chinese sources"。译文中以 should 来译"应当",似有不妥。因为 should 表示法律义务,只表示一般义务或道义上的义务,而 shall 在法律文件中有其特殊的含义,意为"应当承担的责任和义务",带有指令性和强制性,是一种法律义务,不如此则产生违反法律义务的后果。由此可见,原译文用 should 来强调当事人的责任和义务,并没有体现合营企业在此问题上所应承担的严格责任,从而有损法律的严肃性。相反,此处以 shall 来代替 should,更能明确当事人的义务。

从事法律文本翻译,要遵循以下步骤和要点。

第一,要谨慎选词,注意法律语言的庄严性。

在一般的情况下,中西方法律词汇之间总会存在内涵最为接近的对应词汇,这时可以选用该词而不会导致太大的误读。但由于中西法律文化之间存在的固有差异,有一部分词的含义是不可能完全一致的。通常情况下,译者们在面临一种文化中有而另一种文化中无的事物时,会采用音译或直译的办法,翻译法律英语时也需要进行一种创造性的加工和想象,如罗马法系中的 legal person 最初被译成"法人",due procedure 译成"正当程序"等都是一种建设性的创新。

第二,注意把握当事人的法律关系,围绕该法律关系并注意区分主体、内容、客体展开翻译。

比如说,在翻译英语合同中,当事人权利义务的分配与当事人在合同所处的地位(主体)、合同的性质种类(涉及内容)密切相关。同所有其他领域的翻译工作一样,法律法规等法律文献的翻译也要求译者仔细地研读原文并全面准确地理解原文。在充分了解本文第一部分法律英语关于词汇、词法、语法等方面的特点之后,可以较为迅速有效地把握其主旨。比如说,法律英语中定语后置、分隔现象普遍,有时法律文件或条文中往往是一个

句子就构成一段或一个条款,或者在一个定语从句中又嵌套着另外一个定语从句,在理解或翻译此类句子时思维要敏捷、清晰,要通过各种连接标志来理解句子意思。例如:Substantive due process reaches the situation where the deprivation of life, liberty, or property is accomplished by legislation, which can, even if given the fairest procedure, destroy the enjoyment of all three of these rights.(实体法上的正当法律程序适用于那些以立法手段来剥夺生命、自由或财产的情形,而这些情形即使有最公正的程序法作为保障,也可能破坏人们对这三项权利的享受。)

第三,勤查法律英语工具书和参考书,参考借鉴香港同行的翻译。

法律英语的学习是循序渐进,但是翻译工作却是有时间限制的。要在较短时间提高翻译水平,工具书和参考书是不可少的。现在比较权威的法律英汉词典主要有《元照英美法词典》(法律出版社,2003年版),《英汉法律词典》(法律出版社,1998年版)等。由于香港是世界上唯一以中英文立法的司法区,且普通法的历史有100多年的时间,其走在我们前头的法律英语的翻译可以为我们提供一定的借鉴作用。

第四,在直译与意译中作出适当选择。

由于中英法律文化的重大差异和法律专业的特殊性,在更多情形下无法直译,就应该采取意译。有时为了更加符合汉语习惯,译文信息缺失的情况下,还应该适当补译。

比如:The borrower shall not do or cause or suffer anything to be done whereby the lenders' interest may be prejudiced.

如果直译的话是:"借款人不得作出或促使或容许任何事情发生借以使贷款人的利益可能受损。"

显然,上述翻译拗口,不流畅,就应该意译,如下:

"凡可导致贷款人的利益受损的事情,借款人均不得作出,或促使或容许其发生。"

第五,在翻译复杂长句时简化句子结构,先剔除定语、状语等修饰语,寻找主语、谓语、宾语,抓住中心意思。

例如:If the Respondent applies to the court for it to consider the Respondents' financial position after the divorce, the decree nisi can not be made absolute unless the court is satisfied that the Petitioner had made or will make proper financial provision for the Respondent, or else that the Petitioner should not be required to make any financial provision for the Respondent.

整段话虽然看起来非常冗长,但是经过分析,其实主句就是:The decree nisi can not be made absolute. 在掌握原文的结构和意思后,该句话可以译为:"如答辩人提出申请,要求法庭考虑其离婚后的经济状况,则法庭非认为呈请人已经提供或将会提供予答辩人妥善的经济援助,或(因任何理由)呈请人无须为答辩人提供任何经济援助,否则不可将暂准离婚令正式确定为最终/绝对离婚令。"

最后,在翻译初稿完成后,应当进行必要的检查和润色,比如说检查翻译文稿是否搭配不当,句子成分残缺,语序颠倒,用词有无歧义,翻译从句时衔接是否有失当等情形,细加斟酌后才能最终定稿,切不可匆忙收工。

 法律宝典

Lawyer 是"律师"？

lawyer 在英语国家和当代国际社会中是最常用的法律词汇之一，除"律师"一义之外，lawyer 其外延何在？从英美的法律辞典、法律文献到国际法律组织使用这个词汇的情况看，可以分为两层意义。

（一）lawyer "律师"，这是狭义；其次是广义，即包括律师、法官、法学教授等，可以统称为"法律工作者"或"法律家"。

主要依据：

美国《布莱克法律词典》(Black's Law Dictionary) (15th ed, 1983): "lawyer: a person learned in the law; as an attorney, counsel, or solicitor; a person licensed to practice law." 这里，lawyer 的定义是"精通法律的人"。（原文: "a person licensed to practice law. Any person who prosecutes or defends causes in course of record or other judicial tribunals of the United States… or whose business it is to give legal advice or assistance in relation to any cause or matter whatever"）

上述引文表明 lawyer 有两层意义：在 lawyer 词目一开始给 lawyer 界定为"一个精通法律的人"，它简明地概括了所有精通法律的知识界，不论是实际的法律工作者或者法学教师。这是 lawyer 的广义。

该辞典列举不同称谓、不同职能的几种律师，即 attorney, counsel, solicitor, 这是 lawyer 的狭义，也是日常更多使用的关于律师的统称。

该词条最后提出 lawyer 包括在法院从事检控和辩护工作和提供法律意见的人，这就为 lawyer 一词扩大范围给自己所作的定义提供一个内容。

（二）英国《牛津法律辞典》(The Oxford Companion to Law, Oxford, 1980): "lawyer, a general term for one professionally qualified to practice law in some capacity, and including judges…, legal practitioners and law teachers…The term is sometimes restricted to those enrolled as practitioners, excluding judges and law teachers. The category of legal practitioners may be undifferentiated, in the U.S. and Canada, or differentiated into barristers (or advocates) and solicitors as in the U.K. and other jurisdiction."

上述引文同样表明，lawyer 有狭义和广义之分，引文认为 lawyer 一词，是在专业上合格以某种身份从事法律业务的人的总括的名称。它指出，"包括法官（非法律专业法官除外）、开业律师和法学教师"都在这范畴之内。此即广义的 lawyer。

该辞典还指出，lawyer 有时局限于那些已经注册的法律事务开业者（即律师），这就是狭义的律师。

术语积累

legal profession　法律职业；律师界
barrister　诉讼律师

solicitor 非讼律师
bench 法官席；法院；法庭
client 委托人
law firm 律师事务所
private practioner 私人开业律师
Chamber 出庭律师事务所
contempt of court 藐视法庭
hearing 聆讯
advocacy 出庭辩护；代理诉讼
single practitioner 单独开业者
house counsel 专职法律顾问
litigation 诉讼
instrument 文书，文件
inter alia 其他以外
intra vires 权力以内
interlocutory 中途的指令
lapse 失去时效
limitation period 时限
merits 法律理据
next friend 诉讼保护人
pardon 赦免
petition 请求
plaintiff 原告
Power of Attorney 委托书
Prohibition Order 禁制令
reconciliation 和解
refresher fee 大律师上庭之额外费用
specific performance 强制履行
案件 case
案件受理费 litigation fee
打官司 initiate legal proceeding
大律师的收费 counsel's fees
大律师 barrister
大律师事务所 barristers' chambers, chambers of counsel
大律师书记 barrister's clerk
代理检察员 acting prosecutor
代理审判员 acting judge
法律顾问处 Legal Consultant Office
法官考评委员会 Committee for the Examination and Appraisal of Judges

法律服务所　Legal Service Office
法案　bill
法定代表人　legal representative
法定代理人　legal agent

Section III　巩固练习

词汇与短语

1. 从业者
2. 律师界
3. 审问
4. 准则
5. 诉讼律师（英）
6. 事务律师（英）
7. 出庭辩护
8. 审理中的案件
9. 法律学术论文
10. 将律师永久除名
11. indictment
12. jury
13. bench
14. client
15. law firm
16. hearing
17. house counsel
18. litigation
19. Attorney General
20. prosecutor

句子与段落

1. The regulation of the legal profession primarily the concern of the states, each of which has its own requirements for admission to practice.
2. The rules for admission to practice before the federal courts vary with the court, but generally those entitled to practice before the highest court of a state may be admitted before the federal courts upon compliance with minor formalities.
3. It is not uncommon for the practicing lawyer to serve on boards of directors of corporate clients, to engage in business, and to participate actively in public affairs.
4. The American lawyer's domain includes advocacy, counseling, and drafting.
5. A parallel development has taken place in government and out of twenty lawyers who are not in private practice are employees of the federal, state, country, and municipal governments, exclusive of the judiciary.
6. No tradition of our profession is more cherished by lawyers than that of its leadership in public affairs.

7. The distinction between barristers and solicitors found in England did not take root in the United States, and there is no branch of the profession that has a special or exclusive right to appear in court, nor is there a branch that specializes in the preparation of legal instruments.
8. The growth of corporations, the complexity of business, and the multitude of problems posed by government regulation make it desirable for such firms to have in their employ persons with legal training who, at the same time, are intimately familiar with the particular problems and conditions of the firm.
9. 诉讼律师代表委托人参与诉讼，咨询律师则准备文件，对企业提供咨询，处理财产。
10. 律师不仅对法律事务提供咨询，而且也对其他事项提供咨询，如企业决策和家庭事务。
11. 律师应该力求避免诉讼，以谈判求妥协。
12. 咨询律师为委托人利益作出的辩护不是针对法官和陪审团的。
13. 律师在为一项不得人心的案由提供辩护时，必须明白他同时也是在维护法制。
14. 通过地方、州和全国律师协会的发展，通过职业道德规范、纪律规则程序的颁行，以及对法学院入学条件的界定与紧控，法律职业得以控制律师来源并限制对该职业的接近与进入。
15. 由于年轻一代的律师在今后 10 年至 20 年内不可能占据掌权的位置以及该组织管理上那突出的老年统治特征，所以在统治者和被统治者之间的不同利益、风格和人数分布就很可能生成相当紧张的关系。
16. 现在妇女大量地进入法律职业并不一定导致妇女将获得诸如高级合伙人、终身教授、重要法官以及高级政府官员等"有权力的职位"。
17. 在被邀请的 400 家律师事务所中，只有两家出席了听证会。那些律师事务所对未能出席所给出的解释包括：听证会时间不方便，以及由于其事务所没有或几乎没有雇用少数民族律师所以相信它们对听证会做不出什么贡献。
18. 要想成为一位成功的律师，灵活的头脑和雄辩的口才是非常重要的，尤其是在一世纪，几乎所有著名的律师都能说会道。在现在看来，他们当时在法庭上的演说显得过分华丽而夸大其词。但是在那个还没有收音机和电视的时代，律师们的演说更像是一场表演秀。这也是他们赢得声望的关键所在，也许能为他们赢得下一个委托人。

Unit Four

Administrative Law
行 政 法

Section I 译例研究

>> **Passage One**
Introduction to Administrative Law

Administrative law is concerned with the powers and procedures of those organs of government, other than legislatures and courts that affect private interests either by rule or by decision. The field is relatively young and is still in a stage of rapid development. It is heavily procedural in its emphasis and does not include the substantive law created by administrative agencies. It deals chiefly though not exclusively with the discharge by public officials of functions related to rule-making and adjudication, and focuses on control of administrators by courts. Although administrative agencies abound on the state and local levels, the federal agencies are the widest impact and are the easiest to describe.

The administrative process on the federal level goes back as far as 1789, but its modern origins date from the establishment in 1877 of the interstate Commerce Commission to deal with the problems of the railroad industry. The Commission sets the pattern for those independent regulatory agencies — functioning outside of the executive departments and regulating some aspects of private activity — that are the most distinctive species of administrative body in the United States. Federal administrative agencies of all kinds multiplied rapidly under New Deal legislation enacted in the 1930's during the administration of President Roosevelt. There are now one hundred and twenty federal agencies, with such diverse concerns as airlines, nuclear energy, banking, farm prices, immigration, labor relations, and old age pensions.

Administrative law is compounded of constitutional law, statutes, case law, and agency rules and decisions. On the constitutional plane, the effect of the due process clause upon administrative procedure is of chief importance. Most significance on the statutory level is the Federal Administrative Procedure Act of 1946, which sought to regularize administrative procedure and to clarify the scope of judicial review of administrative action. Case law also plays a surprisingly large role, due in part to the general nature of many of the constitutional and statutory directives. Because there is no separate system of courts that dispense administrative law, its judicially developed principles are similar to those of other fields.

Agency procedures may be formal or informal. The vast bulk of decisions are reached by informal proceedings with nothing resembling a formal hearing. As for the small fraction of cases where formal proceedings are held, the variety of agencies and the scope of their activities defy both general description and uniform regulation. Although the Federal Administrative Procedure Act lays down general guidelines of procedure on matters common to most agencies, the dominant theme of the due process clause of the federal Constitution runs throughout administrative procedure. The chief requirements of procedural due process are notice and an opportunity to have a fair hearing, and there is a growing view that one is entitled to notice and a hearing analogous to a trial on disputed facts involved in an adjudication of one's rights. Hearings are commonly held before agency employees known as administrative law judges, whose initial findings are subject to the final decision of the agency.

The judicial control of administrative actions is one of the most significant topics of American administrative law. Because no special system of courts handles administrative matters, judicial review is carried out within the framework created for conventional litigation in the regular courts. Most federal regulatory statutes specifically authorize review of particular actions of the agency charged with their administration. Review is commonly appellate in nature, before a federal court of appeals on the record below; less often it is by an original action in federal district court. Furthermore, there is a general statutory authorization of review in the Federal Administrative Procedure Act as well as non-statutory review in some areas. Review may also be possible under other circumstances, as when agency action requires court enforcement.

Administrative agencies, in spite of their considerable independence, are also subject to some control by the legislative and executive branches. Although there is no general provision for congressional review of administrative rules and regulations, Congress has not hesitated to intervene in agency affairs through its control over agency budgets and through investigation by congressional committees. The President has the power, subject to the consent of the Senate, to appoint agency heads, but his power of removal before the end of a fixed term is severely circumscribed.

词汇提示

legislature   n. 立法机关；议会
procedural   adj. 程序上的
discharge   v. 卸下；放出；解雇；免除   n. 卸货；排放；解雇

rule-making　　*n.* 做出决定
adjudication　　*n.* 裁判，裁决
regulatory agency　管理机关
enact　　*v.* 制订，颁布
age pension　　养老金
(be) compounded of...= composed of...　由……组成
constitutional law　宪法
statutory　　*adj.* 法定的；法令的；可依法惩处的
regularize　　*v.* 使……正式化
(in) formal proceedings　　（非）正式程序
dispense　　*v.* 分配，分发；执行；免除　*vi.* 免除，豁免
juridically　　*adv.* 法律上
formal hearing　　正式审理
lay down　　放下；制定；铺设；主张
entitle　　*v.* 称作；使……有权利
analogous　　*adj.* 类似的；[生] 同功的；可比拟的
adjudication　　*n.* 破产之宣告；判决；裁定
appellate　　*adj.* [律] 受理上诉的；上诉的
original action　　原诉（区别于上诉诉讼而言）；第一审案件
(non-) statutory　　*adj.*（非）法定的
congressional　　*adj.* 国会的；会议的；议会的
consent　　*v.* 同意；答应；赞成
circumscribe　　*v.* 限制

法律术语

substantive law　　实体法
The Interstate Commerce Commission　　州际商业委员会
New Deal legislation　　新政立法
statute　　*n.* 制定法
case law　　案例法
judicial review　　司法审查
congressional committee　　国会委员会
judicial control　　司法监督
the Federal Administrative Procedure Act of 1946　《1946年联邦行政诉讼法》

要点解析

1. Administrative law is concerned with the powers and procedures of those organs of

government, other than legislatures and courts that affect private interests either by rule or by decision.

行政法所调整的，是立法机关和法院之外，以规定或决定影响私人利益的那些政府机关的权利和程序。be concerned with 是"关于"的意思，但在此处，联系上下文和语境，不宜这样翻译，"调整"则更符合原文的意思。powers and procedures 后面的内容很长，结构也比较复杂，翻译成汉语时，可以把它们都作为"权利和程序"的定语，起修饰作用。汉语的特点是把定语放在被修饰词前，而英语则是放在先行词后，用定语从句连接，要符合各自的语言习惯。

2. The Commission sets the pattern for those independent regulatory agencies — functioning outside of the executive departments and regulating some aspects of private activity — that are the most distinctive species of administrative body in the United States.

该委员会为美国行政机关中最具特色的，在行政部门之外行使其职能并管理某方面私人活动的那些独立的管理机关定下了模式。executive 译为"行政"。按上文"行政机关"的"行政"是 administrative，而此处的 executive 则是泛指"立法、行政、司法"三权或三部门之一的"行政"；function 译为"行使职能"而不是"功能"；此外，标点符号的翻译也应当注意，不难发现，原文中的破折号在翻译过程中被转为逗号了，将破折号引出的内容译为定语。

3. The chief requirements of procedural due process are notice and an opportunity to have a fair hearing, and there is a growing view that one is entitled to notice and a hearing analogous to a trial on disputed facts involved in an adjudication of one's rights.

在这方面，人们日益认为：人们有权被通知和接受审理——这种审理，同对裁决有关人们权利的有争议事实的审理，颇有雷同之处。"There is a growing view that…"这一形式经常出现，它是一个没有主语的结构，表示"有"，"存在"，然而在翻译时，我们通常补充主语，表达人们的观点，使句义更加明确；be entitled to 译为"有资格，有权利"。要注意，在翻译过程中，应当适当调整语序，使其符合中文的表达习惯。

4. As for the small fraction of cases where formal proceedings are held, the variety of agencies and the scope of their activities defy both general description and uniform regulation.

至于采用正式程序的那一小部分案件，则机关五花八门，其活动范围又广，既无法概述，也不能统一规定。

defy 原为"挑战，对抗"之意，在此句中表示否定，可译为"既无法……，也不能……"；名词短语 the variety of agencies and the scope of their activities 转换为动词，译为"五花八门、其活动范围又广"。

5. Hearings are commonly held before agency employees known as administrative law judges, whose initial findings are subject to the final decision of the agency.

上述审理一般在称作行政法法官的行政机关职员面前进行，他们的初步决定尚有待于该行政机关做出最终决定。subject 含义多种多样，以 subject to 搭配的形式使用在词典中只有形容词和副词两种情况。subject 一般有两种用法：① 以介词短语形式出现，后跟 agreement，contract，regulations 等法律文件名或文件中特定条款名等名词配合使用，通常可翻译成"根据……规定"及"在不抵触……的情况下"；② 以介词短语/动词短语（be subjected to，较少见）出现，后接法律文书或条款以外的其他名词，一般译为"使……面临/遭受……"或"……服从或接受"等。

6. The judicial control of administrative actions is one of the most significant topics of American administrative law. Because no special system of courts handles administrative matters, judicial review is carried out within the framework created for conventional litigation in the regular courts.

行政行为的司法监督乃是美国行政法上最重要的课题之一。由于没有专门的法院系统处理行政案件,司法审查是在一般法院的传统诉讼的范围内进行的。

control 有"控制"之意,但在法律英语中多译为"监督",本文不止一次出现这个词,如在句子"Administrative agencies, in spite of their considerable independence, are also subject to some control by the legislative and executive branches"中,control 也同样表示"监督"的意思。我们不难发现,很多日常生活中常用的动词,在法律英语中被赋予了特殊、特定的意思,对于这些词,在翻译中要尤其注意。

7. Although there is no general provision for congressional review of administrative rules and regulations, Congress has not hesitated to intervene in agency affairs through its control over agency budgets and through investigation by congressional committees.

虽然关于国会审查行政规则和规章尚无总的规定,但国会对行政机关的事务进行干预,从未迟疑不决;其方法是通过对行政机关预算的监督和国会委员会的调查活动。provision 译为"规定"而不是"供给";hesitate to 后面的结构较长,若译为中文时按照英文的顺序,没有停顿,一译到底,则会显得冗长又杂乱,因此,我们可以把 hesitate to 后面的内容断开,另成一小句。congressional committees 译为"国会委员会"。

参考译文

行 政 法

行政法所调整的,是立法机关和法院之外,以规定或决定影响私人利益的那些政府机关的权利和程序。这个领域比较年轻,而且仍处于迅速发展的阶段。它非常着重程序,排斥行政机关所订立的实体法。它所处理的,主要(虽然不是全部)是公务员如何行使其涉及订立规则和进行裁决的职能,以法院对行政官员的监督为其重点。虽然州和地方两级行政机关多如牛毛,但影响最大且又最易描述的却是联邦机关。

联邦一级的行政程序虽一直可追溯到 1789 年,但其现代起源,则始于 1887 年成立洲际商业委员会以处理铁道业问题的那一天。该委员会为美国行政机关中最具特色的,在行政部门之外行使其职能并管理某方面私人活动的那些独立的管理机关定下了模式。根据 30 年代罗斯福总统任内颁布的新政立法,各种联邦行政机关迅速地成倍增长。现在联邦机关共约 120 个,其涉及范围广泛包括航空、核能、银行活动、农田价格、移民、劳资关系和养老金等。

行政法由宪法、制定法、案例法和机关的规定与决定等构成。在宪法这一级上,以正当法律程序条款对行政诉讼的影响最为重要。在制定法这一级,最重要的是《1946 年联邦行政诉讼法》(该法旨在使行政诉讼正规化,使对行政行为进行司法审查的范围明朗化)。部分地区由于许多宪法上和制定法上的各项指示的笼统性,案例法的作用也大得惊人。因为没有专门办理行政法案件的法院系统,所以行政法在审判上形成的原则同其他领域中的原则相似。

行政机关的程序可以是正式的,也可以是非正式的。大部分决定都是按非正式程序做出的——与正式审理毫无共同之处。至于采用正式程序的那一小部分案件，则机关五花八门、其活动范围又广，既无法概述，也不能统一规定。虽然《联邦行政诉讼》对大多数机关都有的那些事项规定了指导诉讼的总原则，但贯穿在行政诉讼中的中心主题，却是联邦宪法的"正当程序"条款。诉讼程序上"正当程序"，主要是要求给予通知并给予公正审理的机会。在这方面，人们日益认为：人们有权被通知和接受审理——这种审理，同对裁决有关人们权利的有争议事实的审理，颇有雷同之处。上述审理一般在称作行政法法官的行政机关职员面前进行，他们的初步决定尚有待于该行政机关做出最终决定。

行政行为的司法监督乃是美国行政法上最重要的课题之一。由于没有专门的法院系统处理行政案件，司法审查是在一般法院的传统诉讼的范围内进行的。联邦的大多管理立法，都具体授权对（负责贯彻各该立法的）机关的特定行为进行审查。上述审查通常是上诉性的——根据下面的卷宗，在联邦上诉法院进行，在联邦区法院提出原诉的较少。除了在某些案件中的非法定审查外，《联邦行政诉讼法》中还规定了审查的一般的法定授权。在其他情况下（如机关的行为要求由法院执行），也可能进行审查。

行政机关虽然拥有相当大的独立权，却也得受立法和行政两个部门的某种监督。虽然关于国会审查行政规则和规章尚无总的规定，但国会对行政机关的事务进行干预，从未迟疑不决；其方法是通过对行政机关预算的监督和国会委员会的调查活动。总统则有权经参议院的同意委派行政机关的首长，但在这些首长任期届满前总统予以免职的权力却是有限的。

Passage Two
行政法的概念和基本原则

行政，是指组织、管理等活动。行政法领域的行政是指国家与公共事务的行政，即行政主体依法对国家与公共事务进行的决策、组织与管理活动，通常称为公共行政。

行政法则是调整因行政主体行使行政职权而发生的各种社会关系的法律规范和原则的总称。

下面我来谈谈行政法的基本原则。这一问题是行政法学的基本理论问题之一，是指导行政法制定和实施的基本准则。基本原则主要包括合法性原则和合理性原则。

（1）合法性原则是行政法的首要原则，是指行政主体必须按照法定的授权、形式和程序实施行政行为，并对其违法行政行为承担相应的法律责任。合法性原则的基本内容是：第一，行政主体的行政职权依法设定或被授予；第二，行政主体的行政行为必须符合行政法律规范；第三，行政主体的违法行为无效；第四，行政主体必须对其违法行政行为承担相应的法律责任。

（2）合理性原则是对合法性原则的补充。它要求行政主体的行政行为不仅要合法，而且要合理。这一原则的具体要求是：第一，行政行为要符合客观规律；第二，行政行为要符合制定有关法律的目的；第三，行政行为要符合国家和人民的利益；第四，行政行为要有充分客观的依据；第五，行政行为要符合正义和公正；第六，不合理的行政行为要承担相应的法律责任。行政合理性原则是行政法的原则，而不是行政诉讼法的原则，所以它对行政主体的行政行为是适用的，但不适用于司法机关的行政诉讼活动。

行政法的基本原则越来越支配和约束着我国各种行政法律制度。随着社会主义市场经济的发展和社会主义法治国家的建设，这些原则的内容将会不断得到完善。

词汇提示

管理　regulation, management
决策　decision-making
公共行政　public administration
规范　norms
行使　implementation
行政职权　administrative power
基本准则　elementary theoretical issues
制定　enactment
实施　application
合法性　legality
合理性　reasonableness
首要　foremost
法定的　lawful
实施　implement
承担　undertake
相应的　corresponding
授予　confer
符合　comply with
行政法律规范　administrative legal specifications
无效　invalid
补充　supplement
客观规律　objective rules
有关　relevant
充分的　sufficient
正义　justice
公正　fairness

法律术语

行政主体　administrative subject
行政诉讼法　administrative procedural law
诉讼活动　judicial action
支配　control
行政法　administrative law

适用　applicable
司法机关　judicial department
约束　bind

要点解析

1. 行政，是指组织、管理等活动。行政法领域的行政是指国家与公共事务的行政，即行政主体依法对国家与公共事务进行的决策、组织与管理活动，通常称为公共行政。Administration refers to those activities such as organization and regulation. The concept of administration in administrative legal system refers to the regulation of state and public affairs, namely, decision-making, organization and management of state and public affairs by administrative subject according to law, which is often referred to as public administration.

"行政法领域"译为 administrative legal system；"公共行政"译为 public administration。这个句子比较长，但是处理起来并不困难，采取顺译法表达出意思即可。

2. 这一问题是行政法学的基本理论问题之一，是指导行政法制定和实施的基本准则。基本原则主要包括合法性原则和合理性原则。

This problem is one of the elementary theoretical issues in administrative jurisprudence, which denotes the fundamental rules guiding the enactment and application of administrative law. The basic principles mainly consist of legality and reasonableness.

"合法性原则"和"合理性原则"可分别译成 legality 和 reasonableness。

3. 合法性原则是行政法的首要原则，是指行政主体必须按照法定的授权、形式和程序实施行政行为，并对其违法行政行为承担相应的法律责任。

Legality is the foremost principle of administrative law, which means that administrative subject must implement administrative activities according to lawful authorization, form and procedure, and undertake corresponding legal responsibility for its illegal administrative activities.

"依照"译为 according to。这是一个长句，在翻译时应注意，汉语的特点是把定语放在被修饰词前，而英语则是放在先行词后，用定语从句连接，要符合各自的语言习惯。

4. 合法性原则的基本内容是：第一，行政主体的行政职权依法设定或被授予；第二，行政主体的行政行为必须符合行政法律规范；第三，行政主体的违法行为无效；第四，行政主体必须对其违法行政行为承担相应的法律责任。

The basic content of the principle of legality is as follows. Firstly, the administrative authority of administrative subject shall be set or conferred by law. Secondly, administrative activities carried out by administrative subject must comply with administrative legal specifications. Thirdly, administrative subject's activities against law are invalid. Fourthly, administrative subject must undertake corresponding legal responsibility for its illegal administrative activities.

在表达合法性原则的基本内容时，汉语罗列了四点，通过分号，用一个完整的句子表达了很多意思。然而，由于英汉的表达形式不同，在翻译过程中，我们不仅要译出意思。还应当注重形式——在翻译这四点时，可以用 as follows 引出一个句子，分别表达出每层意思，这样处理既简洁又清晰。

5. 合理性原则是对合法性原则的补充。它要求行政主体的行政行为不仅要合法，而且要合理。

The principle of reasonableness is a supplement to the principle of legality. It requires administrative activities of administrative subject be not only legal, but also reasonable.

"补充"可以译为supplement to。"要求"可以用require表达，require等词语后面用虚拟语气require (that) sb. do sth."。

6. 行政法的基本原则越来越支配和约束着我国各种行政法律制度。随着社会主义市场经济的发展和社会主义法治国家的建设，这些原则的内容将会不断得到完善。

The basic principles of administrative law are controlling and binding the various administrative legal systems of our country more and more. Along with the development of socialist market economy and the construction of the socialist rule-of-law country, the content of those principles will be increasingly improved.

"支配"和"约束"分别译为control和bind；"社会主义法治国家"可译成the socialist rule-of-law country。

 参考译文

The Concept and Basic Principles of Administrative Law

Administration refers to those activities such as organization and regulation. The concept of administration in administrative legal system refers to the regulation of state and public affairs, namely, decision-making, organization and management of state and public affairs by administrative subject according to law, which is often referred to as public administration.

Administrative law is the general term of all legal norms and principles that regulates the different kinds of social relations occurring in the course of implementation of administrative power by administrative subject.

Then I would like to introduce the basic principles of administrative law. This problem is one of the elementary theoretical issues in administrative jurisprudence, which denotes the fundamental rules guiding the enactment and application of administrative law. The basic principles mainly consist of legality and reasonableness.

(1) Legality is the foremost principle of administrative law, which means that administrative subject must implement administrative activities according to lawful authorization, form and procedure, and undertake corresponding legal responsibility for its illegal administrative activities. The basic content of the principle of legality is as follows. Firstly, the administrative authority of administrative subject shall be set or conferred by law. Secondly, administrative activities carried out by administrative subject must comply with administrative legal specifications. Thirdly, administrative subject's activities against law are invalid. Fourthly, administrative subject must undertake corresponding legal responsibility for its illegal administrative activities.

(2) The principle of reasonableness is a supplement to the principle of legality. It requires

administrative activities of administrative subject be not only legal, but also reasonable. The specific requirements of this principle are: Firstly, administrative activities should comply with objective rules. Secondly, administrative activities should comply with the aim of the enactment of relevant laws. Thirdly, administrative activities should comply with the benefit of state and people. Fourthly, administrative activities should have sufficient objective basis. Fifthly, administrative activities should comply with justice and fairness. Sixthly, unreasonable administrative activities should undertake corresponding legal responsibility. The principle of administrative reasonableness is the principle of administrative law instead of administrative procedural law; so, it is applicable to administrative activities of administrative subject rather than the judicial action of judicial departments.

The basic principles of administrative law are controlling and binding the various administrative legal systems of our country more and more. Along with the development of socialist market economy and the construction of the socialist rule-of-law country, the content of those principles will be increasingly improved.

Section II 技能拓展

 翻译技巧

法律文本翻译中的转换

根据语言类型学，汉语属分析型语言，英语属分析综合参半型语言。在语序上汉语和英语均属"主谓宾"语言，但也存在殊异性。转换是指法律文本翻译中语言的词性和表现方法的改变。

由于英语和汉语的表达习惯、句子结构和词的搭配关系均有差异，在翻译中往往难以做到词性和表现方法一致。为了适应译文语言的表达习惯和语法规则，在法律文本翻译中必须运用词类和表现方法的转换技巧。

1. 词性的转换

1）动词和名词的转换

例如：

① We regret to inform you that the result of examination was the emergence of disagreement between the shipment and the bill of lading.

遗憾地通知你方，检查的结果是出现了装运的货物与提单不一致的情况。

② 美国与德国汽车制造商在欧洲市场竞争得异常激烈，迫使我们不得不改变投资计划。

Extremely keen competition between American and German vehicle manufacturers in the

European market has compelled us to change our investment plan.

③ The "Events of Default", as used in this Contract, shall mean the occurrence, from time to time, of any of the following circumstances.

合同中使用的"违约事项"是指发生以下情形。

分析：本句的 occurrence 本为名词，但在译成汉语时，转换成动词译成"发生"更通达。

④ The establishment of a joint venture in China is subject to examination and approval by the Ministry of Commerce of PRC.

在中国境内设立合营企业，必须经中华人民共和国商务部审批。

⑤ Until the publication or public announcement of a patent application, staff members of the Patent Office and persons involved shall have the duty to keep the contents of the patent application confidential.

在专利申请公布或公告之前，专利局的工作人员以及有关人员对其内容负有保密义务。

⑥ 绝对不允许合同任何一方违反合同支付条款的行为。

No violation by either party hereto of any payment clause or clauses can be tolerated.

⑦ 卖方声明并保证，卖方将向买方交付完整、准确、有效的系统。该系统能够达到产品说明与规格中规定的技术指标，并通过成功完成系统验收检测予以证明。

The Seller represents and warrants that it will deliver to The buyer a complete, correct and valid system, capable of accomplishing the technical targets specified in Product Description and Specification, and proved by successful completion of the Acceptance Test of the System.

⑧ 招揽订单时，代理商应将卖方成交条件，合同的一般条款充分通知顾客，也应该告知顾客，任何合同的订立都要由卖方确认。代理商应将其收到的订单立即转交给卖方，供卖方选择是否接受订单。

When soliciting orders, the Agent shall adequately advise customers of the general terms and conditions of the Seller's sales note or contractual note and that any contract is subject to the confirmation of acceptance by the Seller. Agent shall immediately dispatch any order received to the Seller for its acceptance or rejection.

2）名词和形容词或副词转换

例如：

① The fair price connected with the superiority of varieties of our products will be able to guarantee our competitive edge in the international market.

我方各种各样的产品价格公平，品质优良，能够确保在国际市场的竞争优势。

② We find difficulty in raising a great number of funds when the government executes the tight money policy.

当政府实行紧缩银根政策时，我们觉得难以筹集大量资金。

③ The rights conferred upon the respective parties by the provisions of this Clause are additional to and do not prejudice any other rights the respective parties may have.

本条款的规定赋予各方权利，是对各方可能享有的其他权利的补充，而不是损害。

④ The supplier shall ensure that it is the lawful owner of the technology to be proved and that the technology provided is complete, accurate, effective and capable of attaining the technical targets specified in the contract.

供方应保证自己是所提供技术的合法拥有者，并且保证所提供的技术具有完整性、准确性、有效性，能够达到合同规定目标。

3）副词和形容词转换

例如：

① 如合同一方实质性违反本合同或其项下的陈述与保证，另一方可终止合同，并向违约方提出索赔。

If either party commits any material breach of this Contract or its representations and warranties, the other party may terminate this contract and file a claim against the breaching party.

② 甲方必须真实、完整地向律师叙述案情、提供证据。在接受委托后，如发现甲方捏造事实、弄虚作假，乙方有权终止代理，依本合同所收费用不予退还。

The statement made and proofs provided by Party A shall be true and complete. Where Party A is found fabricating fact, Party B is free to terminate this Agreement and retain payment already collected from Party A according to this Agreement.

③ Either party shall provide the same care to prevent the other Party's Confidential Information from disclosure or unauthorized use thereof as it provides to protect its own similar proprietary information.

合同各方应如同保护自己的类似专有信息一样，谨慎行事，以防披露或擅自使用另一方的机密信息。

④ The China National Offshore Oil Corporation shall have exclusive and overall responsibility for the work of exploiting offshore petroleum resources in the PRC in cooperation with foreign enterprises.

中华人民共和国对外合作开采海洋石油资源的业务，专门由中国海洋石油总公司全面负责。

⑤ 甲方在此不可撤销地委托乙方，在甲方签署货物交接单据后，立即将货物价款直接支付到供货商的账户。

Party A hereby irrevocably authorizes Party B to make a direct payment for the Goods into the account of the supplier immediately after Party A signs the Delivery Note.

4）介词转化为动词

例如：

Preference shareholders are entitled to a priority in the assets if the company is wound up.

如果公司被解散，优先股东有优先分得公司资产的权利。

2. 词义转换

正常的情况下，在将原文翻译成译文时，译者只需按照原文中各个词的词典含义就能准确而地道地把原文翻译成译文。然而，在一些特殊情况下，尽管按照词典含义对等地翻译，译文也总会让人觉得别扭，词的表达总是很不妥当。这种情况下，译者就必须按照译文的表达习惯，改变词典含义，用地道的译文用词来表达原文作者的真正含义，这就是词义转换。

例如：

① Each Party shall have the right to change its legal or authorized representative and shall promptly notify the other Party of such change and the name, position and nationality of its new legal or authorized representative.

双方有权撤换其各自的法定代表人或授权代表，并应将新法定代表人或授权代表的姓名、职位和国籍及时通知另一方。

分析：原文中 change 的原意为"变化"，但为了符合中文的表达习惯，将它翻译成"撤换"。

② The Company may establish branch offices inside China and overseas with the consent of the Board and approval from the relevant governmental authorities.

合营公司经董事会决议并经有关政府机关批准可在国内外成立分支机构。

分析：原文中 consent 的原意为"同意"，但为了中文法律语言的表达习惯，在译文中将其翻译为"决议"。

③ The purpose of the joint venture shall be to utilize the combined technology, management, operation and marketing strengths of the Parties within the approved scope of business of the Company to achieve good economic results and a return on investment satisfactory to the Parties.

合营公司的宗旨是结合双方在技术、管理、运营以及营销方面的优势，在合营公司经批准的经营范围内开展业务，以取得良好的经济效益及令双方满意的投资回报。

分析：原文中的 strength 的原意为"实力，力量"，但在译文中，为了符合中文表达习惯的需要，它被改译为"优势"。

3. 句型的转换

1）肯定句和否定句的转换

由于英语和汉语表达思想、遣词造句的方式和所用的形象均不相同，因此，我们在翻译时应按照习惯用法决定是否改变表现方法。最为常用的方式是将英语中某些肯定和否定形式的句子在汉译时作句式转换处理。例如：

① They were very few, fewer than at the last meeting of the board of directors. The chairman didn't say much at the meeting, but every word was to the point.

他们没有几个人到会，比董事会上次到会的人还要少。董事长在会上说话不多，但每句话都很中肯。

② It is not rarely that they collect the feedback information of their products directly from the market from all angles.

他们常常从各种角度收集市场直接反馈的产品信息。

2）语态的转换

英语惯用被动语态，而汉语则多用主动语态。因此，英译汉时宜按照汉语的表达习惯作改组，这样的改组常见于那些以人的动作和活动为主语、而动作的执行者已表明或暗示的句子里。例如：

① Everything possible has been done to save their enterprise and to carry on the entire reform of their management and control.

他们已采取了一切可能的措施，以便挽救他们的企业，并对他们的经营管理进行彻底的改革。

② Confidential Information must be kept by the receiving Party in a secure place with access only to both Parties' employees or agents.

机密信息的接受方必须将其存放在安全地方,仅限合同双方雇员、代理人知晓。

③ This Contract shall be signed in four counterparts and all such counterparts shall be deemed to constitute one and the same instrument.

本合同签署本一式四份,视为共同构成同一份文件。

④ 如果一方因不可抗力而无法履行其合同义务,该义务的履行时间应延长,延长的时间应当与该不可抗力事件导致的延误时间相等。

Where one Party is prevented from performing any of its contractual obligations due to an event of force majeure, the time for performing such obligations shall be extended by a period equal to the period of delay caused by such event of force majeure.

⑤ 三名仲裁员应在收到中国国际经济贸易仲裁委员会仲裁员名册后30天内,按照其仲裁规则规定的程序选定。

The three arbitrators shall be selected within thirty (30) days after receiving the arbitrators list delivered by CIETAC pursuant to procedures prescribed by CIETAC's arbitration rules.

⑥ All proceeds of realization of the security right hereby shall be applied in payment of all costs, charges, expenses incurred by the Pledgee in respect of the exercise of any rights hereunder or in preserving the validity of the Pledge.

所有因担保权利实现获得的收入应用于支付质押人为实施本合同权利或保持质押有效性而承担的所有费用、收费和开支。

⑦ 由于一方违约,使本合同不能履行或不能完全履行时,违约一方应承担违约责任;如属于双方违约,则根据实际情况,由双方分别承担各自的违约责任。

Where this Contract or any part of this Contract can not be performed as a result of any Party's default, the Party in breach shall bear the liability; in case of both Parties' default, each Party shall take its liability respectively according to actual situations.

⑧ 没有合法根据,取得不当利益,造成他人损失的,应当将取得的不当利益返还受损失的人。

If profits are acquired improperly and without a lawful basis, resulting in another person's loss, the illegal profits shall be returned to the person who suffered the loss.

⑨ 公民、法人依法取得的专利权受法律保护。

The patent rights lawfully obtained by citizens and legal persons shall be protected by law.

 法律宝典

行政法的过去与现在

严格意义的行政法只是法国行政法院建立以后的事情,其产生、发展的历史不过200年左右。作为一个独立法律部门的行政法,只是到19世纪末20世纪初,随着"行政国家"的兴起而逐步形成起来的。如今,行政法的调整范围已扩展到"从摇篮到坟墓",对人们的生

活和社会的发展也起到了日益深远的影响。所谓行政法是指调整行政关系的、规范和控制行政权的法律规范系统。行政法的研究范围主要包括：行政法的一般原理、原则及行政法、行政法学的历史发展；行政主体的一般理论及其职责、职权、管理手段与行政相对人的权利、义务；行政行为的性质、特征、构成要件及其运作程序；行政救济的一般理论及行政复议、行政诉讼的性质、功能及其受案范围、管辖、程序与裁判标准；行政赔偿责任构成要件，归责原则，赔偿范围、方式、标准和程序等。

美国的法学家认为，行政法是管理政府行政活动的部门法。它规定行政机关可以行使的权力，确立行使这些权力的原则，以及对受到行政行为侵害的人给予法律上的补救。行政法一般被认为是属于公法的范畴，但是在美国，公法和私法之间的区别不像在大陆法系国家中那么严格。因此，美国的行政法案件也由受理私法案件的普通法院审判。

行政法包括实体法和程序法（Procedural Law）的内容。美国行政法研究的主要对象是后者。就联邦一级而言，美国的行政程序法可追溯至 1789 年的联邦宪法修正案，但是实质意义上的行政法程序则始于 1887 年为处理铁路工业问题而成立的州际商业委员会。该委员会是美国联邦行政部门中最早的独立规制机构（Independent Regulatory Agency）。20 世纪 30 年代，在罗斯福总统推行的"新政"（The New Deal）时期，各种联邦行政机关如雨后春笋般建立，美国的行政程序法也得到长足的发展。

美国的行政法是由宪法、法律、判例、行政规章等组成的。其中，最为重要的是联邦宪法第五修正案中的正当程序（Due Process）条款和 1946 年的联邦行政程序法（Federal Administrative Procedure Act）。诚然，判例法的作用亦十分重要。

术语积累

《1946 年联邦行政诉讼法》 The Federal Administrative Procedure Act of 1946
案例法　case law
裁决程序　adjudicatory process
标准程序　paradigmatic procedures
程序上的　procedural
程序法　procedural law
法人　juristic person
自然人　natural person
法定的；法令的；可依法惩处的　　statutory
非正式法规制定程序　informal rulemaking
（非）法定的　(non-) statutory
（非）正式程序　(in) formal proceedings
复审法院　reviewing court
告知和评论程序　notice-and-comment procedure
公共行政　public administration
公民自由　civil liberty
公民权利　civil right

《联邦登记》 Federal Register
裁决性听证 adjudicatory hearing
单方面的;为一方利益的 ex parte
管理机关 regulatory agency
过失的;疏忽的 negligent
公正 fairness
国会委员会 congressional committee
(规章的)解释 interpretation
合理依据 probable cause
合法性 legality
合理性 reasonableness
豁免 immunity
豁免权的放弃 waiver of immunity
基本准则 elementary theoretical issues
检察官 prosecutor
立法机关;议会 legislature
立法权 legislative power
联邦行政程序法 Federal Administrative Procedure Act
《联邦侵权赔偿法》 Federal Tort Claims Act (FTCA)
令状 writ
明确列举的权力 enumerated power
殴打 battery
判决;裁判 adjudication
起诉,检控 prosecute
认为有理,认为正当 justification
实施 application
实体法 substantive law
契约 contract
侵犯 trespass
授权原则 delegation doctrine
授权法 enabling statute
受理上诉的;上诉的 appellate
司法权 judicial power
司法机关 judicial department
司法监督 judicial control
司法审查 judicial review
诉讼活动 judicial action
听证(会) hearing
调解制度 conciliation

Unit Four Administrative Law 行政法

宪法　constitutional law
新政立法　New Deal legislation
行使　implementation
行政裁量　administrative discretion
行政程序法　Administrative Procedure Act(APA)
行政法　administrative law; executive law
行政法律规范　administrative legal specifications
行政法规制定程序　rulemaking
行政法法官　administrative law judge
行政法规　administrative laws and regulations
行政法学　administrative jurisprudence
行政解释　administrative interpretation
行政救济　administrative remedy
行政诉讼法　administrative procedural law
行政权　executive power
行政听证程序　administrative hearing
行政行为　agency action
行政职权　administrative power
行政主体　administrative subject
训令令状　mandamus
一般法定方法　general statutory measures
有记录的　on the record
原诉（区别于上诉诉讼而言）；第一审案件　original action
正当程序　due process
正式裁决　formal adjudication
正式法规制定程序　formal rulemaking
正义　justice
治安管理　security administration
治安条例　security regulation
制定　enactment
制定法　statute
制约与平衡　checks and balance
执行性的（任务）　ministerial
执行民事法典　civil enforcement
州际商业委员会　the Interstate Commerce Commission
准（类）法律规范　statute-like norm
自由裁量的　discretionary
自证其罪　self-incrimination
作出决定　rule-making

Section III 巩固练习

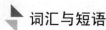 词汇与短语

1. agency action
2. administrative unit
3. enumerated power
4. paradigmatic procedures
5. formal (informal) adjudication
6. administrative law judge
7. bureaucratic routine
8. statutory law
9. case law
10. probable cause
11. 告知和评论程序
12. 司法审查
13. 司法机关
14. 授权原则
15. 行政裁量
16. 行政诉讼法
17. 诉讼活动
18. 国会委员会
19. 裁决性听证
20. 实体法

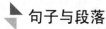 句子与段落

1. Administrative lawyers now realize that not only are traditional concepts of the rule of law inadequate tools for dealing with issues of legality and legitimacy in the modern state, but also that issues of administrative law are connected directly and inescapably to issues of constitutional and political theory.
2. The response to the challenge of these wider horizons had been enthusiastic and illuminating, although perhaps still in its formative years, administrative law already shows signs of maturing onto a subject broad in its scope and vital in its concerns.
3. Much of judicial review has been about the nature and scope of natural justice, which in practice means the hearing principle and the principle against bias. The American doctrine of due process, together with a tendency for similar principles to be adopted in other jurisdictions, has added to the interests in procedural fairness.
4. Another avenue of accountability is to be found in the creation of special authorities, especially tribunals of one kind or another. Special authorities are now a familiar feature of the administrative landscape and their range is so considerable.
5. Methods of accountability extend beyond notions of participation. One such method, American in its inception, is the "hard look doctrine" which has been taken up with some enthusiasm by others. The hard look doctrine means, briefly, that administrative decisions should be examed rigorously to ensure that they are the most rational available.

6. 一方面，行政法是立法、行政与裁决的主体部分，而且它创造和维护了福利的程序和规则。在这个意义上的法仅仅是一个实现福利和秩序目的的工具，它包括法律、惯例和用于实现立法目的的机构。
7. 然而，法律和行政的特定领域的研究带来了更为广泛的关注。每一个监管都是独特的吗？或者说有没有可能确定一个普遍适用的框架？在所有行政领域的基础上是否存在普识的，而且可以概括为一个完整的法律框架的价值和原则？
8. 也就是说，行政法主要关心下列问题：如何实现不同的行政任务？不同行政主体针对不同行政任务的适应性如何？行政和管理的天然属性是什么？
9. 事实上，该学科发展的核心问题，无论是从理论层面还是从实际层面上看，都是如何进一步扩大法治，以提供一套适合现代国家的价值理念。
10. Legal ideas and doctrines sometimes provoke social change, but more often they follow a safe distance behind. Administrative law fits this general pattern. The great social and economic transformations of the twentieth century have only recently begun to be reflected in administrative law. The rise of the welfare and the regulation of social and economic activity have meant a substantial expansion of government in the middle and later years of the twentieth century. New and wide-ranging legislative programmers have been developed, a host of new authorities have been created, and the lives of citizens have been much controlled and regulated. As the close of the century approaches, administrative law continues to develop and mature as it strives to find the doctrines and values, the ideas and institution's, necessary to bring the administrative state within a framework of law.

Unit Five

Civil Law
民　法

Section I　译例研究

▶▶ Passage One
The Institutes of Justinian

Of The Law of Nature, The Law of Nations, and The Civil Law

The law of nature is that which she has taught all animals; a law not peculiar to the human race, but shared by all living creatures, whether denizens of the air, the dry land, or the sea. Hence comes the union of male and female, which we call marriage; hence the procreation and rearing of children, for this is a law by the knowledge of which we see even the lower animals are distinguished.

(1) The civil law of Rome, and the law of nations, differs from each other thus. The laws of every people governed by statutes and customs are partly peculiar to itself, partly common to all mankind. Those rules which a state enacts for its own members are peculiar to itself, and are called civil law, those rules prescribed by natural reason for all men are observed by all people alike, and are called the law of nations. Thus the laws of the Roman people are partly peculiar to itself, partly common to all nations; a distinction of which we shall take notice as occasion offers.

(2) Civil law takes its name from the state wherein it binds, for instance, the civil law of Athens, it being quite correct to speak thus of the enactment of Solon or Draco. So too we call the law of the Roman people the civil law of the Romans, or the law of the Quirites, the law, that is to say, which they observe, the Romans being called Quirites after Quirinus. Whenever we speak, however, of civil law, without any qualification, we mean our own, exactly as, when "the poet" is spoken of, without

addition or qualification, the Greeks understand the great Homer, and we understand Vergil. But the law of nations is common to the whole human race, for nations have settled certain things for themselves as occasion and the necessities of human life required. For instance, wars arose, and then followed captivity and slavery, which are contrary to the law of nature, for by the law of nature all men from the beginning were born free. The law of nations again is the source of almost all contracts, for instance, sale, hire, partnership, deposit, loan for consumption, and very many others.

(3) Our law is partly written, partly unwritten, as among the Greeks. The written law consists of statutes, plebiscites, senate's consults, enactments of the Emperors, edicts of the magistrates, and answers of those learned in the law.

(4) A statute is an enactment of the Roman people, which it used to make on the nation of a senatorial magistrate, as for instance a consul. A plebiscite is an enactment of the commonalty, such as was made on the motion of one of their own magistrates, as a tribune. The commonalty differs from the people as a species from its genus, for "the people" includes the whole aggregate of citizens, among them patricians and senators, while the term "commonalty" embraces only such citizens as are not patricians of senators. After the passing, however, of the statue called the lex Hortensia, plebiscites acquired for the first time the force of statutes.

(5) A Senate's consult is a command and ordinance of the senate, for when the Roman people had been so increased that it was difficult to assemble it together for the purpose of enacting statutes, it seemed right that the senate should be consulted instead of the people.

(6) Again, what the Emperor determines has the force of a statute, the people having conferred on him all their authority and power by the "lex regia", which was passed concerning his office and authority. Consequently, whatever the Emperor settles by rescript, or decides in his judicial capacity, or ordains by edicts, is clearly a statute, and these are what are called constitutions. Some of these of course are personal, and not to be followed as precedents, since this is not the Emperor's will, for a favour bestowed on individual merit, or a penalty inflicted for individual wrongdoing, or relief given without a precedent, do not go beyond the particular person, though others are general, and bind all beyond a doubt.

(7) The edicts of the praetors too have no small legal authority, and these we are used to call the "ius honorarium", because those tribunes have given authority to this branch of law. The curule aediles also used to issue an edict relating to certain matters, which forms part of the ius honorarium.

(8) The answers of those learned in the law are the opinions and views of persons authorized to determine and expound the law, for it was of old provided that certain persons should publicly interpret the laws, who were called jurisconsults, and whom the Emperor privileged to give formal answers. If they were unanimous the judge was forbidden by imperial constitutions to depart from their opinion, so great was its authority.

(9) The unwritten law is that which usage has approved, for ancient customs, when approved by consent of those who follow them, are like statute.

(10) And this division of the civil law into two kinds seems not inappropriate, for it appears to have originated in the institutions of two states, namely Athens and Lacedaemon; it having been usual

in the latter to commit to memory what was observed as law, while the Athenians observed only what they had made permanent in written statutes.

(11) But the laws of nature, which are observed by all nations alike, are established, as it were, by divine providence, and remain ever fixed and immutable, but the municipal laws of each individual state are subject to frequent change, entirely by the tacit consent of the people, or by the subsequent enactment of another statute.

(12) The whole of the law which we observe relates either to persons, or to things, or to actions. And first let us speak of persons, for it is useless to know the law without knowing the persons for whose sake it was established.

▶ 词汇提示

peculiar   *adj.* 特有的
denizen   *n.* 居民
union   *n.* 联合
enact   *v.* 颁布；制定法律
procreation   *n.* 繁殖
rearing   *n.* 教养
statute   *n.* 法规，法令
wherein   *adv.* 在其中；在何处
bind   *v.* 绑；约束；装订
the civil law of Athens   雅典的市民法
Solon   梭伦
enactment   *n.* 制定，颁布；通过；法令
Quirites   古罗马市民，奎里特斯
Quirinus   奎利努斯
qualification   *n.* 资格；条件；限定条件；赋予资格
Homer   荷马
Vergil   维吉尔
contract   *n.* 合同，契约
deposit   *n.* 寄存
loan for consumption   可以实物偿还的借贷
(un)written   *adj.* （不）成文的
edict   *n.* 法令；布告
senatorial   *adj.* 参议院的；参议员的
magistrate   *n.* 地方法官；文职官员
consul   *n.* 领事；（古罗马的）两执政官之一
commonalty   *n.* 平民；法人团体；团体
tribune   *n.* 护民官

genus   *n.* 类，种；[生物] 属
aggregate   *v.* 集合；聚集；合计
patrician   *n.* 贵族
senator   *n.* 参议员；（古罗马的）元老院议员
ordinance   *n.* 条例；法令；圣餐礼
confer   *v* 授予；给予
rescript   *n.* 法令；布告；抄件
precedent   *n.* 先例；前例
ordain   *v.* 颁布命令
bestow   *v.* 赠给，赐予
wrongdoing   *n.* 坏事；不道德的行为
praetor   *n.* 长官；执政官
aediles   *n.* 市政官
expound   *v.* 解释；详细说明
jurisconsult   *n.* 法律专家；法学学者
Lacedaemon   古斯巴达的别称，拉塞戴蒙
divine   *adj.* 神圣的；非凡的；天赐的；极好的
providence   *n.* 天意；深谋远虑
immutable   *adj.* 不变的；不可变的
tacit consent   默许，默示同意

法律术语

The Institutes of Justinian   查士丁尼法学阶梯
the law of nature   自然法
the civil law   市民法
Senate's consult   元老院决议
lex regia   君王法，王权法，国王法
unwritten law   不成文法
the law of nations   万民法
plebiscite   *n.* 公民投票；平民表决
The Lex Hortensia   《霍尔滕西法》
ius honorarium   长官法

要点解析

1. The law of nature is that which she has taught all animals, a law not peculiar to the human race, but shared by all living creatures, whether denizens of the air, the dry land, or the sea. Hence comes the union of male and female, which we call marriage; hence the procreation and rearing of children.

自然法是自然界教给一切动物的法律。因为这种法律不是人类所特有，而是一切动物都具有的，不论是天空、地上或海里的动物。由自然法产生了男与女的结合，我们把它叫做婚姻；从而有子女的繁殖及其教养。

The law of nature 为专业术语，译为"自然法"；procreation and rearing 译成"繁殖及其教养"。英语的结构比较紧凑，翻译时可以根据逻辑关系调整，将原文的长句译为小句。

2. Those rules which a state enacts for its own members are peculiar to itself, and are called civil law, those rules prescribed by natural reason for all men are observed by all people alike, and are called the law of nations.

每一个民族专为自身法理制定的法律，是这个国家所特有的，叫作市民法，即该国本身特有的法。至于处于自然理性而为全人类制定的法，则受到所有民族的同样尊重，叫作万民法。civil law 译成"市民法"；the law of nation 则译成"万民法"。

3. Our law is partly written, partly unwritten, as among the Greeks. The written law consists of statutes, plebiscites, Senate's consult, enactments of the Emperors, edicts of the magistrates, and answers of those learned in the law.

我们的法律或是成文的，或是不成文的，正如希腊的法律，有些是成文的，有些是不成文的。成文法包括法律、平民决议、元老院决议、皇帝的法令、长官的告示和法学家的解答。

written 和 unwritten 分别是"成文"和"不成文"的意思；plebiscite 译为"平民决议"；Senate's consult 译为"元老院决议"。本句中出现的法律专业术语较多，在翻译时应注意表达准确和严谨。

4. A plebiscite is an enactment of the commonalty, such as was made on the motion of one of their own magistrates, as a tribune. The commonalty differs from the people as a species from its genus, for "the people" includes the whole aggregate of citizens, among them patricians and senators, while the term "commonalty" embraces only such citizens as are not patricians of senators.

平民决议是平民根据平民长官例如护民官的提议而制定的。平民不同于人民，正如人种不同于人类，因为人民是指全体公民，包括贵族和元老在内，而平民则是指贵族和元老以外的其他公民而言。

plebiscite 是"公民投票；平民表决"之意；the commonalty differs from the people as a species from its genus 可译为"平民不同于人民，正如人种不同于人类"的句式。

5. Again, what the Emperor determines has the force of a statute, the people having conferred on him all their authority and power by the "lex regia", which was passed concerning his office and authority.

皇帝的决定也具有法律效力，因为根据赋予他权力的王权法，人民把他们的全部权威和权力转移给他。

force 一词在法律英语中经常出现，应当译为"效力"而非"力量"；conferred on 译成"授给（授予）"；lex regia 为专业术语，译为"王权法，国王法"。这个句子不长，结构也不复杂，顺译即可。

6. The answers of those learned in the law are the opinions and views of persons authorized to determine and expound the law; for it was of old provided that certain persons should publicly interpret the laws, who were called jurisconsults, and whom the Emperor privileged to give formal

answers.

　　法学家的解答是那些被授权判断法律的人们所做出的决定和表示的意见。古时规定应该有人公开解释法律，这些人由皇帝赋予权力就法律问题做出解答，成为法学家。

　　answers 译为"解答"而不是"答案"，在翻译时要注意联系语境，注意用词的准确性；"jurisconsults"是"法律专家，法学学者"的意思。这句话是个长句，在翻译时应灵活处理，可分开翻译，不然会显得过于冗长。

　　7. And this division of the civil law into two kinds seems not inappropriate, for it appears to have originated in the institutions of two states, namely Athens and Lacedaemon; it having been usual in the latter to commit to memory what was observed as law, while the Athenians observed only what they had made permanent in written statutes.

　　因此，把市民法区分为两种，是合宜的。这看来是起源于雅典和拉塞戴蒙这两个国家的不同习惯，因为这两个国家的一贯做法是：拉塞戴蒙人宁愿把作为法律来遵守的东西，记在心里，雅典人则宁愿把成文法中所载的东西妥善地保存下来。

　　not inappropriate 是双重否定，译为"合宜"；Lacedaemon 译成"拉塞戴蒙"，是古斯巴达的别称；written statutes 译成"成文法"。

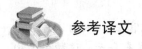 参考译文

查士丁尼法学阶梯

自然法、万民法和市民法

　　自然法是自然界教给一切动物的法律。因为这种法律不是人类所特有，而是一切动物都具有的，不论是天空、地上或海里的动物。由自然法产生了男与女的结合，我们把它叫作婚姻；从而有子女的繁殖及其教养。的确我们看到，除人而外，其他一切动物都被视为同样知道这种法则。

　　（1）市民法与万民法有别，任何受制于法律和习惯的民族都部分适用自己特有的法律，部分适用全人类共同的法律。每一个民族专为自身法理制定的法律，是这个国家所特有的，叫作市民法，即该国本身特有的法。至于处于自然理性而为全人类制定的法，受到所有民族的同样尊重，叫作万民法，因为一切民族都适用它。因此，罗马人民所适用的，一部分是自己特有的法律，另一部分是全人类共同的法律。组成我们法律的这两部分的性质，我们将在适当场合阐述。

　　（2）每一个国家的市民法是以它适用的国家命名的，例如雅典的市民法。如果把梭伦或德拉古的法律称为雅典的市民法，也没有错。因此，我们把罗马人民或奎利迭人民适用的法律叫作罗马人民的市民法或奎利迭人民的市民法。其实罗马人亦称奎利迭人，这名字是从奎利努斯（Quirinus）一字而来的。但若谈到法律而不加上哪个民族时，那么，所指的是我们自己的法，正如我们谈到"诗人"而不说姓名，在希腊人那里就是指杰出的荷马，在我们这里是指维吉尔。至于万民法是全人类共同的。它包含着各民族根据实际需要和你生活必需而制定的一些法则，例如战争发生了，跟着发生俘虏和奴役，而奴役是违背自然法的（因为根据自然法，一切人都是生而自由的）；又如几乎全部契约，如买卖、租赁、合伙、寄存、可以实

物偿还的借贷以及其他等,都起源于万民法。

（3）我们的法律或是成文的,或是不成文的,正如希腊的法律,有些是成文的,有些是不成文的。成文法包括法律、平民决议、元老院决议、皇帝的法令、长官的告示和法学家的解答。

（4）法律是罗马人民根据元老院长官例如执政官的提议制定的。平民决议是平民根据平民长官例如护民官的提议而制定的。平民不同于人民,正如人种不同于人类,因为人民是指全体公民,包括贵族和元老在内,而平民则是指贵族和元老以外的其他公民而言。但从《霍尔滕西法》通过以来,平民协议已经开始具有和法律相等的效力。

（5）元老院决议是元老院所命令和制定的,因为罗马人口已增长到了这样的程度,以致很难把他们召集在一起通过法律,所以向元老院咨询代替向人民咨询,似乎是对的。

（6）皇帝的决定也具有法律效力,因为根据赋予他权力的王权法,人民把他们的全部权威和权力转移给他。因此,凡是皇帝批复中的命令,审理案件时的裁决,诏令中的规定,当然都是法律,这些统称宪令。显然其中有些是个人性质的,而不构成先例,因为皇帝无意使其成为先例。如皇帝因某人有功而给予恩赐,或因某人有罪而予以惩罚,或赐予某人额外救助,这些行为都不超越这一特定人的范围。至于其他宪令,由于它们是普遍的,无疑对一切人都有约束力。

（7）大法官告示同样具有法律权威。我们惯常把这些告示叫作"长官法",因为这种法是由佩戴勋章的人,即长官的批准而生效的。市政官就某些事项有事也发布告示,这种告示构成长官法的一部分。

（8）法学家的解答是那些被授权判断法律的人们所作出的决定和表示的意见。古时规定应该有人公开解释法律,这些人由皇帝赋予权力就法律问题做出解答,成为法学家。他们的一致决定和意见具有这样的权威,根据宪令规定,审判员也不得拒绝遵从。

（9）不成文法是习惯确立的法律,因为古老的习惯经人们加以沿用同意而获得效力,就等于法律。

（10）因此,把市民法区分为两种,是合宜的。这看来是起源于雅典和拉塞戴蒙这两个国家的不同习惯,因为这两个国家的一贯做法是:拉塞戴蒙人宁愿把作为法律来遵守的东西,记在心里,雅典人则宁愿把成文法中所载的东西妥善地保存下来。

（11）各民族都遵守的自然法则是上帝神意制定的,因此始终是固定不变的。至于每一国家为自身所制定的法律则经常变动,其变动或由于人民的默示同意,或由于以后制定的其他法律。

（12）我们所适用的全部法律,或是关于人的法律,或是关于物的法律,或是关于诉讼的法律。首先考察人,因为如果不了解作为法律对象的人,就不可能很好地了解法律。

Passage Two
民法法系

民法（法系）是区别于普通法系的法律制度或法律体系,它起源于古罗马查士丁尼皇帝主持编纂的《罗马民法大全》。普通法系诉讼的结果取决于先前判例的裁决。大多数欧洲国家与南美国家属于民法法系，英国与大多数被其征服和殖民的国家（包括加拿大和美国）都属于普通法系。但是，在这些普通法系国家里，路易斯安那州、魁北克省和波多黎各因受到法国和西班牙殖民者的影响，采用了民法法系的法律制度。

在美国，"民法"（civil law）一词有两种含义。民法第一种含义指流行于欧洲的、建立在成文法典基础上的法律制度，这种意义上的民法区别于英国和美国大多数州所采用的普通法法律制度。普通法系根据判例法而不是成文法典解决法律纠纷。民法的第二种含义指调整私人之间纠纷的法律规范的总称，区别于以侵犯公共利益的犯罪行为为规制对象的刑法。也就是说，此种意义上的民法，与刑法构成相对应的关系。

民法法系起源于古罗马，法律学者总结与创制的法律原则制约着民法法系的发展。在属于民法法系传统的国家中，立法人员与行政人员利用这些原则制定旨在解决所有法律纠纷的法典。

《1804年法国民法典》是民法传统的集大成者。1712年，法国征服路易斯安那，同时把民法输入到该地区。1762年，法国把路易斯安那割让给西班牙，新任西班牙总督以西班牙民法典取代了法国民法典。1803年法国重新获得这一地区的控制权。美国在法国取得控制权20天后，从法国手中购买了路易斯安那。在法国统治路易斯安那的短暂时间里，法国任命的行政长官废除了全部西班牙法院，但是并没有引入法国法。因此，美国路易斯安那州州长克莱伯恩（Claiborne）控制这一地区时，该地区的法律制度付之阙如。

克莱伯恩州长决心把路易斯安那美国化，企图强制推行普通法，但遭到了路易斯安那人民的激烈反对，他们已经适应了法国西班牙相互混合的法律与文化传统。路易斯安那州人民的反对使克莱伯恩州长认识到，不能强制推行普通法。于是，他领导州立法机构，在现有法律的基础上，起草了一部民法典。路易斯安那州第一部民法典制定于1808年，这部法典主要是借鉴了拿破仑民法典，法典使用的语言也是法语。这部法典被1825年制定的一部更加全面与详细的法典所取代。1870年制定的民法典的大部分条文至今仍然有效，该法典使先前的法律更加系统，也较先前的法律更加简明。该法典用英文制定，使路易斯安那州仍是美国唯一属于民法法系而非普通法系的州。

▶ 词汇提示

查士丁尼皇帝　Emperor Justinian
魁北克省　Quebec
波多黎各　Puerto Rico
流行　prevalent
起源于　trace their roots to
纠纷　controversies
美国化　Americanize
违法　offence
长官　prefect
制定　enact

法律术语

《罗马民法大全》 the Roman Corpus Juris Civilus
民法 civil law
判例法 case law
《1804年法国民法典》 French Civil Code of 1804
普通法 common law
成文法典 written codes

要点解析

1. 第一种含义指流行于欧洲的、建立在成文法典基础上的法律制度，这种意义上的民法区别于英国和美国大多数州所采用的普通法法律制度。普通法系根据判例法而不是成文法典解决法律纠纷。

One meaning of civil law refers to a legal system prevalent in Europe that is based on written codes. Civil law in this sense is contrasted with the common-law system used in England and most of the United States, which relies on prior case law to resolve disputes rather than written codes. "成文法"可译为 written law 或 written code；"区别于"译成 contrast with；"普通法系根据判例法而不是成文法典解决法律纠纷"用 which 引导的定语从句连接，更符合英语长句的习惯。

2. 民法的第二种含义指调整私人之间纠纷的法律规范的总称，区别于以侵犯公共利益的犯罪行为为规制对象的刑法。也就是说，此种意义上的民法，与刑法构成相对应的关系。

The second meaning of civil law refers to the body of law governing disputes between individuals, as opposed to those governing offenses against the government — that is, civil law as opposed to criminal law.

对于文中不止一次出现的短语，在翻译时可以用不同的英语来表达，显得语言丰富多样，不重复。上文的"区别于"译成 contrast with，此处"区别于"可译为 opposed to；"以侵犯公共利益的犯罪行为为规制对象"译为 those governing offenses against the government。

3. 民法系起源于古罗马，法律学者总结与创制的法律原则制约着民法法系的发展。在属于民法法系传统的国家中，立法人员与行政人员利用这些原则制定旨在解决所有法律纠纷的法典。

Civil law systems, which trace their roots to ancient Rome, are governed by doctrines developed and compiled by legal scholars. Legislators and administrators in civil law countries use these doctrines to fashion a code by which all legal controversies are decided.

"起源于"可译为 trace their roots to；"立法人员"与"行政人员"分别译为 legislators 和 administrators。

4. 《1804年法国民法典》是民法传统的集大成者。1712年，法国征服路易斯安那，同时把民法输入到该地区。1762年，法国把路易斯安那割让给西班牙，新任西班牙总督以西班牙民法典取代了法国民法典。1803年法国重新获得这一地区的控制权。美国在法国取得控制权20天后，从法国手中购买了路易斯安那。

  In France, the civil law is set forth in the comprehensive French Civil Code of 1804, also known as the Code Napoleon. France exported this legal system to the New World when it settled Louisiana in 1712. When the French ceded Louisiana to Spain in 1762, the new Spanish governor replaced French civil law with Spanish civil law. France regained control of the territory in 1803, and the United States purchased it a mere twenty days later.

  《1804年法国民法典》为专业术语，译成 French Civil Code of 1804；"集大成者"在翻译时要注意表达，可以 set forth 表示；"割让"译为 cede。

  5. 在法国统治路易斯安那的短暂时间里，法国任命的行政长官废除了全部西班牙法院，但是并没有引入法国法。因此，美国路易斯安那州州长克莱伯恩（Claiborne）控制这一地区时，该地区的法律制度付之阙如。

  During that brief period of French rule, the French prefect abolished all Spanish courts but did not reintroduce French law. Hence, the new U.S. governor of Louisiana William Claiborne took control of a territory that lacked a legal system.

  "行政长官"译为 prefect；"废除了全部西班牙法院"在翻译时要注意，不可以采用直译的方法译为 fly out of all Spanish courts，原文要表达的意思是"废除、取消"，因此翻译时可以采用意译的方法译为 abolish；"付之阙如"在理解时按照意思翻译即可，不要翻译得太复杂，可译成 lack。

 参考译文

Civil Law

  Civil Law is a legal system derived from the Roman Corpus Juris Civilus of Emperor Justinian I. It differs from a common-law system, which relies on prior decisions to determine the outcome of a lawsuit. Most European and South American countries have a civil law system. England and most of the countries it dominated or colonized, including Canada and the United States, have a common-law system. However, within these countries, Louisiana, Quebec, and Puerto Rico exhibit the influence of French and Spanish settlers in their use of civil law systems.

  In the United States, the term "civil law" has two meanings. One meaning of civil law refers to a legal system prevalent in Europe that is based on written codes. Civil law in this sense is contrasted with the common-law system used in England and most of the United States, which relies on prior case law to resolve disputes rather than written codes. The second meaning of civil law refers to the body of law governing disputes between individuals, as opposed to those governing offenses against the government — that is, civil law as opposed to criminal law.

  Civil law systems, which trace their roots to ancient Rome, are governed by doctrines developed and compiled by legal scholars. Legislators and administrators in civil law countries use these doctrines to fashion a code by which all legal controversies are decided.

In France, the civil law is set forth in the comprehensive French Civil Code of 1804, also known as the Code Napoleon. France exported this legal system to the New World when it settled Louisiana in 1712. When the French ceded Louisiana to Spain in 1762, the new Spanish governor replaced French civil law with Spanish civil law. France regained control of the territory in 1803, and the United States purchased it a mere twenty days later. During that brief period of French rule, the French prefect abolished all Spanish courts but did not reintroduce French law. Hence, the new U.S. governor of Louisiana William Claiborne took control of a territory that lacked a legal system.

Determined to Americanize Louisiana, Claiborne attempted to impose common law but met fierce resistance from Louisianans who had grown accustomed to their mixture of French and Spanish laws and cultural system, he directed the state's legislature to draft a civil code based on existing law. Louisiana' first civil code, enacted in1808, drew heavily from the Code Napoleon and was even written in French. It was replaced in 1825 by a more comprehensive and detailed code. Finally, the Louisiana Civil Code, enacted in 1870 and still largely in force, clarifies and simplifies the earlier laws. The 1870 code is written in English, signaling a shift toward a partial Americanization of Louisiana's legal culture. To this day, Louisiana enjoys the distinction of being the only state in the United States to have a civil law system rather than a common-law system.

Section II 技能拓展

翻译技巧

法律文本翻译中的增补和省略

一、增补

增补也是法律文本翻译中不可忽视的重要技巧之一。所谓增补，"就是要根据上下文的意思、逻辑关系以及目的语的表达习惯，增加词量，以表达原文字面没有出现但已经包含的意思"。增补主要是因为英汉两种语言在遣词造句以及思维方法上的不同特点造成的。法律语言的表述，失之毫厘，谬以千里。某些法律英语的表述虽然简单，但丝毫不会影响其内容的准确性。因此，在翻译成汉语时，为避免引起误解，就需要根据汉语的习惯和语法规则对这些词或句子予以重述。

1. 增加实义词汇

鉴于法律语言的严谨性和规范性特点，在法律英语汉译过程中需要适当添加一定的词汇，以限定范围，提高表述的准确性。例如：

① This Agreement is made by and between ___Company having its registered office in___(place) and___Company, address of which is___ (house number, street, city).

本协议由__公司（注册营业地__）和__公司（法定地址是__市__街__号）之间达成。

分析：地址有多处，在通常的法律语言环境下，address 即表示"法定地址"，因此翻译成汉语时，需在"地址"前增加"法定"一词。

② The proposal indicates the offeror to be bound by the proposal thereof in case of acceptance.

该意思表明经受要约人承诺，要约人即受该意思表示约束。

分析：增加"受要约人"，表示不能是任何第三人的承诺，这是由合同权利义务的相对性决定的。

③ Court actions fall into two broad categories — civil and criminal.

法院的诉讼可分为两类：民事诉讼和刑事诉讼。

分析：如果在译文中省略"诉讼"一词，则句意欠妥帖。

④ The contract looks upon party A as having rights and duties thereof.

该合同视甲方为享有合同权利和承（负）担合同义务的主体。

分析："享有"和"承（负）担"虽然意思相反，但在法律英语中都可用 have 一词表达，而汉语找不到一个能够准确表达双重含义的对等词，所以应当用两个汉语动词分别表达。

法律英语使用被动结构的语序，而中国人惯用主动句，下面两例是因语序变化而需要加词的情况。

⑤ Civil actions generally are brought for breach of a contract, or for a wrong or tort.

一般来说，当事人都是因为对方违约、违法或侵权而对其提起民事诉讼的。

⑥ IN WITNESS whereof the Carrier or his Agents has signed the above stated number of Bills of Lading, all of this tenor and date, one of which being accomplished, the others to stand void.

证明以上各项，承运人或其代理人已签署各份内容和日期一样的上述正本提单，其中一份如已完成提货手续，则其余各份均告失效。

2. 增补连词

汉语偏正复句，很多时候不出现连词，如果原文中有表示"时间""假设""条件""让步""目的""原因"等关系的"偏句"，可以用相应的英语连词连接表示上述各种关系的从句。立法语言中最为典型的是以"的"结构的假设句，英译时必须添加显示主句和从句逻辑关系的连接词。例如：

① 合同对科技成果的使用权没有约定的，当事人都有使用的权利。(《中华人民共和国民法通则》第 88 条）

If the contract does not contain an agreed term regarding rights to the use of scientific and technological research achievements, the parties shall all have the right to use such achievements.

② 同一诉讼的几个被告住所地、经常居住地在两个以上人民法院辖区的，各该人民法院都有管辖权。(《中华人民共和国民事诉讼法》第 22 条）

Where the domiciles or habitual residences of several defendants in the same lawsuit are in the areas under the jurisdiction of two or more People's Courts, all of those People's Courts shall have jurisdiction over the lawsuit.

分析：上述两例原文都是属于以"的"收尾的假设句，汉译英时，形式上缺失的关联词，需要根据对汉语原句的理解，在英语译文中予以增补，使用 if 和 where 引导的从句来表示假设，从句子形式上清楚地表明英语句子中主从句的逻辑关系。

3. 增补同义词

英语有一词多义的特点，同一个词可以同时与若干个词进行搭配，修饰它们或被它们修饰，语言仍自然流畅，如下文中的 decrease 和 negotiations，因此，翻译多义词时就应该将其多义性表述清楚。例如：

① The innovation of products is one of the reform measures of the state-owned enterprises because it can decrease loss, cost and budget.

产品的革新是国企改革措施之一，因为它可以减少损失，降低成本和递减预算。

② Both the buyer and the seller are busy at negotiations of business, contract and draft.

买卖双方正忙于交易磋商，合约谈判和汇票议付。

4. 增补句子成分

1）增补主语

英语和汉语主语均是句子的主体，但按照汉语的表达习惯和文体特征，省略主语的情况较多，而英语句中的主语则通常不能省略。因此，在汉译英时运用增补技巧，可以补充汉语句中省略的主语。例如：

如蒙尽快惠告美国计算机详细的情况，不胜感激。

We should be grateful if you would give us further details of American computers at the earliest time.

分析：原文中，收信人是卖方，询问计算机情况的人是买方，译文中增补"我方"和"你方"，不仅使英语的句子结构完整，而且表明了买方和卖方的关系。

2）增补宾语

汉语和英语的及物动词后面都有宾语，表示动作的对象，动作关系涉人或事物。在某些情况或一定的上下文的条件下，汉语句子中的宾语可省略，而英语及物动词在任何情况下都须带宾语。运用增补技巧，以补充汉语中省略的宾语。例如：

我们觉得在这个时候延长信用证有效期和更改卸货港口是不恰当的。

We don't think it proper to extend the validity of L/C and amend the discharging port at this time.

分析：译文中增补宾语 it，代表复合结构中的"不定式"，使英语句子结构完整无缺。如果不采用增补技巧，上述两个英语句子均不能成立。

二、省略

省略就是把原文中的某些冗余成分略去不译，或去掉不符合译文表达习惯的无用之词，以保证译文内容准确、文字简洁、结构规范。

1. 省略表示重复、多余概念的词汇

例如：

① Within(…)days after the effective date of this contract, the Owner shall pay the Contractor as full and complete compensation for accomplishing the Works and assuming all obligations under this contract the contract price in the amount of_____.

在本合同生效后××天内，业主应向承包商支付金额_____为合同价格，作为承包商完成该工程并承担本合同规定的所有义务的全部报酬。

分析：full and complete 如直译为"全部和所有的"。而在汉语中，这两个概念几乎没有区别，因此译文用其中一词即可。

② 影响市场对商品需求的变化情况有内因和外因两方面的因素。

The changes of requirement for the commodities in the market are affected by the internal and external factors.

分析：上述汉语句中的范畴词"情况、方面"可使前面的抽象名词更加具体、明确，符合汉语的修辞需要。但译成英语后不省略这些范畴词，译文便显得累赘，概念模糊。

③ If any guarantee is required as security for any external financing of the Company approved by the Board in accordance with Article 8.2(c)(v), and if the Parties agree to provide guarantees in relation to such financing, the Parties shall severally guarantee the obligations of the Company under such external financing in proportion to their respective interests in the registered capital of the Company at such time as the guarantee is given (unless otherwise agreed in writing by the Parties).

如果合营公司董事会依照第 8.2（c）（v）条批准的外部融资需要以保证形式提供担保，并且双方同意对该融资提供保证，则（除非双方另有书面协议）双方应按当时在合营公司注册资本中所占份额的比例分别各自对合营公司的义务提供保证。

分析：在原文中，such time as the guarantee is given 本来是个定语从句，但在对其进行翻译时，根据上下文意思和逻辑关系就直接把它翻译成了"当时"。尽管作者省略了一个从句，但并没有改变原文的意思。在经过这样的省词后，译文反而更加通顺，更加符合中文的表达习惯。

④ The growth of capitalism and the competition for domestic and international business have led to a never-ending stream of new business instruments and techniques and sophisticated markets, each with its own communication system, its trading rules and its procedures for clearance and settlement.

随着资本主义的发展以及国内、国际业务的竞争的加剧，新的交易手段和商业技术层出不穷，市场变得更加专业化、更加成熟，每种市场都拥有自己的通信系统，自己的贸易规则和自己的清算结算程序。

分析：原文中有 has led to 这个动词，但在译文中译者省略了它的中文对应词。译者这样省略的目的是为了使译文更加通顺，更加符合中文的表达习惯。尽管译者这样省略，其译文并没有改变原文的意思。

2. 省略修饰词

例如：By a loan agreement dated___made between___Co. (Borrower) and___Co. (Lender), the Lender has agreed to make available to the Borrower a loan facility of up to $___.

根据__年__公司（借款方）和__公司（贷款方）签署的贷款协议，贷款方同意向借款方提供__美元的贷款。

分析：up to 在句中表示"直到，多达"之意，为使译文更加精练，翻译成汉语时可以省略。

3. 省略连接词

例如：The parties must act in accordance with the principle of good faith, no matter in exercising rights or in performing obligations.

当事人行使权利、履行义务应当遵循诚实信用原则。

分析：原文中的 or 在翻译成汉语时用顿号代替，可以达到简练的目的。

4. 省略介词

例如：The contract is made by and between the Buyer, ____ Co. and the Seller, ____ Co.

本合同是由买方____公司和卖方____公司之间签订的。

分析：between 在这句话中用来限定范围，以表明合同是在特定的买卖双方之间签订的，但在译文中，其意思已经由于汉语内在的逻辑关系而得到明确体现，因此可以不译。

5. 省略 here, there, where+介词或副词的表达

法律英语当中有一套惯用的副词。严格地说，这类副词并不是法律术语，但从修辞和文体的角度来看，这类词的广泛使用既使句子简练严密，又使句子严肃庄重，具有法律文体的风格。因而法律条文和著作中大量运用，在翻译成汉语时有时可以省略不译。例如：

In accordance with the "Law of the People's Republic of China on Chinese-foreign Equity Joint Venture" and other relevant PRC laws and regulations, party A and party B hereby agree to set up a joint venture limited liability company.

根据中华人民共和国中外合资经营企业法和其他相关的法律法规，甲方和乙方同意共同组建合资经营有限责任公司。

分析：句中的 hereby 即 under the Law of the People's Republic of China on Chinese-foreign Equity Joint Venture and other relevant PRC laws and regulations，可理解为"据此"。而汉语表达的连贯性已经使得译文忠实地再述了原文的含义，所以 hereby 可省略不译。

6. 省略时态词

例如：Where the seller sells the subject matter which has been delivered to a carrier for transportation and is in transit, unless otherwise agreed by the parties, the risk of damage or loss is borne by the buyer as from the time of formation of the contract.

出卖人出卖交由承运人运输在途的标的物，除当事人另有约定的以外，毁损、灭失的风险自合同成立时起由买受人承担。

分析：英语时态区分细微、习惯性强，动作的进行过程通过固定的丰富的语法手段描绘得非常精确，相比之下，汉语的时态有时则可模糊表达，在保持句意流畅的同时也忠实地反映了原文的意思。

法律宝典

民　　法

民法是调整平等主题的自然人、法人、其他组织之间的财产关系和人身关系的法律规范的总称。

民法法系与普通法法系是西方两大主要法律文化传统，具有历史悠久、影响广泛的特点。法系是比较法学常用的概念，指若干国家和地区具有共同传统的法律的总称。民法法系（civil law system of family）的起源可以追溯到古罗马的市民法，其法典化的传统可以追溯到罗马《十二表法》和《查士丁尼民法大全》。公元 533 年公布的《查士丁尼法学总论》，又名《查士丁

尼法学阶梯》，它以法学家盖尤斯的同名著作为蓝本，是《查士丁尼民法大全》的重要组成部分。古罗马法学家乌尔比安提出："公法是关于罗马国家的法律，私法是关于个人利益的法律。"民法法系国家在学理上沿用公法与私法划分的观点。

1804年《法国民法典》、1900年《德国民法典》是民法法系形成发展过程中具有重要意义的两部法典。该法系首先在法、德等欧洲大陆国家出现与发展，因此也称"大陆法系"。法学家在民法法系法律制度发展进程中起着举足轻重的作用，法学家基于法秩序创制的法律原则影响着法律的发展，立法机构以这些法律原则为基础制定法典，以解决法律纠纷，因此民法法系具有法典化的特征。

普通法起源于12世纪的英国，具有遵循先例（或先例约束）的特点。在美国法早期发展过程中，法官通过司法活动创造的判例法（case law）是最重要的法律渊源，因此普通法又有法官法（judge-made law）之别称。

在美国法语境中，民法（civil law）一词有两种含义。一是指与"遵循先例"为特征的普通法法系相区别的、建立在成文法典基础上的民法法系；一是指调整私人之间人身关系、财产关系的法律规范的总称，其外延涵盖了美国法中契约法、财产法、遗嘱法、侵权法、家庭法等内容，与刑法或公法形成对比，此种含义上的"民法"不同于大陆法系上作为一个独立法律部门的"民法"。

美国宪法确立的联邦主义原则决定了美国法由联邦法和州法组成。美国法是一个分散的系统，50个州拥有各自的宪法和法律。美国法总体上属于普通法法系，但路易斯安那州属于融合了普通法因素的民法法系法律制度。《路易斯安那民法典》使该州成为美国唯一属于民法法系的州。

▶ 术语积累

补充规定　supplementary provision
补救办法　remedial measures
不成文法　unwritten law
不作为　abstain from an act; act of omission
查士丁尼法典　Code Justinian; Codex Justinianus
查士丁尼法规汇编　Authenticum
成文法　written law
次要规则　secondary rule
从宽解释原则　doctrine of liberal construction
基本法　the fundamental law
大法官　Lord High Chancellor
大法官法院　Court of Chancery
大陆法系　Continental Legal System
地方法官　magistrate
法律渊源　source of law
法典　code; statute book

法典编纂　codification of codes
法定程序　legal procedure
法定处罚　statutory penalty
法定代理人　agent ad litem
法定解释　statutory interpretation
法定量刑情节　legally prescribed circumstances of sentencing
法定时效　statutory prescription
法定条件　legal condition
法定限制　statutory restrictions
法定效力　statutory force
法律保护　legal protection
法律编纂　codification
法律标准　legal standards
法律制裁　legal sanction
高级法官　senior judge
客观条件　objective condition
客观因素　objective factor
高级人民法院　Higher People's Court
高级人民检察院　Higher People's Procuratortate
格式条款　clause of style
公民投票；平民表决　plebiscite
规避义务　evade obligations
规范性法律文件　normalizative document of law
国际法学　international jurisprudence
过错方　tort-feasor; wrongdoer
过错推定原则　doctrine of presumption
《霍尔滕西法》　The Lex Hortensia
《罗马民法大全》　The Roman Corpus Juris Civilus
《民法大全》　Corpus Juris Civilis
民法典　civil code
民法法系　Civil-Law System
民法通则　General Principles of the Civil Law
民法学　science of civil law
民事案件中"占有优势证据"的原则　"by a preponderance of evidence" in civil cases
民事权利能力　the capacity for civil rights
民事权益　civil rights and interests
民事诉讼法　Civil Procedure Law
民事制裁　civil punishment; civil sanction
民政部门　the civil affairs department

民事上的占有　civil possesion
民事上的没收　civil forfeiture
民事上诉　civil appeal
民事主体　civil subject
民事法律关系　civil legal relationship
民事活动　activity relating to civil law
民事纠纷　civil dispute
民事客体　civil object
民事原告　civil plaintiff
民事被告　civil defendant
民事指控　civil charge
民事案件　civil case
民事过失　civil negligence
民事责任事故　accident involving civil liability
民事补偿　civil remedy
民事诉讼　civil action
民事损害　civil injury
民事债务　civil debt
民事管辖　civil jurisdiction
民事制裁　civil sanction
民事审判　civil trial
民事调解　civil mediation
民事罚款　civil penalty
民事权利争议　dispute concerning private rights
民事权利剥夺　deprived of private rights
《拿破仑法典》　The Napolean Code
判例法系　Case Law System
判例汇编　reports; reports of judgments
普通法　common law
普通法上的过失　common-law negligence
普通法学　general jurisprudence
强制规定　mandatory provisions
万民法　jus gentium
王权法，国王法　lex regia
违法构成要件　essential condition of delict
元老院决议　Senate's consult
长官法　ius honorarium
正当权益　justified rights; legitimate interests
正式渊源　formal source

执法人员　law enforcement officials
执行权　enforcement power
直接故意　actual intent; direct intent
直接客体　direct object

Section III　巩固练习

词汇与短语

1. binding force
2. jurisprudence constant
3. oral argument
4. stare decisis
5. The Law of Nature
6. civil law system of family
7. general principles of the civil law
8. ius honorarium
9. The Roman Corpus Juris Civilis
10. The Civil Law

11. 民事权利能力
12. 民事行为
13. 民事法律行为
14. 判例法
15. 万民法
16. 法官法
17. 不成文法
18. 王权法
19. 刑事诉讼程序
20. 上诉法院

句子与段落

1. Article 3 defines custom as a "practice repeated for a long time and generally accepted as having acquired the force of law". However, Article 3 makes it clear that custom may not abrogate or conflict with legislation.
2. Here, Louisiana judges do not make law with their decisions; rather, the code charges them with interpreting, as closely as possible, what has been written and passed by the legislature or long established by custom.
3. The second meaning of civil law refers to the body of law governing disputes between individuals, as opposed to those governing offenses against the government — that is, civil law as opposed to criminal law.
4. Civil Law is a legal system derived from the Roman Corpus Juris Civilis of Emperor Justinian I. It differs from a common-law system, which relies on prior decisions to determine the outcome of a lawsuit.
5. For example, whereas European judges actively elicit the facts in a controversy and seldom use a jury, Louisiana judges operate more like their common-law colleagues, assuming the

role of neutral and passive fact finder or arbiter, and leaving the final decision a jury.

6. 路易斯安那州法官与普通法法官同行不同之处在于,他们不受司法先例的约束,而普通法法官必须坚持"遵守先例"的原则,该原则要求依据先前类似案件的判决确立的法律原则裁决当下的案件。

7. 在路易斯安那州,陪审团的裁决可能被上诉法院推翻,因此证据充分的原告可能希望在适用普通法的州提起诉讼。此外,如果原告不确定在初审法院能否胜诉,则选择路易斯安那州起诉更好,因为该州上诉法院拥有更加广泛的审查权。

8. 1870年制定的民法典的大部分条文至今仍然有效,该法典使先前的法律更加系统,也较先前的法律更加简明。该法律用英文制定,使路易斯安那州仍是美国唯一属于民法法系而非普通法系的州。

9. 民法系起源于古罗马,法律学者总结与创制的法律原则制约着民法法系的发展,在属于民法法系传统的国家中,立法人员与行政人员利用这些原则制定旨在解决所有法律纠纷的法典。

10. 第一种含义指流行于欧洲的、建立在成文法典基础上的法律制度,这种意义上的民法区别于英国和美国大多数州所采用的普通法法律制度。普通法系根据判例法而不是成文法典解决法律纠纷。

11. In the United States, the term civil law has two meanings. One meaning of civil law refers to a legal system prevalent in Europe that is based on written codes. Civil law in this sense is contrasted with the common-law system used in England and most of the United States, which relies on prior case law to resolve disputes rather than written codes. The second meaning of civil law refers to the body of law governing disputes between individuals, as opposed to those governing offenses against the government — that is, civil law as opposed to criminal law.

12. 民法法系和普通法系还有一个重要的区别,即在普通法系,上诉法院在多数情况下,只就法律问题的裁决进行复核,但是,民法法系的上诉法院既复核法律问题,又复核事实问题。路易斯安那州上诉法院可以宣布陪审团的裁决错误,重新认定事实,甚至可能减少损害赔偿金数额。这对于既可以在路易斯安那州起诉,又可以在其他州起诉的原告来说意义重大(在特定的州起诉,原告必须证明案件与该州有某种关系)。

Unit Six

Criminal Law
刑　　法

Section I　译例研究

>> Passage One
The Legal Definition of Crime

The traditional legal definition of a crime is restated in the statutes of most states. While that restatement varies slightly from jurisdiction to jurisdiction, the definition contained in The California Penal Code is typical:

A crime or public offense is an act committed or omitted in violation of a law forbidding or commanding it, and to which is annexed, upon conviction, either of the following punishments: (1) Death; (2) Imprisonment; (3) Fine; (4) Removal from office; or (5) Disqualification to hold and enjoy any office honor, trust, or profit in this State.

Several features of this definition help to explain the legal principles underlying the concept of "crime". First, a crime, as a creature of the law, requires an act that violates the law as opposed to violating customs, religious standards, or some other means of social control. There are, however, many acts that violate the law, but are not crimes. *Breach of contract,* for example, is illegal, yet not ordinary criminal. To turn an illegal act into a criminal offense, further elements are needed. The California definition also describes a crime as a "public offense". A crime, in other words, is viewed as an illegality against the interests of the public as a whole as opposed to an illegality only against the individual victim of the violation. As we noted in Chapter Two, it is this factor which largely distinguishes the criminal law from the civil law, and explains why the judicial enforcement of the criminal law is pursued by a public official (the prosecuting attorney) on behalf of the state. The concept of the crime as an act against the public also explains a third element of the traditional definition — that a crime is an act which may lead to the imposition of punishment.

The California provision lists five different forms of punishment. Each of these is designed to vindicate the interests of the public (largely by preventing future offenses) rather than to compensate the individual victim. As a particular matter, the court's authority to impose the second and third of the mentioned punishments (imprisonment and fine) are the crucial elements of identifying most crimes. The death penalty is limited to a narrow class of homicides which clearly are crimes. The two other categories of punishment, both relating to the holding of public office, almost always are provided for under laws that also provide for imprisonment or fine. If a question arises as to whether some act prohibited by law is a crime, the court will look to the potential consequences that may be imposed upon the violator. If it finds that imprisonment or a punitive fine may be imposed, it recognized that the behavior is viewed as an offense against the public and, hence, a crime.

Although the concept of a criminal offense is well established today, this was not always the case. The recognition of a class of illegal acts known as crimes was a product of a gradual historical development. Society made several crucial determinations in accepting the concept of crime, some of which are still being reexamined today. First, society has to determine that there were some factions that should be viewed as injurious to the public as a whole rather than just to the individual victim. This decision, in turn, was followed by the conclusion that such actions were appropriated subject to punishment. Finally, various determinations had to be made as to what punishment could legitimately be imposed.

▶ 词汇提示

restate　　*v.* 重新叙述；重讲；重申
jurisdiction　　*n.* 司法权，审判权，管辖权；权限，权力
commit to　　交付，把……投入；把……置于
omit　　*v.* 省略；遗漏；删除；疏忽
violation　　*n.* 违背；违反；妨碍，侵害；强奸
annex　　*v.* 附加；并吞；获得　　*n.* 附加物；附属建筑物
conviction　　*n.* 定罪；确信；[法] 证明有罪
fine　　*n.* 罚金
disqualification　　*n.* 不合格；取消资格；[体] 被罚下场
office honor　　荣誉职位
violate　　*v.* 违反；侵犯，妨碍；亵渎
underlying　　*adj.* 潜在的；根本的；在下面的；优先的
opposed to　　反对；反对……的
illegality　　*n.* 违法；非法行为；犯规
judicial enforcement　　审判强制权
public official　　国家公职人员

imposition　*n.* 强加；征收；欺骗；不公平的负担
provision　*n.* 供应品；准备；条款；规定 *v.* 供给……食物及必需品
vindicate　*v.* 维护；证明……无辜；证明……正确
identify　*v.* 认同；一致；确定
homicide　*n.* 杀人；杀人犯
public office　公共职务
violator　*n.* 违背者；违反者；妨碍者
reexamine　*v.* 重考，复试；再调查
faction　*n.* 派别；小集团；内讧；纪实小说
injurious　*adj.* 有害的；诽谤的

▶ 法律术语

statute　*n.* 成文法
public offense　公罪
imprisonment　*n.* 监禁
the civil law　民法
legal principles　法定原则
The California Penal Code　《加利福尼亚刑法典》
death（penalty）　*n.* 死刑
removal from office　免除公职
prosecuting attorney　公诉律师
breach of contract　不履行合同

▶ 要点解析

1. A crime or public offense is an act committed or omitted in violation of a law forbidding or commanding it, and to which is annexed, upon conviction, either of the following punishments: (1) Death; (2) Imprisonment; (3) Fine; (4) Removal from office; or (5) Disqualification to hold and enjoy any office honor, trust, or profit in this State.

犯罪或公罪是一种侵犯了法律所禁止或强制性规定的侵害行为或过失行为。并且，如果被判定有罪，将会附加下例任何一种刑罚：（1）死刑；（2）监禁；（3）罚金；（4）免除公职；或（5）取消在政府中担任和享有任何荣誉职位、信托，或者收益的资格。

trust 和 profit 分别是"托管"和"收益"的意思。这里应注意，五种刑罚均为专业的法律名词，翻译时应弄清楚意思，做到严谨。此外，这是一个长句，在翻译时要注意，不要让译文显得冗长。我们可以分开处理：前半段首先表述犯罪的定义，"犯罪是一种……的行为"，然后对它进行说明，将五种刑罚译出。

2. First, a crime, as a creature of the law, requires an act that violates the law as opposed to violating customs, religious standards, or some other means of social control.

第一，犯罪作为法律的创造物，需要具备一种侵犯法律的行为。这种行为不是侵害习俗、宗教标准和其他社会控制手段的。在翻译 control 一词时可以用增词法，将其译为"控制手段"。此外，我们可以将长句断开，以便清楚、简洁地表达出意思。

3. A crime, in other words, is viewed as an illegality against the interests of the public as a whole as opposed to an illegality only against the individual victim of the violation.

换句话说，相对于只针对单个被害者的违法侵害行为，犯罪总体上可以看作是一种危害公共利益的行为。

as opposed to 有"相对于"的意思，这里表示前后的对比。整个句子在翻译时，可以适当调整语序，强调出前后的对比 against 可以灵活处理，译为"危害"。

4. As we noted in Chapter Two, it is this factor which largely distinguishes the criminal law from the civil law, and explains why the judicial enforcement of the criminal law is pursued by a public official (the prosecuting attorney) on behalf of the state. The concept of the crime as an act against the public also explains a third element of the traditional definition — that a crime is an act which may lead to the imposition of punishment.

正是这个因素很大程度地把刑法与民法区分开来，并解释了国家公职人员（公诉律师）基于政府利益要求的刑法审判强制权的原因。犯罪，作为危害公共利益行为的这个概念，也解释了犯罪的传统定义中的第三个要素——犯罪是一种可能导致强制性刑罚的行为。

judicial enforcement 译成"审判强制权"; public official 译为"国家公职人员"; prosecuting attorney 则译成"公诉律师"; imposition 是"征收；强加"的意思，在此处 imposition of punishment 中译成"强制性刑罚"较适合。

5. As a particular matter, the court's authority to impose the second and third of the mentioned punishments (imprisonment and fine) are the crucial elements of identifying most crimes. The death penalty is limited to a narrow class of homicides which clearly are crimes.

作为一种实践性事务，法庭所具有的采取上述第二种、第三种刑法措施（监禁和罚金）的权力，在认定大部分犯罪中，是决定性因素。死刑仅限于明确是杀人犯罪的狭窄范围内。

a particular matter 译为"实践性事务"; homicide 是"杀人"的意思。

6. The California provision lists five different forms of punishment. Each of these is designed to vindicate the interests of the public (largely by preventing future offenses) rather than to compensate the individual victim.

加利福尼亚刑法典中列举了五种不同的刑罚措施，每一种都是为了维护公共利益（大部分为了预防将来的侵害），而不是集中于单个的被害者。

provision 有"规定""条款"的意思。The California 根据上下文宜译为"加利福尼亚刑法典"而不是简单地译为"加利福尼亚"; compensate the individual victim 直译是"补偿单个的被害者"，但是似乎过于直白，本句强调的是刑罚措施的目的和作用，着重在于强调它们对集体利益的维护，因此译为"集中于单个的被害者"更妥。

7. The two other categories of punishment, both relating to the holding of public office, almost always are provided for under laws that also provide for imprisonment or fine.

另两类刑罚措施都与担任公共职务有关，而且它们几乎总是被法律规定许可与监禁或罚金这两种措施合并执行。

hold 有"举办，支持"之意，而联系句意，holding 在此处译为"担任"；public office 译为"公共职务"；under laws 则译为"根据法律"。

8. If a question arises as to whether some act prohibited by law is a crime, the court will look to the potential consequences that may be imposed upon the violator. If it finds that imprisonment or a punitive fine may be imposed, it recognized that the behavior is viewed as an offense against the public and, hence, a crime.

如果有人提出某种被法律禁止的行为是否为犯罪的问题，法庭将考察可能强加于该违法者的可能结果。如果发现可能强制采用监禁或惩罚性罚金，表明这种行为应看作是对公共利益的侵害，因此，是犯罪。

If a question arises as to 这种句式不仅在法律英语中，在日常翻译也经常可见。在翻译时，我们可以将人作为主语，译为"如果有人提出"，be imposed 这一被动句式译成主动形式，更符合汉语表达习惯。翻译时注意词性的转换。原文的主语 recognition 在翻译时转换成动词，更符合汉语的习惯。

9. First, society has to determine that there were some factions that should be viewed as injurious to the public as a whole rather than just to the individual victim. This decision, in turn, was followed by the conclusion that such actions were appropriated subject to punishment.

首先，社会必须确认有一些行为应当视为对公众总体的侵害，而不是仅针对个人的侵害。因此，这个决定伴随着这样一个结论，即上述的行为是相应地易受到刑罚的。

subject 含义多种多样，以 subject to 搭配的形式使用的在词典中只有形容词和副词两种情况。subject to 一般有两种用法：① 以介词短语形式出现，后跟 agreement, contract, regulations 等法律文件名或文件中特定条款名等名词配合使用；通常可翻译成 "根据……规定"及"在不抵触……的情况下"；② 以介词短语/动词短语（be subjected to，较少见）出现，后接法律文书或条款以外的其他名词，一般译为"使……面临/遭受……"或"……服从或接受"等。

 参考译文

犯罪的法律定义

犯罪的传统法律定义在许多国家的成文法中都有表述。虽然这些表述在不同的司法管辖区内有轻微的差异，但加利福尼亚州刑法典中的犯罪定义仍很有代表性：

犯罪或公罪是一种侵犯了法律所禁止或强制性规定的侵害行为或过失行为。并且，如果被判定有罪，将会附加下例任何一种刑罚：（1）死刑；（2）监禁；（3）罚金；（4）免除公职；或（5）取消在政府中担任和享有任何荣誉职位、信托，或者收益的资格。

这个定义的几个特征可以用来帮助解释"犯罪"这个概念中的法定原则。第一，犯罪作为法律的创造物，需要具备一种侵犯法律的行为。这种行业是禁止侵害习俗、宗教标准和其他社会控制手段的。将违法行为归为犯罪，还需要另外一些要素。加利福尼亚州刑法典中的定义也把犯罪描述成"公罪"。换句话说，相对于只针对于单个被害者的违法侵害行为，犯罪总体上可以看作是一种危害公共利益的行为。正是这个因素很大程度地把刑法与民法区分开来，并解释了国家公职人员（公诉律师）基于政府利益要求刑事的审判强制权的原因。犯

罪，作为危害公共利益行为的这个概念，也解释了犯罪传统定义中的第三个要素——犯罪是一种可能导致强制性刑罚的行为。

　　加利福尼亚刑法典中列举了五种不同的刑罚措施，每一种都是为了维护公共利益（大部分为了预防将来的侵害），而不是集中于单个的被害者。作为一种实践性事务，法庭所具有的采取上述第二种、第三种刑法措施（监禁和罚金）的权力，在认定大部分犯罪中，是决定性因素。死刑仅限于明确是杀人犯罪的狭窄范围内。另两类刑罚措施都与担任公共职务有关，而且它们几乎总是被法律规定许可与监禁或罚金这两种措施合并执行。如果有人提出某种被法律禁止的行为是否为犯罪的问题，法庭将考察可能强加于该违法者的可能结果。如果发现可能强制采用监禁或惩罚性罚金，表明这种行为应看作是对公共利益的侵害，因此是犯罪。

　　虽然刑法中违法的概念已经很好地建立起来，但事情并非总是如此。把一部分违法行为看作是犯罪是历史不断发展的产物。社会在接受犯罪这个概念的过程中做了几个重要的决定，今天，其中一些还一直在被检验着。首先，社会必须确认有一些行为应当视为对公众总体的侵害，而不是仅针对个人的侵害。因此，这个决定伴随着这样一个结论，即上述的行为是相应地易受到刑罚的。最后，各种不同的判决做出强制刑罚要合法。

▶▶ *Passage Two*
我国刑法中的正当防卫

　　正当防卫是排除犯罪性的行为，也就是说，这种行为在表面上给合法权益造成了损害，实质上却是保护了合法权益。因此，我国刑法明文规定这种行为不构成犯罪。根据刑法，为了使国家、公共利益、本人或者他人的人身、财产和其他权利免受正在进行的不法侵害，而采取的制止不法侵害的行为，对不法侵害人造成损害的，属于正当防卫，不负刑事责任。

　　正当防卫必须具备以下条件：

　　第一，这种行为的目的是为了保护国家、公共利益、本人或者他人的人身、财产和其他权利免受正在进行的不法侵害；

　　第二，必须存在不法侵害行为，包括犯罪行为和其他违法行为；

　　第三，不法侵害必须正在进行，即不法侵害已经开始且尚未结束；

　　第四，防卫必须针对不法侵害人本人；

　　最后，正当防卫行为不能明显超过必要限度造成重大损害，正当防卫明显超过必要限度造成重大损害的，属于防卫过当，应当负刑事责任，但是应当减轻或者免除处罚。

　　此外，为了有效地保护合法权益，鼓励公民积极进行正当防卫，我国刑法规定对于正在进行的行凶、杀人、抢劫、强奸、绑架以及其他严重危及人身安全的暴力犯罪，采取防卫行为造成不法侵害人伤亡的，属于正当防卫而不是防卫过当，不负刑事责任。据此，对严重危及人身安全的暴力犯罪进行防卫，不存在防卫过当的问题。

　　正当防卫是刑法学的一个重要问题，是保护国家和人民合法权益的有效手段。但是在实践中，有时也很难判断正当防卫的限度，这就需要刑法学专家不断进一步地研究。

词汇提示

排除　exempt
合法权益　lawful rights and interests
规定　prescribe
构成　constitute
侵害　infringe
正在进行的　on-going
减轻　mitigate
行凶　assault
杀人　murder
强奸　rape
人身安全　personal safety

法律术语

正当防卫　justifiable defence
刑法　criminal law
刑事责任　criminal responsibility
不法侵害　unlawful infringement
不法侵害人　perpetrator
防卫过当　undue defence
刑法学　criminal jurisprudence

要点解析

1. 正当防卫是排除犯罪性的行为，也就是说，这种行为在表面上给合法权益造成了损害，实质上却是保护了合法权益。因此，我国刑法明文规定这种行为不构成犯罪。

Justifiable defence is the act being exempted from crimes, namely, this act appears to cause damage to lawful rights and interests, but in essential it protects lawful rights and interests. Therefore, Chinese Criminal Law definitely prescribes that this act doesn't constitute crimes.

"排除"应译成 be exempted from；"明文"应译为 definitely；"规定"译为 prescribe。

2. 根据刑法，为了使国家、公共利益、本人或者他人的人身、财产和其他权利免受正在进行的不法侵害，而采取的制止不法侵害的行为，对不法侵害人造成损害的，属于正当防卫，不负刑事责任。

According to Criminal Law, an act that a person commits to stop an unlawful infringement in order to prevent the interests of the state and the public, or his own or other people's individual rights, rights of property or other rights from being infringed upon by the on-going infringement, thus harming the perpetrator, is justifiable defence, and he shall not bear criminal responsibility.

在汉译英中，在翻译像"应""应该""必须""非……不可"以及表示此类意思的中文时，表示法律上可以强制执行的义务的时候，应该用 shall 来翻译；"负责任"可译为 bear。

3. 最后，正当防卫行为不能明显超过必要限度造成重大损害，正当防卫明显超过必要限度造成重大损害的，属于防卫过当，应当负刑事责任，但是应当减轻或者免除处罚。

Finally, the act of justifiable defence cannot obviously exceed the limit of necessity and cause serious damage. If a person's act of justifiable defence obviously exceeds the limits of necessity and causes serious damage, which is considered as undue defence, he shall bear criminal responsibility. However, he shall be given a mitigated punishment or be exempted from punishment.

"防卫过当"为专业术语，译作 undue defence；"减轻"译为 be exempted from。此句难度不大，在最后半句的表达上稍微注意即可。

4. 此外，为了有效地保护合法权益，鼓励公民积极进行正当防卫，我国刑法规定对于正在进行的行凶、杀人、抢劫、强奸、绑架以及其他严重危及人身安全的暴力犯罪，采取防卫行为造成不法侵害人伤亡的，属于正当防卫而不是防卫过当，不负刑事责任。

Moreover, in order to effectively protect lawful rights and interests and encourage citizens to carry out actively justifiable defence, our Criminal Law prescribes that if a person acts in defence against an on-going assault, murder, robbery, rape, kidnap and other crime of violence that seriously endangers his personal safety, thus causing injury or death to the perpetrator, it is justifiable defence instead of undue defence, and he shall not bear criminal responsibility.

与"正当防卫"进行搭配的动词可以用 carry out；在法律英语中，常用 prescribe 表示"规定"的意思；"正在进行的"译为 on-going。另外，此句比较长，可以用顺译法，依次表达出意思。

5. 正当防卫是刑法学的一个重要问题，是保护国家和人民合法权益的有效手段。但是在实践中，有时也很难判断正当防卫的限度，这就需要刑法学专家不断进一步地研究。

Justifiable defence is an important problem in criminal jurisprudence. It is an effective way to protect the rights and interests of the state and people. However, in practice, it is also difficult to judge the limits of justifiable defence sometimes. It needs further research by experts of criminal jurisprudence gradually.

"刑法学"译为 criminal jurisprudence，在句子"这就需要刑法学专家不断进一步地研究"中，转换词性，将动词"研究"译为名词。

参考译文

About Justifiable Defence in Chinese Criminal Law

Justifiable defence is the act being exempted from crimes, namely, this act appears to cause damage to lawful rights and interests, but in essential it protects lawful rights and interests. Therefore, Chinese Criminal Law definitely prescribes that this act doesn't constitute crimes.

According to Criminal Law, an act that a person commits to stop an unlawful infringement in order to prevent the interests of the state and the public, or his own or other people's individual rights, rights of property or other rights from being infringed upon by the on-going infringement, thus harming the perpetrator, is justifiable defence, and he shall not bear criminal responsibility.

Justifiable defence must include the following conditions:

Firstly, the purpose of this act is to prevent the interests of the state and the public, or a person's own or other people's individual rights, rights of property or other rights from being infringed upon by the on-going infringement.

Secondly, there must exist an unlawful infringement, including criminal acts as well as other illegal acts.

Thirdly, the unlawful infringement must be on going, which means an unlawful infringement has begun and has not finished yet.

Fourthly, an actor can only defend against the person who himself commits unlawful infringement.

Finally, the act of justifiable defence cannot obviously exceed the limit of necessity and cause serious damage. If a person's act of justifiable defence obviously exceeds the limits of necessity and causes serious damage, which is considered as undue defence, he shall bear criminal responsibility. However, he shall be given a mitigated punishment or be exempted from punishment.

Moreover, in order to effectively protect lawful rights and interests and encourage citizens to carry out actively justifiable defence, our Criminal Law prescribes that if a person acts in defence against an on-going assault, murder, robbery, rape, kidnap and other crime of violence that seriously endangers his personal safety, thus causing injury or death to the perpetrator, it is justifiable defence instead of undue defence, and he shall not bear criminal responsibility. According to this provision, it is not undue defence to the acts in defence against crime of violence that seriously endangers one's personal safety.

Justifiable defence is an important problem in criminal jurisprudence. It is an effective way to protect the rights and interests of the state and people. However, in practice, it is also difficult to judge the limits of justifiable defence sometimes. It needs further research by experts of criminal jurisprudence gradually.

Section II 技能拓展

翻译技巧

法律文本程式化、固定结构的翻译

法律文本中程式化语言结构是人们在长期使用民族共同语的过程中，由于立法和司法工作的需要，逐渐形成的一套具有法律专业特色的语言结构。

从语篇结构这个层次上看，古今中外立法语篇的结构大致相同，最突出的特点是它的高度程式化。整体结构形式上都采用了分条列款的方式，"条"以下设"款""项""目""点"，内容都是由描写性成分过渡到规定性成分；由颁布命令和/或前言过渡到具体条文；其结构层次分明，都是采用从宏观到微观；从总论/总则到条文；从重要条文到次要条文的语篇结构。这种程式化语篇是保持法律规范的庄严性及其内容的严谨合理和准确规范的必要手段，能使法律规范的内涵得到最充分的体现。程式化的语篇结构的另一个重要优点是它可以给所涉及的法律条文、专业术语和概括性词语设定具体的阐释语境，减少曲解或误解法律条文和概括性词语的可能性，瓦解那些想钻法律漏洞者的企图。

下面首先从四个方面谈谈立法语言的程式化语言结构。

一、表达禁止性的程式化语言结构

禁止性规范是指禁止法律关系主体为某种行为的法律规范。汉语的表达方式通常是"严禁""禁止""不得""不能"等。其英语的程式化语言结构有：

（1）be prohibited/not allowed
（2）be not obliged/permitted
（3）shall / may / must not+*v.*

例如：

① 禁止对任何民族的歧视和压迫，禁止破坏民族团结和制造民族分裂的行为。

Discrimination against and oppression of any nationality are prohibited; any act which undermines the unity or instigates division between or among any nationalities is prohibited.

② A person cannot at the same time be both landlord and tenant of the same premises.

任何人不得在同一项地产上同时既是出租人又是承租人。

③ No security may be offered or sold to the public unless it is registered with the SEC.

如未在证券交易（管理）委员会登记，任何证券不得上市或向大众出售。

④ 国家保护野生动物及其生存环境，禁止任何单位和个人非法猎捕或者破坏。

The state shall protect wildlife and the environment for its survival, and shall prohibit the illegal hunting, catching or destruction of wildlife by any unit or individual.

⑤ The state ensures the rational use of natural resources and protests rare animals and plants. Appropriation or damaging of natural resources by any organization or individual by whatever means is prohibited.

国家保障自然资源的合理利用，保护珍贵动物和植物。禁止任何组织或者个人用任何手段侵占和破坏自然资源。

⑥ 被认为（入境后）可能危害中国国家安全、社会秩序的外国人，不准入境。

Aliens who are considered a possible threat to China's state security and public order shall not be permitted to enter into China.

⑦ State property is sacred and inviolable, and no organization or individual shall be allowed to seize, encroach upon, privately divide, retain or destroy it.

国家财产神圣不可侵犯，禁止任何组织或者个人侵占、哄抢、私分、截留或破坏。

二、表达义务性的程式化语言结构

义务性规范，是指规定人们必须依法作出一定行为的法律规范。汉语表达方式为"有……义务""必须"等。其英语的程式化语言结构有：

(1) must / shall + *v.*
(2) fulfill one's obligation to+*v.*

(3) have the duty to+*v.*
(4) it is the duty of /to+*v.*

例如：

① 公司必须保护职工的合法权益，加强劳动保护，实现安全生产。

Companies must protect the lawful rights of their staff and workers, and strengthen labor protection so as to achieve safety in production.

② The seller owes a duty to the buyer to use due care in production, packing, and sale of his or her goods so that foreseeable harm, …, will be avoided.

为使可预见的伤害……得以避免，卖方在其生产、包装、销售中负有做到适当谨慎之义务。

③ 中华人民共和国公民有维护国家统一和全国各民族团结的义务。

It is the duty of citizens of the People's Republic of China to safeguard the unification of the country and the unity of all its nationalities.

④ Parents have the duty to rear and educate their children who are minors, and children who have come of age have the duty to support and assist their parents.

父母有抚养教育未成年子女的义务，成年子女有赡养扶助父母的义务。

⑤ 夫妻双方有实行计划生育的义务。

Both husband and wife shall fulfill their obligation to practice family planning.

三、表达授权性的程式化语言结构

授权性规范指的是"规定法律关系主体依法有权自己为某种行为以及要求他人为或不为某种行为的法律规范"。其汉语的表达方式为"享有……的权利""有权……"等。其英语的程式化语言结构为：

(1) have the right/power to +*v.*
(2) enjoy the right of…
(3) be entitled to+*v.* /*n.*
(4) be authorized to+*v.*
(5) may / shall +*v.*

例如：

① 当事人依法享有自愿订立合同的权利，任何单位和个人不得非法干预。

The parties shall have the right to be voluntary to enter into a contract in accordance with law. No unit or individual may illegally interfere.

② When one of the parties to the Contract fails to perform his or her obligations under the contract and the other party thereby sustains some injury, the injured party is entitled to be put, as nearly as possible, in the same position as if the contract had been performed.

当一方未按约履行其义务并使对方由此受到损害，该受损方享有获取（尽可能）接近于合同已履行之（有利）状况。

③ Enterprises as legal persons, individual businesses and individual partnerships shall have the right to use and lawfully assign their own names.

企业法人、个体工商户、个人合伙有权使用、依法转让自己的名称。

④ 公民、法人享有著作权（版权），依法有署名、发表、出版、获得报酬等权利。

Citizens and legal persons shall enjoy the right of authorship (copyrights) and shall be entitled to sign their names as authors, issue and publish their works and obtain remuneration in accordance with law.

⑤ Under any of the following circumstances, an enterprise as legal person shall bear liability, its legal representative may additionally be given administrative sanctions and fined and, if the offence constitutes a crime, a criminal responsibility shall be investigated in accordance with the law.

企业法人有下列情形之一的,除法人承担责任外,对法定代表人可以给予行政处分、罚款,构成犯罪的,依法追究刑事责任。

四、表达法律效力的程式化语言结构

表达法律效力的汉语表达方式为"施行(实施)"和"废止(废除)"等。其英语的程式化语言结构为:

(1) come / enter into force
(2) become effective
(3) go into effect
(4) be put into effect
(5) be abolished
(6) be abrogated
(7) be null and void

例如:

① 本法自公布之日起施行。

This law shall come/enter into force as of its promulgation.

② These Regulations shall become effective as of July 1, 2002.

本条例自 2002 年 7 月 1 日起施行。

③ 本通则经国务院发布施行。过去各地原有检查办法与本通则有抵触者,即予以废除。

These General Rules shall go into effect after their promulgation by the Government Administration Council. If any former inspection procedures adopted in various regions conflict with these General Rules, the former shall be abolished.

法律宝典

正 当 防 卫

正当防卫(又称自我防卫,简称自卫),是大陆法系刑法上的一种概念,表示"对于现实不法之侵害,为防卫自己或他人之权力所为之行为"。

正当防卫的本质在于制止不法侵害,保护合法权益。它有以下基本特征。

1. 正当防卫是目的正当性和行为的防卫性的统一

目的正当性是指正当防卫的目的是为了保护国家、公共利益、本人或者他人的人身、财产和其他权利免受正在进行的不法侵害。行为的防卫性是指正当防卫是在合法权益受到不法侵害的时候,同不法侵害做斗争的行为。他既是法律赋予公民的一种权利,又是公民在道义上应尽的义务,是一种正义行为,应受到法律的保护。目的正当性与行为的防卫性具有密切的联系。首先，目的的正当性制约着行为的防卫性。其次，行为的防卫性体现着目的的正当性，是目的正当性的客观表现。

2. 正当防卫是主观的防卫意图和客观上的防卫行为的统一

防卫意图，是指防卫人意识到不法侵害正在进行，为了保护国家、公共利益、本人或者他人的人身、财产等合法权利，而决意制止正在进行的不法侵害的心理状态。正当防卫在客观上对不法侵害人造成了一定的人身或者财产的损害，因此具有犯罪的外观。但是，正当防卫与犯罪具有本质的区别，我们只有看到正当防卫制止不法侵害、保护国家和其他合法权益的本质，才能真正把握住正当防卫不负刑事责任的依据。

3. 正当防卫是社会政治评价和法律评价的统一

正当防卫的目的是为了使国家、公共利益、本人或者他人的人身、财产和其他权利免受正在进行的不法侵害，而且客观上具有制止不法侵害、保护合法权益的性质。因此，正当防卫没有法益侵害性，这是我国刑法对正当防卫的肯定的社会政治评价；正当防卫不具备犯罪构成，没有刑事违法性，因此，正当防卫不负刑事责任，这是我国刑法对正当防卫的肯定的法律评价。在这个意义上说，正当防卫是排除社会危害性和阻止刑事违法性的统一。

▶ 术语积累

帮助当事人毁灭、伪造证据罪　crime of aiding a client to destroy or forge evidence
绑架妇女儿童罪　crime of kidnapping women and children
包庇、纵容黑社会性质组织罪　crime of harboring a mafia-style syndicate
包庇毒品犯罪分子罪　crime of harboring drug criminals
报复陷害罪　case of retaliation and frame-ups
必要共同犯罪　indispensable joint crime
并科原则　doctrine of cumulating punishments
剥夺权利　deprival of rights
参加恐怖活动组织罪　crime of taking part in an organization engaged in terrorist activities
超越管辖权　excess of jurisdiction
超越职权范围　overstep one's authority
惩办和宽大相结合　combine punishment with leniency
惩办少数、改造多数的原则　principle of punishing the few and reforming the many
惩罚措施　punitive measure
惩罚性制裁　punitive sanction
抽逃出资罪　crime of flight of capital contribution
抽象行政行为　abstract administrative act
出口骗税犯罪活动　criminal activities of cheating out of tax rebates in export
出售伪造发票罪　crime of selling counterfeit currency
出于恶意　from malevolence
从轻处罚　give a lesser punishment

从重处罚　give a severer punishment
单位受贿罪　crime of bribe taken by a unit
单一犯罪构成　single constitution of crime
定罪　conviction
罚金　fine
法定原则　legal principles
罚不当罪　punishment does not fit the crime
犯意　criminal intent
犯罪低龄化　lowering ages of criminal offenders
犯罪动机　criminal motive
犯罪构成　constitution of a crime; constitutive elements of a crime
犯罪构成要件　special constitutive elements of crime
犯罪集团　criminal gang; criminal group
犯罪学　criminology
犯罪预防　crime prevention
犯罪中止　discontinuance of crime; desistance of crime
犯罪主体　subject of crime
犯罪组织　criminal organization
贩卖毒品罪　drug offense; crime of drug trafficking
防卫过当　unjustifiable self-defense
防卫挑拨　instigation of defense; provocation of defense
防卫限度　limit of defense
妨碍公务罪　crime of disrupting public service
妨害公共安全罪　crime of impairing public security
放弃权利　withdraw a claim; waive a right
非法持、私藏枪支、弹药罪　crime of illegally holding or hiding a firearm or ammunition
非法持有毒品罪　crime of illegally holding drugs
非法干预　unlawful interference
非法教唆他人作伪证　subornation of perjury
非法出售增值税专用发票罪　crime of illegal selling invoice for exclusive use of VAT
非法利益　unlawful interests
非法手段　illegal means
诽谤罪　crime of defamation
隔地犯　offense of segregation by location
隔时犯　offense of segregation by time
工具不能犯　impossibility of instruments
公罪　public offense
故意犯罪　calculated crime; intentional crime
故意杀人罪　crime of intentional homicide

故意伤害罪　crime of willful and malicious injury
故意醉酒　voluntary intoxication
管辖　jurisdiction
惯犯　habitual criminal
惯例　custom and usage
过失犯罪　criminal negligence; involuntary crime; negligent crime
国家赔偿案件　case of state compensation
国家赔偿的归责原则　principle of culpability for state compensation
国家赔偿的双重过错原则　principle of dual faults for state compensation
国家赔偿法　state compensation law
国家赔偿主体　subject of state compensation
国家权力机关　state authority
国家审判机关　state judicial organs
国家行政机关　state administrative organs
国家意志　state's will
国家职能　function of the state
国民待遇　national treatment
黑社会性质的犯罪集团　gangland criminal syndicate
缓期二年执行　with a two-year reprieve
缓刑　probate execution
基于综合症的犯罪　syndrome-based defense
集合犯　aggregate offense; collective offense
既遂犯　accomplished crime
继续犯　continuous crime
加重处罚　give an aggravated punishment beyond the maximum prescribed
假冒他人注册商标罪　crime of counterfeiting the registered trademark of another
假释　parole
假想数罪　imaginatively several crimes
监禁　imprisonment
简单共同犯罪　simple joint crime
间接故意　indirect intent; indirect intention
教唆未遂　attempt of solicitation
劫持船只、汽车罪　crime of hijacking a ship or an automobile
劫持航空器罪　crime of skyjacking
结果犯　consequential offense
结果加重犯　aggregated consequential offense
结合犯　combinative crime; integrated offense
具结悔过　make a statement of repentance
具体行政行为　specific administrative act

具体罪名　concrete accusation
军人违反职责罪　crimes of soldiers violating military duties
抗税罪　offense of resisting taxes
客体不能犯　object impossibility
空白罪状　blank facts about a crime
滥伐林木罪　crime of illegal denudation
累犯　recidivist; repeat offender; cumulative offense
连续犯罪　continuing crime
量刑　criterion for sentencing; sentencing criterion
量刑幅度　extent for discretionary action of sentencing
虐待罪　crime of abusing member of one's family
挪用公款案　case of misappropriation of public funds
偶犯　casual offender; casual offense
情节加重犯　aggravated offense by circumstances
情节特别严重　when the circumstances are particularly wicked
取保候审　post a bail and await trial with restricted liberty of moving
扰乱公共场所秩序罪　crime of disturbing order at public places
死刑　death（penalty）
实体法（规定基本权利及义务）　substantive law
实体刑法　substantive criminal law
实质措施　substantial step
严格责任　strict liability
刑法　criminal law
刑罚　penalty; punishment
刑事责任能力　criminal capacity
预防犯罪　anti-crime
治安管理　security administration
治安条例　security regulations

Section III　巩固练习

词汇与短语

1. capital felony
2. mala prohitita
3. juvenile offense
4. defense of infancy

5. excusable homicide
6. forcible felony
7. gross negligence
8. criminal homicide
9. element of crime
10. separate statute
11. 正当杀人
12. 刑法典
13. 死刑
14. 无致命抢劫
15. 通奸行为
16. 刑事处分
17. 一级杀人罪
18. 重刑
19. 法定罪
20. 有罪答辩

句子与段落

1. The concept of criminal law emerged only when the custom of private vengeance was replaced by the principle that the community as a whole is injured when one of its members is harmed. Thus the right to act against a wrongdoing was, indeed, granted to the state as the representative of the people.

2. Punishment originally consisted of either fines, the infliction of bodily harm (known as corporal punishment), or execution (capital punishment). The primary formals of corporal punishment were branding, flogging, and mutilation. Still another early form of punishment was banishment — exclusion from the community.

3. Imprisonment had been initialed substantially before the late eighteenth century, but early punishment was used only to retain a prisoner pending trial or to hold vagrants.

4. That decision has been a matter of continuing concern to scholars studying the criminal law, and many books have been written addressed to the two basic issues presented by our use of punishment: "What are the legitimate objectives of punishment?" and "What are the moral justifications for imposing punishment?"

5. The severe character of most punishments, even in their modern forms, also underscores the significance of the issues that society faces when it decides to impose punishment on fellow human beings.

6. 今日的美国，对很大一部分的轻微犯罪，监禁、缓刑和假释是刑罚的主要方式（这也是保持刑罚制度的重要意义之所在）。

7. 死刑，如我们将看到的，在一些州已一同废除了，而在另外的各州中只对一类犯罪还采用（如杀人罪），肉体刑罚也已被废止。然而，在某些情况下，监狱中仍然采用"禁闭"措施。

8. 虽然刑法中违法的概念已经很好地建立起来，但事情并非总是如此。把一部分违法行为看作是犯罪是历史不断发展的产物。社会在接受犯罪这个概念的过程中做了几个重要的决定，在今天，其中一些一直还在被检验着。

9. 我们今天认为是犯罪的行为，在起初被认为是非法行为；换句话说，所有罪过在过去都认为是私错。在法律的早期历史中，政府（那时为国王所统治）没有把它自己与刑罚考虑到一起，除非这些行为是直接反对政府的，例如谋反。

10. 在现阶段，重要的是知晓过去和今天采用的刑罚措施的一般本质。各种强制性刑罚措施的性质，明显地影响着我们对作为重大罪错行为—犯罪的一致看法。

11. Just as prisons were the primary development in penology in the 1880's, the use of probation and parole were the primary developments in the 1990's. Both involve supervised control of the convict in a community setting rather than in a prison. Under probation, the convicted person is released into the community under supervised control without first having served any time in a penitentiary. Under parole, the individual first serves as a term of imprisonment and then is released for supervised control. Under both procedures, if the individual violated the terms of his supervised control, he can be imprisoned to serve the remainder of his sentence.

12. 在美国刚摆脱了英国殖民地的地位时，英国的法律规定了超过200项的重罪，并且，每个重罪都会导致判处死刑。许多重罪，即使是死刑，都是些按我们今天的划分标准来看不过是些轻罪的犯罪。80%的死刑是侵犯财产罪，也包括一些小偷小摸。死刑的执行是公众事务，要有大量的人围观，并且在执行时尽可能惨不忍睹。在美国和英国，正如人们会预见到的那样，有许多对滥用死刑的不满存在。法庭和陪审团都在尽力地用各种方式来避免宣判死刑。

Unit Seven

Contract Law
合 同 法

Section I 译例研究

>> Passage One
Introduction to Contract Law

A contract is defined by Trietel in his book *The Law of Contract* as "an agreement giving rise to obligations which are enforced or recognized by the law." Agreements are fundamental to business practices.

Classification of Contracts

The law has developed several ways of classifying contracts. They can be classified according to formation, validity and performance.

Formation

One method of classification is according to the way in which a contract is formed. Contracts can be formed expressly or impliedly.

Contracts formed expressly are created by express words, either written or spoken. For example, a contract for the sale of a house for $200,000 is created by a standard form written contract. An example of an express verbal agreement would be an agreement made by Sandra to sell her car to Peter for $10,000.

A contract created impliedly is created not by words, either written or spoken, but by the conduct or actions of the parties. The conduct of the parties leads to the implication that there is a contract.

A third way of creating a contract is independent of the wishes of the parties, by operation of law. The term used for such contracts is quasi-contracts.

Validity

Contracts can be classified according to their validity into several categories: valid, void, voidable or illegal.

It is common for people to believe that a contract will not be legally enforceable unless it is in writing. This is not so. Very few contracts are required to be in writing or evidenced in writing to be valid. Apart from this very small group, contracts made verbally will be valid and enforceable by the law. Obviously, it will be easier to prove the existence and terms of a written contract. Problems will arise when seeking to enforce a verbal contract. It will be necessary to decide which party is telling the truth. For these reasons it is recommended that contracts should be placed in writing.

A contract is valid when all elements are present and the law will enforce the contract. A void contract is one that is of no legal effect. A contract falling into this category cannot be enforced by a party to the contract. Examples of void contracts are where the consideration for the contract is immoral or where a party enters a contract under a mistaken belief. Only certain instances of mistaken belief will make a contract void.

A voidable contract is one that a party will be entitled to rescind (i.e. not be bound by the contract). This right will usually be given to the injured party. Examples of voidable contracts are those entered as a result of misrepresentation, duress or undue influence.

An unenforceable contract is one where all the essential elements are present. However, a technicality may make it impossible for the contract to be enforced. For example, a contract for the assignment of copyright has to be in writing [Copyright Act 1968(Cwlth)]. If such an assignment is not in writing the contract will be unenforceable.

An illegal contract is one where the purpose or object of the contract is illegal, either pursuant to common law or statute. Contracts that are in restraint of trade are illegal at common law unless reasonable.

An example of a contract illegal by statute would be a contract that involved a restrictive trade practice. For example, price fixing between a wholesaler and a retailer is prohibited by The Trade Practices Act 1974(Cwlth).

Performance

The final way of classifying a contract is according to performance. A contract can be either executed or executory. An executed contract is one where one party to the contract has performed their side of the bargain.

Another way of classifying contracts is into *simple and formal contracts*. Formal contracts can be divided into two broad categories: contracts of record and contracts under seal (deeds). Simple contracts are all contracts that are not formal contracts and they are not required to be in any particular form but are required to have consideration. Formal contracts do not have to possess consideration. They are enforceable because of their form.

Sources of contract law

Contract law has its sources in both common law and statute. The rules in respect to the essential elements of a contract are predominantly common-law based but some have been modified by statute.

For example, there are numerous statutes protecting consumers. The majority of these are state rather than federal statutes. The reason is that the federal Constitution restricts the law-making power of the federal parliament to certain matters.

▶ 词汇提示

agreement　　*n.* 合约，合同，协议
validity　　*n.* 有效，正当，合法性
performance　　*n.* 履行，执行，清偿
expressly　　*adv.* 明示地，明确地
impliedly　　*adv.* 默示地
implication　　*n.* 推断，含义
valid　　*adj.* 有效的
void　　*adj.* 无效的
voidable　　*adj.* 可撤销地
illegal　　*adj.* 违法的
verbal　　*adj.* 口头的
rescind　　*v.* 解除（合同）
misrepresentation　　*n.* 讹传，虚假陈述
duress　　*n.* 胁迫，威胁
undue　　*adj.* 不当的，非法的
unenforceable　　*adj.* 不能强制的，不能执行的
technicality　　*n.* 程序性问题，技术性问题
pursuant to　　依照，根据，按照
common law　　普通法
statute　　*n.* 成文法，法令，法规
wholesaler　　*n.* 批发商
retailer　　*n.* 零售商
executed　　*adj.* 已执行的，已生效的
executory　　*adj.* 执行中的，实施中的
bargain　　*n.* 买卖合同，协议，成交条件
source　　*n.* 渊源，出处
parliament　　*n.* 议会

▶ 法律术语

express contract　　明示合同
implied contract　　默示合同
quasi-contract　　*n.* 准合同
valid contract　　有效合同

void contract　无效合同
voidable contract　可撤销合同
unenforceable contract　不可强制执行合同
executory contract　待履行合同
executed contract　已履行合同
simple contract　简单合同
formal contract　正式合同
contract of record　有记录的合同
contract under seal　盖印合同
consideration　*n.* 对价

要点解析

1. an agreement giving rise to obligations which are enforced or recognized by the law

在此句中，obligations 指法律意义上的义务/责任。which 引导的从句限定这种责任和义务。在英语中，限定成分通常放在所限定词语的后面，翻译时注意适当调整到所限定词语前面，以符合汉语行文习惯。所以此句翻译为"引起法律上认可的可执行的债的关系的协议"。

2. A contract created impliedly is created not by words, either written or spoken, but by the conduct or actions of the parties.

"not...but..."表示"不是……而是……"，本句中前后两部分是平等的地位。either written or spoken 修饰 words。此句翻译为："默示合同不是通过口头的或书面的言辞，而是通过双方的行动或行为产生的。"

3. For these reasons it is recommended that contracts should be placed in writing.

英语和汉语一个很大区别在于英语频繁使用被动句，这些被动句大多是无主句。而在汉语中，习惯使用主动句，句中包含明确的主语。翻译这种英语句子的关键在于确定句子的主语，从而给句子添加适当的主语。此句翻译为："出于上述原因，（我们）建议在订立合同时应采用书面形式。"

4. Examples of void contracts are where the consideration for the contract is immoral or where a party enters a contract under a mistaken belief.

这句话可以这样来看：If the consideration for the contract is immoral, or if a party enters a contract under a mistaken belief, then the contracts formed are examples of void contracts. 所以此句可译为："显失公平的合同和基于误解签订的合同都是无效合同的范例。"

5. Contracts that are in restraint of trade are illegal at common law unless reasonable.

that 引导的从句修饰 contract。此句的主语是 contracts that are in restraint of trade, are 是整个句子的谓语。unless reasonable 此处可以添词理解为 unless there are good reasons。所以此句可译为："按照普通法，除非有正当理由，限制贸易的合同属于违法合同。"

6. The rules in respect to the essential elements of a contract are predominantly common-law based but some have been modified by statute.

common-law based 意思为 based on the common-law。这种表达在英语中很常见，简洁有力。此句可译为："有关合同必备要素的规则主要来自普通法，但制定法对其作了一些修改。"

 **参考译文**

合同法简介

Trietel 在他的专著《合同法》中把合同定义为"引起法律上认可的可执行的债的关系的协议"。这种协议是商业活动的基本形式。

合同的分类

法律上合同分类的方法很多。合同可按下列标准分类：形式、效力和履行。

形式

合同的分类方法之一就是按照合同成立的形式来分类。合同可以明示地或默示地产生。

合同的明示产生必须通过言辞，不论是书面的还是口头的。例如，通过一份标准格式合同来订立一个标的为二十万美金的房屋买卖合同。又如，桑德拉把她的汽车作价一万美金卖给了彼得，这是一个口头的明示合同。

默示合同不是通过口头的或书面的言辞，而是通过双方的行动或行为产生的。人们可以从双方的行为中推断出合同的存在。

产生合同的第三种方法独立于当事人的意愿而依存于法律的运作。这类合同被称为准合同。

效力

合同按照其效力不同可以分为下列几种：有效的、无效的、可撤销的、违法的。

人们通常认为口头合同不具备法律上强制执行的效力，其实并非如此。只有极少数合同要求书面形式或以书面形式加以证明，否则无效。除了这些极少数合同以外，口头合同有效且具备法律上强制执行的效力。很明显，证明书面合同的存在和合同条款内容都比较容易。（但是），执行口头合同时常会产生一些问题。我们有必要来决定哪一方讲的是事实。出于上述原因，（我们）建议在订立合同时应采用书面形式。

当所有要素都具备时，合同有效且依法可强制执行。无效合同是缺乏法律效力的合同。这类合同的一方当事人不能强制执行合同。显失公平的合同和基于误解签订的合同都是无效合同的范例。但只有一些特定的误解可以导致合同无效。

在可撤销合同中，合同一方有权废止合同（即不受合同约束）。受损失的一方通常享有这一权利。因欺诈、胁迫和乘人之危而签订的合同属于可撤销合同。

在不能强制执行的合同中，所有的合同必备要素也都存在。但是，一个技术性细节问题就可使合同无法强制履行。例如，版权转让合同必须采用书面形式（《1968年版权法》）。如果某一版权转让合同没有采用书面形式，那么这个合同就不能强制执行。

违法的合同是指依照普通法或制定法规定的合同的目的或标的物违法。按照普通法，除非有正当理由，限制贸易的合同属于违法合同。

按照制定法，限制贸易的合同是违法合同。例如，根据1974年《贸易法》，禁止零售商和批发商之间确定价格。

履行

合同分类的最后一种方法是以合同是否履行为标准。合同可分为已履行的和待履行的。

已履行的合同是指该合同的一方当事人已经履行了该方的义务。

合同还可以分为简单合同和正式合同。正式合同还可以分为两类：有记录的合同和盖印合同。简单合同包括所有非正式合同和不要求特定形式的合同，但必须有对价。正式合同并非必须有对价。正式合同的强制性在于它的形式。

合同法的渊源

合同法的渊源来自于普通法和制定法。有关合同必备要素的规则主要来自普通法，但制定法对其作了一些修改。例如，出现了许多保护消费者的制定法。这种类型的法律大多数是州立法而非联邦立法。原因在于联邦宪法严格限制了联邦议会的立法事项。

Passage Two
中华人民共和国合同法

总 则

第一章 一般规定

第一条 为了保护合同当事人的合法权益，维护社会经济秩序，促进社会主义现代化建设，制定本法。

第二条 本法所称合同是平等主体的自然人、法人、其他组织之间设立、变更、终止民事权利义务关系的协议。

婚姻、收养、监护等有关身份关系的协议，适用其他法律的规定。

第三条 合同当事人的法律地位平等，一方不得将自己的意志强加给另一方。

第四条 当事人依法享有自愿订立合同的权利，任何单位和个人不得非法干预。

第五条 当事人应当遵循公平原则确定各方的权利和义务。

第六条 当事人行使权利、履行义务应当遵循诚实信用原则。

第七条 当事人订立、履行合同，应当遵守法律、行政法规，尊重社会公德，不得扰乱社会经济秩序，损害社会公共利益。

第八条 依法成立的合同，对当事人具有法律约束力。当事人应当按照约定履行自己的义务，不得擅自变更或者解除合同。

依法成立的合同，受法律保护。

第二章 合同的订立

第九条 当事人订立合同，应当具有相应的民事权利能力和民事行为能力。

当事人依法可以委托代理人订立合同。

第十条 当事人订立合同，有书面形式、口头形式和其他形式。

法律、行政法规规定采用书面形式的，应当采用书面形式。当事人约定采用书面形式的，应当采用书面形式。

第十一条 书面形式是指合同书、信件和数据电文（包括电报、电传、传真、电子数据交换和电子邮件）等可以有形地表现所载内容的形式。

第十二条 合同的内容由当事人约定，一般包括以下条款：

（一）当事人的名称或者姓名和住所；

（二）标的；

（三）数量；

（四）质量；

（五）价款或者报酬；

（六）履行期限、地点和方式；

（七）违约责任；

（八）解决争议的方法。

当事人可以参照各类合同的示范文本订立合同。

第十三条 当事人订立合同，采取要约、承诺方式。

第十四条 要约是希望和他人订立合同的意思表示，该意思表示应当符合下列规定：

（一）内容具体确定；

（二）表明经受要约人承诺，要约人即受该意思表示约束。

第十五条 要约邀请是希望他人向自己发出要约的意思表示。寄送的价目表、拍卖公告、招标公告、招股说明书、商业广告等为要约邀请。

商业广告的内容符合要约规定的，视为要约。

第十六条 要约到达受要约人时生效。

采用数据电文形式订立合同，收件人指定特定系统接收数据电文的，该数据电文进入该特定系统的时间，视为到达时间；未指定特定系统的，该数据电文进入收件人的任何系统的首次时间，视为到达时间。

第十七条 要约可以撤回。撤回要约的通知应当在要约到达受要约人之前或者与要约同时到达受要约人。

第十八条 要约可以撤销。撤销要约的通知应当在受要约人发出承诺通知之前到达受要约人。

第十九条 有下列情形之一的，要约不得撤销：

（一）要约人确定了承诺期限或者以其他形式明示要约不可撤销；

（二）受要约人有理由认为要约是不可撤销的，并已经为履行合同作了准备工作。

第二十条 有下列情形之一的，要约失效：

（一）拒绝要约的通知到达要约人；

（二）要约人依法撤销要约；

（三）承诺期限届满，受要约人未作出承诺；

（四）受要约人对要约的内容作出实质性变更。

第二十一条 承诺是受要约人同意要约的意思表示。

第二十二条 承诺应当以通知的方式作出，但根据交易习惯或者要约表明可以通过行为作出承诺的除外。

第二十三条 承诺应当在要约确定的期限内到达要约人。

要约没有确定承诺期限的，承诺应当依照下列规定到达：

（一）要约以对话方式作出的，应当即时作出承诺，但当事人另有约定的除外；

（二）要约以非对话方式作出的，承诺应当在合理期限内到达。

词汇提示

制定　formulate
自然人　natural person
法人　legal person
变更　alter
自愿地　voluntarily
干涉　interfere with
遵循　abide by
公平原则　the principle of fairness
确定（权利、义务、合同条款）　prescribe
社会公德　social ethics
依照　in accordance with
擅自　arbitrarily
合同变更、解除　amend or terminate the contract
代表　on behalf of sb/ on sb's behalf
合同书　a memorandum of contract
有形的　tangible
报酬，酬金　remuneration
责任，义务　liability for sth.
争议　dispute
符合，遵从　comply with
拍卖公告　announcement of auction
招标公告　call for tender
招股说明书，招股章程　prospectus
商业广告　commercial advertisement
收件人　recipient
撤销　revoke
失效　extinguish
实质性的，重要的　material
通知，通告，告示　notification

法律术语

订立合同　enter into a contract
标的物　subject matter

违约　breach of the contract
要约　offer
承诺　acceptance
受要约人　offeree
要约人　offeror
不可撤销的　irrevocable

要点解析

1. 为了保护合同当事人的合法权益，维护社会经济秩序，促进社会主义现代化建设，制定本法。

This Law is formulated in order to protect the lawful rights and interests of contract parties, to safeguard social and economic order, and to promote socialist modernization.

翻译此句时，原来的主动句译成了被动句，用 in order to 短语将原文次序颠倒，以更符合英语行文习惯。

2. 当事人订立、履行合同，应当遵守法律、行政法规，尊重社会公德，不得扰乱社会经济秩序，损害社会公共利益。

In concluding or performing a contract, the parties shall abide by the relevant laws and administrative regulations, as well as observe social ethics, and may not disrupt social and economic order or harm the public interests.

"in concluding or performing..." 表伴随状态，与主句形成并列关系。此句应注意用词的准确性，"订立""履行""遵守""尊重""扰乱""损害" 等词留意意义的区分，选择最合适的表达。

3. 当事人应当按照约定履行自己的义务，不得擅自变更或者解除合同。

The parties shall perform their respective obligations in accordance with the contract, and neither party may arbitrarily amend or terminate the contract.

"各自的"译为 respective，"按照"用 in accordance with 来表达，"变更"译为 amend，"终止"译为 terminate。两个分句之间是并列的关系，第二个分句翻译的时候注意添加主语。

4. 要约是希望和他人订立合同的意思表示，该意思表示应当符合下列规定。

An offer is a party's manifestation of intention to enter into a contract with the other party, which shall comply with the following.

"订立合同"译为 enter into a contract。which 引导的从句修饰 the manifestation of intention，更符合英语长句的习惯。

5. 表明经受要约人承诺，要约人即受该意思表示约束。

It indicates that upon acceptance by the offeree, the offeror will be bound thereby.

要约人，受要约人是法律英语中的术语，要准确表达。thereby 意为"因此, 由此, 从而"，在法律英语中经常使用，可使行文简洁准确。

6. 承诺应当以通知的方式作出，但根据交易习惯或者要约表明可以通过行为作出承诺的除外。

An acceptance shall be manifested by notification, except where it may be manifested by conduct in accordance with the relevant usage or as indicated in the offer.

翻译时应注意情态动词的恰当使用，"应当"此处译为 shall 较好；"但"没有简单地译为 but，而是用 except where 表示，自然地引出后面的句子。

 参考译文

Contract Law of the People's Republic of China

General Principles

Chapter One: General Provisions

Article 1. This Law is formulated in order to protect the lawful rights and interests of contract parties, to safeguard social and economic order, and to promote socialist modernization.

Article 2. For purposes of this Law, a contract is an agreement between natural persons, legal persons or other organizations with equal standing, for the purpose of establishing, altering, or discharging a relationship of civil rights and obligations.

An agreement concerning any personal relationship such as marriage, adoption, guardianship, etc. shall be governed by other applicable laws.

Article 3. Contract parties enjoy equal legal standing and neither party may impose its will on the other party.

Article 4. A party is entitled to enter into a contract voluntarily under the law, and no entity or individual may unlawfully interfere with such right.

Article 5. The parties shall abide by the principle of fairness in prescribing their respective rights and obligations.

Article 6. The parties shall abide by the principle of good faith in exercising their rights and performing their obligations.

Article 7. In concluding or performing a contract, the parties shall abide by the relevant laws and administrative regulations, as well as observe social ethics, and may not disrupt social and economic order or harm the public interests.

Article 8. A lawfully formed contract is legally binding on the parties. The parties shall perform their respective obligations in accordance with the contract, and neither party may arbitrarily amend or terminate the contract.

A lawfully formed contract is protected by law.

Chapter Two   Formation of Contracts

Article 9. In entering into a contract, the parties shall have the appropriate capacities for civil rights and civil acts.

A party may appoint an agent to enter into a contract on its behalf under the law.

Article 10. A contract may be made in a writing, in an oral conversation, as well as in any other form.

A contract shall be in writing if a relevant law or administrative regulation so requires. A contract shall be in writing if the parties have so agreed.

Article 11. A writing means a memorandum of contract, letter or electronic message (including telegram, telex, facsimile, electronic data exchange and electronic mail), etc. which is capable of expressing its contents in a tangible form.

Article 12. The terms of a contract shall be prescribed by the parties, and generally include the following:

(i) names of the parties and the domiciles thereof;

(ii) subject matter;

(iii) quantity;

(iv) quality;

(v) price or remuneration;

(vi) time, place and method of performance;

(vii) liabilities for breach of contract;

(viii) method of dispute resolution.

The parties may enter into a contract by referencing a model contract for the relevant contract category.

Article 13. A contract is concluded by the exchange of an offer and an acceptance.

Article 14. An offer is a party's manifestation of intention to enter into a contract with the other party, which shall comply with the following:

(i) Its terms are specific and definite;

(ii) It indicates that upon acceptance by the offeree, the offeror will be bound thereby.

Article 15. An invitation to offer is a party's manifestation of intention to invite the other party to make an offer thereto. A delivered price list, announcement of auction, call for tender, prospectus, or commercial advertisement, etc. is an invitation to offer.

A commercial advertisement is deemed an offer if its contents meet the requirements of an offer.

Article 16. An offer becomes effective when it reaches the offeree.

When a contract is concluded by the exchange of electronic messages, if the recipient of an electronic message has designated a specific system to receive it, the time when the electronic message enters into such specific system is deemed its time of arrival; if no specific system has been designated, the time when the electronic message first enters into any of the recipient's systems is deemed its time of arrival.

Article 17. An offer may be withdrawn. The notice of withdrawal shall reach the offeree before or at the same time as the offer.

Article 18. An offer may be revoked. The notice of revocation shall reach the offeree before it has dispatched a notice of acceptance.

Article 19. An offer may not be revoked:

(i) if it expressly indicates, whether by stating a fixed time for acceptance or otherwise, that it is irrevocable;

(ii) if the offeree has reason to regard the offer as irrevocable, and has undertaken preparation for performance.

Article 20. An offer is extinguished in any of the following circumstances:

(i) The notice of rejection reaches the offeror;

(ii) The offeror lawfully revokes the offer;

(iii) The offeree fails to dispatch its acceptance at the end of the period for acceptance;

(iv) The offeree makes a material change to the terms of the offer.

Article 21. An acceptance is the offeree's manifestation of intention to assent to an offer.

Article 22. An acceptance shall be manifested by notification, except where it may be manifested by conduct in accordance with the relevant usage or as indicated in the offer.

Article 23. An acceptance shall reach the offeror within the period prescribed in the offer.

Where the offer does not prescribe a period for acceptance, the acceptance shall reach the offeror as follows:

(i) Where the offer is made orally, the acceptance shall be dispatched immediately, unless otherwise agreed by the parties;

(ii) Where the offer is made in a non-oral manner, the acceptance shall reach the offeror within a reasonable time.

Section II 技能拓展

 翻译技巧

英语贸易合同汉译技巧的探讨

贸易合同是在贸易活动中进行技术引进和输出或货物的买卖时采用的，在国际贸易活动中通常用英语签订。贸易合同作为保证国际贸易活动顺利进行的法律文件，在国际贸易中起着十分重要的作用。中国加入了世界贸易组织（WTO），与世界各国的贸易往来更加频繁，会更多地接触各种英语贸易合同。规范英语贸易合同的汉译在当今显得更加迫切。

英语贸易合同主要应用于经济领域,有特殊的语体特征。译者必须使用一定的翻译技巧,忠实再现原文的内容,并保持原文的语体特征和风格。下面从英语贸易合同的语体特征和具体翻译实践,探讨英语贸易合同的汉译,包括词语的翻译、长句的处理和篇章的转换,归纳出英语贸易合同汉译的一些基本技巧。

一、英语贸易合同的语体特征

英语贸易合同作为一种法律性文件主要是用于经济领域,这一特定语域决定了其自身的语体特征,主要表现在四个方面。

1. 用词准确

作为有法律效应的正式文件,英语贸易合同的词语使用严谨,力求准确,以避免对方利用词义差别产生诉讼纠纷,例如:

In the event that there is any discrepancy or ambiguity…

discrepancy 指某一差异或合同的两种文本不一致,而 ambiguity 指某一内容意义模糊、表达不明确,因此概括了两种可能。

2. 词语专业化

英语贸易合同的词语受特定语域限制。语域的差异和特点大量反映在词语上,因此合同中有许多专业化词语,如:Force Majeure(不可抗力),Jurisdiction(诉讼管辖)。

3. 语句的复杂化

为使文字表达严谨、精确、避免歧义,合同常采用一些复杂语句。并列句和复杂句交叉使用,插入成分频繁出现,使合同中的语句趋向复杂化,一个明显特点就是长句多,如:"In case no amicable settlement can be reached between the two parties, the case on dispute shall be submitted to arbitration, which shall be held in the country where the defendant resides."(若双方不能友好解决争议,争议案应提交仲裁,仲裁在被诉一方国家举行。)

4. 篇章的严谨性

一份合同就是一个信息语篇,作为一个完整的语篇,应该具有一定的严谨性。主要体现为结构紧凑、语义连贯、格式规范。

二、英语贸易合同的翻译要求

鉴于英语贸易合同的语篇严谨、语句复杂、用语专业和表达精确的特点,其翻译也相应具有独特的要求。

1. 词语翻译的准确性

对英语贸易合同词语的理解影响到对句子乃至整个语篇的理解,在翻译时要确保词语翻译的准确性,主要涉及专业词汇和普通词汇。

1)专业词汇的翻译

专业词汇主要指专门用于某个领域的词汇,具有排他性。在英语贸易合同中,语域的差异和特点绝大部分反映在专业词汇上。翻译时首先要确保意义明确、无偏差,如:Force Majeure 译为"不可抗力",duplicate 译为"一式二份"。专业词汇的翻译不仅意义要明确,还要专业化,如 invoice 译为"发票",turnover 译为"营业额",credit sales 译为"赊销"。一些常见的缩略词及字母大写的词或词组,翻译起来既要准确,又要专业化,如:EXW (ex works)译为"工厂交货价",B/L(bill of lading)译为"提单",DDP(delivered duty paid)译为"完税后交货"。

2）普通词汇的翻译

普通词汇指大多数文本中使用的、没有严格语域限制的词汇。在英语贸易合同中语义转向特殊化，甚至专业化。翻译时要根据合同实际情况确定意义，注意选词专业化。例如：terms 和 conditions 同时出现要译为"条款"；territory 在销售代理合同中应译为"代理区域"或"销售区域"。

2. 长句的处理

考虑到文字表达的严谨和精确，英语贸易合同常采用长句。主要由并列成分、复合成分和插入成分交织形成。翻译时可将原句拆散，变更句子顺序，再按汉语习惯重新组合。具体而言，主要有四种方法：顺译、倒译、扩充和合并。

1）顺译

如果长句的语法结构、时间顺序和逻辑顺序与汉语的表达习惯相符，可采用顺译法，按原句的结构和顺序进行翻译。例如：

Party B shall present to Party A the relevant document on the industrial property including photocopies of the patent certificates and trademark registration certificate, statements of validity, their technical characteristics, practical value, the basis for calculating the price, etc.

乙方向甲方提供工业产权的技术资料包括影印本的专利证书和注册商标证书、有效期说明、技术特点、实际价值、价格计算等。

2）倒译

如果长句的语法结构、时间、逻辑顺序与汉语表达习惯相反，应按汉语表达习惯颠倒原句顺序重新组合。例如：

The Seller shall be responsible for any infringement with regard to patent, utility model, trademark, design or copyright of the merchandise, whether in the Buyer's country or any other country or place.

若在买方国家或其他国家或地区关于契约货物产生专利、实用模型、商标、设计或版权的侵犯事件，由卖方负责。

句子前半部分表达了判断或观点，如"The Seller shall be responsible for…"，具体内容则放在句子后半部分，符合英语开门见山的表达习惯；而译文中遵循汉语"主题—评论"的表达习惯，同英语表达习惯刚好相反。

3）扩充

英语贸易合同的长句往往包含多层意思，为表达通顺、意义明确，可将这类句子拆散，译成数个汉语句子。例如：

Any dispute or difference arising out of relating to this Purchase Confirmation, or the breach thereof which cannot be settled amicably shall be arbitrated in Beijing, China, in accordance with the Provisional Rules or procedure of the Foreign Trade Arbitration Commission of the China Council for the Promotion of International Trade.

有关本协议所产生的争议和分歧或违约，若未得到友好解决，则会在中国北京进行仲裁。仲裁根据中国国际贸易促进委员会对外贸易仲裁委员会的仲裁程序或暂行规则进行。

In accordance with 引导的介词短语复杂冗长，在译文中不宜单独译成一个句子。

4）合并

当几个长句的意思相关联或有一定的逻辑联系，可译成一个句子，使句子更紧凑和严谨。例如：

We learned from the Chamber of Commerce in your country that you have changed to deal in electric appliances. We think that your firm is not represented in this district and are writing to offer our services as your agents here.

从贵国商会得悉，贵公司已改为经营电器，想必贵方在此地尚无代理，故函告愿担任你方代理。

3. 语篇的转换

英语贸易合同作为一个严谨完整的信息语篇，不仅要表达清楚、信息传递准确，还要结构紧凑、语义连贯。汉译要从语篇的角度出发，使译文的语法结构和语义结构既忠实地传递原文的信息，又符合汉语的表达习惯。

1）时态的处理

现在时具有泛时性，在语篇中可以发挥概括功能，使语篇内容在叙事人看来不仅真实可信，而且适用于任何时间。所以合同中的条款虽然是准备实施的事项，但采用一般现在时叙述。译者要注意这一语篇的特点，在译文中采用一般现在时。在原文语篇中有时会出现 when，after 之类的连词，并不是表示将来时态，而是指出情况、状态或条件。例如：

The duration of Joint Venture is＿＿＿years, which begins when Joint Venture is issued the business license.

合同期限为＿＿＿年。合营企业的成立日期为合营公司营业执照签发之日。

when 指出了合营企业成立的条件或是对合营企业在营业执照签发后成立这一客观情况的说明。

另外，shall，will 这类的词，也并非表示将来时的助动词，而是情态动词。例如：

The Buyer will take necessary steps to obtain import license and to arrange letter of credit for the performance of the contract with reasonable business practices. The Buyer shall not be responsible for any failure or delay in obtaining such important license, if caused by reason beyond the control of the Buyer.

买方应该采取必要措施，以获得进口许可证，并按照合理的商业惯例开具执行合同的信用证。若买方因无法控制的原因未能开出或迟开出信用证，买方不负责。

will 和 shall 都表达一种强制语气，在译文中也得到了体现。

2）语态的处理

英语贸易合同中主动语态使用较多，尤其是涉及合同双方时。合同双方作为动作的执行者放在主位上充当主语，使权利和责任一目了然。主动语态使合同的表述明确、直接，语篇显得更加严谨。主动语态这一特点要引起重视，译文应根据实际情况尽量采用主动语态。例如：

Party B shall forward once every three months to Party A detailed reports on current market conditions and of consumers' comments.

乙方每三个月向甲方提供一次有关当时市场情况和用户意见的详细报告。

有时原文中用被动语态，译文还是应该采用主动语态。例如：

The Seller shall not be held responsible for any delay in delivery or non-delivery of the goods due to Force Majeure.

由于不可抗力事件卖方延迟交货或未能交货，卖方不负责。

英语贸易合同作为一种法律性文件在国际贸易活动中起着越来越重要的作用，英语贸易合同的汉译在当前也显得尤其重要。在英语贸易合同汉译进程中，首先要明确其语体特征，其次把握重点词语的翻译，并妥善处理长句。另外，还要从语篇的角度比较原文和译文，正确处理语篇中的某些结构以及时态和语态。总之，掌握一些英语贸易合同汉译的技巧，不仅能提高翻译的质量，更重要的是能促进贸易双方交际以及贸易活动的顺利进行。

 **法律宝典**

合同法的形成和发展

合同法是调整合同关系的法律规范，而合同是商品经济的产物，是与商品交换相伴而生，相伴而发展的。考察合同立法及实践的历史可以发现，合同法的形成和发展大致经历了三个时期。

古代合同法

古代时期包括原始时期、奴隶制时期和封建时期。这一时期由于社会经济不发达，商品交换有限，所以调整商品交换的规则简陋，不存在近现代意义的合同法。因此，在古代合同法时期，虽然也诞生了简单商品生产条件下最完备的罗马法，但由于这个时期的任何法必然受制于它特定的经济基础，于是也就不可能把合同法推向一个超脱或跨越时代的较高层次。于是，尽管罗马法在古代已有了各种合同的若干规则，与其他国家比较有了相当的发展，甚至对现代合同法产生了重大影响，但整个古代合同法是落后的，包括罗马法在内的合同法也尚未达到真正的系统、完备的理论水平，更与现代合同法精神相去甚远。

古代合同法具有以下共同特点：其一，合同主体受到严格限制，范围狭窄。在奴隶社会，奴隶如牛马、工具和物品属主人所有，只是合同的标的物，任其买卖或租赁；合同主体只限于奴隶主和自由民。家庭中，法律也仅赋予家长享有订立合同的权利能力。在封建社会的"家长"制下，农民附属于封建土地的所有者，家属附属于家长，没有独立的人格，无权进入市场进行商品交换。其二，合同形式复杂，程序烦琐。当时的商品经济不甚发达，在商品交换中，当事人特别关心交易的安全与可靠，尽可能切实地取得财产。因而，合同的手续或形式甚至比当事人间的合意重要得多。古代的汉谟拉比法典规定，在某种场合下，没有书面契约而取得财产的被当作犯罪。而"单纯的契约不能发生诉权"甚至是罗马法的一个原则，由此订立合同的形式十分严格。我国古代也不例外，《周礼·天官·小宰》曰"所称责以傅别"，"听买卖以质剂"，"听取予以书契"，其中"傅别""质剂""书契"均为借贷、买卖等关系不同的书面合同形式。

近代合同法

合同法虽然产生于简单商品经济，但其真正发育成长却是在近代时期完成的。在近代时期，资产阶级夺取政权后，商品生产和商品交换蓬勃发展，在经济上奉行自由放任主义，在法律上推崇私法自治为指导原则，导致了资本主义的近代合同制度的空前繁荣。

17—18世纪是自由资本主义阶段，自由竞争替代了古老的传统束缚，为了和封建等级特权抗衡，资本主义的思想家推崇的个人主义、自由主义哲学、放纵主义经济和自然法学都在这个时期发展到顶峰。历史把所有权神圣不可侵犯、契约自由和过错责任原则推到了全部民法（私法）的基础地位上。为此，合同自由就成为合同法上的铁律。"从身份到契约"，这意味着现在任何人均可通过自由的合同关系创造一切，人人有为自己缔结合同的不可剥夺的权利，法律应尽可能少地干预人们的活动。合同关系遍及于社会各个角落。根据契约自由的私法原则，订立合同自由，选择对方当事人自由，决定合同内容自由，合同方式自由，协议变更合同自由。相比之下，法律甚至法官起的作用都是次要的、消极的，它们的主要目的是使人们能够实现自己的意志，不受政府干预，或在一方当事人违反了缔约规则或不履行义务时帮助救济另一方，仅此而已。为此，合同当事人的真实的意思自治置于至高无上的地位。契约自由原则对促进资本主义商品经济的竞争和繁荣功不可没。可以说，合同自由和合同神圣是近现代合同法不可动摇的基石，是近现代合同法的灵魂，体现了现代合同法的价值。

现当代合同法

19世纪末20世纪初，随着工业革命的完成，世界历史进入现当代时期。这个时期，资本主义内在的缺陷，导致资本主义周期性经济危机频繁发生，社会各阶层之间利益冲突表面化、白热化。为协调这种利益冲突，克服频繁和严重的经济危机，维持良好的经济秩序与交易安全，统治者在主客观上都不得不对交易自由进行限制，契约自由原则在立法上、司法上和契约的实践中均受到了修正和束缚，由此带给合同法的冲击是强有力的。首先是合同内容得到了前所未有的拓展，合同法调整社会交易关系的涵盖面宽广了许多。如资本主义国家在第一次世界大战以后出现了继续供应、分期付款、租售、售货机买卖等新的合同形式，出现了因旅游、科研、技术转让等引发的交易。国际贸易中许多新型的合同形式也纷纷出台。其次，垄断经济导致了合同的格式化趋势，单方条款置对方当事人于无可选择的地位，近代合同法建立的朴素的公平性受到损害。此外，国家对合同关系的干预在合同法领域和其他方面均有加强，例如，大陆法系国家的司法上出现了诚实信用、情势变更原则，英美法系国家有了合同落空规则，学理上则出现了"审判官形成权"的理念，这些都使法官取得了近似于变更或解除合同的司法裁量权。契约就是法律的观念被冲淡了，合同自由原则受到了怀疑，甚至有人惊呼"合同死亡了"。从近现代到当代，对合同自由的限制渐在各国中成为普遍的事实，表明了国家在法律上对经济活动的干预，法律开始注重保护经济上处于弱者的个人及中小企业的利益。这种干预当然缘于维护各国所有制的需要。随着现代科技的日益进步，可以想见，合同法作为调整合同交易关系的法律，也必将随之变化和发展。

术语积累

contract　合约；合同；契约
bilateral contract　双方合同
unilateral contract　单方合同
void agreement　无效协议
consideration　对价；约因
make an offer　报盘

make a quotation　报价
firm offer　实盘
non-firm offer　虚盘
counter-offer　还盘
counter-bid　还价
offer sheet　报盘单
quotation sheet　报价单
counter-sign　副署；会签
counter-signature　连署签名
revocation of offer　撤销要约
substantial performance　实质性履行；基本履行
right of demurrer for concurrent performance　同时履行抗辩权
right of demurrer for security　不安抗辩权
right of subrogation　代位权
deposit the object　提存标的物
terms of payment　支付条款
time of shipment　装运期限
inspection and claims　检验索赔
arbitration　仲裁
arbitration clause　仲裁条款
make up the order　备货
maximum discount　最大折扣
volume discount　总购量折扣
quantity discount　数量折扣
cash discount　现金折扣
trade discount　同业折扣；批发折扣
specific inquiry　具体询价
commercial counselor　商务参赞
obtain indemnity　获得赔偿
a cover note　承保单
document of title　产权单证
days of grace　宽限期
expiry date　失效期
without recourse　无追索权
breach of the contract　违反合同；违约
compulsory arbitration　强制性仲裁
voluntary arbitration　自愿仲裁
settlement of claims　理赔
contract by post　通信订立的合同

without qualification　毫无保留地
bill of exchange　汇票
doctrine of part performance　部分履行原则
contractual capacity　立约能力
void ab initio　自始无效
non est factum　否认订立合同的答辩
auctioneer　拍卖商；拍卖人
subject to contract　以签订合同为条件
the doctrine of promissory estoppel　允诺后不得否认的原则
express terms　明示的条件
implied terms　默示的条件
equitable defence　衡平抗辩
oral warranty　口头担保
exemption clause　免责条款
internal contradiction　自相矛盾；内在矛盾
contractual relationship　合同关系
contributory negligence　共同过失
comparative negligence　比较过失
absolute liability　绝对责任；绝对赔偿责任；无过失责任
accommodation endorsement　通融背书；在保单上加注条件
accommodation party　签署通融票据的当事人
act of God　天灾；不可抗力和无法避免的自然灾害
adhesion contract　附议合同；附加契约
bill of lading　提单；提货单
blank endorsement　不记名背书；空白背书
buy-sell agreement　交易协议
certificate of deposit　存单；存款单
consignment　发货；交运货物
consignor　发货人；寄售人
estoppel by deed　契据不容否认规则
estoppel by laches　因迟延而丧失求偿权
expectation damages　估计海损
free exercise clause　免除货物税条款
freight forwarder　货物转运商
fringe benefit　小额优惠
products liability　产品赔偿责任
severable contract　可分契约

Section III 巩固练习

词汇与短语

1. defective performance
2. estoppel
3. force majeure
4. option contract
5. firm offer
6. promissory estoppel
7. the principle of fairness
8. the principle of honesty and credibility
9. contract object
10. contractual obligation
11. 一般交易条件
12. 临时订单
13. 购物合同
14. 订单
15. 起草合同
16. 无效
17. 格式条款
18. 欺诈或胁迫
19. 权利人；债权人
20. 义务人；债务人

句子与段落

1. An acceptance occurs where the offeree agrees to the proposal of the offeror on the terms required by the offeror.
2. Examples of void contracts are where the consideration for the contract is immoral or where a party enters a contract under a mistaken belief.
3. A domestic agreement is one made between members of the same family or household, whereas a social agreement is one made between friends or acquaintances.
4. A contract made with a minor that is not for necessaries nor a beneficial contract of service may be voidable.
5. A person who signs a written document and is mistaken as to the nature of the document may be able to rely on a defence called non est factum.
6. The essential feature of an offer is that the person making it must intend to be bound without further negotiation, by a simple acceptance of his terms.
7. 承诺最重要的原则是它必须与要约相符。
8. 沉默无承诺的原则并不意味着向要约人传递"承诺"的言辞是必需的。
9. 格式的第三作用是通过提供合同条款的书面声明来保护交易中弱的一方。
10. 这个文件会使建立合法不动产的目的失效，但它会是一个可以由佃户强制实施的有效租赁契约。
11. 交际习惯默示条款之所以被包含进合同中的最好解释是因为便利,而不管当事人的意图如何。
12. 口头证据规则仅适应于在书面合同履行之前或履行之时做出的陈述。

Unit Eight

The Law of Property
财　产　法

Section I　译例研究

>> ### *Passage One*
Real Property Law

　　There are two basic classes of property in modern law, real property and personal property. Real property consists of fixed, immovable things, such as lands. The terms "land", "real estate" and "real property" are generally used synonymously. The old phrase, "lands, tenements and hereditaments", covered all kinds of real property and all interests therein. Included in the definition of real property are such incorporeal rights as easements and rights of profit a prendre.

　　Buildings, fixtures, fences, and other improvements affixed to land are generally a part of the real estate. Standing timber is a part of the land and is real property until it is severed from the land. Whether a growing crop is real property or personalty depends upon the nature of the crop, the relationship of the parties raising the question, and upon other circumstances. One primary distinction in determining this question classifies crops as either fructus naturales or fructus industriales. The latter class consists of products of the earth which are annual and owe their existence to yearly planting and cultivation by man. For most purposes such crops are treated as personal chattels, even while still annexed to the soil. On the other hand, fructus naturales, such as grasses growing from perennial roots, and according to some courts, the fruit and other products of trees, bushes, vines, and plants growing from perennial roots, are regarded as realty while they are un-severed from the soil. However, courts now tend to regard as fructus industriales growing fruit and other products of trees, etc., which depend largely upon the care and cultivation of man.

Minerals in place are a part of the real estate, and in the absence of a contrary provision in a grant, belong to the owner of the land. Oil and gas underlying land are classified as minerals and are a part of the land, subject to "capture" and to loss by escape. Water also, in its natural state and before appropriation, is regarded as a part of the land in or upon which it is found.

An ancient maxim of the common law states, "cujus est solum, ejus est usque ad coelum et ad inferos," meaning that the owner of the soil owns to the heavens and to the lowest depths. Applied literally, this would give the landowner exclusive dominion over the air space above his land to an infinite vertical distance, as well as ownership of minerals and other things beneath the surface. The modern development of air navigation, however, has required a qualification of these rights with respect to the upper space. The landowner's ownership of such space is no longer regarded as exclusive and unlimited. It is now settled that the flight of aircraft over land does not constitute trespass or nuisance so long as such flights are at a proper height and do not unreasonably interfere with the landowner's use and enjoyment of his property. The owner's rights extend upward only so far as is necessary for the full use and enjoyment of the land, and the space beyond is regarded as open and navigable air space. The owner has a superior right to erect structures extending upward to any distance necessary for the full enjoyment of his property, however. And any flight over his land at such low altitude or in such manner as to interfere unreasonably with his enjoyment of his property, as by endangering his structures, frightening his domestic animals, or impairing the health and tranquility of his family, will generally constitute a trespass or nuisance.

Fixtures have been variously defined as objects which were originally personal property but which, by reason of their annexation to or use in association with real property, have become a part of the realty; as chattels so attached to realty that, for the time being, they become a part thereof; and as chattels annexed to realty in such manner that they cannot be removed without injury to the freehold. However, there is no single statement defining such use which is capable of application in all situations. The principal significance of a determination that an object is a fixture is that it is thereafter treated as part and parcel of the land and may not generally be removed therefrom except by the owner of the realty.

The general tests for determining whether a particular object has become a fixture are usually said to comprise annexation to the realty, adaptation to the use to which the realty is devoted, and intention that the object become a permanent accession to the freehold. There is some disagreement, however, on the relative importance to be assigned to each of these several factors.

Annexation in this connection refers to the act of attaching or affixing personal property to real property. Although annexation or affixation to the soil was the primary or main test under the early common law in determining whether an object had assumed the character of a fixture, it is no longer the controlling factor in many situations. While the exact manner in which an object is annexed to the realty is a matter of diminishing relevance in the modern decisions, it may still be important under some circumstances. Slight attachment to the realty may be sufficient to constitute an article a fixture if other tests are met. There may be an annexation even though the object is held in place only by gravity, as a building upon its foundation or heavy machinery in a factory. The relative ease with which an object annexes to realty may be removed is often considered in determining whether the object has become a fixture. Thus, where an object which is physically attached to realty may be easily removed, it may be held to have retained its character as personalty notwithstanding the annexation. Conversely, if the object cannot be removed without injury to itself or to the realty, the object is usually deemed to be a fixture and a part of the realty.

Adaptation to the use of the realty, the second of the three factors generally held to comprise the test in determining whether an object has become a fixture, refers to the relationship between a chattel and the use which is made of the realty where it is located. According to the adaptation principle, an object introduced onto realty may become a fixture if it is a necessary adjunct to the realty, considering the purposes to which the latter is devoted. This principle, sometimes called the "institution doctrine," is often given great weight in determining whether a particular object has assumed the status of a fixture. The adaptation principle is often applied where a factory, plant, mill, or similar industrial establishment is involved. In such cases, it is frequently held that chattels placed in such an industrial establishment for permanent use and necessary to the operation of the plant become fixtures and hence a part of the real estate, regardless of whether they are physically attached thereto. As early as the sixteenth century it was held that millstones passed on a conveyance of the mill though temporarily detached at the time.

Intention, the third of the three factors comprising the general test, refers to the intent of the parties that the object being introduced onto realty become a permanent accession thereto. This is an important criterion in determining the character of property as fixtures, and it is frequently given controlling weight, at least where the other criteria leave the matter in doubt. It has been said that the mode of annexation is of little consequence as it bears on the question of intent.

The parties may by contract determine the status of an object as a fixture or personalty. They may by agreement provide that, as between themselves, an object which would normally become a fixture shall remain personalty, or that an object which would normally retain its character as personalty shall become a fixture. As a general proposition, such special agreements are binding only on the contracting parties and their privies, and are not binding on third parties, such as a subsequent purchaser or mortgagee of the land without notice of the agreement.

An object may lose its status as a fixture by severance from the land and, provided the rights of third parties are not involved, may reacquire the character of personal property. An effective severance can be made only by the owner of the realty and must be effected under such circumstances that an intention to separate the object permanently from the realty may be presumed.

▶ 词汇提示

immovable   *adj.* 不能移动的，固定的
synonymous   *adj.* 同义的，等同的
incorporeal *adj.* 无形体的，无形的
cultivation *n.* 耕种，种植，栽培

perennial *adj.* 多年生的
subject to 可能受……影响的，易遭受……的
appropriation *n.* 占有
maxim *n.* 格言，箴言，座右铭
literally *adj.* 按字面，字面上
exclusive *adj.* 独有的，独占的
dominion *n.* 统治权，管辖，支配
qualification *n.* 限定条件
interfere with 干扰
navigable *adj.* 可航行的，适于通航的
altitude *n.* 海拔，高度
domestic *adj.* 驯养的，家养的
tranquility *n.* 安静，安宁
principal *adj.* 最重要的，主要的
part and parcel of sth. 重要部分，基本部分
diminish *v.* 减少，削弱
sufficient *adj.* 足够的，充足的
heavy machinery 重型设备
notwithstanding *prep.* 虽然，尽管
the institution doctrine 组合原则
the adaptation principle 适合性原则
industrial establishment 工业设施
permanent *adj.* 永久的，长久的
binding *adj.* 必须遵守的，有法律约束力的
provided *conj.* 如果，假如，在……条件下

法律术语

real property law 不动产法
real property 不动产
personal property 动产
chattel *n.* （个人的）财产，动产
easement *n.* 地役权
profit a prendre 土地收益权
fructus naturales 自然成果
fructus industriales 劳动成果
realty *n.* 不动产
trespass *v.* 非法侵入
nuisance *n.* 妨害行为
mortgagee *n.* 受抵押人，抵押权人

要点解析

1. Included in the definition of real property are such incorporeal rights as easements and rights of profit a prendre.

incorporeal rights 指"无形权利"；easement 指"地役权"；profit a prendre 指"土地收益权"。此句翻译时还应注意适当调整句子后半部分顺序。所以本句可译为："在不动产概念中还包括地役权、先占权这样的无形权利。"

2. However, courts now tend to regard as fructus industriales growing fruit and other products of trees, etc., which depend largely upon the care and cultivation of man.

which 引导的从句修饰 growing fruit and other products of trees, etc. fructus industriales 意为"劳动成果"。本句译为："但是，法庭现在倾向于将主要靠人工看护和培育而得到的产于树木的果实和其他产品，视为劳动成果。"

3. Applied literally, this would give the landowner exclusive dominion over the air space above his land to an infinite vertical distance, as well as ownership of minerals and other things beneath the surface.

as well as 前后两部分是并列的关系。翻译时拆分为两个句子，避免把英语的长句套到汉语里。此句译为：从字面上讲，它赋予土地所有者对土地上空无限远的空间的排他支配权。对矿藏和其他地下物的所有权也是如此。

4. It is now settled that the flight of aircraft over land does not constitute trespass or nuisance so long as such flights are at a proper height and do not unreasonably interfere with the landowner's use and enjoyment of his property.

so long as 意为"只要"；interfere with 意为"干扰"。句子顺序也需调整。此句翻译为："现在已成定论的是，航空器飞过土地上空，只要在一合适高度并没有不适合地干扰地主对其财产的使用和享有，就不构成非法侵入或滋扰。"

5. The principal significance of a determination that an object is a fixture is that it is thereafter treated as part and parcel of the land and may not generally be removed therefrom except by the owner of the realty.

本句中有两个 that 引导的从句，第一个 that 从句修饰 determination，第二个 that 引导句子的主干。此句翻译为："我们决定某物属附属物的主要意义是，此后它将被视为土地的一部分，除不动产的所有人，一般不允许把它移走。"

6. Thus, where an object which is physically attached to realty may be easily removed, it may be held to have retained its character as personalty notwithstanding the annexation.

which 引导的从句修饰 an object, notwithstanding 意为"虽然、尽管"。此句翻译为："因此，一个仅在形体上附于不动产上、却又可轻易被移走的小物体，尽管存在附属关系，可能仍然被认定还保持着其动产性质。"

7. It has been said that the mode of annexation is of little consequence as it bears on the question of intent.

bear on sth. 意为"和（某事物）有关，涉及"。原文的被动译为主动，同时添加主语。

此句翻译为：人们认为动产与不动产附着的方式并无意义，除非它体现了某种意图。

参考译文

不 动 产 法

现代法律中财产有两个基本类型：不动产与动产。不动产由固定的、不可移动的东西组成，如土地。"Lands""real estate""real property"一般作为同一概念使用。古老的习惯用语"地产、房产、不动产"囊括了所有的不动产及其权益。在不动产概念中还包括地役权、先占权这样的无形权利。

建筑及其附属物、围栏和其他附着于土地之上以提高其效用的物体通常包括在不动产内，固定在土地上的树木，在其于土地分离之前作为土地一部分，也属不动产。判断正在生长的农作物是不动产还是动产要视农作物的性质，提出这一问题的双方当事人的关系，以及其他条件而定。决定农作物这种有争议的分类时，最主要的区别是该农作物被划为自然成果，还是劳动成果。后者包括土地上每年收获的由人们栽种培育的果实。在大多数情况下，这种农作物被视为动产，即使它们仍附着在土地上。另一方面，自然成果，如从多年生的根系上长出来的草，根据一些法庭的意见，还有水果等从树木、灌木、藤蔓及其他多年生根系植物上获得的产品，在其未脱离土地时，应被视为不动产。但是，法庭现在倾向于将主要靠人工看护和培育而得到的产于树木的果实和其他产品，视为劳动成果。

地下的矿藏是不动产的一部分，如果让与时没有相反的规定，它属于该土地的所有人。蕴藏在地下的石油和天然气，作为矿藏，是土地的一部分，可供采集，也可因逸漏而丧失。水，在其未被占有和处于自然状态时，也视为储藏它的土地的一部分。

一句古代普通法格言说："土地为谁所有，其上的空间与地下也归谁所有。"它意味着土地所有人拥有该土地从天顶到地底的支配权。从字面上讲，它赋予土地所有者对土地上空无限远的空间的排他支配权。对矿藏和其他地下物的所有权也是如此。然而，现代航空的发展已要求对这些权利有关高空部分加以限制。土地所有人对这部分空间的所有权不再被认为是排他的和无限的。现在已成定论的是，航空器飞过土地上空，只要在一合适高度并没有不适当地干扰地主对其财产的使用和享有，就不构成非法侵入或滋扰。所有权向上扩展以充分使用和享有该土地之必要为限。超过此范围的空间被认为是公共的和可供航空使用的空间。但所有人拥有为充分享用其财产修建建筑物至任何必要高度的优先权。任何越过其上空的飞行，如高度过低或以某种特别方式，以至不合理地干涉了他对财产的充分享用，危及他的建筑物，惊扰了他的禽畜，或损害了他的家人健康与安宁，一般将构成非法侵入或滋扰。

附属物有各种不同的定义。有的定义为：原为动产，因依附或与不动产使用上的联系而成为不动产的一部分之物；有的定义为：作为动产，因长期附着于不动产而成其一部分的动产。还有的定义为：作为动产，联系紧密地附着于不动产上至不损及财产的完好不能将之分离。不过，没有任何一个单独的定义能适用所有情形。我们决定某物属附属物的主要意义是，此后它将被视为土地的一部分，除不动产的所有人，一般不允许把它移走。

决定某一特定物是否已成为附属物的一般标准，通常认为包括三方面：与不动产的附属关系；是否符合于不动产设定的用途；是否适合成为不动产永久添附的意图。当然，对上述

Unit Eight The Law of Property 财产法

各因素之间的相对重要性,也存在一些不同意见。

"附属"在这里的意义,指将动产固定、附着于不动产上。尽管对于土地的附着或添附是早期普通法决定是否某物已具有附属物性质的主要标准,但现在它在许多情况下已不再占主导地位。关于物体附着于不动产的具体方式,在现代判决中,其影响虽日益削弱,但在某些情况下,它仍有重要意义。在符合其他标准的情况中,对不动产轻微的附着关系,就可能使某一物品成为附着物,甚至就像地基上的建筑物和工厂里的重型设备那样,仅因重力而固定于某地点,也能构成附属关系。可分离的不动产附着物与不动产之间结合的紧密程度,常常被作为决定该物体是否已成为附属物时的考虑。因此,一个仅在形体上附于不动产上、却又可轻易被移走的小物体,尽管存在附属关系,可能仍然被认定还保持着其动产性质。反之,如物体不能在不伤及自身或不动产价值的情况下被分开,那它通常就被认定为附属物,成为不动产的一部分。

衡量或决定某物附属物性质的三因素中的第二个因素,即是否合适于不动产所设定的用途,是指一项动产和它所依附的不动产的用途之间的关系。依适合用途的原则,附于不动产上的物,可能成为附属物,如果考虑到不动产的用途,它是不动产的必要添附。这一原则,有时被称为"组合原则",在决定某一特定物是否具有附属物性质时常起重要作用。适合性原则常常被用于涉及工厂、农场、制造厂或工业设施的场合。在那种情形里,动产如果被安置在工业设施上永久使用,并且它对工厂的生产是必需的,那么无论它是否与不动产连为一体,法庭通常都认为它已成为附属物,因而是不动产的一部分。早在16世纪,人们就认为磨石是被转让的磨坊的一部分,尽管它时常与之分离。

三个决定因素中的第三个因素,即使某物成为附属物的意图,涉及当事人是否有意使一件加之于不动产上的物体成为前者的永久添附。在决定某项财产是否是附属物时,这是一个重要的标准,常常具有举足轻重的地位,至少在其他标准不能解决问题时如此。人们认为动产与不动产附着的方式并无意义,除非它体现了某种意图。

当事人可以通过合同约定某物是动产或附属物。他们可以通过双方合意,设定一件在正常情况下被看成附属物的物体仍为动产,或一件正常情况下具有动产性质的物体成为附属物。但作为一个前提,这种特殊约定只能约束合同的双方当事人及相关人,而不能约束第三人,如不知此约定的后手购买人或不动产抵押权人。

物体如与土地分离就失去附属物的地位。假如没有涉及第三人权利,它可重新成为动产,有效的分离只能由不动产所有人作出,且必须在他已有使该物永久与不动产分离的意图的情况下生效。

Passage Two
中华人民共和国民法通则

第五章 民事权利

第一节 财产所有权和与财产所有权有关的财产权

第七十一条 财产所有权是指所有人依法对自己的财产享有占有、使用、收益和处分的权利。

第七十二条 财产所有权的取得，不得违反法律规定。

按照合同或者其他合法方式取得财产的，财产所有权从财产交付时起转移，法律另有规定或者当事人另有约定的除外。

第七十三条 国家财产属于全民所有。

国家财产神圣不可侵犯，禁止任何组织或者个人侵占、哄抢、私分、截留、破坏。

第七十四条 劳动群众集体组织的财产属于劳动群众集体所有，包括：

（一）法律规定为集体所有的土地和森林、山岭、草原、荒地、滩涂等；

（二）集体经济组织的财产；

（三）集体所有的建筑物、水库、农田水利设施和教育、科学、文化、卫生、体育等设施；

（四）集体所有的其他财产。

集体所有的土地依照法律属于村农民集体所有，由村农业生产合作社等农业集体经济组织或者村民委员会经营、管理。

已经属于乡（镇）农民集体经济组织所有的，可以属于乡（镇）农民集体所有。

集体所有的财产受法律保护，禁止任何组织或者个人侵占、哄抢、私分、破坏或者非法查封、扣押、冻结、没收。

第七十五条 公民的个人财产，包括公民的合法收入、房屋、储蓄、生活用品、文物、图书资料、林木、牲畜和法律允许公民所有的生产资料以及其他合法财产。

公民的合法财产受法律保护，禁止任何组织或者个人侵占、哄抢、破坏或者非法查封、扣押、冻结、没收。

第七十六条 公民依法享有财产继承权。

第七十七条 社会团体包括宗教团体的合法财产受法律保护。

第七十八条 财产可以由两个以上的公民、法人共有。

共有分为按份共有和共同共有。按份共有人按照各自的份额，对共有财产分享权利，分担义务。共同共有人对共有财产享有权利，承担义务。

按份共有财产的每个共有人有权要求将自己的份额分出或者转让。

但在出售时，其他共有人在同等条件下，有优先购买的权利。

第七十九条 所有人不明的埋藏物、隐藏物，归国家所有。接收单位应当对上缴的单位或者个人，给予表扬或者物质奖励。

拾得遗失物、漂流物或者失散的饲养动物，应当归还失主，因此而支出的费用由失主偿还。

第八十条 国家所有的土地，可以依法由全民所有制单位使用，也可以依法确定由集体所有制单位使用，国家保护它的使用、收益的权利；使用单位有管理、保护、合理利用的义务。

公民、集体依法对集体所有的或者国家所有由集体使用的土地的承包经营权，受法律保护。承包双方的权利和义务，依照法律由承包合同规定。

土地不得买卖、出租、抵押或者以其他形式非法转让。

第八十一条 国家所有的森林、山岭、草原、荒地、滩涂、水面等自然资源，可以依法由全民所有制单位使用，也可以依法确定由集体所有制单位使用，国家保护它的使用、收益的权利；使用单位有管理、保护、合理利用的义务。

国家所有的矿藏，可以依法由全民所有制单位和集体所有制单位开采，也可以依法由公民采挖。国家保护合法的采矿权。

公民、集体依法对集体所有的或者国家所有由集体使用的森林、山岭、草原、荒地、滩涂、水面的承包经营权，受法律保护。

承包双方的权利和义务，依照法律由承包合同规定。

国家所有的矿藏、水流，国家所有的和法律规定属于集体所有的林地、山岭、草原、荒地、滩涂不得买卖、出租、抵押或者以其他形式非法转让。

第八十二条 全民所有制企业对国家授予它经营管理的财产依法享有经营权，受法律保护。

第八十三条 不动产的相邻各方，应当按照有利生产、方便生活、团结互助、公平合理的精神，正确处理截水、排水、通行、通风、采光等方面的相邻关系。给相邻方造成妨碍或者损失的，应当停止侵害，排除妨碍，赔偿损失。

词汇提示

有，拥有　possess
使用，运用　utilize
违反，违背　violation
转让，让与　transfer
同时发生（或进行）的，同步的　simultaneous
国家财产　state property
神圣的　sacred
不容亵渎的，不可侵犯的，不容破坏的　inviolable
集体组织　collective organization
劳动群众　the working masses
荒地　unreclaimed land
滩涂　beach
水库，蓄水池　reservoir
水利设施　irrigation facility
农业生产合作社　agricultural production cooperatives
农业集体经济组织　collective agricultural economic organization
村民委员会　villages' committee
（尤指作为惩罚）没收，把……充公　confiscate
文物　object d'art
盗用，挪用，占用，侵吞　appropriate
财产继承权　the right of inheritance
关于　respecting
相称，协调　in proportion to
优先采购，先行购买　pre-emption
（尤指公开地）赞扬，称赞，表扬　commend

给予物质奖励　give a material reward
漂流物　flotsam
（长指宠物）走失的，无主的　stray
引致，带来（成本、花费等）　incur
偿还，补偿　reimburse
使用单位　usufructuary
有义务的，有责任的，必须地　be obligated to
租用，租借，出租　lease
抵押　mortgage
自然资源　natural resources
矿藏　mineral resources
开矿，采矿　mine
全民所有制单位　units under ownership by the whole people
集体所有制单位　units under collective ownership
采矿权　the mining right
全民所有制企业　enterprises under ownership by the whole people
经营权　the right of management
便利的，方便的　convenient
互助　mutual assistance
排水，放水　drainage
通风　ventilation
采光　lighting
妨碍　obstruction
排除，清除，消除　eliminate
赔偿　compensate

▶ 法律术语

财产所有权　property ownership
集体所有　collective ownership
集体所有的财产　collectively owned property
共有　joint ownership
按份共有　co-ownership by shares
共同共有　common ownership
共有财产　joint property

▶ 要点解析

1. 财产所有权是指所有人依法对自己的财产享有占有、使用、收益和处分的权利。

"Property ownership" means the owner's rights to lawfully possess, utilize, profit from and dispose of his property.

翻译时注意"占有""使用""收益""处分"四个词语及介词搭配。dispose of sth. 意为"处理，解决"。

2. 集体所有的财产受法律保护，禁止任何组织或者个人侵占、哄抢、私分、破坏或者非法查封、扣押、冻结、没收。

Collectively owned property shall be protected by law, and no organization or individual may seize, encroach upon, privately divide, destroy or illegally seal up, distrain, freeze or confiscate it.

这句话中出现了较多的两字词语，它们的准确翻译是重点。

3. 按份共有人按照各自的份额，对共有财产分享权利，分担义务。

Each of the co-owners by shares shall enjoy the rights and assume the obligations respecting the joint property in proportion to his share.

"承担责任"用 assume the obligation 来表达；"共有财产"译为 joint property；"按照各自的份额"译为 in proportion to the share。

4. 国家保护它的使用、收益的权利；使用单位有管理、保护、合理利用的义务。

The state shall protect the usufruct of the land, and the usufructuary shall be obligated to manage, protect and properly use the land.

在法律文件的英译中，情态动词 shall 使用频繁，注意根据情况选择恰当的情态动词，以合适的表达语气。"使用单位"译为 usufructuary，"有……的义务"用 be obligated to 来表达。

5. 全民所有制企业对国家授予它经营管理的财产依法享有经营权，受法律保护。

Enterprises under ownership by the whole people shall lawfully enjoy the rights of management over property that the state has authorized them to manage and operate, and the rights shall be protected by law.

"全民所有制企业"译为 enterprises under ownership by the whole people，"批准，授权"译为 authorize。that 引导的从句修饰 property。

6. 应当按照有利生产、方便生活、团结互助、公平合理的精神

in the spirit of helping production, making things convenient for people's lives, enhancing unity and mutual assistance, and being fair and reasonable

"有利生产""方便生活""团结互助""公平合理"，后两个四字词组翻译时需要添词 enhancing 和 being，这样翻译出来的英文形式上更整齐，意思上也更完整。

 参考译文

General Principles of the Civil Law of the People's Republic of China

Chapter V Civil Rights

Section 1. Property Ownership and Related Property Rights

Article 71. "Property ownership" means the owner's rights to lawfully possess, utilize, profit from and dispose of his property.

Article 72. Property ownership shall not be obtained in violation of the law.

Unless the law stipulates otherwise or the parties concerned have agreed on other arrangements, the ownership of property obtained by contract or by other lawful means shall be transferred simultaneously with the property itself.

Article 73. State property shall be owned by the whole people.

State property is sacred and inviolable, and no organization or individual shall be allowed to seize, encroach upon, privately divide, retain or destroy it.

Article 74. Property of collective organizations of the working masses shall be owned collectively by the working masses. This shall include:

(1) land, forests, mountains, grasslands, unreclaimed land, beaches and other areas that are stipulated by law to be under collective ownership;

(2) property of collective economic organizations;

(3) collectively owned buildings, reservoirs, farm irrigation facilities and educational, scientific, cultural, health, sports and other facilities;

(4) other property that is collectively owned.

Collectively owned land shall be owned collectively by the village peasants in accordance with the law and shall be worked and managed by village agricultural production cooperatives, other collective agricultural economic organizations or villages' committees.

Land already under the ownership of the township (town) peasants' collective economic organizations may be collectively owned by the peasants of the township (town).

Collectively owned property shall be protected by law, and no organization or individual may seize, encroach upon, privately divide, destroy or illegally seal up, distrain, freeze or confiscate it.

Article 75. A citizen's personal property shall include his lawfully earned income, housing, savings, articles for daily use, cultural relic, books, reference materials, trees, livestock, as well as means of production the law permits a citizen to possess and other lawful property.

A citizen's lawful property shall be protected by law, and no organization or individual may appropriate, encroach upon, destroy or illegally seal up, distrain, freeze or confiscate it.

Article 76. Citizens shall have the right of inheritance under the law.

Article 77. The lawful property of social organizations, including religious organizations, shall be protected by law.

Article 78. Property may be owned jointly by two or more citizens or legal persons.

There shall be two kinds of joint ownership, namely co-ownership by shares and common ownership. Each of the co-owners by shares shall enjoy the rights and assume the obligations respecting the joint property in proportion to his share. Each of the common owners shall enjoy the rights and assume the obligations respecting the joint property.

Each co-owner by shares shall have the right to withdraw his own share of the joint property or transfer its ownership.

However, when he offers to sell his share, the other co-owners shall have a right of pre-emption if all other conditions are equal.

Article 79. If the owner of a buried or concealed object is unknown, the object shall belong to the state. The unit that receives the object shall commend or give a material reward to the unit or individual that turns in the object.

Lost-and-found objects, flotsam and stray animals shall be returned to their rightful owners, and any costs thus incurred shall be reimbursed by the owners.

Article 80. State-owned land may be used according to law by units under ownership by the whole people; it may also be lawfully assigned for use by units under collective ownership. The state shall protect the usufruct of the land, and the usufructuary shall be obligated to manage, protect and properly use the land.

The right of citizens and collectives to contract for management of land under collective ownership or of state-owned land under collective use shall be protected by law.

The rights and obligations of the two contracting parties shall be stipulated in the contract signed in accordance with the law.

Land may not be sold, leased, mortgaged or illegally transferred by any other means.

Article 81. State-owned forests, mountains, grasslands, unreclaimed land, beaches, water surfaces and other natural resources may be used according to law by units under ownership by the whole people; or they may also be lawfully assigned for use by units under collective ownership. The state shall protect the usufruct of those resources, and the usufructuary shall be obliged to manage, protect and properly use them.

State-owned mineral resources may be mined according to law by units under ownership by the whole people and units under collective ownership; citizens may also lawfully mine such resources. The state shall protect lawful mining rights.

The right of citizens and collectives to lawfully contract for the management of forests, mountains, grasslands, unreclaimed land, beaches and water surfaces that are owned by collectives or owned by the state but used by collectives shall be protected by law.

The rights and obligations of the two contracting parties shall be stipulated in the contract in accordance with the law.

State-owned mineral resources and waters as well as forest land, mountains, grasslands, unreclaimed land and beaches owned by the state and those that are lawfully owned by collectives may not be sold, leased, mortgaged or illegally transferred by any other means.

Article 82. Enterprises under ownership by the whole people shall lawfully enjoy the rights of management over property that the state has authorized them to manage and operate, and the rights shall be protected by law.

Article 83. In the spirit of helping production, making things convenient for people's lives, enhancing unity and mutual assistance, and being fair and reasonable, neighbouring users of real estate shall maintain proper neighbourly relations over such matters as water supply, drainage, passageway, ventilation and lighting. Anyone who causes obstruction or damage to his neighbour, shall stop the infringement, eliminate the obstruction and compensate for the damage.

Section II 技能拓展

翻译技巧

法律英语词汇的特点及其翻译

随着中国加入世界贸易组织,世界经济一体化,中国与世界的交往和联系越来越多。法律文件的翻译将会在社会生活中扮演很重要的角色。要做好法律文件的英汉翻译,我们必须了解法律英语的一些特点。所谓法律英语,"是指法律界通用的书面英语(包括法律、法规、条例、规章、协定、判定和裁定等),尤其是指律师起草法律文件(合同、章程、协议、契约等)惯常使用的语言。"法律英语在词汇、句式等方面都有它自己的特点。本文尝试归纳出法律英语在词汇方面的四大特点,并进而探讨一些具体的翻译方法和策略。

1. 专业性

"法律语言部分是由具有特定法律意义的词组成,部分是由日常用语组成。具有特定法律意义的词,在日常用语中即使有也很少使用,如预谋、过失、非法侵害等。"除了具有特定法律意义的词之外,很多在日常生活中普遍应用的词汇,一旦到了法律文本中,便具有了区别于日常意义的法律意义。这也就是我们常说的法律词汇的"专业性"。下表列举部分英语单词的普通意义和法律意义。

英语单词	日常意义	法律意义
adverse	相反的	非法的
battery	电池	伤害、人身攻击
condemn	谴责	判刑、定罪
declaration	声明、宣言	申诉书
exhibit	展出	物证
hear	听见	听审
immunity	免疫力	豁免权
leave	离开	休庭
proceed	进行	起诉
report	报告	揭发
sentence	句子	判决
undo	解开	勾引、诱奸
vacation	假期	休庭期
warrant	保证	拘捕令

除了这些普通词汇所具有的专业意义之外，法律英语中还保留了一些外来词和旧体词，这也是法律词汇专业性的一个体现和标记。

外来词：现代法律词汇中保留一些来自拉丁文的词汇，如下表所示。

ad hoc	专门地	bona fide	真诚地
de facto	事实上的	inter alia	除了别的因素以外
in re	关于	mutatis mutandis	已作了必要的修订
pari passu	按相同比例	per se	自身
pro hono	为了公益	pro rata	按比例

此外，法律英语词汇中还保留着一些旧体词，常见的旧体词主要是由 here、there、where 和介词合成的，如下表所示。

hereby	由此，以此，特此	hereinafter	在下文
herein	其中，在此处	hereinbefore	在上文
hereof	至此，由此	heretofore	直到此时
hereto	至此，关于这个	hereinabove	在上文
hereunder	在下面	hereunto	于是
therein	其中	thereafter	此后，据此
therefore	因此	therefrom	由此，从那里
thereof	由此，因此	thereto	在那里
thereon	关于那，在其上	whereof	关于那个
wherein	在那方面	whereby	靠那个
aforesaid	上述的		

在翻译时译者需要充分了解、熟悉一些普通词语的法律意义，并适当地运用上述外来词和旧体词。例如下面译文中的斜体部分。

① 依照《中外合资经营企业法》批准在中国境内设立的中外合资经营企业（以下简称合营企业）是中国的法人，受中国法律的管辖和保护。

Chinese-foreign equity joint ventures (*hereinafter* referred to as joint ventures) established within Chinese territory upon approval in accordance with the Law on Chinese-Foreign Equity Joint Ventures are Chinese legal persons, who shall be governed and protected by Chinese law.

② A contract shall be an agreement *whereby* the parties establish, change or terminate their civil relationship. Lawfully established contracts shall be protected by law.

合同是当事人之间设立、变更、终止民事关系的协议。依法成立的合同，受法律保护。

2. 正式性

法律语言和普通语言相比，还体现在它的正式性上。在词汇层面上的正式性主要体现在法律英语会使用一些较正式的词。比如在合同中，表示"在……之前"，用 prior 而不用 before；表示"在……之后"，用 subsequent，而不用 after。例如：

合同的权利义务终止后,当事人应当遵循诚实信用原则,根据交易习惯履行通知、协助、保密等义务。

After the rights and obligations under a contract are terminated, the parties shall follow the principle of honesty and trustworthiness and the appropriate trading practice to perform the obligations of notification, assistance and confidentiality.

原文中"终止""原则""通知""协助"四个词分别被译成正式的英语词汇 terminate, principle, notification, assistance, 而不是日常使用较多的 end, rule, notice, help。下表中的正式词汇一般常见于法律文本中。

非正式词汇	正式词汇
buy	purchase
change	modify/alter
end	terminate
go	proceed
make	render
begin/start	commence
show	demonstrate

法律英语正式性的特点要求译者翻译时尽量选用正式的用词。

3. 客观性

法律文本应该是一种客观的叙述,这种客观性当然可以通过一些特定的句式,比如被动语态的使用等来实现。在词汇层面上,我们在翻译过程中,要避免带有感情色彩的词语。如 die 一词,在其他的文本中,根据具体情况,可以译为"死亡、逝世、牺牲、上西天、离开"。但在法律文本中,我们只把它译为表述事实的"死亡"。

4. 准确性(精确性)

法律术语的精确性是指"语义与所反映的客观事物(现象)完全相符,不仅是正确的,而且是准确的、精密的;不仅准确地反映事物(现象)的主要特点,而且准确地反映事物(现象)的一般特点。"准确性(精确性)可以说是法律文本的灵魂。因为一词之差导致官司的例子在历史和现代生活中并不鲜见。例如,美国阿肯色州的一起遗产纠纷案,其争论主要就是围绕遗嘱中所使用的 between 一词。这份遗嘱是:The remainders of the testator's property should be divided equally between all of our nephews and nieces on my wife's side and my niece.

立遗嘱人妻子一方的外甥及外甥女共有 22 人。上述遗嘱到底是立遗嘱人遗产的一半归其妻一方的 22 个外甥及外甥女,另一半归其自己的侄女,还是将遗产在双方外甥、外甥女、侄女之间平均分配呢?最后法官裁定为前者,其理由是"只有表示'在两者之间'或'在两方之间',才用 between。如按后一种理解,即在 23 人中平均分配,就必须用 among"。这个例子充分说明了准确性(精确性)对法律文本的重要性。在具体翻译过程中,译者如何在用词上再现精确性呢?大致说来,有如下几种。

1)具体化

翻译时,将细微的差别加以具体化,从而使表述更加准确。如 executor 和 administrator

在法律英语中的意思都是指"死者的遗产代理人",负责管理和处理死者的遗产。但二者有一点细微的区别,前者指的是死者已经定下遗嘱的,后者则指的是死者没有留下遗嘱的情形。因而,executor 应该翻译成"遗嘱执行人",而 administrator 则为"遗产管理人",此外这两个词主要指的都是男性,如果是女性,则分别为 executrix 和 administratrix,可分别译为"女遗嘱执行人"和"女遗产管理人"。

2）合并法

法律语言是精确的,同时也应该尽量的简洁。要做到精确和简洁的统一,有时我们需要将不同层面的意义合并,以便使法律词汇表达得更加精确。如 condition 一词在合约中,指的是较重要的条款和条文,违反它,则另一方有权取消合同或追讨赔款。所以这个词事实上含有"很重要的条件"之意,因而一般翻译成"要件",而不译简单的"条件"。再如,covenant 指的是在契约中所做出的承诺,它不同于一般的承诺或是协定,它包含"契约"和"承诺"两种意义在里面,因而可以译为"契诺"。

3）并置法

有时为了表达更加准确,将两个意义相近的词并列使用。如"诚实信用"就被译成了 honesty and trustworthiness,而在早先则被翻译成 good faith。常见的还有:terms and conditions（条款）、rules and regulations（规章制度）、damage or injury（损害或损伤）、losses and damages（损坏）、null and void（无效）、transfer and convey（转让）、heirs and devisees（继承人）。这些同义词在程度上,或是在使用范围等方面有些细微的差别,将它们组合在一起使用,从而使所表达的意义更加完整、精确。如 heirs and devisees 中,heir 一般可以指根据法律或是根据遗嘱继承另外一方之财产者,而 devisee 则指的是根据遗嘱接受另外一方之财产者。将这两个词合并在一起使用则完整地包含了这两方面的意义,避免引起法律纠纷。

4）增添法

增加一些解释性的话语,使得表述更加准确。如 environmental law 可以照字面意思翻译成"环境法";而 environmental lawyer 若直译成"环境律师",则有些让人不知所云,而应该按照其意义增添解释性的话语,译为:"从事环境法律事务的律师"。

再如前例"当事人应当遵循诚实信用原则,根据交易习惯履行通知、协助、保密等义务",其中的"交易习惯"译成了 the appropriate trading practice,很显然这里添加了 appropriate 一词,这是以前的合同法翻译中所没有的。这样的添加,就排除了那些非合同、非正当渠道的习惯做法,从而使翻译更加准确和合理。

翻译时,除了可以根据具体情况使用上述方法以使表述更加准确之外,还有两点也需要引起译者的重视。其一,要做到术语统一。有些术语可能有好几个译法,但在同一份文件中,前后所使用的术语要一致。比如,insured 一词可以译为"保险人""受保人""投保人"。尽管这三种表达都是可以接受的,但在同一份文件中,就只能择其一而用。其二,法律英语的术语在不同的法域其含义可能会有些差别,如 dominion 在民法中指的是完全的所有权;而在国际法中,则指的是主权。再如,estoppel 在合同法中是"不可反悔"之意,而在刑事诉讼法中则为"禁止翻供"。

法律宝典

两大法系财产法的差异

一、绝对所有权与相对所有权

许多学者都认为,"两大法系财产法的主要区别在于是否存在绝对所有权"。在他们看来,古罗马社会是以农业为基础的社会,作为经济支柱的生产资料主要是土地等不动产,这决定了法律必须对土地的占有加以保护。同时,土地的不可替代性和不可再生性使对土地处分权的保护成为罗马私法的核心使命。因而土地和动产的个人所有权在古罗马获得了绝对所有权的地位。而早期日耳曼法是在商品经济不发达的条件下,在村落共同体对土地进行团体占有的基础上发展而成。日耳曼物权法的各种观念和制度都以具体的事实为出发点,并基于物资利用的种种形态来规定各种权利。这一法律体系没有严格的所有权概念,各种物权均为具体的相对的,并存于同一块土地上的"高级所有权"和"低级所有权"即所谓"双重所有权"为相对所有权最有力的例证和说明。

二、"以所有为中心"与"以利用为中心"

根据一些研究者的结论,罗马物权法与日耳曼财产法的另一个主要区别是,罗马物权法以所有为中心,日耳曼财产法以利用为中心,日耳曼法比罗马法更注重物的利用。他们认为,在罗马法上,所有权为抽象的支配的权利,对物的利用乃是抽象的支配的作用。对所有权即财产归属的界定,是一切法律关系的前提。他物权人作为利用人,其权利无论多么宽泛,总是受所有人意志的制约。整个罗马物权法从抽象的所有权概念出发,进而最终回到所有权,他物权不过是作为所有权的部分权能而存在。所有权居于中心和基础的地位,各种利用权则处于依附地位。日耳曼财产法的各种观念和制度都以具体的事实关系为出发点,并基于物资利用的种种形态来规定各种权利。法律对这些财产权利均给予平等的保护。

三、"一物一权"与"一物多权"

有人认为,"一物一权"与"一物多权"也是罗马物权法与日耳曼财产法的重要差异之一。"根据罗马法,一物之上只能产生一个所有权","而日耳曼法主要是根据对物的各种利用形态确定各种权利,这样在不动产之上形成了多重所有权关系,而未采纳一物一权原则。"日耳曼法中并存于同一块土地之上的上级所有权和下级所有权以及起源于中世纪并已发展成为英美法系最具特色的制度之一的信托关系中的普通法所有权与衡平法所有权常被学者们引以为日耳曼财产法及当代英美财产法"一物多权"主义的例证。

术语积累

ownership 所有权
legal status 法律地位
leasehold interest 租赁权益
trust 信托
beneficiary 受益人

trustee 受托人
executor 执行人
equitable title 衡平法上的所有权
equitable interest 衡平法上的利益
joint tenancy 共同保有
concurrent estate 共同占有的财产
right of survivorship 生存者财产权
partition action 分割
tenancy by the entirely 夫妻共同保有
tenancy in common 混合共有
possess 占用
priority 优先权
title 所有权；产权证明
security 担保（物）
gift 赠予
account stated 确定欠债清单
undischarged bankrupt 未偿清债务的破产者
trustee in bankruptcy 破产财产管理人
estate agent 地产经纪人
adjoining land 相邻的土地
hiring out 分期付款购买
freehold 完全保有的
leasehold 租赁的；承租的
fee simple 无条件继承的不动产权
fee tail 指定继承人继承的不动产权
reversion 复归权
remainder 残余权
conveyance 要式转移
mere right 非占有财产权
a proprietary right 所有权；所有者权利
proprietor 所有人；所有者
abeyance 土地所有权未定
aboriginal title 原始所有权（指印第安人排他性的继承占用）
abutter 临近的住户；相邻业主
alienation 让与财产权；转移产权
appraise 动产评价；估价；鉴定
bailee 受托保管人
beneficial use 使用收益权
chattel mortgage 动产抵押

conditional fee (or estate)　附条件的不动产物权
contingent estate (or interest)　可变财产；未定利益
conversion　侵占他人财产
corporeal　有形的动产
detainer　非法占有他人财产；扣留
determinable fee (fee simple determinable)　可终止的不动产物权
disseisin　非法强占他人不动产，并将原所有人逐出
distress　扣货还债；扣押私人动产；扣押被告的动产
distribution　动产分配；财产分配
divestiture　（财产、权利等的）剥夺
dominant estate(or tenement)　承役地
donation intent　赠予
donee　受赠人
donor　赠予人
ejectment　请求恢复不动产占有的诉讼
eminent domain　国家征用权
encumbrance　债务负担；不动产的债务
estate　不动产物权
expropriation　征收；没收财产；剥夺所有权
false pretense (pretences)　诈欺取财罪
ferae nature　不属于私产的；野生的
fieri facias　财物扣押令
fraudulent conveyance　欺诈性财产让与
free and clear　不动产无抵押权负担的
tangible property　有形财产
tenure　土地保有制
unlawful detainer　非法扣押他人动产
vandalism　破坏他人财产的行为
vested remainder　既定的残余财产权
future estate　将来的不动产物权
future interest　将来财产权
gift tax　赠予税
hypothecate　抵押（财产）
implied easement　默示地役权
lessee　承租人
lessor　出租人
marital life estate　终身财产
mortgage　抵押；抵押权
mortgagor　抵押债务人

possibility of reversion　取得财产复归权的可能性
proprietary interest　财产及附随于该财产权的所有者的利益
right of eminent domain　征用权（国家将私有财产作为公用的权力）
hereditament　不动产
principal　本人，委托人
creator of trust　信托受益人
express trust　明示信托
public trust　公益信托
implied trust　默示信托
private trust　私人信托
discretionary trust　任意决定的信托
constructive trust　推定信托

Section III　巩固练习

词汇与短语

1. testamentary trusts
2. inter vivos trust
3. chose in action
4. chose in possession
5. without recourse
6. proprietary
7. lease
8. leasehold
9. negative easement
10. non-exempt property

11. 共同租赁；共同租借权
12. 终身地产
13. 未来权益
14. 分时段享用权
15. 抵押权人
16. 永久管业权
17. 剩余财产
18. 直接物权关系
19. 身份保证金；不动产租赁押金
20. 单独保有的物权

句子与段落

1. Estates in land are divided into two broad categories according to the duration of the estate: freehold estates and leasehold estates.
2. There are two basic classes of property in modern law, real property and personal property.
3. The principal significance of a determination that an object is a fixture is that it is thereafter treated as part and parcel of the land and may not generally be removed therefrom except by

the owner of the realty.

4. The adaptation principle is often applied where a factory, plant, mill, or similar industrial establishment is involved.
5. Estates in expectancy are of two sorts, those created by act of the parties, called "remainders", and those created by operation of law, called "reversions".
6. A life estate is an estate of freehold but not of inheritance created by deed or will.
7. 复归权是法律设立的一项可期待的地产权。
8. 残余权是在不动产的某部分权益转让后，被处分的残余部分。
9. 终生地产，正常情况下，因享有人或约定的第三人的死亡而中止。
10. 复归权人并不拥有对地产的实际占有或抑制占有，或主张其中一种的权利，他仅享有一项可期待的地产权。
11. 残余权的本质在于，它于特定的地产因期限届满或其他中止条件而中止后，立刻产生，而不是该地产的翻版。
12. 普通法上，收回权是不可流转、转让或遗赠的。

Unit Nine

The Intellectual Law
知识产权法

Section I 译例研究

Passage One
Copyright Protection

A copyright is a governmental grant, an acknowledgement that original writings are owned by the author. A copyright is the legal recognition of the special "property rights" in an author's work.

Copyright protection is available for almost all writing and books, short stories, magazine articles, newspaper columns, poetry, plays, screenplays, and songs. Both fictional and nonfictional works are covered, and copyright protection is even available for such writings as an index, a master's thesis, a map, even an original directory, such as the phone book, or a name and address guide to vegetarian restaurants.

A copyright protects the specific way that you develop, detail and express your idea in writing. That is, if you have an idea for an article about nuclear-powered musical instruments of the future, you can't obtain protection for your concept. Anyone can use your idea, and write, copyright and publish his or her own article about nuclear-powered musical instruments of the future.

However, if somebody else wants to write an article dealing with the same subject or idea of your copyrighted article, that second somebody had better not lift sentences or paragraphs from your article, and had better not even paraphrase your article, or parts of it, because that would be copyright infringement.

"Words and short phrases" are not protected by copyright. A catchy slogan, a clever word if you are using these in business as a brand name for a product, or as the name of your musical group or other business, protection for the single word or short slogan may be available under the trademark laws, but not the copyright laws.

What else is not protected? Lists of ingredients are not, hence, the major part of most recipes. Does this mean that you have no protection if you write a cooking article or cookbook? No, because your article or book as a whole presumably contains more text than a string of ingredients, affording you a basis for copyright protection.

The same principle applies to chemical formulae, and to math problems. Copyright law won't allow these to be removed from the "public domain", so an individual equation, even if developed today under the new copyright act, would not be protected under the copyright laws. However, your math book or chemistry text would contain far more than a string of formulae or equations, and would, as a whole, be protected.

Computer program-software is an area where copyright laws are up in the air. Right now, software is not adequately protected under the copyright laws, but this situation may soon change. However, depending on the circumstances, protection is sometimes available under the "common law" of unfair competition and trade secrets.

The Copyright Office does not make an extensive examination of the substance of your work, because what you are keeping from the public domain is your way of expressing a concept, which concept anyone is entitled to use in his or her own words. That is, your "monopoly" does not work a serious hardship on the public, so your work does not have to pass a serious muster to earn its copyright protection. Obviously, if your work was primarily copied from a public domain work and you find yourself holding a certificate of copyright registration nonetheless, an "infringer" you seek to sue over the matter can raise a public domain defense, despite your registration.

Now, what about "fair use"? Fair use, as defined by Marybeth Peters, senior attorney/advisor to the Copyright Office, "allows copying without permission from or payment to, the copyright owner where the use is reasonable and not harmful to the rights of the copyright owner." However, what is "reasonable" and "not harmful" is not necessarily determined by your personal beliefs.

Fair use is one of the most nebulous, tricky areas viewed differently depending on who is taking the copyrighted material from where, and to what end!

For example, your use of chunks of material from a copyrighted work, properly credited to the copyright owner might be "fair use" in your doctoral thesis. But your use of the exact same chunk of quoted material, even if credited to the copyright owner, could get you into hot water if it is included in your article for the Chicago Tribune.

Why? In determining "fair use", the courts look to the "purpose and character of the use, including whether such use is of commercial nature, or for educational purposes."

Because of the ill-defined, continuum nature of fair use, there is no rule advising how many words you may quote before crossing the border from fair to unfair use. Another factor is timeliness. If you've had 6 months' lead time, you're expected to have had the opportunity to contract the copyright owner whose work you'd like to quote. If your article is due at the printers in two days, however, and you want to add a quoted sentence or two from somebody's article published this morning, the courts may conclude that your failure to obtain permission for use of the small quote was reasonable.

Does attributing the quoted portion to the author relieve you of liability for copyright infringement? No, but the reverse—omitting the author credit—may well make your copying appear to be intentional plagiarism so that the equitable defense of fair use won't apply. Fair is fair. Also, as a practical matter, a quoted author is less likely to feel ripped off if properly credited, and, accordingly, is less likely to sue you.

Fair use does not automatically prevent an irate author or publisher from suing you and/or your publisher for copyright infringement with respect to the quoted material. It merely permits you a defense—an excuse—to tell the judge if suit is filed.

词汇提示

acknowledgement   *n.* 承认
cover   *v.* 包括，包含
a master's thesis   硕士论文
a vegetarian restaurant   素食餐馆
detail   *v.* 详细列举，详细说明，详述
musical instrument   乐器
ingredient   *n.* 成分，烹饪原料
recipe   *n.* 烹饪法，食谱
chemical formulae   化学公式
equation   *n.* 等式
up in the air   悬而未决
unfair competition   不正当竞争
trade secret   商业秘密
the Copyright Office   版权局
an extensive examination   全面审查
monopoly   *n.* 垄断
a public domain work   某种公有的著作
infringer   *n.* 侵权人
sue   *v.* 控告，提起诉讼
senior   *adj.* 资深的
attorney   *n.* 律师
advisor   *n.* 顾问
personal beliefs   个人信念
nebulous   *adj.* 模糊的，不清楚的
tricky   *adj.* 难办的，难对付的
end   *n.* 目的，目标

a doctoral thesis　博士论文
credit ... to ...　说明……是属于……的
Chicago Tribune　《芝加哥论坛报》
cross the border　越过界线
timeliness　*n.* 及时性
liability　*n.* 责任，义务
plagiarism　*n.* 剽窃
irate　*adj.* 极其愤怒的，暴怒的

▶ 法律术语

copyright　*n.* 版权，著作权
property right　财产权
copyright protection　版权保护
copyright infringement　侵犯版权
the trademark law　商标法
the copyright law　版权法
public domain　（不受版权保护的）公有财产
the common law　普通法
a certificate of copyright registration　版权登记证
copyright owner　版权（所有）人

▶ 要点解析

1. A copyright protects the specific way that you develop, detail and express your idea in writing.

that 引导的从句在此修饰 the specific way, protect 的对象是"the specific way that..."。detail 可用作动词，意为详细说明，具体落实。因此此句可译为："版权所保护的，是用书面来构思、具体落实并予以表达的那种特定的方式。"

2. that second somebody had better not lift sentences or paragraphs from your article, and had better not even paraphrase your article, or parts of it, because that would be copyright infringement

had better not 意为"最好不要"，这里注意把握语气。lift sentences or paragraphs 译为"摘句取段"，四字结构简洁清楚。此句可译为"那么这第二个写作者还是别从你的文章里摘句取段，甚至别诠释你文章的全部或几部分为好，因为那样做会侵犯版权的"。

3. Copyright law won't allow these to be removed from the "public domain", so an individual equation, even if developed today under the new copyright act, would not be protected under the copyright laws.

此句先因后果，理解时可适当调整句子后面部分的顺序：so, even if developed today under the new copyright act, an individual equation would not be protected under the copyright laws. "even if..." 作为一个插入成分，可调整位置以利于理解。此句可译为："版权法是不会让化学公式

和数学题从'公有'的范围中排斥出去的。因此,个别的等式即使是今天在有新版权法的情况下列出的,也不能受到版权法的保护。"

4. what you are keeping from the public domain is your way of expressing a concept, which concept anyone is entitled to use in his or her own words

英语中用 which 引导的从句将两个句子连在一起。翻译时,可运用拆分,将原句译成两个并列的小句。所以原句可译为"你要求保护的,是你表达思想的方式;至于思想本身,则是任何人都有权以自己的语言加以利用的。"

5. Fair use is one of the most nebulous, tricky areas viewed differently depending on who is taking the copyrighted material from where, and to what end!

英语中惯用长句,其逻辑关系复杂,正确的分析是翻译的关键,可重新组织为:Fair use is one of the most nebulous, tricky areas. It is viewed differently by people, depending on who is taking the copyrighted material from where and to what end. 所以此句可译为:"正当使用,是最模糊、最复杂的领域之一。对此,人们看法不同,要根据谁以什么目的从哪里挪用了旁人拥有版权的材料而定。"

6. No, but the reverse—omitting the author credit—may well make your copying appear to be intentional plagiarism so that the equitable defense of fair use won't apply.

the equitable defense of fair use 是表达的难点,可添词译为"以正当使用为理由提出衡平法上的辩护"。apply 此处意为"应用,适用"。所以此句可译为:"不是的。但从反面——不注明版权所属——倒很可能使你的引用成为故意剽窃,从而你就无法以正当使用为理由提出衡平法上的辩护了。"

参考译文

版 权 保 护

版权由政府授予,即确认原著归作者所有。版权是在法律上承认对于作者著作的特殊"财产权"。

几乎所有的著作——书、短篇小说、杂志文章、报纸专栏、诗、剧、电影剧本和歌曲——都享有版权保护。这里,虚构的和非虚构的作品都包括在内;而且,索引、硕士论文、地图,甚至像电话簿或蔬菜馆便览那样原版的指南书,也都享有版权保护。

版权所保护的,是用书面来构思、具体落实并予以表达的那种特定的方式。这就是说,你灵机一动,要写一篇关于未来的一种原子能乐器的文章,那么你是无法为你的设想获得保护的。任何人都可以利用你的设想,写作、出版自己关于未来的那种原子能乐器的文章和取得其版权。

但是,如果有人写文章谈论与你拥有版权的那篇文章相同的题材或思想,那么这第二个写作者还是别从你的文章里摘句取段,甚至别诠释你文章的全部或几部分为好,因为那样做会侵犯版权的。

"词和短语"不受版权保护。一个吸引人的口号、一个俏皮的词儿——如果是在商业上用作产品的品牌名、乐队或其他行业名字——可以受商标法的保护,却不受版权法的保护。

还有什么是不受版权保护的呢？制品的成分表不受保护，因此大部分食谱的主要部分是不受保护的。这是不是说，如果你写一本烹饪书或一篇关于烧饭做菜的文章，你就得不到保护呢？不是，因为你的文章或书作为整体，不只是列出一系列配料的成分而已，从而为你提供了受版权保护的根据。

同样的原则也适用于化学公式和数学题。版权法是不会让化学公式和数学题从"公有"的范围中排斥出去的。因此，个别的等式即使是今天在有新版权法的情况下列出的，也不能受到版权法的保护。但你写的数学书或化学文章的内容远远不止一些公式和等式，因此，作为整体是会受到版权保护的。

电脑程序（软件）是版权法上还不明确的领域。就目前而论，软件没有受到版权法的充分保护，但这一情况很快就会改变。但是，根据各种情况，有时候可以按照"普通法"关于不正当竞争和商业秘密的规定得到保护。

版权局对你著作的内容不作全面审查，因为你要求保护的，是你表达思想的方式；至于思想本身，则是任何人都有权以自己的语言加以利用的。这就是说，你的"垄断"并不对公众构成严重的障碍，因此，你的著作是不必通过严格的审查就能获得版权保护的。不言而喻，如果你的著作主要是从某种公有的著作中抄袭得来的，而你却照样取得了版权登记证；那么尽管你已经登了记，你想控告的版权"侵犯者"仍然可以以版权属公有为辩护理由。

那么，"正当使用"又是怎么回事呢？按版权局资深律师兼顾问马里贝思·彼得氏的定义，正当使用乃"允许不经版权人许可或不给版权人费用而翻印，但使用必须合理且无损于版权人的权利"。但什么是"合理"且"无损于"，那就未必是你个人的信念所能判定的了。

正当使用，是最模糊最复杂的领域之一。对此，人们看法不同，要根据谁以什么目的从哪里挪用了旁人拥有版权的材料而定。

例如，你把版权人某著作中一段段的材料，用于你的博士论文，并适当地说明这些材料是属于其版权人的，这可以是"正当使用"。但是如果你把上述材料用于发表在《芝加哥论坛》报上的文章里，那么即使声明了版权人是谁，也会给你惹出麻烦来的。

为什么呢？在判定"正当使用"时，法院要研究"使用的目的和性质"——包括商业性的使用和用于教育。

由于"正当使用"定义不清，在数量上又连续不断，所以，没有什么规则能说明可引用多少个词儿才不算越过正当使用与不正当使用的界线。

另一个因素就是及时性。如果你有六个月付印准备期，人们就指望你有机会同你要援引作品的作者去联系。但是如果你的文章两天内就必须付印，而你想从人家在今天早上发表的文章中援引一两个句子，那么法院会作出结论：你未能取得使用那短小引文的许可是符合情理的。

是不是引文注明了原作者就可以免除你侵犯版权的责任了呢？不是的。但从反面——不注明版权所属——倒很可能使你的引用成为故意剽窃，从而你就无法以正当使用为理由提出衡平法上的辩护了。正当就是正当。此外，从实务来说，如果恰当地说明了版权所属，那么被引用的作者也就不大会感到自己已经被夺去了什么，因而也就不大会来告你了。

正当使用，并不当然阻止一位发火的作者或出版者来告你，你的出版者或许告你们俩引用的材料侵犯了他的版权。如果对方起诉，正当使用只能作为你向法官提出的一个抗辩理由（辩解）而已。

Passage Two
中华人民共和国专利法

第一章 总 则

第一条 为了保护发明创造专利权,鼓励发明创造,有利于发明创造的推广应用,促进科学技术进步和创新,适应社会主义现代化建设的需要,特制定本法。

第二条 本法所称的发明创造是指发明、实用新型和外观设计。

第三条 国务院专利行政部门负责管理全国的专利工作;统一受理和审查专利申请,依法授予专利权。

省、自治区、直辖市人民政府管理专利工作的部门负责本行政区域内的专利管理工作。

第四条 申请专利的发明创造涉及国家安全或者重大利益需要保密的,按照国家有关规定办理。

第五条 对违反国家法律、社会公德或者妨害公共利益的发明创造,不授予专利权。

第六条 执行本单位的任务或者主要是利用本单位的物质技术条件所完成的发明创造为职务发明创造。职务发明创造申请专利的权利属于该单位;申请被批准后,该单位为专利权人。

非职务发明创造,申请专利的权利属于发明人或者设计人;申请被批准后,该发明人或者设计人为专利权人。

利用本单位的物质技术条件所完成的发明创造,单位与发明人或者设计人定有合同,对申请专利的权利和专利权的归属作出约定的,从其约定。

第七条 对发明人或者设计人的非职务发明创造专利申请,任何单位或者个人不得压制。

第八条 两个以上单位或者个人合作完成的发明创造、一个单位或者个人接受其他单位或者个人委托所完成的发明创造,除另有协议的以外,申请专利的权利属于完成或者共同完成的单位或者个人;申请被批准后,申请的单位或者个人为专利权人。

第九条 两个以上的申请人分别就同样的发明创造申请专利的,专利权授予最先申请的人。

第十条 专利申请权和专利权可以转让。

中国单位或者个人向外国人转让专利申请权或者专利权的,必须经国务院有关主管部门批准。

转让专利申请权或者专利权的,当事人应当订立书面合同,并向国务院专利行政部门登记,由国务院专利行政部门予以公告。专利申请权或者专利权的转让自登记之日起生效。

第十一条 发明和实用新型专利权被授予后,除本法另有规定的以外,任何单位或者个人未经专利权人许可,都不得实施其专利,即不得为生产经营目的制造、使用、许诺销售、销售、进口其专利产品,或者使用其专利方法以及使用、许诺销售、销售、进口依照该专利方法直接获得的产品。

外观设计专利权被授予后,任何单位或者个人未经专利权人许可,都不得实施其专利,即不得为生产经营目的制造、销售、进口其外观设计专利产品。

第十二条　任何单位或者个人实施他人专利的，应当与专利权人订立书面实施许可合同，向专利权人支付专利使用费。被许可人无权允许合同规定以外的任何单位或者个人实施该专利。

第十三条　发明专利申请公布后，申请人可以要求实施其发明的单位或者个人支付适当的费用。

第十四条　国有企业事业单位的发明专利，对国家利益或者公共利益具有重大意义的，国务院有关主管部门和省、自治区、直辖市人民政府报经国务院批准，可以决定在批准的范围内推广应用，允许指定的单位实施，由实施单位按照国家规定向专利权人支付使用费。

中国集体所有制单位和个人的发明专利，对国家利益或者公共利益具有重大意义，需要推广应用的，参照前款规定办理。

第十五条　专利权人有权在其专利产品或者该产品的包装上标明专利标记和专利号。

第十六条　被授予专利权的单位应当对职务发明创造的发明人或者设计人给予奖励；发明创造专利实施后，根据其推广应用的范围和取得的经济效益，对发明人或者设计人给予合理的报酬。

第十七条　发明人或者设计人有在专利文件中写明自己是发明人或者设计人的权利。

第十八条　在中国没有经常居所或者营业所的外国人、外国企业或者外国其他组织在中国申请专利的，依照其所属国同中国签订的协议或者共同参加的国际条约，或者依照互惠原则，根据本法办理。

▶ 词汇提示

发明　invention
专利行政部门　the Patent Administration Department
国务院　the State Council
专利申请　patent application
自治区　autonomous region
自治市，自治区　municipality
有害的，不利的　detrimental
实行，执行，实施　in execution of
申请　apply for
专利申请　file an application for a patent
批准，通过　approve
转让，让与　assign
生效　take effect
（法律、规定等）作出规定，使有据可依　provide for
外观设计专利权　the patent right for a design
利用　exploitation
合适的，恰当的　appropriate
应用，运用　application
附上，贴上　affix

专利标记　a patent marking
专利号　the number of the patent
酬金，报酬　remuneration
住所　residence
（国家之间的）条约，协定　treaty

▶ 法律术语

发明创造　inventions-creations
实用新型　utility model
外观设计　design
职务发明创造　a service invention-creation
非职务发明创造　a non-service invention-creation
专利权人　patentee
专利权　the patent right
发明专利　a patent for invention
互惠原则　the principle of reciprocity

▶ 要点解析

1. 本法所称的发明创造是指发明、实用新型和外观设计。

In this Law，"inventions-creations" mean inventions, utility models and designs.

此句注意专业术语的准确翻译。"发明创造"译为 inventions-creations，"实用新型"译为 utility models，"外观设计"译为 designs。

2. 申请专利的发明创造涉及国家安全或者重大利益需要保密的，按照国家有关规定办理。

Where an invention-creation for which a patent is applied for relates to the security or other vital interests of the State and is required to be kept secret, the application shall be treated in accordance with the relevant prescriptions of the State.

英语句子讲究形合，整个句子之间的逻辑联系必不可少，造成句子乍看上去关系复杂，其实并非如此，仔细分析即可，本句主要有三层意思：the invention-creation applying for the patent relates to the security or other vital interests of the State；so it is required to be kept secret；in this case the application shall be treated in accordance with the relevant prescriptions of the State.

3. 对违反国家法律、社会公德或者妨害公共利益的发明创造，不授予专利权。

No patent right shall be granted for any invention-creation that is contrary to the laws of the State or social morality or that is detrimental to public interest.

本句的翻译用 no 和 any 强调出了"绝不"的态度。两个 that 引导的从句之间是并列的关系，表示不授予专利权的两种情况。

4. 利用本单位的物质技术条件所完成的发明创造，单位与发明人或者设计人定有合同，对申请专利的权利和专利权的归属作出约定的，从其约定。

In respect of an invention-creation made by a person using the material and technical means of an entity to which he belongs, where the entity and the inventor or creator have entered into a contract in which the right to apply for and own a patent is provided for, such a provision shall apply.

此句主要是修饰成分的位置，英语中的修饰成分通常放在所修饰的事物的后面，翻译时注意表达的地道性和清楚性。

5. 中国单位或者个人向外国人转让专利申请权或者专利权的，必须经国务院有关主管部门批准。

Any assignment, by a Chinese entity or individual, of the right to apply for a patent, or of the patent right, to a foreigner must be approved by the competent department concerned of the State Council.

"国务院"译为 the State Council。句子本身信息量并不是很大，但小成分很多，翻译时注意不要漏掉任何一个意思，同时注意句子的组织。

6. 中国集体所有制单位和个人的发明专利，对国家利益或者公共利益具有重大意义，需要推广应用的，参照前款规定办理。

Any patent for invention belonging to a Chinese individual or an entity under collective ownership, which is of great significance to the interest of the State or to the public interest and is in need of spreading and application, may be treated alike by making reference to the provisions of the preceding paragraph.

英语句子主干分明，逻辑关系清楚，翻译时就要注意主句从句的安排和衔接。此句翻译时首先用了 belonging to，又用了一个 which 引导的从句，将整个句子层次清晰地连为一个整体。

 参考译文

Patent Law of the People's Republic of China

Chapter One: General Provisions

Article 1. This Law is enacted to protect patent rights for inventions-creations, to encourage inventions-creations, to foster the spreading and application of inventions-creations, and to promote the development and innovation of science and technology, for meeting the needs of the construction of socialist modernization.

Article 2. In this Law, "inventions-creations" mean inventions, utility models and designs.

Article 3. The Patent Administration Department under the State Council is responsible for the patent work throughout the country. It receives and examines patent applications and grants patent rights for inventions-creations in accordance with law.

The administrative authority for patent affairs under the people's governments of provinces, autonomous regions and municipalities directly under the central government are responsible for the administration work concerning patents in their respective administrative areas.

Article 4. Where an invention-creation for which a patent is applied for relates to the security or other vital interests of the State and is required to be kept secret, the application shall be treated in accordance with the relevant prescriptions of the State.

Article 5. No patent right shall be granted for any invention-creation that is contrary to the laws of the State or social morality or that is detrimental to public interest.

Article 6. An invention-creation, made by a person in execution of the tasks of the entity to which he belongs, or made by him mainly by using the material and technical means of the entity is a service invention-creation. For a service invention-creation, the right to apply for a patent belongs to the entity. After the application is approved, the entity shall be the patentee.

For a non-service invention-creation, the right to apply for a patent belongs to the inventor or creator. After the application is approved, the inventor or creator shall be the patentee.

In respect of an invention-creation made by a person using the material and technical means of an entity to which he belongs, where the entity and the inventor or creator have entered into a contract in which the right to apply for and own a patent is provided for, such a provision shall apply.

Article 7. No entity or individual shall prevent the inventor or creator from filing an application for a patent for a non-service invention-creation.

Article 8. For an invention-creation jointly made by two or more entities or individuals, or made by an entity or individual in execution of a commission given to it or him by another entity or individual, the right to apply for a patent belongs, unless otherwise agreed upon, to the entity or individual that made, or to the entities or individuals that jointly made, the invention-creation. After the application is approved, the entity or individual that applied for it shall be the patentee.

Article 9. Where two or more applicants file applications for patent for the identical invention-creation, the patent right shall be granted to the applicant whose application was filed first.

Article 10. The right to apply for a patent and the patent right may be assigned.

Any assignment, by a Chinese entity or individual, of the right to apply for a patent, or of the patent right, to a foreigner must be approved by the competent department concerned of the State Council.

Where the right to apply for a patent or the patent right is assigned, the parties shall conclude a written contract and register it with the Patent Administration Department under the State Council. The Patent Administration Department under the State Council shall announce the registration. The assignment shall take effect as of the date of registration.

Article 11. After the grant of the patent right for an invention or utility model, except where otherwise provided for in this Law, no entity or individual may, without the authorization of the patentee, exploit the patent, that is, make, use, offer to sell, sell or import the patented product, or use the patented process, and use, offer to sell, sell or import the product directly obtained by the patented process, for production or business purposes.

After the grant of the patent right for a design, no entity or individual may, without the authorization of the patentee, exploit the patent, that is, make, sell or import the product incorporating its or his patented design, for production or business purposes.

Article 12. Any entity or individual exploiting the patent of another shall conclude with the patentee a written license contract for exploitation and pay the patentee a fee for the exploitation of the patent. The licensee has no right to authorize any entity or individual, other than that referred to in the contract for exploitation, to exploit the patent.

Article 13. After the publication of the application for a patent for invention, the applicant may require the entity or individual exploiting the invention to pay an appropriate fee.

Article 14. Where any patent for invention, belonging to any state-owned enterprise or institution, is of great significance to the interest of the State or to the public interest, the competent departments concerned under the State Council and the people's governments of provinces, autonomous regions or municipalities directly under the central government may, after approval by the State Council, decide that the patented invention is spread and applied within the approved limits, and allow designated entities to exploit that invention. The exploiting entity shall, according to the regulations of the State, pay a fee for exploitation to the patentee.

Any patent for invention belonging to a Chinese individual or an entity under collective ownership, which is of great significance to the interest of the State or to the public interest and is in need of spreading and application, may be treated alike by making reference to the provisions of the preceding paragraph.

Article 15. The patentee has the right to affix a patent marking and to indicate the number of the patent on the patented product or on the packing of that product.

Article 16. The entity that is granted a patent right shall award to the inventor or creator of a service invention-creation a reward and, upon exploitation of the patented invention-creation, shall pay the inventor or creator a reasonable remuneration based on the extent of spreading and application and the economic benefits yielded.

Article 17. The inventor or creator has the right to be named as such in the patent document.

Article 18. Where any foreigner, foreign enterprise or other foreign organization having no habitual residence or business office in China files an application for a patent in China, the application shall be treated under this Law in accordance with any agreement concluded between the country to which the applicant belongs and China, or in accordance with any international treaty to which both countries are party, or on the basis of the principle of reciprocity.

Section II 技能拓展

 翻译技巧

法律语言的语言特征

法律语言是民族共同语在长期的法律科学和法律实践中逐步形成的、服务于一切法律活

动而且具有法律专业特色的一种社会方言，是在法制发展过程中，按法律活动（立法、司法、法律科研）的要求逐步磨砺、逐步构建的一种有别于日常语言的"技术语言"，是全民语言的一个社会功能变体，具有很强的功用性特点，如社会价值、逻辑性、技术性，也具有很强的语言性特点。

法律语言包括表述各种法律规范的用语和为诉讼活动、非诉讼的法律事务服务的司法用语。司法用语又表现为司法口语和司法书面语。司法书面语主要表现为诉讼和非诉讼法律活动中普遍运用的具有法律效力或法律意义的非规范性的法律文书的语言。一般而言，法律语言具有以下特征：

准确性与模糊性

法律之目的即为"定分止争"。因此作为法律外在形式的法律语言其法定原则就是语言的准确性，即要求法律语言务必清晰明确，不模棱两可，以达明确各方权利义务的要求。准确是法律语言的灵魂与生命，也是法律语言的基本风格格调。立法中强调一个词语应当只有一个义项而不能有两种或多种含义，强调意义固定，不能作多种解释，如缓刑、假释、正当防卫等术语，在刑法中有其固定的含义。《刑法》第三章第四十一条：

拘役的刑期，从判决执行之日起计算；判决执行以前先行羁押的，羁押一日折抵刑期一日。

本条采用具体的词语表达，对拘役的刑期进行限定，"判决执行之日""一日折抵刑期一日"等具体表达时间，保证准确。

另一方面，法律语言具有模糊性。在法律条文中以及司法实践中，法律语言运用模糊词语的现象俯拾皆是。Pearce（Maley, 1994: 28）指出，在澳大利亚和英格兰约 40% 的法庭活动需要对特定的立法条款的意义做出裁决；在美国各级法院普遍用词典作为一种审理案件的辅助工具，对法律文本进行文义解释；在我国有学者初步统计我国《刑法》法条，从《总则》到《分则》运用模糊词语共一百余条，占全部条文的 50% 以上。

法律语言的模糊性在于有限的法律规范不可能尽数对应所有的社会行为。现实社会生活千姿百态，人们用来约束社会行为的法律条文极为有限，为了调整现实生活中的相互关系，法律应尽可能地包容这些关系，因此，就必须保证法律语言的概括性，以达到法律的规范性指引的目的。如"善良风俗""社会公共利益""诚实信用""公平原则"等概括条款，本身包容性较强，涵盖多重社会价值。法律语言的模糊性还在于客观事物自身的模糊性和人对客观事物认识的不确定性。客观事物本身的模糊性，这是自然普遍现象，人们认识事物把握对象时，无法运用语言准确定义、指称或描述，采用多种解释的表达手段进行表达。"模糊"作为人们认知世界的一条重要途径，不同于"含混不清"，后者常指人们运用语言不当而产生的消极结果，是尽量要避免的现象。模糊性则是不确定性，有消极的效应，也有积极的作用。在《中华人民共和国和美利坚合众国建交联合公报》中有这么一段：

... and that it intends gradually to reduce its sale of arms to Taiwan, leading, over a period of time, to a final resolution. [……它（美国）准备逐步减少它对台湾的武器出售，并经过一段时间导致最后的解决。]

The two sides will maintain contact and hold appropriate consultations on bilateral and international issues of common interest. （双方将就共同关心的双边问题和国际问题保持接触并进行适当的磋商。）

对于究竟何时停止向台出售武器，用 gradually reduce（逐步减少），而未说明具体时间

maintain contact（保持接触）和 hold appropriate consultations（进行适当的磋商）都是模糊词语，用来表示一些未定的概念。谁也说不出它们究竟意味着多大程度，但在这里用却是恰如其分，非常贴切，这比用精确的数字表示得更准确，也更有说服力。

在法庭辩论中的控辩双方律师或合议庭中的法官出于对他人的尊重及体现自身的修养，也常使用委婉语或模糊用语以表述自己的不同意见。例如：

My lord, I take the strongest possible objection to the course proposed by my learned friend.

在此，strongest/objection 表达了不同意见，而 possible/learned/friend 显示了对他人的尊重。

Unless this account is paid within next ten days, we will take further measures.

除非在 10 天内把账付清，否则我们就要采取进一步的措施。

这句话中的 take further measures 就是模糊词语。律师完全可以用 start legal proceedings 或 bring suit 等词语来取代，但律师并没有这样做，因为他认为这个时候把话说得如此肯定，还为时过早，就采取一种模糊的说法。类似的例子在法律事务中数不胜举。

我国 1997 年的刑法第一百一十四条：

Whoever commits arson, breaches a dike, causes explosion, spreads poison or uses other dangerous means to sabotage any factory, mine, oilfield, harbor, river, water source, warehouse, house, forest, farm, threshing grounds, pasture, key pipeline, public building or any other public or private property, thereby endangering public security but causing no serious consequences, shall be sentenced to fixed-term imprisonment of not less than three years but not more than ten years.

放火、决水、爆炸、投毒或者以其他危险方法破坏工厂、矿场、油田、港口、河流、水源、仓库、住宅、森林、农场、谷场、牧场、重要管道、公共建筑物或者其他公私财产，危害公共安全，尚未造成严重后果的，处三年以上十年以下有期徒刑。

这里使用的 other 就是一个典型模糊词语，在列举了主要的犯罪手段和破坏项目之后，再加上 other dangerous means 和 other public of private property 这样的模糊词语，就使这一规定有了一定的限定性与概括性，使表义更加严密，从而更大限度地打击犯罪。如果把模糊词语省略掉或改用确切词语，这一方面会使立法失去严谨性，另一方面也很有可能使现实生活中的大量违法犯罪逃脱法律的制裁。

通用性与专门性

法律语言是服务于法律的，也是服务于生活的。所以，一方面，在语言上，它得体现统治阶级的意图，服务于法律与统治阶级；另一方面，又必须给生活以可行的指导、约束，体现生活的要求。这表现在法律语言所规定的内容上，如："国家为了公共利益的需要，可以依照法律规定对土地实行征收或者征用并给予补偿。"这个内容就规定了国家可以为了公共利益需要而依法征收或征用土地，因为法律语言是服务于国家的；同时，也规定了这种情况下的被征收或被征用者可以获得补偿，因为法律语言也是服务于公众的。法律语言中有大量的法律工作常用词语、民族共同语中的其他基本词与非基本词、文言词语和普通词语。

另外，法律沿袭发展至今，形成了一套相对固定的模式，具备了一套专用的术语，用特定的表达形式表达具体的内容，因此有很大程度的专门性。例如：术语的采用，除了对古旧语言的继承，拉丁语汇的借用，还及时地从科学技术领域术语和概念。例如：sadism（性虐待狂）源自心理学，abortion（堕胎）源自医学，artistic work（艺术作品）源自艺术，continental shelf（大陆架）源自地理学，heredity（遗传）源自生物学，ratio（比率）源自数学，incest（乱伦罪）源自社会学，monogamy（一夫一妻制）源自人口学，tariff（关税）源自经济学，average（海损）源自运输，claims（索赔）源自对外贸易，life insurance（人寿保险）源自保险等。

繁复周密与简洁明快

法律具有强制性、规范性和权威性，因此，法律语言须表达得繁复周密，让人无漏洞可钻。但繁复周密有时也会啰嗦冗赘。1835年，一位名叫Arthur Symonds的人就曾严厉批评过法律语言的啰嗦冗赘。他说："I give you that orange."（我把那个橘子给你。）这样简单的一句话在律师那里就会变成下面这个样子：

I give you all and singular, my estate and interest, right, title, claim and advantage of and in that orange, with all its rind, skin, juice, pulp and pips, and all right and advantage therein, with full power to bite, cut, suck, and otherwise eat the same, or give the same away as fully and effectively as I the said A. B. am now entitled to bite, cut, suck, or otherwise eat the same orange, or give the same away, with or without its rind, skin, juice, pulp, and pips, anything hereinbefore, or hereinafter, or in any other deed, or deeds, instrument or instruments of what nature or kind soever, to the contrary in any wise, notwithstanding.

我把所有的、独一的、属于这个橘子的和包含在这个橘子中的地产、利益、权利、资格、主张和优势都给你，包括它的外皮、内皮、橘汁、橘肉、籽粒及其内含的所有权利和优势；并赋予你充分的权力完全地有效地咬它、切它、吸它、吃它或者拿他送人，不管是带上外皮、内皮、橘汁、橘肉、籽粒还是不带这些东西，就像我，即上面所说的××，那样有权去咬它、切它、吸它、吃它或者拿他送人一样，不管是在此前，还是在此后，不管是使用什么样的文据，一个文据还是多个文据，一个契据还是多个契据，也不管是什么类型的和性质的文据或者契据。

法律语言繁复周密的特征主要体现在长句和主谓句的使用上。从法律汉语看，长句结构复杂，词语较多，形体较长，表意细致周密。例如《中华人民共和国经济合同法》第30条：

当事人一方由于不可抗力的原因不能履行经济合同的，应及时向对方通报不能履行或者需要延期履行、部分履行经济合同的理由，在取得有关证明后，允许延期履行、部分履行或者不履行，并可根据情况部分或全部免于承担违约责任。（共计103个字）

与中国立法语言的长句相比，英美法律条文则更为冗长。例如：

2A-519. LESSEES DAMAGES FOR NON-DELIVERY, REPUDIATION, DEFAULT, AND BREACH OF WARRANTY IN REGARD TO ACCEPTED GOODS.

Except as otherwise provided with respect to damages liquidated in the lease agreement (Section 2A-504) or otherwise determined pursuant to agreement of the parties (Section 1-102(3) and 2A-503)，if a lessee elects not to cover or a lessee elects to cover and the cover is by lease agreement that for any reason does not qualify for treatment under Section 2A-518(2)，or is by purchase or otherwise, the measure of damages for non-delivery or repudiation by the lessor or for rejection or revocation of acceptance by the lessee is the present value, as of the date of the default, of the then market rent minus the present value as of the same date of the original rent, computed for the remaining lease term of the original lease agreement, together with incidental and consequential damages, less expenses saved in consequence of the lessor's default.

《美国统一商法典》(UNIFORM COMMERCIAL CODE)本款由一个句子组成,共 145 个单词,包括一系列分句及其他形式的修饰语,句子结构复杂,容纳的信息量大。

主谓句表意完备周密,能准确地叙述和说明,在法律语言中也被普遍使用。在立法条文中,有时为了强调行为的主体,更不惜笔墨地一再重复主语,如《中华人民共和国宪法》第十九条至第二十六条共 16 句,它们的主语都是"国家",可谓是不厌其烦地述说,显示了法律语言的准确严密性。在司法文书中,由于大部分篇幅是叙述事实和说明理由的,为了确保得出正确的审判结论,就需要对每句话中的每一个成分都写清楚,不可有丝毫的歧义和疏漏,表意完备周密的主谓句也大量使用。

另外,法律又具有时效性和约束力,所以,法律语言又须表述得简洁明快,使人一目了然。法律语言简洁明快的特征主要体现在特定句式(如短句、短语句、非主谓句)的大量使用。法律语言表示命令、禁止语气的祈使句及结构简单、表意单纯的陈述句,都常用短句表述,如"禁止重婚""实行计划生育""刑罚分为主刑和附加刑"等。此类短句的使用,保证了法律语言的简洁性,也体现了法律的不可抗拒性。

非主谓句的使用在立法语言中占有一定的比重。非主谓句有名词性、动词性、形容词性非主谓句和叹词句,由于法律是庄重严肃的,不需要形象描绘和抒发感情,因此,法律语言一般选用动词性非主谓句。如下例:

实行婚姻自由、一夫一妻、男女平等的婚姻制度。

保护妇女、儿童和老人的合法权益。

实行计划生育。

(《婚姻法》第二条)

禁止用任何方法对公民进行侮辱、诽谤和诬告陷害。

(《宪法》第三十八条)

对于涉及国家秘密的证据,应当保密。

(《刑事诉讼法》第四十五条第二款)

在司法文书中,有时因制作司法文书的机关不言自明,也常采用非主谓句,如"现查明……""依照……,判决如下""判处被告人,……"等。

总而言之,无论是用繁复周密的长句和主谓句,还是用简洁明快的短句和非主谓句,都体现了法律语言庄重性和严谨性的特点。

法律宝典

知识产权分类与保护

知识产权,指"权利人对其所创作的智力劳动成果所享有的专有权利",一般只在有限时间期内有效。各种智力创造比如发明、文学和艺术作品,以及在商业中使用的标志、名称、图像以及外观设计,都可被认为是某一个人或组织所拥有的知识产权。

智慧财产为无形资产,包括专利、商标、著作权及经注册或未注册的设计权。知识产权事实上并非真正意义上的产权,它更像是一种垄断特权——在一段时间内对于智慧活动成果的垄断。实证经验表明,知识产权的保护能够确保智慧活动创造者的利益受到保护,并鼓励更多智慧活动的产生，从而对社会经济的发展起到推进作用，其他公众也能从知识产权保护中受益。知识产权所有者的利益可以通过对使用者收取费用，或在一段时间内禁止他人抄袭、竞争来获得保护。

通过授予这种垄断权利，智慧活动的创造者能够获得对其劳动成果的补偿。例如一个厂商可能为了开发一种新产品而投入了 10 年的精力与资金，如果没有知识产权对其新产品的保护，则最后的结果很可能是在其新产品推出后，其他厂商可以在没有任何成本的情况下立即抄袭其成果，从而也因此能够以更低价格出售相同或类似产品，损害原创作者的利益。

知识产权分为两类：

（1）工业产权，它包括发明（专利）、商标、工业品外观设计以及原产地地理标志等。专利保护期一般 20 年，工业设计保护至少 10 年，而商标则可无限期保护；

（2）著作权，它包括文学和艺术作品，诸如小说、诗歌和戏剧、电影、音乐作品；艺术作品诸如绘画、摄影和雕塑以及建筑设计。与著作权相关的权利包括表演艺术家对其表演的权利、录音制品制作者对其录音制品的权利以及广播电视组织对其广播和电视节目的权利。著作权持续到作者逝世后至少 50 年。

此外还有一种特殊的知识产权：商业秘密。企业可以认定任何信息为"商业秘密"，禁止能够接触这些机密的人将秘密透露出去，一般是通过合约的形式来达到这种目的。只要接触到这些秘密的人在获取这些机密前签署合约或同意保密，他们就必须守约。商业秘密的好处是没有时限，而且任何东西都可被认定为商业秘密。例如可口可乐的配方就属商业秘密，100 多年来外界都无法获知可口可乐的全部成分。

▶ 术语积累

intangible personal property　无形的人身财产（权）
patent law　专利法
trade marks　商标
patentable　可获得专利的
monopoly right　专有权
database right　数据权
performers' right　表演权
goodwill　信誉
confidential information　保密信息
negative form of protection　否定（或消极）形式的保护
derogatory treatment of the work　对作品的贬毁性处理（或使用）
industrial property　工业产权
compulsory licenses　强制许可
delegated legislation　授权立法
novel　新颖性
originality　独创性
passing off　假冒经营；冒名经营

appropriation 窃取；非法挪用；盗用
imitate 仿制
authorize 授权
right of priority 优先权
forfeiture of the patent 丧失专利权
ex officio 依职权
industrial design 外观设计
examination for and approval of 审批
retroactive effect 追溯力
novelty 新颖性
inventiveness 创造性
practical applicability 实用性
duration, cessation and invalidation of patent right 专利权的期限、终止和无效
preliminarily approve 初步审定
the Trademark Review and Adjudication Board 商标评审委员会
copyright collective administration organizations 版权集体管理组织
commissioned work 委托作品
a work of joint authorship 合作作品
a copyright licensing contract 版权许可合同
neighboring rights 邻接权
indications of source 货源标记
appellation of origin 原产地标记
the infringing act 侵权行为
deliberation 深思熟虑
de minimis 法律不计较琐细小事
prima facie 乍看起来
typeface 铅字字体
graphic work 图解作品
exploiter of works 著作的利用者
World Intellectual Property Organization 世界知识产权组织
publishing contract 出版合同
statutory bar 法定障碍
statutory classes 法定分类
Patent and Trademark Office 专利与商标局
licensee 被许可人；被许可方
franchise 特许
common-law trademark 共同法商标；事实商标；不注册商标
U.S. Patent Office 美国专利署
declaratory judgment 确认判决

common-used name　通用名称
registration　注册；登记
patent attorney　专利律师
technology transfer　技术转让
know-how　诀窍；专有技术
abstract of title　所有权证书摘要；产权说明书
certificate of title　所有权证明书；所有权凭证
freedom of press　出版自由
imprimatur　出版许可；出版执照

Section III　巩固练习

词汇与短语

1. certification trade marks
2. defensive trade marks
3. co-ownership
4. copyrightable
5. copyright royalty
6. injunction
7. infringement action
8. three-dimensional marks
9. the principle of reciprocity
10. infringement
11. 反垄断法；反托拉斯法
12. 专利联营（制）
13. 认证标志
14. 注册商标
15. 商品商标
16. 服务商标
17. 集体商标
18. 证明商标
19. 驰名商标
20. 联号商标

句子与段落

1. Intellectual property law is the legal right that relates to intangible property such as copyright, registered designs, trade marks and patents.
2. Copyright is a right to prevent the unauthorized reproduction by a third party of the tangible form in which a person has chose to express his ideas, for example, in a book, a musical composition, a painting or a cinematograph film.
3. A trade mark enables providers of goods and services to distinguish their goods and services from those of others.
4. Patent law gives an inventor the sole and exclusive right to exploit and to authorise another

to exploit an invention.
5. It is a basic rule of copyright law that copyright does not protect ideas but only the expression of ideas.
6. A trade mark is the mark of a particular type of property.
7. Registration will initially be for seven years.
8. 对已注册的商品，以同一或类似性商标使用于商品或服务，即构成对商标的侵权。
9. 专利法的理论基础是对新颖发明的保护。
10. 发明必须具有新颖性，并有一定实用性。
11. 小型发明会在 12 个月内得到保护。
12. 标准专利如交纳更新费，自申请之日起 16 年内得到保护。
13. 著作权不会因对产品所依据的设计文件的周期的草拟而每次都产生。
14. 图画作品包括任何的绘画、图画、图表、地图、海路图或说明书以及任何的雕刻、蚀刻画、石版画、木刻画或类似的作品。

Unit Ten

Law of Succession
继 承 法

Section I 译例研究

Passage One
Last Will of Michael Joseph Jackson

I, MICHAEL JOSEPH JACKSON, a resident of the State of California, declare this to be my last Will, and do hereby revoke all former wills and codicils made by me.

I

I declare that I am not married. My marriage to DEBORAH JEAN ROWE JACKSON has been dissolved. I have three children now living, PRINCE MICHAEL JACKSON, JR., PARIS MICHAEL KATHERINE JACKSON and PRINCE MICHAEL JOSEPH JACKSON, II. I have no other children, living or deceased.

II

It is my intention by this Will to dispose of all property which I am entitled to dispose of by will. I specifically refrain from exercising all powers of appointment that I may possess at the time of my death.

III

I give my entire estate to the Trustee or Trustees then acting under that certain Amended and Restated Declaration of Trust executed on March 22, 2002 by me as Trustee and Trustor which is called the MICHAEL JACKSON FAMILY TRUST, giving effect to any amendments thereto made prior to my death. All such assets shall be held, managed and distributed as a part of said Trust according to its terms and not as a separate testamentary trust.

If for any reason this gift is not operative or is invalid, or if the aforesaid Trust fails or has been revoked, I give my residuary estate to the Trustee or Trustees named to act in the MICHAEL JACKSON FAMILY TRUST, as Amended and Restated on March 22,2002，and I direct said Trustee or Trustees to divide, administer, hold and distribute the trust estate pursuant to the provisions of said Trust, as hereinabove referred to as such provisions now exist to the same extent and in the same manner as though that certain Amended and Restated Declaration of Trust, were here in set forth in full, but without giving effect to any subsequent amendments after the date of this Will. The Trustee, Trustees, or any successor Trustee named in such Trust Agreement shall serve without bond.

IV

I direct that all federal estate taxes and state inheritance or succession taxes payable upon or resulting from or by reason of my death (herein "Death Taxes") attributable to property which is part of the trust estate of the MICHAEL JACKSON FAMILY TRUST, including property which passes to said trust from my probate estate shall be paid by the Trustee of said trust in accordance with its terms. Death Taxes attributable to property passing outside this Will, other than property constituting the trust estate of the trust intentioned in the preceding sentence, shall be charged against the taker of said property.

The term "my executors" as used in this Will shall include any duly acting personal representative or representatives of my estate. No individual acting as such need post a bond.

V

I appoint JOHN BRANCA, JOHN MCCLAIN and BARRY SLLIGEL as co-Executors of this Will. In the event of any of their deaths, resignations, inability, failure or refusal to serve or continue to serve as a co-Executor, the other shall serve and no replacement need be named. The co-Executors serving at any time after my death may name one or more replacements to serve in the event that none of the three named individuals is willing or able to serve at anytime.

I hereby give to my Executors, full power and authority at any time or times to sell, lease, mortgage, pledge, exchange or otherwise dispose of the property, whether real or, personal comprising my estate, upon such terms as my Executors shall deem best, to continue any business enterprises, to purchase assets from my estate, to continue in force and pay insurance premiums on any insurance policy, including life insurance, owned by my estate, and for any of the foregoing purposes to make, execute and deliver any and all deeds, contracts, mortgages, bills of sale or other instruments necessary or desirable therefor. In addition, I give my Executors full power to invest and reinvest the estate funds and assets in any kind of property, real, personal or mixed, and every kind of investment, specifically including, but not by way of limitation, corporate obligations of every kind and stocks, preferred or common, and interests in investment trusts and shares in investment companies, and any common trust fund administered by any corporate executor hereunder, which men of prudent discretion and intelligence acquire for their own account.

VI

Except as otherwise provided in this Will or in the Trust referred to in Article III hereof, I have intentionally omitted to provide for my heirs. I have intentionally omitted to provide for my former wife, DEBORAH JEAN ROWE JACKSON.

VII

If at the time of my death I own or have an interest in property located outside of the State of California requiring ancillary administration, I appoint my domiciliary Executors as ancillary Executors for such property. I give to said domiciliary Executors the following additional powers, rights and privileges to be exercised in their sole and absolute discretion, with reference to such property: to cause such ancillary administration to be commenced, carried on and completed; to determine what assets, if any, are to be sold by the ancillary Executors; to pay directly or to advance funds from the California estate to the ancillary Executors for the payment of all claims, taxes, costs and administration expenses, including compensation of the ancillary Executors and attorneys' fees incurred by reason of the ownership of such property and by such ancillary administration; and upon completion of such ancillary administration, I authorize and direct the ancillary Executors to distribute, transfer and deliver the residue of such property to the domiciliary Executors herein, to be distributed by them under the terms of this Will, it being my intention that my entire estate shall be administered as a unit and that my domiciliary Executors shall supervise and control, so far as permissible by local law, any ancillary administration proceedings deemed necessary in the settlement of my estate.

VIII

If any of my children are minors at the time of my death, I nominate my mother, KATHERINE JACKSON as guardian of the persons and estates of such minor children. If KATHERINE JACKSON fails to survive me, or is unable or unwilling to act as guardian, I nominate DIANA ROSS as guardian of the persons and estates of such minor children.

I subscribe my name to this Will this 7th day of July, 2002.

MICHAEL JOSEPH JACKSON

On the date written below, MICHAEL JOSEPH JACKSON, declared to us, the undersigned, that the foregoing instrument consisting of five (5) pages, including the page signed by us as witnesses, was his Will and requested us to act as witnesses to it. He thereupon signed this Will in our presence, all of us being present at the same time. We now, at his request, in his presence and in the presence of each other, subscribe our names as witnesses.

Each of us is now more than eighteen(18) years of age and a competent witness and resides at the address set forth after his name.

Each of us is acquainted with MICHAEL JOSEPH JACKSON. At this time, he is over the age of eighteen(18) years and, to the best of our knowledge, he is of sound mind and is not acting under duress, menace, fraud, misrepresentation or undue influence.

We declare under penalty of perjury that the foregoing is true and correct.
Executed on July 7th, 2002 at 5:00pm, Los Angeles

▶ 词汇提示

codicil   *n.* 遗嘱的附件
deceased   *adj.* 亡故的
dispose   *v.* 准备做
refrain   *v.* 克制
estate   *n.* 遗产
Trustee   *n.* 受托人
Trustor   *n.* 委托人
testamentary   *adj.* 遗嘱中有的
invalid   *adj.* 无效的
aforesaid   *adj.* 上述的
revoke   *v.* 取消
residuary   *adj.* 剩余的
pursuant   *adj.* 依据的
provision   *n.* 条款
hereinabove   *adv.* 在上文
successor   *n.* 继任者
bond   *n.* 合同，契约
payable   *adj.* 应付的
attributable   *adj.* 可归于……的
probate   *n.* 遗嘱检验
pledge   *v.* 抵押
hereunder   *adv.* 在下文
prudent   *adj.* 谨慎的
discretion   *n.* 慎重
heir   *n.* 继承人
ancillary   *adj.* 附属的
domiciliary   *adj.* 家庭的
residue   *n.* 剩余财产
deem   *v.* 相信
duress   *n.* 威胁
menace   *n.* 胁迫
undue   *adj.* 不适当的
penalty   *n.* 惩罚
perjury   *n.* 伪证

要点解析

1. a resident of "居住于"。此处翻译关系到一种翻译方法：转性译法。resident 原本是名词，为了表达更加清晰，译文就使用了动词。

2. ... declare this to be my last Will, and do hereby revoke all former wills and codicils made by me.

我宣布这是我最终的遗嘱，下列所有的条款都是我本意授权的。

此处的翻译使用了省略法，原文中 revoke all former wills 意味着 last Will，意思重复，所以译文中省去不译。

3. I have three children now living, PRINCE MICHAEL JACKSON, JR.，PARIS MICHAEL KATHERINE JACKSON and PRINCE MICHAEL JOSEPH JACKSON, II.

我有三名子女，普林斯·迈克尔·杰克逊，帕里斯·迈克尔·凯瑟琳·杰克逊，普林斯·迈克尔·杰克逊 II。

此处使用了省略法。为了使表达更加自然，译文将原文中的 now living 省去了。

4. It is my intention by this Will to dispose of all property which I am entitled to dispose of by will. I specifically refrain from exercising all powers of appointment that I may possess at the time of my death.

此遗嘱代表了我处置全部财产的意愿，并且我愿意放弃我死亡时的财产处置权。

此处涉及的翻译方法是增词译法。原文本是两个以句号隔开的独立句子，而译文中则增用了"并且"这一连词将两个句子衔接起来，使表达更为顺畅。

5. If for any reason this gift is not operative or is invalid, or if the aforesaid Trust fails or has been revoked...

如果因为任何原因导致这份遗产失效，或上述信托基金破产或被撤销。

此处用的翻译法为正反译法。原文中 not operative 本是否定，而译文则从正面进行了翻译，相比原文表达的"没有作用"，译文的"失效"更为精简流畅。

6. I hereby give to my Executors, full power and authority at any time or times to sell, lease, mortgage, pledge, exchange or otherwise dispose of the property.

我在此授予我的执行人完全权力在任何时间出售、出租、抵押、交换或以其他方式处理财产。

此处运用了合词译法，power 和 authority 意思相近，故译文就取其共同的意思"权力"，更贴合读者的习惯。

7. ... I have intentionally omitted to provide for my heirs. I have intentionally omitted to provide for my former wife, DEBORAH JEAN ROWE JACKSON.

我是有意没有留遗产给我的继承人以及前妻黛博拉·简·罗薇·杰克逊。

此处用了省略法，原文很明显可以看出重复的句式，而译文中为了使表达更为清晰，省略了重复句式。

8. ... and upon completion of such ancillary administration, I authorize and direct the ancillary Executors to distribute, transfer and deliver the residue of such property to the domiciliary Executors herein...

当附件遗产监管结束时,我授权并且制定我的附加遗产监管人将剩余财产转到遗产执行人名下。

此处的翻译方法也是合词译法,原文中三个词义有重复的"distribute, transfer and deliver"都被合译成"转移",显得简洁明了。

9. If KATHERINE JACKSON fails to survive me, or is unable or unwilling to act as guardian, I nominate DIANA ROSS as guardian of the persons and estates of such minor children.

如果凯瑟琳·杰克逊已经去世,没有能力或者不愿意担当监护人,那么我指定戴安娜·罗斯作为监护人。

这句话里用了两种翻译方法,第一种是正反译法,原文中 fails to survive me 意味"没有活过我",而译文则从正面翻译成"去世"以让表达更为自然;第二种是省略法,as guardian of the persons and estates of such minor children 曾在上文出现过一次并且进行了完整的翻译,而在这句话里译文仅以"监护人"带过。

10. Each of us is now more than eighteen(18) years of age and a competent witness and resides at the address set forth after his name.

我们都已经过了18周岁,可以胜任见证人一职,我们也都居住在加州。

此处的翻译方法是转性译法,原文中的 competent 本是形容词,而译文则使用了动词"胜任"使表达自然。

11. We declare under penalty of perjury that the foregoing is true and correct.

我们宣誓没有触犯伪证罪条款,上述所有内容都属实。

此处运用了合词译法,原文 true 和 correct 二词都有"真实的"的意思,所以译文将其合译成"属实",更加简练利落。

 **参考译文**

迈克尔·杰克逊最终遗嘱

我,迈克尔·杰克逊,居住于加利福尼亚州,我宣布这是我最终的遗嘱,下列所有的条款都是我本人授权的。

一

我宣布我目前没有婚姻关系,我和黛博拉·简·罗薇·杰克逊的婚姻关系已经解除。我有三名子女,普林斯·迈克尔·杰克逊、帕里斯·迈克尔·凯瑟琳·杰克逊、普林斯·迈克尔·杰克逊 II,我没有其他子女在世或死亡。

二

此遗嘱代表了我处置全部财产的意愿,并且我愿意放弃我死亡时的财产处置权。

三

我将全部财产交付委托管理人管理,我曾做出一份修改和重新表述的信托声明并于2002年3月22日执行,通过迈克尔·杰克逊家庭信托明确了委托人和委托管理人关系,在我死前所作的任何修正都是有效的。委托管理的全部财产的保有、管理和分配都将根据规章执行，不能视为单独依遗嘱建立的信托基金。

如果因为任何原因导致这份遗产失效，或上述信托基金破产或被撤销，我将剩余财产转交给迈克尔·杰克逊家庭基金任命的其他委托管理人，该信托基金于2002年3月22日进行了章程修改和重新表述。我授权委托管理人按信托基金条款分割、管理、保有和分配信托基金，上述条款同修订和重新表述的信托宣言一样适用同样范围和同等方式。修订和重新表述的信托宣言在此全文表述，但并没有规定可以进行任何的后续修改。委托管理人或任何继承委托管理人应依照执行。

四

我指定所有因我死亡或在我死亡之时需支付的联邦遗产税和州继承税（简称"遗产税"）由迈克尔·杰克逊家庭信托基金财产支付，包括由我的遗嘱检验财产归入以上基金的财产部分应由上述受托人按照相关条款进行。本遗嘱所涉遗产之外的遗产税，除了构成基金财产的部分，应由上述财产获得者支付。

"我的执行人"一词在此遗嘱中应包括任何适时行为的财产个人代表。有此行为的个人无须签署任何契约。

五

我指定约翰·布兰卡、约翰·麦克兰和巴里·西格尔作为此遗嘱共同执行人。如出现他们死亡、放弃、无行为能力、未能或者拒绝继续作为遗嘱共同执行人的情形，其他执行人应继续履行，不得指定其他代执行人。共同执行人在我死后可指定一名或多名代执行人履行此三名执行人不愿或不能实现的行为。

我在此授予我的执行人完全权力在任何时间出售、出租、抵押、交换或以其他方式处理财产，不论是不动产，还是个人财产，以继续企业贸易、购买资产、购买保险，包括人寿保险，或为以上目的而缔约、履行或交付契约、合同、抵押、抵押证券或其他必要的形式。另外，我赋予我的执行人完全权力对财产基金以任何形式的财产、不动产、个人或混合财产进行投资、再投资，包括但不限于各种形式的公司债务，首选或普通股，对信托基金投资和投资公司股份的投资，以及由共同执行人管理的任何普通信托基金。

六

除了在遗嘱中提到的信托基金外，我是有意没有留遗产给我的继承人以及前妻黛博拉·简·罗薇·杰克逊。

七

在我去世时，如果我拥有加州以外的房产，或者享有加州以外房产的收益需要做附加遗产监管，我指定我的遗嘱执行人作为这些财产的附加遗产监管人。我给予遗嘱执行人以下额外的权利和义务，他们可以自行处理以下提到的财产：

当有遗产需要附加遗产监管时，他们可以决定是否要出售部分遗产；他们可以从遗产中直接获得，或是洛杉矶地产的预付经费中获得来支付所有的债权，税务，花费以及管理费用，其中也包括补偿附加遗产监管人以及律师的费用；当附件遗产监管结束时，我授权并且制定我的附加遗产监管人将剩余财产转到遗产执行人名下，由他们监管和控制，并且在当地法律允许的情况下，可以对这些附加财产做出任何有必要的处置。

八

如果在我死时我的孩子仍未成年，那么我指定我的母亲，凯瑟琳·杰克逊为孩子的监护人，并且保管属于这个未成年孩子的遗产。如果凯瑟琳·杰克逊已经去世，没有能力或者不愿意担当监护人，那么我指定戴安娜·罗斯作为监护人。

签名时间：2002年7月7日

迈克尔·约瑟夫·杰克逊

在签名时间下面，迈克尔·约瑟夫·杰克逊向我们宣布，以上的5页，包括我们签名作为见证人的那页，将会成为他的遗嘱，并且要求我们作为他的遗嘱见证人。他随后当着我们的面签名，当时我们所有人都在场。而我们应他的请求，当着他的面也签下我们的名字，作为遗嘱的见证人。

我们都已经年满18周岁，可以胜任见证人一职，我们也都居住在加州。

我们都和迈克尔·约瑟夫·杰克逊意见一致。此时，他已经年满18周岁，就我们所知，意识健全，并没有受到束缚，胁迫，欺骗或是在过度压力下曲解意思。

我们宣誓没有触犯伪证罪条款，上述所有内容都属实。

此遗嘱从2002年7月7日下午5点开始生效，洛杉矶。

>> Passage Two
中华人民共和国继承法

第一章 总 则

第一条 根据《中华人民共和国宪法》规定，为保护公民的私有财产的继承权，制定本法。

第二条 继承从被继承人死亡时开始。

第三条 遗产是公民死亡时遗留的个人合法财产，包括：

（一）公民的收入；

（二）公民的房屋、储蓄和生活用品；

（三）公民的林木、牲畜和家禽；

（四）公民的文物、图书资料；

（五）法律允许公民所有的生产资料；

（六）公民的著作权、专利权中的财产权利；

（七）公民的其他合法财产。

第四条 个人承包应得的个人收益，依照本法规定继承。个人承包，依照法律允许由继承人继续承包的，按照承包合同办理。

第五条 继承开始后，按照法定继承办理；有遗嘱的，按照遗嘱继承或者遗赠办理；有遗赠扶养协议的，按照协议办理。

第六条 无行为能力人的继承权、受遗赠权，由他的法定代理人代为行使。

限制行为能力人的继承权、受遗赠权，由他的法定代理人代为行使，或者征得法定代理人同意后行使。

第七条 继承人有下列行为之一的，丧失继承权：

（一）故意杀害被继承人的；

（二）为争夺遗产而杀害其他继承人的；

（三）遗弃被继承人的，或者虐待被继承人情节严重的；

（四）伪造、篡改或者销毁遗嘱，情节严重的。

第八条 继承权纠纷提起诉讼的期限为二年，自继承人知道或者应当知道其权利被侵犯之日起计算。但是，自继承开始之日起超过二十年的，不得再提起诉讼。

第二章 法定继承

第九条 继承权男女平等。

第十条 遗产按照下列顺序继承：

第一顺序：配偶、子女、父母。

第二顺序：兄弟姐妹、祖父母、外祖父母。

继承开始后，由第一顺序继承人继承，第二顺序继承人不继承。没有第一顺序继承人继承的，由第二顺序继承人继承。

本法所说的子女，包括婚生子女、非婚生子女、养子女和有扶养关系的继子女。

本法所说的父母，包括生父母、养父母和有扶养关系的继父母。

本法所说的兄弟姐妹，包括同父母的兄弟姐妹、同父异母或者同母异父的兄弟姐妹、养兄弟姐妹、有扶养关系的继兄弟姐妹。

第十一条 被继承人的子女先于被继承人死亡的，由被继承人的子女的晚辈直系血亲代位继承。代位继承人一般只能继承他的父亲或者母亲有权继承的遗产份额。

第十二条 丧偶儿媳对公、婆，丧偶女婿对岳父、岳母，尽了主要赡养义务的，作为第一顺序继承人。

第十三条 同一顺序继承人继承遗产的份额，一般应当均等。

对生活有特殊困难的缺乏劳动能力的继承人，分配遗产时，应当予以照顾。

对被继承人尽了主要扶养义务或者与被继承人共同生活的继承人，分配遗产时，可以多分。

有扶养能力和有扶养条件的继承人，不尽扶养义务的，分配遗产时，应当不分或者少分。

继承人协商同意的，也可以不均等。

第十四条 对继承人以外的依靠被继承人扶养的缺乏劳动能力又没有生活来源的人，或者继承人以外的对被继承人扶养较多的人，可以分给他们适当的遗产。

第十五条 继承人应当本着互谅互让、和睦团结的精神，协商处理继承问题。遗产分割的时间、办法和份额，由继承人协商确定。协商不成的，可以由人民调解委员会调解或者向人民法院提起诉讼。

 词汇提示

家禽　　poultry

文物　cultural object
生产资料　means of production
法定代理人　statutory agent
婚生子女　legitimate children
非婚生子女　illegitimate children
生父母　natural parents
养父母　adoptive parents
遗产分割　partition the estate
人民调解委员会　People's Mediation Committee
继承人　successor

要点解析

1. 根据《中华人民共和国宪法》规定，为保护公民的私有财产的继承权，制定本法。

This Law is enacted pursuant to the provisions of the Constitution of the People's Republic of China with a view to protecting the right of citizens to inherit private property.

此处涉及的翻译方法是换序译法，原文中目的在前事件在后，而译文中则是事件在前目的在后，使表达更为顺畅。

2. 个人承包，依照法律允许由继承人继续承包的，按照承包合同办理。

Contracting by an individual, if permitted by law to be continued by the successor, shall be treated in accordance with the terms of the contract.

此处用到的翻译法是转态译法。原文中"办理"是主动态，而译文中则使用了被动态 be treated。

3. 有遗嘱的，按照遗嘱继承或者遗赠办理；有遗赠扶养协议的，按照协议办理。

Where a will exists, it shall be handled in accordance with testamentary succession or as legacy; where there is an agreement for legacy in return for support, the former shall be handled in accordance with the terms of the agreement.

此处用了增词两次译法，原文中第一个分号后的两个句子都是无主句，但是译文中则用了 it 和 the former 加以补足，使得表达更加自然，更加贴合读者习惯。

4. "故意杀害被继承人的"译为 intentional killing of the decedent。

此处翻译涉及的翻译方法是转性译法。原文中"杀害"是动词，而译文则使用了名词"killing"。

5. 但是，自继承开始之日起超过二十年的，不得再提起诉讼。

No legal proceedings, however, may be instituted after the expiration of a period of 20 years from the day succession began.

此处的翻译方法是换序译法，原文是转折词位于句首，而译文的转折副词 however 则位于句中。

6. 丧偶儿媳对公、婆，丧偶女婿对岳父、岳母，尽了主要赡养义务的，作为第一顺序继承人。

Widowed daughters-in-law or sons-in-law who have made the predominant contributions in maintaining their parents-in-law shall, in relationship to their parents-in-law, be regarded as successors first in order.

此句的翻译中涉及两种翻译方法，第一种是合译法，原文中"丧偶儿媳"和"丧偶女婿"是分开说的，而译文中则是 Widowed daughters-in-law or sons-in-law 将二者合并；第二种是增词译法，原文中并未明示，而译文中则增加了 in relationship to their parents-in-law 以充分表明关系。

7. 对生活有特殊困难的缺乏劳动能力的继承人，分配遗产时，应当予以照顾。

At the time of distributing the estate, due consideration shall be given to successors who are unable to work and have special financial difficulties.

此处也用到了两种翻译方法，第一种是换序译法，原文是时间状语"分配遗产时"位于句中，而译文则是把时间状语 At the time of distributing the estate 提前至句首；第二种是转态译法，原文中"予以"是主动态，而译文中 be given 则是被动态。

8. 对继承人以外的依靠被继承人扶养的缺乏劳动能力又没有生活来源的人，或者继承人以外的对被继承人扶养较多的人，可以分给他们适当的遗产。

An appropriate share of the estate may be given to a person, other than a successor, who depended on the support of the decedent and who neither can work nor has a source of income, or to a person, other than a successor, who was largely responsible for supporting the decedent.

此句中有两处地方共同涉及了换序译法。"……的人"，两处原文都是定语置于中心词"人"之前，而译文中"... to a person, other than a successor, who..."两处都是将定语置于中心词 person 之后。

9. 继承人应当本着互谅互让、和睦团结的精神，协商处理继承问题。

Questions pertaining to succession should be dealt with through consultation by and among the successors in the spirit of mutual understanding and mutual accommodation, as well as of amity and unity.

此处用到的翻译方法是转态译法，原文中"处理"本是主动态，而译文中则使用了被动态 be dealt with。

参考译文

Law of Succession of the People's Republic of China

Chapter I   General Provisions

Article 1. This Law is enacted pursuant to the provisions of the Constitution of the People's Republic of China with a view to protecting the right of citizens to inherit private property.

Article 2. Succession begins at the death of a citizen.

Article 3. Estate denotes the lawful property owned by a citizen personally at the time of his death, which consists of:

(1) his income;
(2) his houses, savings and articles of everyday use;
(3) his forest trees, livestock and poultry;
(4) his cultural objects, books and reference materials;
(5) means of production lawfully owned by him;
(6) his property rights pertaining to copyright and patent rights;
(7) his other lawful property.

Article 4. Personal benefits accruing from a contract entered into by an individual are heritable in accordance with the provisions of this Law. Contracting by an individual, if permitted by law to be continued by the successor, shall be treated in accordance with the terms of the contract.

Article 5. Succession shall, after its opening, be handled in accordance with the provisions of statutory succession; where a will exists, it shall be handled in accordance with testamentary succession or as legacy; where there is an agreement for legacy in return for support, the former shall be handled in accordance with the terms of the agreement.

Article 6. The right to inheritance or legacy of a competent person shall be exercised on his behalf by his statutory agent.

The right to inheritance or legacy of a person with limited capacity shall be exercised on his behalf by his statutory agent or by such person himself after obtaining the consent of his statutory agent.

Article 7. A successor shall be disinherited upon his commission of any one of the following acts:
(1) intentional killing of the decedent;
(2) killing any other successor in fighting over the estate;
(3) a serious act of abandoning or maltreating the decedent;
(4) a serious act of forging, tampering with or destroying the will.

Article 8. The time limit for institution of legal proceedings pertaining to disputes over the right to inheritance is two years, counting from the day the successor became or should have become aware of the violation of his right to inheritance. No legal proceedings, however, may be instituted after the expiration of a period of 20 years from the day succession began.

Chapter II   Statutory Succession

Article 9. Males and females are equal in their right to inheritance.

Article 10. The estate of the decedent shall be inherited in the following order:

First in order: spouse, children, parents.

Second in order: brothers and sisters, paternal grandparents, maternal grandparents.

When succession opens, the successor(s) first in order shall inherit to the exclusion of the successor(s) second in order. The successor(s) second in order shall inherit in default of any successor first in order.

The "children" referred to in this Law include legitimate children, illegitimate children and adopted children, as well as step-children who supported or were supported by the decedent.

The "parents" referred to in this Law include natural parents and adoptive parents, as well as step-parents who supported or were supported by the decedent.

The "brothers and sisters" referred to in this Law include blood brothers and sisters, brothers and sisters of half blood, adopted brothers and sisters, as well as step-brothers and step-sisters who supported or were supported by the decedent.

Article 11. Where a decedent survived his child, the direct lineal descendants of the predeceased child inherit in subrogation. Descendants who inherit in subrogation generally shall take only the share of the estate their father or mother was entitled to.

Article 12. Widowed daughters-in-law or sons-in-law who have made the predominant contributions in maintaining their parents-in-law shall, in relationship to their parents-in-law, be regarded as successors first in order.

Article 13. Successors same in order shall, in general, inherit in equal shares.

At the time of distributing the estate, due consideration shall be given to successors who are unable to work and have special financial difficulties.

At the time of distributing the estate, successors who have made the predominant contributions in maintaining the decedent or have lived with the decedent may be given a larger share.

At the time of distributing the estate, successors who had the ability and were in a position to maintain the decedent but failed to fulfil their duties shall be given no share or a smaller share of the estate.

Successors may take unequal shares if an agreement to that effect is reached among them.

Article 14. An appropriate share of the estate may be given to a person, other than a successor, who depended on the support of the decedent and who neither can work nor has a source of income, or to a person, other than a successor, who was largely responsible for supporting the decedent.

Article 15. Questions pertaining to succession should be dealt with through consultation by and among the successors in the spirit of mutual understanding and mutual accommodation, as well as of amity and unity. The time and mode for partitioning the estate and the shares shall be decided by the successors through consultation. If no agreement is reached through consultation, they may apply to a People's Mediation Committee for mediation or institute legal proceedings in a people's court.

Section II 技能拓展

 翻译技巧

法律翻译的基本原则

法律语言是一种具有规约性的语言分支，因此在翻译中，综合翻译的总体标准同样适用

于法律翻译。如严复的"信、达、雅",奈达的"功能对等"及翻译界广泛接受的"忠实""通顺""流畅"等翻译标准,在法律翻译中都起着重要的指导作用。但是,与其他语言相比,法律语言最重要的特点是准确、严密。当然法律语言也注重文采,但当法律翻译中文采与准确不可兼得时,必须舍雅而求信;另一方面,好的译文应当能正确反映出原文的内容和风格,即语言功能对等。但法律翻译中更应当注重的是法律功能对等(legal function),法律功能对等指原语和目的语在法律上所起的作用和效果的对等。

一、准确性与对等性原则

准确性是法律语言的生命,更是法律语言的灵魂。法律翻译处理法律语言材料时,必须固守准确性这一首要原则。例如:reasonable person 是"普通正常人",而非"通情达理的人"。香港遗产法中的 personal representative 不能误译作"个人代表",而是指"遗嘱执行人",它包括 executor(男遗嘱执行人)、executrix(女遗嘱执行人)或遗产管理人,包括 administrator(男遗产管理人)、administratrix(女遗产管理人),都是由法庭指定管理死者遗产的人。

看下面的例子:

The contents of contract should be agreed upon by the parties thereto **and generally** shall include the following causes:

(1) Designation or names and domicile of the parties
(2) The targeted matter
(3) Quantity
(4) Quality

合同的内容由当事人协商并达成一致,一般包括以下条款:

(一)当事人的名称或者姓名和住所
(二)目标物
(三)数量
(四)质量

上例的翻译中有两处不太好。agreed upon 应该被译为"协商"吗?The suggested matter 是"目标物"的意思吗?这样的翻译就不够准确,没有明确的表达出原意。agreed upon 的原意应该是经过协商而达到统一的意见,所以应该翻译为"约定";而 The suggested matter 在法律英语中的准确译法应该是"标的物"。

法律翻译中所谓准确性,就是要求翻译法律文件应当表达清楚具体,多注意两种语言在表达上的差异,绝对避免因使用错误的词语而失去准确性,从而产生不同的法律后果。对法律专业术语的翻译要词义准确,最忌望文生义。例如:Royalty payments,不是王室支付费用,而是使用费,指在每次复制或利用受版权或专利权保护的作品或专利发明时,应当向作者或发明人支付的报酬。"国际公约"就不能译成 public international treaty,因为这里的"国际公约"是指许多国家为解决某一重大问题而举行国际会议最后缔约的多边条约,所以应译成 general multilateral convention;"互不侵犯条约"应译成 treaty of mutual non-aggressions,而不译成 pact of mutual non-aggression,因为 pact 常被认为比 treaty 较不重要或是约束力较弱的协定。"诉讼参加人"不应译成 litigant,而应译成 litigant participant,因为它是指参与诉讼的人,包括"当事人、第三人、共同诉讼人"等;而 litigant 主要指"诉讼当事人",即"原告和被告"。"法人权限"不译成 authority of legal body,应译为 corporate power,这里 power

是指"权利范围"。

法律翻译的对等性,指在具体翻译过程中,译者应该在原文法律语言中(source legal language,SLL)寻找与译文法律语言(target legal language,TLL)相匹配的对等语。由于中西法律文化的巨大差异,要真正做到"所谓'全面严格对等'仅仅是一种理想",在翻译过程中总会有大大小小的差异和矛盾。根据 Varo 和 Hughes 等人的观点,做到译语与源语法律效果的对等,翻译者要经历三个步骤(three stages),其一,"充分把握源语文本(source text)的思想以及表达思想的工具";其二是语言,即用"相同目的语的术语表达源语思想";其三,是其他方面如目的语的归化标准问题(criterion of naturalness)。(Varo & Hughes,2002:29)如果一个法律文本的译文(parallel text)达到了相同的法律效果,就达到了法律对等(equivalence)的目的。使译文的权威性不仅在意义上,而且在法律效果上达到相同。

原文:The law holds that the individual is responsible for his acts. The law also indicates what is good and right, and what may and should be done. It also indicates what is evil and wrong, and should not and may not be done. The law further holds that what is evil and wrong is a crime and may not be done, and if done, renders the doer liable to punishment. The law also recognizes the principle that man has free will and that, with certain exceptions, he exercises free will in commission of any crime that he may commit.

译文 1:法律认为公民应对自己的行为负责。法律还规定什么是美好的和正确的,规范了哪些事是允许做或应该做的。同样,法律规范了什么是邪恶的和错误的,法律还进一步明确规定哪些邪恶的错误的事是不能做的犯罪行为,如果某人做了这样的事,那么该行为人就要受到惩罚。同样,法律还承认这样一个原则,每个公民除犯罪自由外都具有自由意志,如果某人在各种违法活动中实施其自由意志,那么他就可能触犯法律。

译文 2:法律规定人人应对自己的行为承担责任,分清善良和正义,规范了人们的行为准则;法律还认为,作孽枉法即是犯罪,法不可恕,谁要以身试法,必将受到严惩。法律所主张的原则是人人享有自由意志的权利,同时也认为,除特殊情况外,人们的自由往往表现在因滥施自由意志而受到惩罚的行为上。

从上述两例译文可见,第一种译文语言显得松散,句法不够严谨,甚至有些口语化,与严密的法律条文不吻合;第二种译文用词严谨,表述准确简练,确能体现出法律的庄严和对等性。

法律翻译的对等性,除了文体特征,专门的法律知识是必备的。简单的 go to the bar,普通人会译成"去酒吧"或"到栅栏那里去",只有具备专门法律知识的人才知道应该译成"当律师"或"进入司法系统"。"物证"翻译成 material evidence,译文看似正确表达了原文的含义,但实质上却和原文的指示意义截然不同。根据我国三大诉讼法的有关规定,证据按表现形式可分为言词证据和实物证据两种。而"物证"是指"对查明案件真实情况有证明作用的有关物品或物质痕迹",显然这个定义不包括证人证言、当事人的陈述等言词证据。而 material evidence 是指"与案件的事实或结果存在逻辑关系的证据",不论是言词证据还是实物证据,只要能推理出案件的事实即可。因此,"物证"译为 real evidence 或 physical evidence 要更妥当一些。

二、一致性与同一性原则

某些领域的翻译,特别是文学翻译,同一个概念、内涵或同一事物可用不同的词语来表达，以免译文词语贫乏。但是对于法律翻译，为了维护同一概念、内涵或事物在法律上始终如一，以免引起歧义，词语一经选定就必须前后统一。在法律翻译中只要认准并用准了某词语，就千万别怕反复使用该词语。如果怕重复用同一个词表示同一个事物或概念有伤文采，那肯定会牺牲法律的准确性。（陈忠诚，2000：214）

一致性与同一性原则是指在法律翻译的过程中用同一法律术语表示同一法律概念的原则。法律语言翻译如果缺乏一致性和同一性，无疑会使法律概念混淆，也会使受众不必要地去揣测不同词语的差别，从而影响法律信息传递的精度。正如 Henry Weihofen 在其所著《法律文体》中所说的："Exactness often demands repeating the same term to express the same idea. where that is true, never be afraid of using the same word over and over again. Many more sentences are spoiled by trying to avoid repetition and repetition."（如果您怕重复用同一个词表示同一个事物或概念有伤文采，那您肯定会牺牲法律的精确性。）

因此，法律翻译过程中，为了维护同一概念、内涵或事物在法律上始终同一，避免引起歧义，词语一经选定后就必须前后统一，就千万别怕反复使用同一词语。例如：

① 被告（宝洁公司）从未以任何方式向原告（雇员）施加精神压力，被告可以拿走原告的文档和他使用的计算机，这是公司的规章制度所规定的，其目的是防止公司的商业秘密被泄露。

…the defendant (P&G)never exerted any spiritual pressure in any form on the claimant, the defendant was free to take away all the plaintiff's files and the computer he had been using, strictly in accordance with the company's stipulations, and that such actions were aimed at preventing the company's trade secrets from being disclosed.

分析：译文中对原文中的"原告"用了两个不同的词，即 claimant（索赔者，严格来讲，应指的是仲裁案件中的"申诉人"）和 plaintiff（民事案件中的原告），这种现象在法律英语翻译当中是被禁止的，否则，读者会以为是两个不同的主体。

② 前款所指的支付各种应纳税的款项，包括现金支付，汇款支付，转账支付和有价证券或实物支付时折算的金额。

The various kinds of taxable payments referred to in the proceeding paragraph include payments in cash, payments by remittance, payments through transfer accounts and payments in marketable securities or in kind, which are rendered into equivalent amount of money.

分析：译文中的 payment 重复五次，为的是译名同一。不能因为注重修辞而使用另一个近义词 disbursement。payment 和 disbursement 两者表达的意思有所不同，前者包括"支付"和"缴纳"（paying or being paid），而后者则仅指"支付"（paying out）。

同样的道理，"未成年人"在英文中有 infant 和 minor 两个词，当我们在翻译同一材料时若选定 infant，在下文中就不能随意用 minor。英文中的 minor offence 既有"轻罪，小罪"之意，又有"未成年人犯罪"之意。若不注意术语的一致性，歧义在所难免。

三、专业性与规范化原则

随着人类社会的发展，行业的划分也越来越复杂和细致。在所有的行业中，法律行业对专业性有着很高的要求。首先，法官和律师要在法律方面拥有很丰富的知识和技能，同样，法律英语翻译者也是如此。因为法律英语翻译是法律专业和英语语言专业的结合。对于法律英语翻译者而言，同时掌握良好的语言能力和法律知识是一个很重要的标准。

例如,"不可抗力"应该被翻译为 force majeure,而不应该被翻译为 beyond human power、force controlled by good 或者 irritable force;"包办婚姻"应该被翻译为 arranged marriage;unfair competition 不应该被翻译为"不公平比赛",应当译成"不正当竞争";obviously unfair civil act 译成"显失公平的民事行为",不译成"明显不公平民事行为";unjust enrichment 译成"不当得利",不应该译成"不正义的致富";disturb the socio-economic order 译成"扰乱社会经济秩序"比"搞乱社会经济秩序"更专业化;pro-choice of abortion 译成"支持堕胎"比"赞同选择打掉孩子"更具法律的严肃性。

① The seller shall present the following documents to the negotiation bank for payment.
售方应向经办支付货款的银行交付下列文件。

分析:译者由于不懂法律专业术语,把 seller 译成"售方"(应为"卖方"),把 the negotiation bank for payment 译成了"经办支付货款的银行"(实际上,negotiation bank 在法律上为"议付行")。所以,本句应译为:"卖方应向议付行递交下列文件要求付款。"

② 举证责任由被告承担。
The responsibility of proof rests with the defendant.

分析:在法律英语中,"举证责任"有其专门的术语,即 burden of proof 或 onus of proof。所以,本句应译为:"The onus of proof/burden of proof rests with the defendant."

再举几个翻译句子,注意画线部分的专业表达:

① Party A is a company duly organized, validly existing and <u>in good standing</u> as a legal person under the laws of the PRC.
甲方(公司)是依据中华人民共和国法律正式成立、有效存续和<u>资格完备</u>的法人

② Now therefore, in consideration of the premises, and the representations, warranties, covenants, and undertakings of the parties hereinafter set forth, and for other <u>good</u> and valuable <u>consideration</u>, the parties agree among themselves as follows.
鉴于上述事实和各方在下文所做的陈述、保证、立约和承诺,及其他<u>有效</u>的有价<u>约因</u>,现各方达成协议如下。

③ The vendor shall procure that the Purchaser acquires <u>good title</u> to the Shares free from all charges, lines, encumbrances, equities and claims whatsoever.
卖方应保证买房获得<u>绝对的</u>股份所有权,且该股份不带任何收费、抵押、留置、权益和主张。

规范性是对语言最基本的要求,语言规范化原则就是指在法律英语翻译过程中使用官方认可的规范化语言或书面语,以及避免使用方言和俚语。虽然在法律文书的起草和翻译中有许许多多的清规戒律(如慎用被动语态、外来词、缩略词等);但有一点必须强调,那就是必须使用官方用词(语),尤其是现行法律中已有界定的词语。如 target 在法律上为"标的"(不译为"目标"),subject matter 为"标的物"(不译为"主题"),cause of action 为"案由"(不译为"行为原因")。

四、精练性与简明性原则

法律语言翻译应遵循精练性与简明性的原则,即用最少的语词传递最大量的信息(Giving a lot of information in few words)。

我国某些法律文本的英译文有拖沓累赘、衍生歧义之弊,从某种程度上说,有损我法治

之国的形象。

① 女职工违反国家有关计划生育规定的，其劳动保护应当按照国家有关计划生育规定办理，不适用本规定。

原译：Labour protection of those women staff and workers that run counter to state stipulations concerning family planning should be treated according to State stipulations concerning family planning. The Regulations are thus inapplicable。

很明显，此译文冗赘笨拙，让人读来颇生烦累。原文本来是一句完整的话（主语为"本规定"，谓语为"不适用"，宾语为"女职工违反国家有关计划生育规定"），而译文却分为两句，因而不能明朗地表达原文内涵。拟译为：

These Regulations do not apply to any violation of state family-planning measures by a woman employee whose labor protection is regulated by the said measures.

② CONTRIBUTOINS TO COLLECTIVE WORKS—Copyright in each separate contribution to a collective work is distinct from copyright in the collective work as a whole, and vests initially in the author of the contribution. In the absence of an express transfer of the copyright or of any rights under it, the owner of copyright in the collective work is presumed to have acquired only the privilege of reproducing and distributing the contribution as part of that particular collective work, any revision of that collective work, and any later collective work in the same series.

原译：集体作品中可分割使用的作品——集体作品中每一可分割使用的作品的版权不同于作为整体的集体作品的版权，属于该可分割使用的作品的作者。在无明确转让版权或依版权享有的任何其他权利的情况下，推定该集体作品的版权所有人获得的权利仅限于复制、发行作为该特定集体作品构成部分的可分割使用的作品和修订该集体作品及同一序列中任何未来创作的集体作品。

分析：在保证原文意义不受损害的前提下，还要考虑如何使译文符合目标语言的表达习惯，因此译者完全有自由而且有必要对原文进行增删。原译译文完全按照原来的语序，致使指代不明确，信息凌乱。在第一句中"可分割使用的作品的版权，属于该可分割使用的作品的作者"是主要信息，不应该离得太远。第二句中的"推定"没有实施者，原文也没有给出此类信息，对于此类被动句，翻译时我们一般转为主动句。最后，"修订该集体作品及同一序列中任何未来创作的集体作品"完全是错译，the contribution as part of that particular collective work，any revision of that collective work，any later collective work in the same series 是平行结构，都是 reproducing and distributing 的宾语；"同一序列中任何未来创作的集体作品"是对 any later collective work in the same series 的翻译，不仅啰嗦烦琐，而且口语化。

改译：集体作品中可分割使用的作品——集体作品中每一可分割使用的作品的版权，属于该可分割使用的作品的作者，这不同于作为整体的集体作品的版权。在无明确转让版权或依版权享有的任何其他权利的情况下，该集体作品的版权所有人的特权仅限于复制和发行集体作品的可分割使用的作品、该集体作品的修订本以及同一丛书中任何集体作品续编的稿件。

③ A transfer of copyright ownership, other than by operation of law, is not valid unless an instrument of conveyance, or a note or memorandum of the transfer, is in writing and signed by the owner of the rights conveyed or such owner's duly authorized agent.

原译：版权的所有权除因法定转让外，非经转让的权利的所有人或该所有人之适当授权的代理人签署书面让与文件、转让记录或备忘录的，版权所有权的转让无效。

分析：duly authorized agent 正当授权代理人：经明示或默示授权，于特定场合从事代理行为的人。按照法律语言的习惯，"除……之外"经常放在句首，信息传达清楚明了。"转让的权利的所有人"带有翻译腔，不精练，译为"版权原权利所有人"。

试译：除因法定转让外，非经版权原权利所有人或该所有人之正当授权代理人签署让与文件、转让记录或备忘录的，版权所有权的转让无效。

④ Copyright protection under this title is not available for any work of the United States, but the United States Government is not precluded from receiving and holding copyrights transferred to it by assignment, bequest, or otherwise.

原译：合众国政府之任何作品依本篇不受版权保护，但不得妨碍合众国政府接受及持有因转让、赠予或者以其他方式转移给它的版权。

分析：译文中"不得妨碍合众国政府接受及持有……版权"的权利主张的主体不明确。两个分句的衔接不连贯，但是我们稍稍调整语序，译文效果就不一样了。

试译：本篇版权不适用于合众国之任何作品，但不妨碍合众国政府接受及持有因转让、赠予或者以其他方式转移的版权。

⑤ 英文如与中文有歧义，以中文为准。

译文 1：If the interpretation of the English version is different from that of the Chinese version, the latter shall be taken as the standard.

译文 2：In case of any misinterpretation of the English version, the Chinese one prevails.

译文 3：In case of any discrepancy between the English and the Chinese versions, the latter prevails.

分析：译文 1 可称得上是表达清楚，但有失精练，行文拖沓。译文 2 和译文 3 既符合英文的表达习惯，又体现法律文件精练的原则。

⑥ 房屋购买人应向房地产登记处办理登记手续。

译文 1：The vendee shall effect registration with the real estate registration office.

译文 2：The vendee shall register with the real estate registry.

分析：译文 1 中的 effect registration with（向……办理登记手续）完全可以用 register with，而"登记处"有现成的 registry，为什么非要舍简从繁用 registration office 呢？显而易见，译文 2 既贴近原意又显精练。

⑦ 约翰·史密斯在中国居住期间没有受过刑事制裁。

译文 1：John Smith has no record of committing offences against the Criminal Law during his living in China.

译文 2：John Smith has no record of criminal offence during his living in China.

分析：比较而言，在译文 1 中"没有受过刑事制裁"用了 10 个单词表达，虽然意思明确具体，但欠精练，而译文 2 就言简意赅多了。

 法律宝典

继承法基础知识

1. 继承，在民法上特指财产继承，作为一种民事法律关系，是指将死者生前的合法财产和其他合法权益转归为有权取得该项财产和权益的人所有的法律现象或者法律制度。

2. 继承权，是指公民依照法律的直接规定或者被继承人所立的合法有效的遗嘱享有的继承被继承人遗产的权利。

3. 生理死亡，又称为自然死亡，是指自然人生命的终结。一般以呼吸停止和心脏搏动停止为生理死亡的时间。

4. 宣告死亡，是指经利害关系人申请，由法院宣告下落不明的满一定期间的自然人为死亡的制度。

5. 遗产，是指被继承人死亡时遗留的个人所有财产和法律规定可以继承的其他财产权益，包括积极遗产和消极遗产。积极遗产，是指死者生前个人享有的财务和可以继承的其他合法权益，如债权和著作权中的财产权益等。消极遗产，是指死者生前所欠的个人债务。

6. 承包，即"承包经营管理"，是指企业或农村各级集体组织与承包者间订立承包经营合同，将企业的经营管理权、农林牧渔开发权等属于企业或者集体所有的权利的全部或部分在一定期限内交给承包者，由承包者进行经营管理，并承担经营风险及获取收益的行为。

7. 法定继承，是指被继承人没有对其遗产的处理立有遗嘱的情况下，由法律直接规定继承人范围、继承顺序、遗产分配原则的一种继承形式。

8. 遗嘱继承，是指按照立遗嘱人生前所留下的符合法律规定的合法遗嘱的内容要求，确定被继承人的继承人及各继承人应继承遗产的份额。

9. 遗赠，是指被继承人通过遗嘱的方式，将其遗产的一部分或者全部赠予国家或社会或者法定继承人以外的被继承人的一种民事法律行为。立遗嘱人为遗赠人，接受遗赠的人称遗赠受领人。遗赠是遗赠人死亡后才生效的单方或无偿的民事法律行为。遗赠的标的仅仅是财产权利，遗嘱人不得把债务转移给受赠人。

10. 遗赠抚养协议，是指公民与扶养人、集体所有制组织订立的有关扶养、遗赠的协议。这里的抚养人是指法定继承人以外的人。公民与扶养人之间本来没有法定的权利义务关系，他们之间的遗赠和扶养是通过协议产生的。

11. 无行为能力人，根据民法通则的规定是指不满十周岁的未成年人和不能辨认自己行为的精神病人。无行为能力人对自己行为的性质和后果都无法判断，只能由其法定代理人代为进行各种民事活动。

12. 限制行为能力人，在民法上主要是指以下几类公民：（1）十周岁以上十八周岁以下的未成年人。但年满十六周岁未满十八周岁以自己的劳动作为主要收入来源的是完全民事行为能力人；（2）身体有缺陷（又聋又哑的人或者盲人，心里有缺陷的人不在此列）以及患有间歇性精神病的人是限制民事行为能力人。完全精神病的人是无民事行为能力人。

13. 未成年人的父母是他们的法定代理人。未成年人的父母死亡或者没有监护能力的，由其有监护能力的近亲属担任他们的法定代理人。

14. 继承权的丧失，又称为继承权的剥夺，是指依照法律规定在发生法定事由时取消继承人继承被继承人遗产的资格的法律制度。

15. 遗弃，是指家庭成员中负有赡养、扶养、抚养义务的一方，对需要赡养、扶养和抚养的另一方，不履行其应尽的义务的违法行为。例如，父母不抚养未成年子女，成年子女不赡养无劳动能力或生活困难的父母，配偶不履行扶养对方的义务等。遗弃以不作为的形式出现，该为而不为，致使被遗弃人的权益受到侵害。

16. 虐待，是指一个人以胁迫或暴力的方式控制另一个人的一种行为模式。虐待造成身体上的伤害和心理上的恐惧，它使被虐待人不能做自己想做的事，或强迫其以不情愿的方式做事。虐待包括使用人身暴力和性暴力、威胁和恐吓、情感虐待和经济剥夺。

17. 诉讼时效，是指民事权利受到侵害的权利人在法定的时效期间内不行使权利，当时效期间届满时，人民法院对权利人的权利不再进行保护的制度。在法律规定的诉讼时效期间内，权利人提出请求的，人民法院就强制义务人履行所承担的义务。而在法定的诉讼时效期间届满之后，权利人行使请求权的，人民法院就不再予以保护。值得注意的是，诉讼时效届满后，义务人虽可拒绝履行其义务，权利人请求权的行使发生障碍，权利本身及请求权并不消灭。当事人超过诉讼时效后起诉的，人民法院应当受理。受理后查明无中止、中断、延长事由的，判决驳回其诉讼请求。

18. 男女平等，是指妇女和男子在政治的、经济的、文化的、社会的和家庭的生活各方面享有同等的权利。

19. 代位继承，是与本位继承相对应的一种继承制度，乃法定继承的一种特殊情况，是指被继承人的子女先于被继承人死亡时，由被继承人子女的晚辈直系血亲代替先死亡的长辈直系血亲继承被继承人遗产的一项法定继承制度，又称为间接继承或承租继承。

20. 直系血亲，是指有直系关系的亲属，是与自己同一血缘的亲属。从自身往上数的亲生父母、祖父母（外祖父母）等均为长辈直系血亲。从自身往下数的亲生子女、孙子女、外孙子女均为晚辈直系血亲。

21. 遗产分配，是指财产所有人死亡后根据法定继承、遗嘱或其他法律规定对其遗产的分配制度。遗产分配一般应遵循均等原则。

▶ 术语积累

assets　资产
legacy　遗赠（物），遗产（祖先传下来）
decedent　死者
maltreat　虐待，滥用
heir　继承人，后嗣
forge　铸造，伪造
tamper with　损害，篡改
pertain　适合，属于
inheritance　遗传，遗产
institute　创立，开始，制定，开始（调查），提起（诉讼）

expiration 满期
property entrusting 财产委托
legatee 遗产受赠人
legacy-support agreement 遗赠抚养协议
testamentary 遗嘱的，据遗嘱的，遗嘱中有的
statutory successor 法定继承人
securities 证券
livestock 家畜，牲畜
poultry 家禽
patent 专利权，执照，专利品
heritable 可遗传的，可继承的
creditor 债权人
debtor 债务人
marine 舰队，水兵，海运业
designate 指明，指出，任命，指派
collective ownership 集体所有制
accrue 自然增加，产生
domicile 住所，住宅
nationality 国籍
governing law 管辖法律
derogation 毁损，堕落，减损
applicable 可适用的，可应用的
algorithm 运算法则
hereditary 世袭的，遗传的
vacate 腾出，空出，离（职），退（位）
sibling 兄弟，姐妹，同胞，同属
collateral 间接的
morganatic 贵贱通婚的（指王室，贵族成员与庶民通婚的）
coronation 加冕礼
tanist （爱尔兰）凯尔特族酋长继承人
agnatic 男系亲属的
primogeniture 长子身份，长子继承权
heiress 女性继承人
proximity of blood 近亲，骨肉之亲
incumbent 职责所在的，负有……义务的
electoral 选举人的，选举的
genealogical 宗谱的，系谱的，家系的
seniority 资历
fief holder 封地拥有者

partible   可分的
abeyance   暂时无效，中止，归属待定
ultimogeniture   幼子继承制
lateral   横（向）的，侧面的

Section III   巩固练习

词汇与短语

1. perjury
2. pledge
3. testamentary
4. deceased
5. menace
6. trustee
7. invalid
8. revoke
9. successor
10. provision
11. 生产资料
12. 非婚生子女
13. 生父母
14. 法定代理人
15. 遗产分割
16. 文物
17. 世袭的，遗传的
18. 遗赠抚养协议
19. 近亲，骨肉之亲
20. 法定继承人

句子与段落

1. It is my intention by this Will to dispose of all property which I am entitled to dispose of by will. I specifically refrain from exercising all powers of appointment that I may possess at the time of my death.
2. All such assets shall be held, managed and distributed as a part of said Trust according to its terms and not as a separate testamentary trust.
3. I direct said Trustee or Trustees to divide, administer, hold and distribute the trust estate pursuant to the provisions of said Trust, as hereinabove referred to as such provisions now exist to the same extent and in the same manner as though that certain Amended and Restated Declaration of Trust, were here in set forth in full, but without giving effect to any subsequent amendments after the date of this Will.
4. Death Taxes attributable to property passing outside this Will, other than property constituting the trust estate of the trust intentioned in the preceding sentence, shall be charged against the taker of said property.

5. He thereupon signed this Will in our presence, all of us being present at the same time. We now, at his request, in his presence and in the presence of each other, subscribe our names as witnesses.
6. 公民可以立遗嘱将个人财产赠给国家、集体或者法定继承人以外的人。
7. 无行为能力人的继承权、受遗赠权，由他的法定代理人代为行使。限制行为能力人的继承权、受遗赠权，由他的法定代理人代为行使，或者征得法定代理人同意后行使。
8. 继承人应当本着互谅互让、和睦团结的精神，协商处理继承问题。遗产分割的时间、办法和份额，由继承人协商确定。协商不成的，可以由人民调解委员会调解或者向人民法院提起诉讼。
9. 遗嘱继承或者遗赠附有义务的，继承人或者受遗赠人应当履行义务。没有正当理由不履行义务的，经有关单位或者个人请求，人民法院可以取消他接受遗产的权利。
10. 无行为能力人或者限制行为能力人所立的遗嘱无效。遗嘱必须表示遗嘱人的真实意思，受胁迫、欺骗所立的遗嘱无效。伪造的遗嘱无效。遗嘱被篡改的，篡改的内容无效。

Unit Eleven

Commercial Law
商　法

Section I　译例研究

>> **Passage One**

Convention on Combating Bribery of Foreign Public Officials in International Business Transactions

The Parties,

Considering that bribery is a widespread phenomenon in international business transactions, including trade and investment, which raises serious moral and political concerns, undermines good governance and economic development, and distorts international competitive conditions;

Considering that all countries share a responsibility to combat bribery in international business transactions;

Having regard to the Revised Recommendation on Combating Bribery in International Business Transactions, adopted by the Council of the Organization for Economic Co-operation and Development (OECD) on 23 May, 1997，C(97)123/FINAL, which, *inter alia*, called for effective measures to deter, prevent and combat the bribery of foreign public officials in connection with international business transactions, in particular the prompt criminalization of such bribery in an effective and coordinated manner and in conformity with the agreed common elements set out in that Recommendation and with the jurisdictional and other basic legal principles of each country;

Welcoming other recent developments which further advance international understanding and cooperation in combating bribery of public officials, including actions of the United Nations, the

World Bank, the International Monetary Fund, the World Trade Organization, the Organization of American States, the Council of Europe and the European Union;

Welcoming the efforts of companies, business organizations and trade unions as well as other nongovernmental organizations to combat bribery;

Recognizing the role of governments in the prevention of solicitation of bribes from individuals and enterprises in international business transactions;

Recognizing that achieving equivalence among the measures to be taken by the Parties is an essential object and purpose of the Convention, which requires that the Convention be ratified without derogations affecting this equivalence;

Have agreed as follows:

Article 1: The Offence of Bribery of Foreign Public Officials

1.

Each Party shall take such measures as may be necessary to establish that it is a criminal offence under its law for any person intentionally to offer, promise or give any undue pecuniary or other advantage, whether directly or through intermediaries, to a foreign public official, for that official or for a third party, in order that the official act or refrain from acting in relation to the performance of official duties, in order to obtain or retain business or other improper advantage in the conduct of international business.

2.

Each Party shall take any measures necessary to establish that complicity in, including incitement, aiding and abetting, or authorization of an act of bribery of a foreign public official shall be a criminal offence. Attempt and conspiracy to bribe a foreign public official shall be criminal offences to the same extent as attempt and conspiracy to bribe a public official of that Party.

…

Article 2: Responsibility of Legal Persons

Each Party shall take such measures as may be necessary, in accordance with its legal principles, to establish the liability of legal persons for the bribery of a foreign public official.

…

Article 3: Sanctions

…

Article 5: Enforcement

Investigation and prosecution of the bribery of a foreign public official shall be subject to the applicable rules and principles of each Party. They shall not be influenced by considerations of national economic interest, the potential effect upon relations with another State or the identity of the natural or legal persons involved.

…

词汇提示

combat　　*v.* 反对，打击
bribery　　*n.* 行贿
undermine　　*vt.* 破坏
distort　　*v.* 扭曲
jurisdictional　　*adj.* 司法管辖的
call for　　呼吁
deter　　*vt.* 遏止
equivalence　　*n.* 等效
object　　*n.* 目标
ratified　　*adj.* 批准的
derogation　　*n.* 减损
offence　　*n.* 犯罪
pecuniary　　*adj.* 金钱的
intermediary　　*n.* 中介机构
retain　　*vt.* 保留
complicity　　*n.* 同谋
incitement　　*n.* 煽动
abet　　*vt.* 唆使
authorization　　*n.* 授意
conspiracy　　*n.* 共谋
sanction　　*n.* 制裁
enforcement　　*n.* 执行
investigation　　*n.* 侦查
prosecution　　*n.* 检控
applicable　　*adj.* 适用的
identity　　*n.* 身份
convention　　*n.* 公约
parties　　*n.* 缔约各方
foreign public officials　　外交公职人员
international business transaction　　国际商务交易活动
Revised Recommendation　　修订建议案
OECD　　经济发展与合作组织
the Council　　理事会
inter alia　　特别，尤其
the International Monetary Fund　　国际货币基金组织
the Organization of American States　　美洲国家组织

the Council of Europe　欧洲理事会
trade unions　工会组织
article　条款
refrain from　避免，抑制
in accordance with　一直
subject to　受制于，受到

要点解析

1. Convention on Combating Bribery of Foreign Public Officials in International Business Transactions（国际商务交易活动反对行贿外交公职人员公约），标题介词词组前置和名词后移。英文标题（副标题）中的介词词组译为中文时作定语放在名词之前，英文标题（副标题）题首的名词译为中文时移至题尾。从形式上看，标题与副标题多为名词（动名词）词组，翻译时要注意中英文表达习惯上的差异，针对具体的语言环境，调整语序，灵活处理，使之符合中文习惯。

2. Considering that bribery is a widespread phenomenon in international business transactions, including trade and investment, …

其中 including trade and investment 作为插入语，翻译成中文时应注意语序的调整，译成："鉴于行贿行为已是国际商业交易活动中，包括贸易与投资活动中，普遍存在的现象……"

3. Having regard to the Revised Recommendation on Combating Bribery in International Business Transactions, …

其中"having regard to…"可译成"参照，依据……"。

4. Having regard to the Revised Recommendation on Combating Bribery in International Business Transactions, …and other basic legal principles of each country"

该句是一个长句。首先剖析原文的主句、重心及整个句子含义，并进行拆解，探析句子中的几层含义。"…on 23 May, 1997，C(97)123/FINAL"可划为一个层次，which 之后可划为一个层次，"in particular the prompt criminalization of…"到句尾可划为另一个层次。

5. Recognizing the role of governments in the prevention of solicitation of bribes from individuals and enterprises in international business transactions; …

根据下文，其中 recognizing 可译为赞赏；in the prevention of 为介词词组，将动词 prevent 名词化，也是法律英语中的特点之一。

6. …which requires that…. without derogations affecting this equivalence

这一句中需注意非谓语从句加介词短语的翻译，可译为"这就要求要完整无损地批准本公约，不得有影响实现这种等效的减损条款"。

7. "Have agreed as follows:"汉译时，应补充主语。

8. The Offence of Bribery of Foreign Public Officials 译成汉语后，法律英语条款名称中的介词词组前置和名词后移，按中文语序，译为"行贿外交公职人员罪"。

9. Each Party shall take such measures as may be necessary to establish that…为法律英语中固定专业用语，可译为"缔约方应当采取必要的措施设定……"。

10. it is a criminal offence under its law for... 汉译时可将何为犯罪的具体内容放在前，"依法定为犯罪"后置。

11. 英语短语 subject to...经常出现在商务和法律英语中，有时在句中作状语，但大部分情况下作表语，意为"根据；按照；如果；受……约束等"。例如：

Subject to the provisions of Clause 5.4.1, the contributions of Party A and Party B to the Company's registered capital shall be made in one instalment by no later than six(6) months after the Establishment Date. The Parties shall make their respective capital contributions to the registered capital of the Company on the same date.

根据5.4.1条款的规定，甲乙双方对公司注册资本的出资必须在成立日之后最晚6个月内一次性付清。双方必须在同一天支付各自对注册资本的出资。

参考译文

国际商务交易活动反对行贿外交公职人员公约

缔约各方：

鉴于行贿行为已是国际商业交易活动中，包括贸易与投资活动中，普遍存在的现象，引起了道德和政治方面的严重忧虑，破坏了良好的管理与经济的发展，扭曲了国际竞争条件；

鉴于所有国家在国际商业交易活动中都负有反行贿责任；

参照经济合作与发展组织理事会于1997年5月23日通过的第C(97)123/FINAL号关于在国际商务交易活动中反行贿的修订建议案，该建议案特别呼吁采取行之有效的措施，遏止、预防和打击国际商务交易活动中行贿外国公职人员的行为，尤其呼吁根据该建议案中《公认通则》和各个缔约方司法管辖及其他法律准则，立即采取协调有效的方式对这种行贿行为进行定罪；

采纳了近年来取得的在打击行贿公职人员活动中新成果，包括联合国、世界银行、国际货币基金组织、世界贸易组织、美洲国家组织、欧洲理事会和欧盟等组织反行贿活动中取得的新成果，以进一步促进国际了解与合作；

欢迎各公司、商业组织、工会组织以及其他非政府组织做出努力，参与打击行贿行为；

赞赏各国政府在国际商务交易活动中防止向个人和企业索贿中所发挥的作用；

承认使各个缔约方所采取的措施达到等效是本公约最基本的目标和宗旨，这就要求要完整无损地批准本公约，不得有影响实现这种等效的减损条款。

特此各缔约方约定如下：

第一条：行贿外交公职人员罪

1. 缔约方应当采取必要的措施设定：任何人，无论是直接还是通过中间方，故意向外国公职人员或者为外国公职人员或第三方提议给予、承诺给予或事实上给予不当的金钱或其他利益，以期该外国公职人员在履行其职责中采取行动或不行动，进而在国际商业活动中获得或保留其业务或其他不当利益的行为，依法定为犯罪。

2. 缔约方应当采取必要的措施设定：共同参与，包括煽动、协助、唆使、或授意他人行贿外国公职人员的行为是犯罪行为。企图行贿外国公职人员或共谋行贿外国公职人员与企图行贿本国公职人员或共谋行贿本国公职人员一样，同为犯罪。

……

第二条：法人的责任

缔约方均须依其法律准则采取必要的措施，确立法人行贿外国公职人员应承担的责任。

……

第三条：制裁

……

第五条：执行

行贿外国公职人员案件的侦查与检控应当符合各缔约方适用的法规和法理，不得受国家经济利益，可能影响与另一国关系或相关自然人或法人身份等因素的影响。

……

▶▶ *Passage Two*
个体工商户、个人合伙与法人

第二十六条　公民在法律允许的范围内，依法经核准登记，从事工商业经营的，为个体工商户。个体工商户可以起字号。

第二十七条　农村集体经济组织的成员，在法律允许的范围内，按照承包合同规定从事商品经营的，为农村承包经营户。

第二十八条　个体工商户、农村承包经营户的合法权益，受法律保护。

第二十九条　个体工商户、农村承包经营户的债务，个人经营的，以个人财产承担；家庭经营的，以家庭财产承担。

第三十条　个人合伙是指两个以上公民按照协议，各自提供资金、实物、技术等，合伙经营、共同劳动。

第三十一条　合伙人应当对出资数额、盈余分配、债务承担、入伙、退伙、合伙终止等事项，订立书面协议。

第三十二条　合伙人投入的财产，由合伙人统一管理和使用。

合伙经营积累的财产，归合伙人共有。

第三十三条　个人合伙可以起字号，依法经核准登记，在核准登记的经营范围内从事经营。

第三十四条　个人合伙的经营活动，由合伙人共同决定，合伙人有执行和监督的权利。

合伙人可以推举负责人。合伙负责人和其他人员的经营活动，由全体合伙人承担民事责任。

第三十五条　合伙的债务，由合伙人按照出资比例或者协议的约定，以各自的财产承担清偿责任。

合伙人对合伙的债务承担连带责任，法律另有规定的除外。偿还合伙债务超过自己应当承担数额的合伙人，有权向其他合伙人追偿。

第三十六条　法人是具有民事权利能力和民事行为能力，依法独立享有民事权利和承担民事义务的组织。

法人的民事权利能力和民事行为能力，从法人成立时产生，到法人终止时消灭。

第三十七条　法人应当具备下列条件：

（一）依法成立；

（二）有必要的财产或者经费；

（三）有自己的名称、组织机构和场所；

（四）能够独立承担民事责任。

第三十八条　依照法律或者法人组织章程规定，代表法人行使职权的负责人，是法人的法定代表人。

第三十九条　法人以它的主要办事机构所在地为住所。

第四十条　法人终止，应当依法进行清算，停止清算范围外的活动。

第四十一条　全民所有制企业、集体所有制企业有符合国家规定的资金数额，有组织章程、组织机构和场所，能够独立承担民事责任，经主管机关核准登记，取得法人资格。

在中华人民共和国领域内设立的中外合资经营企业、中外合作经营企业和外资企业，具备法人条件的，依法经工商行政管理机关核准登记，取得中国法人资格。

第四十二条　企业法人应当在核准登记的经营范围内从事经营。

第四十三条　企业法人对它的法定代表人和其他工作人员的经营活动，承担民事责任。

第四十四条　企业法人分立、合并或者有其他重要事项变更，应当向登记机关办理登记并公告。

企业法人分立、合并，它的权利和义务由变更后的法人享有和承担。

第四十五条　企业法人由于下列原因之一终止：

（一）依法被撤销；

（二）解散；

（三）依法宣告破产；

（四）其他原因。

第四十六条　企业法人终止，应当向登记机关办理注销登记并公告。

第四十七条　企业法人解散，应当成立清算组织，进行清算。企业法人被撤销、被宣告破产的，应当由主管机关或者人民法院组织有关机关和有关人员成立清算组织，进行清算。

第四十八条　全民所有制企业法人以国家授予它经营管理的财产承担民事责任。集体所有制企业法人以企业所有的财产承担民事责任。中外合资经营企业法人、中外合作经营企业法人和外资企业法人以企业所有的财产承担民事责任，法律另有规定的除外。

第四十九条　企业法人有下列情形之一的，除法人承担责任外，对法定代表人可以给予行政处分、罚款，构成犯罪的，依法追究刑事责任：

（一）超出登记机关核准登记的经营范围从事非法经营的；

（二）向登记机关、税务机关隐瞒真实情况、弄虚作假的；

（三）抽逃资金、隐匿财产逃避债务的；

（四）解散、被撤销、被宣告破产后，擅自处理财产的；

（五）变更、终止时不及时申请办理登记和公告，使利害关系人遭受重大损失的；

（六）从事法律禁止的其他活动，损害国家利益或者社会公共利益的。

第五十条 有独立经费的机关从成立之日起，具有法人资格。

具备法人条件的事业单位、社会团体，依法不需要办理法人登记的，从成立之日起，具有法人资格；依法需要办理法人登记的，经核准登记，取得法人资格。

第五十一条 企业之间或者企业、事业单位之间联营，组成新的经济实体，独立承担民事责任、具备法人条件的，经主管机关核准登记，取得法人资格。

第五十二条 企业之间或者企业、事业单位之间联营，共同经营、不具备法人条件的，由联营各方按照出资比例或者协议的约定，以各自所有的或者经营管理的财产承担民事责任。依照法律的规定或者协议的约定负连带责任的，承担连带责任。

第五十三条 企业之间或者企业、事业单位之间联营，按照合同的约定各自独立经营的，它的权利和义务由合同约定，各自承担民事责任。

▶ 词汇提示

个体工商户　individual businesses
从事　engage in
工商业经营　industrial or commercial operation
农村承包经营户　lease holding farm households
集体　collective
商品经营　commodity production
合法权益　legitimate rights and interests
个人财产　individual's property
家庭财产　family's property
个人合伙　individual partnership
书面协议　written agreement
盈余分配　distribution of profits
债务承担　responsibility for debt
退伙　withdrawal from partnership
合伙经营　partnership operation
执行　carry out
经营活动　operational activities
民事责任　civil liability
追偿　claim compensation
法人　legal person
法定代表人　legal representative
清算　liquidation
办事机构　administrative office
职权　functions and powers

集体所有制 collective ownership
合资经营企业 joint venture
外资企业 foreign-capital enterprise
破产 bankrupt
刑事责任 criminal responsibility
行政处分 administrative sanctions
经济实体 economic entity
连带责任 joint liability

要点解析

1. 公民在法律允许的范围内，依法经核准登记，从事工商业经营的，为个体工商户。

"Individual businesses" refers to business run by individual citizens who have been lawfully registered and approved to engage in industrial or commercial operation within the sphere permitted by law.

原句前面三个分句都属于主语部分，但在英文的表达习惯里，主语通常较短，所以翻译本句的时候将句子前后顺序颠倒，这样可以避免头重脚轻，同时可以起到下定义的作用。

2. 个体工商户、农村承包经营户的合法权益，受法律保护。

The legitimate rights and interests of individual businesses and lease holding farm households shall be protected by law.

权益包括两个部分，既有权力也有收益，所以译为 rights and interests。用 shall 增强了承诺和规定的意味，符合法律的语言特征。

3. 个体工商户、农村承包经营户的债务，个人经营的，以个人财产承担；家庭经营的，以家庭财产承担。

The debts of an individual business or a lease holding farm household shall be secured with the individual's property if the business is operated by an individual and with the family's property if the business is operated by a family.

前后两个句子结构平行，内容相似，所以在翻译第二句的时候省略了相同的部分，避免了累赘。

4. 个人合伙是指两个以上公民按照协议，各自提供资金、实物、技术等，合伙经营、共同劳动。

"Individual partnership" refers to two or more citizens associated in a business and working together, with each providing funds, material objects, techniques and so on according to an agreement.

此处翻译调整了顺序，将中间部分译为状语，从而强调了句子的主干。

5. 合伙人应当对出资数额、盈余分配、债务承担、入伙、退伙、合伙终止等事项，订立书面协议。

Partners shall make a written agreement covering the funds each is to provide, the distribution of profits, the responsibility for debts, the entering into and withdrawal from partnership, the ending of partnership and other such matters.

此处将列举的事项译为"书面协议"的后置定语，一方面使句子主干更加精短，另一方面阐明了协议的具体内容。

6. 个人合伙的经营活动，由合伙人共同决定，合伙人有执行和监督的权利。

The operational activities of an individual partnership shall be decided jointly by the partners, who each shall have the right to carry out and supervise those activities.

本句含有两个分句，第一句为被动句，第二句为主动句。此处将第二个句子调整为定语从句，不仅没有破坏原句的完整性，还使句子的结构更加紧凑，两句的联系更加紧密。

7. 全民所有制企业、集体所有制企业有符合国家规定的资金数额，有组织章程、组织机构和场所，能够独立承担民事责任，经主管机关核准登记，取得法人资格。

An enterprise owned by the whole people or under collective ownership shall be qualified as a legal person when it has sufficient funds as stipulated by the state; has articles of association, an organization and premises; has the ability to independently bear civil liability; and has been approved and registered by the competent authority.

此处将中间的条件句置于句尾，将主谓结构组织到一起。

8. 依法需要办理法人登记的，经核准登记，取得法人资格。

…if according to law it does need to go through the registration procedures, it shall be qualified as a legal person after being approved and registered.

前文提到了不需要办理法人登记的情况，此处说明需要办理登记的情况，所以用does说明了登记的必要性，起到了强调的作用。

 参考译文

Individual Businesses, Individual Partnership and Legal Person

Article 26. "Individual businesses" refers to business run by individual citizens who have been lawfully registered and approved to engage in industrial or commercial operation within the sphere permitted by law. An individual business may adopt a shop name.

Article 27. "Lease holding farm households" refers to members of a rural collective economic organization who engage in commodity production under a contract and within the spheres permitted by law.

Article 28. The legitimate rights and interests of individual businesses and lease holding farm households shall be protected by law.

Article 29. The debts of an individual business or a lease holding farm household shall be secured with the individual's property if the business is operated by an individual and with the family's property if the business is operated by a family.

Article 30. "Individual partnership" refers to two or more citizens associated in a business and working together, with each providing funds, material objects, techniques and so on according to an agreement.

Article 31. Partners shall make a written agreement covering the funds each is to provide, the distribution of profits, the responsibility for debts, the entering into and withdrawal from partnership, the ending of partnership and other such matters.

Article 32. The property provided by the partners shall be under their unified management and use. The property accumulated in a partnership operation shall belong to all the partners.

Article 33. An individual partnership may adopt a shop name; it shall be approved and registered in accordance with the law and conduct business operations within the range as approved and registered.

Article 34. The operational activities of an individual partnership shall be decided jointly by the partners, who each shall have the right to carry out and supervise those activities.

The partners may elect a responsible person.

All partners shall bear civil liability for the operational activities of the responsible person and other personnel.

Article 35. A partnership's debts shall be secured with the partners' property in proportion to their respective contributions to the investment or according to the agreement made. Partners shall undertake joint liability for their partnership's debts, except as otherwise stipulated by law. Any partner who overpays his share of the partnership's debts shall have the right to claim compensation from the other partners.

Article 36. A legal person shall be an organization that has capacity for civil rights and capacity for civil conduct and independently enjoys civil rights and assumes civil obligations in accordance with the law.

A legal person's capacity for civil rights and capacity for civil conduct shall begin when the legal person is established and shall end when the legal person terminates.

Article 37. A legal person shall have the following qualifications:

(1) establishment in accordance with the law;

(2) possession of the necessary property or funds;

(3) possession of its own name, organization and premises;

(4) ability to independently bear civil liability.

Article 38. In accordance with the law or the articles of association of the legal person, the responsible person who acts on behalf of the legal person in exercising its functions and powers shall be its legal representative.

Article 39. A legal person's domicile shall be the place where its main administrative office is located.

Article 40. When a legal person terminates, it shall go into liquidation in accordance with the law and discontinue all other activities.

Article 41. An enterprise owned by the whole people or under collective ownership shall be qualified as a legal person when it has sufficient funds as stipulated by the state; has articles of association, an organization and premises; has the ability to independently bear civil liability; and has been approved and registered by the competent authority. A Chinese-foreign equity joint venture, Chinese-foreign contractual joint venture or foreign-capital enterprise established within the People's

Republic of China shall be qualified as a legal person in China if it has the qualifications of a legal person and has been approved and registered by the administrative agency for industry and commerce in according with the law.

Article 42. An enterprise as legal person shall conduct operations within the range approved and registered.

Article 43. An enterprise as legal person shall bear civil liability for the operational activities of its legal representatives and other personnel.

Article 44. If an enterprise as legal person is divided or merged or undergoes any other important change, it shall register the change with the registration authority and publicly announce it.

When an enterprise as legal person is divided or merged, its rights and obligations shall be enjoyed and assumed by the new legal person that results from the change.

Article 45. An enterprise as legal person shall terminate for any of the following reasons:

(1) if it is dissolved by law;

(2) if it is disbanded;

(3) if it is declared bankrupt in accordance with the law;

(4) for other reasons.

Article 46. When an enterprise as legal person terminates, it shall cancel its registration with the registration authority and publicly announce the termination.

Article 47. When an enterprise as legal person is disbanded, it shall establish a liquidation organization and go into liquidation. When an enterprise as legal person is dissolved or is declared bankrupt, the competent authority or a people's court shall organize the organs and personnel concerned to establish a liquidation organization to liquidate the enterprise.

Article 48. An enterprise owned by the whole people, as legal person, shall bear civil liability with the property that the state authorizes it to manage. An enterprise under collective ownership, as legal person, shall bear civil liability with the property it owns. A Chinese-foreign equity joint venture, Chinese-foreign contractual joint venture or foreign-capital enterprise as legal person shall bear civil liability with the property it owns, except as stipulated otherwise by law.

Article 49. Under any of the following circumstances, an enterprise as legal person shall bear liability, its legal representative may additionally be given administrative sanctions and fined and, if the offence constitutes a crime, criminal responsibility shall be investigated in accordance with the law:

(1) conducting illegal operations beyond the range approved and registered by the registration authority;

(2) concealing facts from the registration and tax authorities and practicing fraud;

(3) secretly withdrawing funds or hiding property to evade repayment of debts;

(4) disposing of property without authorization after the enterprise is dissolved, disbanded or declared bankrupt;

(5) failing to apply for registration and make a public announcement promptly when the

enterprise undergoes a change or terminates, thus causing interested persons to suffer heavy losses;

(6) engaging in other activities prohibited by law, damaging the interests of the state or the public interest.

Article 50. An independently funded official organ shall be qualified as a legal person on the day it is established.

If according to law an institution or social organization having the qualifications of a legal person needs not go through the procedures for registering as a legal person, it shall be qualified as a legal person on the day it is established; if according to law it does need to go through the registration procedures, it shall be qualified as a legal person after being approved and registered.

Article 51. If a new economic entity is formed by enterprises or an enterprise and an institution that engage in economic association and it independently bears civil liability and has the qualifications of a legal person, the new entity shall be qualified as a legal person after being approved and registered by the competent authority.

Article 52. If the enterprises or an enterprise and an institution that engage in economic association conduct joint operation but do not have the qualifications of a legal person, each party to the association shall, in proportion to its respective contribution to the investment or according to the agreement made, bear civil liability with the property each party owns or manages. If joint liability is specified by law or by agreement, the parties shall assume joint liability.

Article 53. If the contract for economic association of enterprises or of an enterprise and an institution specifies that each party shall conduct operations independently, it shall stipulate the rights and obligations of each party, and each party shall bear civil liability separately.

Section II 技能拓展

翻译技巧

国际商法的语言特点及翻译

法律语言的功能是表现、传播和执行立法者的一致。因此，必须准确无误，前后一致，否则，就会引起混乱和争议。正确把握国际商务法律法规的语言特点，是准确理解和翻译国际商法的关键。

一、国际商法的词汇特征

1. 法律专业术语的使用

国际商法中会涉及大量的专业术语。这些法律术语都有其特定的含义及适用范围，既不能被随意引申，也不能由其他词汇代替。例如：legal person（法人），indict（控告，起诉），

appeal（上诉），damages（损失赔偿金），negotiable instrument（流通票据），obligee（债权人），obligor（债务人），tort（侵权行为）。a material breach（重大违约）不能用 a serious breach 代替；termination（终止）不能用 finish 代替；invoke（援引）不能用 quote 代替；peremptory（最高）不能用 supreme 代替。另外，一个词可能有多种意思，但作为术语，只能作特定理解。例如，article 有多种义项，但在商法条约中，它只能作"条款"解释。convention 也有多种义项，而在商法条约中它只特指"公约"。基于法律术语固定的表达方式、确切的含义以及高频率的使用，从某种意义上而言，它们正是理解和把握法律英语的关键所在。

2. 普通词语含有的法律意义

在法律英语中，也会用到很多日常英语中的普通词汇，但由于长期被法律工作者使用，这些普通词已被赋予了特定的法律含义。例如，attach 在日常英语中的基本意义是"附加、依附"，而法律意义是"逮捕（某人）、扣押、查封（某人的财物）"；cause 的基本意义是"原因"，而法律意义是"诉因"；client 的基本意义是"顾客"，而法律意义是"当事人、委托人"；hear 的基本意义是"听"，而法律意义是"听审，审理"等。此外，与日常英语通常要求的简洁明了不同，法律英语用词经常舍简就繁，语句"累赘""浮夸"，以显其权威、庄严。例如：在法律英语中，一般用 in accordance wit" 来表述"按照，根据"的含义，而少用 according to；用 in compliance with 而不是 comply with 来表示"遵照、遵循"；用 in addition 而较少用 also 来表示"也，并且"。这主要是因为后类词汇较口语化，不够正式，无法彰显法律英语的庄严和权威。

3. 古英语和外来词的使用

国际商法中最突出的古体词是那些由 here, there 和 where 加上一个或几个介词如 after, from, in, of, under, upon 等构成的复合副词，这类古英语能避免重复，使句子结构紧凑精练。常用的有：hereafter（自此以后，此后），hereby（由此、特此，以此方式），herein（于此处，于此文件、声明或事实中），hereof（关于此点），hereto（至此），hereunder（在下面），thereafter（此后，其后），therein（其中），thereof（由是，由此），thereto（附之，随之），thereunder（在那部分之后，在其下），whereon（在上面），whereby（凭此，借以，由于），hereinafter（在下文中），hereinbefore（在上文中），heretofore（直到此时，在此之前，前此），hereinabove（在上文），thereinafter（在下部分，在下文中），therefrom（由此），whereby（靠那个），wherein（在那方面），whereof 的含义是 of the fact that（关于那个）等。

国际商法中也会使用一些来自法语或拉丁语的词汇。西方法律源远流长，希腊的思辨精神和罗马的法律精神对西方文明的形成和发展起着至关重要的作用，加上英语语言的变迁，外来词的使用成为法律英语的特征之一。例如：inte ralia（特别是，除其他以外），de facto（事实上），de jure（法律上），pacta sunt servanda（条约必须被遵守原则），proviso（限制性条款），Proces-Verbal（会谈纪要），ipso facto（依事实本身），Modus Vivendi（临时协定），actus reus（禁止的行为，非法行为），bona fide（真诚的，善意的），consensus adidem（意思一致），ex parte（片面，单方面），in re（对于），inrem（对物，物权），jus naturale（自然法）等。

4. 同义词并列结构

为了表意准确和规范严谨，国际商法的制定者在行文中大量使用词语并列结构，用 and 或 or 把两个或多个短语并列起来。这种并列结构有更强的包容性，避免产生歧义与争端，确保文字表达的准确与严密。经常有如 customs fees and duties（关税），have and hold（持有），rules and regulations（法规），terms and conditions（条款），losses and damages（损坏），sign and issue（签发），null and void（无效），just and fair（公正）等这样同（近）义词并列的词汇，同时也使得语句更加流畅及有气势，更好地彰显了法律英语的正式性及庄严性。

二、国际商法中的句式特点

1. 大量使用长句结构

尽管随着时代的变迁，法律英语呈现出一些简化趋势，但与其他文体相比，法律文件依然存在不少结构复杂、文辞冗长的句子。国际商法中，往往一个句子就是一个段落，长达数十个至上百个单词，有时通篇法律文书就只有一个句子。法律英语中的长句构成是通过各种从属关系把一些连续的短句交织合并成一个复杂庞大的复合句，并同时使用一些修饰成分。这样的长句结构复杂，负载含义多，包含信息量大，叙事具体，说理严密，层次分明，相对逻辑性更强，也就减少了产生歧义的可能性。例如：

If two or more applicants apply for registration of identical or similar trademarks for the same kind of goods or similar goods, the trademark whose registration was first applied for shall be given preliminary examination and approval and shall be publicly announced; if the applicants are filed on the same day, the trademark which was first used shall be given preliminary examination and approval and shall be publicly announced, and the applications of the others shall be rejected and shall not be publicly announced.

两个或者两个以上的申请人，在同一种商品或者类似商品上，以相同或近似的商标申请注册的，初步审定并公告申请在先的商标；同一天申请的，初步审定并公告使用在先的商标，驳回其他人的申请，不予公告。

2. 较多使用被动语态和名词化结构

法律的突出特点是客观公正，不带主观色彩，因而法律文本中较少出现人称主语，而更多的是采用被动语态和名词化结构。例如：

These rules are formulated in accordance with Arbitration Law of the People's Republic of China and the provisions of the relevant laws and...

根据《中华人民共和国仲裁法》和有关的法律条款以及……，制定本仲裁规则。

3. 大量状语的使用

国际商法中，为了使条款明确清晰，排除一切可能产生的歧义和误解，严格界定相关各方的义务和权利，常常使用大量结构复杂，重叠的状语来修饰条款中的动词。多个状语同时修饰一个动词，或者一个状语包含另一个状语的现象也很常见。法律英语中引导条件状语从句最常用的连接词是 if，用来表述先规定条件然后确定权利的基本句型可归纳为：if X, then Y shall do/shall be Z。

三、国际商法的翻译技巧

对国际商法语言特点的分析有助于确立合理的、行之有效的翻译标准。历来传统的法律翻译方法是重"直译"，轻"意译"。法律翻译中忠实原文更多地体现在法律术语的翻译上，对于句子结构，则大可不必拘泥于传统的法律翻译理论，重要的还是要保证译文能够通顺、地道，保证原文的意义能够得到准确的传递，做到形可变而神不变。

1. 词汇的翻译

对于法律专业术语的翻译，必须以准确为先，切忌乱译。遇到把握不准的意义表达时，应借助工具书或网络搜索引擎，查询法律用语的确切含义。常用法律英语工具书有法律出版社的《元照英美法词典》和《牛津现代法律用语词典》。在使用网络搜索引擎查询法律术语含义时，要多做对比，尤其要比对中英文网站的解释有无差别。

对于并非法律语体所独有的术语，如 parties, item, instrument, suspension, resolution, act 等在法律语体中，有其确切含义，翻译时应搞清其特殊法律词义，并坚持"直译"原则：parties 译为"当事人/方/国"；item 译为"款"；instrument 译为"法律文书"；suspension 译为"终止"。

由于不同国家的法律存在差异，有时源语言中所表达的法律含义在目标语言中不存在，或是直译得到的目标语言词汇所表达的含义与源语言不同，在翻译时应特别注意。例如：obligation of a contract 译为"妨碍司法"而不是"合同的义务"；straw man 译为"挂名负责人"而不是"稻草人"；cause of action 在法律文书中应译为"案由"而不是"行为原因"。

2. 状语的翻译

1）目的状语

国际商法用语中的目的状语通常由 in order to, for the purposes of, so as to, so（such）…that 引导，可以位于句首，也可以位于句末。其所在的位置取决于它传递的信息在条约内容中的重要性和目的状语的结构。一般目的为次要信息或者目的状语含有多个平行结构，行文时以位于句末为主。例如：

For the purposes of Paragraph 1

(a) the initialing of a text constitutes a signature of the treaty when it is established that the negotiating states so agreed;

(b) the signature ad referendum of a treaty by a representative, if confirmed by his state, constitutes a full signature of the treaty.

此句中的目的状语简练短小，不妨就用"就"字把其放于句首，译为："就适用第一项而言：（甲）倘经确定谈判国有此协议，约文之草签构成条约之签署；（乙）代表对条约作核准之签署，倘经其本国确认，即构成条约之正式签署。"

2）方式状语

为了避免造成歧义，方式状语通常放于它所修饰的动词之前或之后，由副词或介词短语来充当，结构或简短，或冗长。方式状语通常都是规定性的，作用是规定条约各方履行义务或行使权力时必须采取的方式或手段。因此，方式状语有时尽管简单，但作用却比较重要。

例如：A treaty shall be interpreted in good faith in accordance with the ordinary meaning to be given to the terms of the treaty in their context and in the light of its object and purpose.

此句的方式状语相当冗长，但为了体现其语用特征——国际商法的严密性和庄重性，我们还是要把方式状语放在动词之前："条约应依其用语按其上下文并参照条约之目的及宗旨所具有之通常意义，善意解释之。"为了句子的连贯和顺畅，我们把 in good faith 放得离动词更近。

3）条件状语

条件状语的情况比较复杂，有表假设的条件状语，有表先决条件的条件状语，还有表示例外情况的条件状语。引导条件状语的词语有 if, unless, except, subject to, in case, provided (that) 等,所以在翻译中不可一概而论,针对不同的条件状语要采取不同的翻译技巧。

遇到表假设的条件状语,我们一般考虑将其放到句首,使句子主干部分更加紧凑,结构也更加简化。

常用的 except 的译法:

A ground for invalidating, terminating, withdrawing from or suspending the operation of a treaty recognized in the present convention may be invoked only with respect to the whole treaty except as provided in the following paragraphs or in Article 60。

本句中"except"引导的条件状语,对全句进行了限制,表明了在什么条件下不可以"援引理由",在语用功能上,它是对条款的补充和修正,含有一定的转折意义,翻译时我们把它译为"……不在此限"放在句末。全句可译为:"本公约所承认之条约失效、终止、退出或停止实行条约之理由仅对整个条约援引之,但下列各项或第六十条所规定之情形不在此限。"

3. 长句的翻译

法律英语中较多使用长句是由法律语言的特殊性所决定的。在翻译法律英语长句时要先从语法分析入手,充分理解源语文本的意思,然后将其意思用通顺的汉语翻译出来。换句话说,长句的翻译可以简化为"破"和"立"两个过程。"破"是指剖析出原文的主句、重心及整个句子含义,并进行拆解,探析句子中的几层含义。"立"是指结合所涉专业知识,以汉语的表达习惯方式翻译原句并精心组织目的语。例如:

When there are two or more creditors or debtors to a deal, each of the joint creditors shall be entitled to demand that the debtor fulfill his obligations, in accordance with legal provisions or the agreement between the parties; each of the joint debtors shall be obliged to perform the entire debt, and the debtor who performs the entire debt shall be entitled to ask the other joint debtors to reimburse him for their shares of the debt.

分析:这是一个复合句,共有 78 个单词。全句由三个并列句组成,分别是:each of the joint creditors shall be entitled to…; each of the joint debtors shall be obliged to…; the debtor shall be entitled to…。对于这三个并列句而言,有一个共同的时间状语从句:When there are two or more creditors or debtors to a deal。另外有一个由 who 引导的定语从句修饰 the debtor。通过语法分析,理清脉络后,可组织译文如下:"债权人或债务人一方人数为二人以上的,依照法律的规定或者当事人的规定,享有连带权利的每个债权人,都有权要求债务人履行义务;负有连带义务的每个债务人,都负有清偿全部债务的义务,履行了义务的人,有权要求其他负有连带义务的人偿付他应当承担的份额。"

 **法律宝典**

国际商法基础知识

一、什么是国际商法

国际商法(International Business Law)是调整国际商事关系的法律规范的总称。它的调整对象是国际商事关系,即:各国商事组织在跨国经营中所形成的商事关系。

目前,国际商法在法律渊源方面已形成了国际条约、国际贸易惯例(两者我们可合称为国际法渊源)、国内法并存的局面。具体来讲,凡调整跨国界商事关系的法律规范,不论它以国际公法规范、国际经济法规范表现出来,还是以当事人自愿接受的国际商事惯例、国内商法中的国际性规范形式表现出来,在本质上都属于国际商法的范畴,彼此之间互相依赖、互相补充、互相转化、互相作用。各国之间涉外商法的差异日渐缩小,国际商法的内容也不断丰富和完善,国际商法统一化进程日益加快,为适应并促进国际经济一体化发挥了积极作用。

二、国际商法的特点

国际商法在法律渊源方面具有多样性、复杂性。国际商法的体系不是固定不变的,而是处在不断发展变化过程中,这是由国际商事关系的性质和特点所决定的。当前,国际商事关系发展的国际性、协调性、安全性和便利性趋势,为国际商法的未来发展指明了方向,也使国际商法体系的发展呈现出以下特点:一是国际商法所涉及的领域越来越广泛,尤其在商事行为法方面的规范内容会越来越多,体系会越来越完备。二是在国际条约公约、国际贸易惯例、国内法之间互动机制的基础上,各国涉外商事交易的法律会日渐统一。

三、国际商法的内容

在内容上,国际商法体系的确定取决于跨国界的商事关系的发展。如今,国际商事关系所涉及的已不再是简单的产品交换。根据联合国国际贸易法委员会在起草《国际商事仲裁示范法》时,就"商事"一词所作的注释,具有商事性质的关系包括但不限于下列交易:任何提供或交换商品或劳务的交易;销售协议;商事代表或代理;保付代理;租赁;咨询;设计;许可;投资;融资;银行业;保险;开采协议或特许权;合营企业或其他形式的工业或商业合作;客货的航空、海洋、铁路或公路运输。国际商事关系以生产要素的跨国界流动为主流,再结合商事行为法性质的结构划分,可以系统地划分国际商事活动涉及的领域,这也是国际商法按调整对象进行划分的基础。按照这一思路,国际商事关系涉及四个领域,一是直接媒介钱货交易的动产和不动产买卖、有价证券的买卖,在交易所进行的买卖以及商人间的买卖等;二是间接媒介货物交易的行为,如货物运输、仓储保管、居间、行纪、代办商等;三是为工商提供资金融通的银行、信托,为商业提供产品的制造业、加工业等;四是直接间接为商事活动提供服务的财产保险等。

由此可知,国际商法应包括:商事主体法(包括商事组织、商事代理、商业登记等);商事行为法(包括国际货物买卖法、国际货物运输法、国际货物运输保险法、海商法、国际技术贸易法、产品责任法、票据与国际结算法、国际资金融通法);国际商事争议解决规则(包括国际民事诉讼、国际商事仲裁)。每一组成部分在表现形式上都是由国际法渊源和国内法渊源有机结合组成的。

▶ 术语积累

abandonment of a patent application   放弃专利申请

abuse of patent 滥用专利权
action for infringement of patent 专利侵权诉讼
action of a patent 专利诉讼
allowance 准许
amendment 修改，修正
appeal 上诉
appellation of origin 原产地名称
applicant for patent 专利申请人
application date 申请日期
application documents 申请案文件
application fee 申请费
application laying open for public inspection 公开供公众审查的申请
application number 申请号
application papers 申请案文件
arbitration 仲裁
article of manufacture 制品
assignee 受让人
assignment 转让
assignor 转让人
author of the invention 发明人
author's certificate 发明人证书
basic patent 基本专利
BIRPI 保护知识产权联合国国际局
board of appeals 申诉委员会
burden of proof 举证责任
case law 判例法
certificate of addition 增补证书
certificate of correction 更正证明书
certificate of patent 专利证书
citation 引证
claim 权项
classifier 分类员
海商法 maritime law
船舶国籍证书 certificate of registry; certificate of ship's nationality
船旗国 flag country

船舶所有权证书　certificate of ship ownership
船舶检验　register of ship
船舶保险　insurance on hull
船舶保险单　hull insurance policy
船舶登记证书　certificate of registry
船舶丈量　tonnage measurement of ships
船舶进港费　groundage
船舶抵押　ship mortgage
船舶租赁　ship chartering
船舶转租　ship subchartering
船舶所有人责任限制　limitation of liabilities of ship owners
船舶碰撞　ship collision
船舶遇难　maritime distress
海上灾难　perils of the sea
海上拖航　marine towage
船舶扣押　detention of ship
船舶债权　ship's credit
船级证书　certificate of class
船舶抵押权　maritime mortgage
海上优先请求权　priority claim to seagoing ships
救助优先权　priority claim to salvage
共同海损优先权　priority claim to general average
服务优先权　priority claim to service
货物损害优先权　priority claim to cargo damage
船舶抵押借款和货物抵押借款优先权　priority claim to ship credit and goods credit
海运合同　shipping contract
空舱费　dead freight
租船费　charterage
期租船合同　time charter-party; time CP
航次租船合同　voyage charter-party
定期租船合同　time charter-party
光船租船合同　bareboat charter-party; bareboat CP
包租运输合同　shipping charter-party
远洋拖带合同　contract of ocean towage
港内拖带合同　contract of port towage

Section III 巩固练习

词汇与短语

1. Taxation System of China
2. International Revenue
3. Analysis of Risk Investment
4. Budget Accountancy
5. Cost Accounting
6. International Private Law
7. Litigation Law
8. Theory of Knowledge Property Right
9. Penal Law
10. Lawyer Affairs
11. 仲裁法
12. 金融法
13. 国际商法
14. 基础会计
15. 财务会计
16. 税务管理
17. 管理学
18. 公司法
19. 合同法
20. 税法

句子与段落

1. A patent is a governmental grant of an exclusive monopoly as an incentive and a reward for a new invention.
2. Goods that must bear a registered trademark may not be marketed unless an application therefore has been approved.
3. The court granted the plaintiff an injunction restraining the defendant from breaching copyright.
4. The reproduction of copyright material without the permission of the copyright holder is banned by law.
5. The clause provides that the parties will submit any dispute to arbitration rather than litigation.
6. 财产所有权是指所有人依法对自己的财产享有占有、使用、收益和处分的权利。
7. 财产所有权的取得，不得违反法律规定。按照合同或者其他合法方式取得财产的，财产所有权从财产交付时起转移，法律另有规定或者当事人另有约定的除外。
8. 财产可以由两个以上的公民、法人共有。共有分为按份共有和共同共有。按份共有人按照各自的份额，对共有财产分享权利，分担义务。共同共有人对共有财产享有权利，承担义务。按份共有财产的每个共有人有权要求将自己的份额分出或者转让。但在出售时，其他共有人在同等条件下，有优先购买的权利。

9. 全民所有制企业对国家授予它经营管理的财产依法享有经营权,受法律保护。

10. 对下列所得,免征、减征所得税:

(一)外国投资者从外商投资企业取得的利润,免征所得税;

(二)国际金融组织贷款给中国政府和中国国家银行的利息所得,免征所得税;

(三)外国银行按照优惠利率贷款给中国国家银行的利息所得,免征所得税;

(四)为科学研究、开发能源、发展交通事业、农林牧业生产以及开发重要技术提供专有技术所取得的特许权使用费,经国务院税务主管部门批准,可以减按百分之十的税率征收所得税,其中技术先进或者条件优惠的,可以免征所得税。

除本条规定以外,对于利润、利息、租金、特许权使用费和其他所得,需要给予所得税减征、免征的优惠待遇的,由国务院规定。

Unit Twelve

Securities Law
证 券 法

Section I 译例研究

>> ***Passage One***
Registration of Securities and Taking Effect of Registration Statement

SEC. 6. (a) Any security may be registered with the Commission under the terms and conditions hereinafter provided, by filing a registration statement in triplicate, at least one of which shall be signed by each issuer, its principal executive officer or officers, its principal financial officer, its comptroller or principal accounting officer, and the majority of its board of directors or persons performing similar functions (or, if there is no board of directors or persons performing similar functions, by the majority of the persons or board having the power of management of the issuer), and in case the issuer is a foreign or Territorial person by its duly authorized representative in the United States; except that when such registration statement relates to a security issued by a foreign government, or political subdivision thereof, it need be signed only by the underwriter of such security. Signatures of all such persons when written on the said registration statements shall be presumed to have been so written by authority of the person whose signature is so affixed and the burden of proof, in the event such authority shall be denied, shall be upon the party denying the same. The affixing of any signature without the authority of the purported signer shall constitute a violation of this title. A registration statement shall be deemed effective only as to the securities specified therein as proposed to be offered.

...

(c) The filing with the Commission of a registration statement, or of an amendment to a registration statement, shall be deemed to have taken place upon the receipt thereof, but the filing of a registration statement shall not be deemed to have taken place unless it is accompanied by a United States postal money order or a certified bank check or cash for the amount of the fee required under subsection (b).

(d) The information contained in or filed with any registration statement shall be made available to the public under such regulations as the Commission may prescribe, and copies thereof, photostatic or otherwise, shall be furnished to every applicant at such reasonable charge as the Commission may prescribe.

...

SEC. 8. (a) Except as hereinafter provided, the effective date of a registration statement shall be the twentieth day after the filing thereof or such earlier date as the Commission may determine, having due regard to the adequacy of the information respecting the issuer theretofore available to the public, to the facility with which the nature of the securities to be registered, their relationship to the capital structure of the issuer and the rights of holders thereof can be understood, and to the public interest and the protection of investors. If any amendment to any such statement is filed prior to the effective date of such statement, the registration statement shall be deemed to have been filed when such amendment was filed; except that an amendment filed with the consent of the Commission, prior to the effective date of the registration statement, or filed pursuant to an order of the Commission, shall be treated as a part of the registration statement.

(b) If it appears to the Commission that a registration statement is on its face incomplete or inaccurate in any material respect, the Commission may, after notice by personal service or the sending of confirmed telegraphic notice not later than ten days after the filing of the registration statement, and opportunity for hearing (at a time fixed by the Commission) within ten days after such notice by personal service or the sending of such telegraphic notice, issue an order prior to the effective date of registration refusing to permit such statement to become effective until it has been amended in accordance with such order. When such statement has been amended in accordance with such order the Commission shall so declare and the registration shall become effective at the time provided in subsection (a) or upon the date of such declaration, whichever date is the later.

(c) An amendment filed after the effective date of the registration statement, if such amendment, upon its face, appears to the Commission not to be incomplete or inaccurate in any material respect, shall become effective on such date as the Commission may determine, having due regard to the public interest and the protection of investors.

(d) If it appears to the Commission at any time that the registration statement includes any untrue statement of a material fact or omits to state any material fact required to be stated therein or necessary to make the statements therein not misleading, the Commission may, after notice by personal service or the sending of confirmed telegraphic notice, and after opportunity for hearing (at a time fixed by the Commission) within fifteen days after such notice by personal service or the sending of such telegraphic notice, issue a stop order suspending the effectiveness of the registration statement. When such statement has been amended in accordance with such stop order the Commission shall so declare and thereupon the stop order shall cease to be effective.

(e) The Commission is hereby empowered to make an examination in any case in order to determine whether a stop order should issue under subsection (d). In making such examination the Commission or any officer or officers designated by it shall have access to and may demand the production of any books and papers of, and may administer oaths and affirmations to and examine, the issuer, underwriter, or any other person, in respect of any matter relevant to the examination, and may, in its discretion, require the production of a balance sheet exhibiting the assets and liabilities of the issuer, or its income statement, or both, to be certified to by a public or certified accountant approved by the Commission. If the issuer or underwriter shall fail to cooperate, or shall obstruct or refuse to permit the making of an examination, such conduct shall be proper ground for the issuance of a stop order.

(f) Any notice required under this section shall be sent to or served on the issuer, or, in case of a foreign government or political subdivision thereof, to or on the underwriter, or, in the case of a foreign or Territorial person, to or on its duly authorized representative in the United States named in the registration statement, properly directed in each case of telegraphic notice to the address given in such statement.

词汇提示

security　*n.* 证券
commission　*n.* 委员会
registration statement　注册报告书
in triplicate　一式三份
board of directors　董事会
underwriter　*n.* 包销商
respecting　*prep.* 有关
facility　*n.* 便利
capital structure　资本结构
holders　*n.* 持有人
public interest　公共利益
amendment　*n.* 修正案
postal money order　邮政汇票
bank check　支票
copies　*n.* 副本
photostatic　*adj.* 影印的
on its face　表面上看
take effect　生效
hearing　*n.* 听证
assets and liabilities　资产和负债情况

a balance sheet　损益计算书
public accountant　公共会计师
certified accountant　注册会计师
duly authorized　正当授权

要点解析

1. Any security may be registered with the Commission under the terms and conditions hereinafter provided, by filing a registration statement in triplicate, at least one of which shall be signed by each issuer, its principal executive officer or officers, its principal financial officer, its comptroller or principal accounting officer, and the majority of its board of directors or persons performing similar functions...

根据以下所规定的条件，任何证券都可以以提交注册报告书的形式向委员会注册。报告书一式三份——至少其中一份应由每个发行人、其主要执行官员、主要财务官员、监理官员或主要会计官员、董事会大多数成员或行使类似职能的人签字……

此处英文原文的一句话很长，翻译的时候使用了断句法，将一个长句断成几个短句。另外将原文的定语从句断开，转化成两个部分，用破折号将其连接起来，这样既避免译出的句子太长，又完整地保留了原来句子的关系。

2. ...in case the issuer is a foreign or Territorial person by its duly authorized representative in the United States; except that when such registration statement relates to a security issued by a foreign government, or political subdivision thereof, it need be signed only by the underwriter of such security.

……在发行人是外国人或准州居民时，则由美国经正式授权的代表在上面签字——如果该注册报告书所涉及的证券是由外国政府或其政治机构发行的，则只需要该证券的包销商签字。

此处原句将 except 表示的例外部分用破折号与前面所述的情况相连，起到了强调说明的作用。此外，原句的被动句 need be signed 译成了主动句，符合中文的表达习惯。

3. A registration statement shall be deemed effective only as to the securities specified therein as proposed to be offered.

只有其中规定的证券是提及所要发行的证券时，注册报告书才会被认为有效。

此处译文将条件句前置，后置定语转化为前置定语。

4. The information contained in or filed with any registration statement shall be made available to the public under such regulations as the Commission may prescribe, and copies thereof, photostatic or otherwise, shall be furnished to every applicant at such reasonable charge as the Commission may prescribe.

任何注册报告书中包括的或随报告书一起提交的内容和资料都必须根据委员会规定的有关规则使公众能够得到，并且，注册报告书的副本、影印本或其他都应以委员会规定的合理价格向每一个申请人提供。

此句有两处被动表达在翻译时均转化成主动结构。

5. …and to the public interest and the protection of investors.

……以及对公众利益和保护投资者等方面……

此处应用了"词性转换法",将名词 protection 转化成动词,另外使用了增词译法,补充了"等方面",确保了全面性和准确性。

6. …except that an amendment filed with the consent of the Commission, prior to the effective date of the registration statement, or filed pursuant to an order of the Commission, shall be treated as a part of the registration statement.

……但若经过委员会同意,在注册报告书生效日前提交的修正案,或是根据委员会命令提交的,则可作为注册报告书的一部分对待。

此处原文表示的是跟前文不同的情况,译成转折句恰好说明了前后关系。

7. If it appears to the Commission that a registration statement is on its face incomplete or inaccurate in any material respect, the Commission may, after notice by personal service or the sending of confirmed telegraphic notice not later than ten days after the filing of the registration statement, and opportunity for hearing…

如果委员会认为注册报告书看上去在某些实质性内容上有不完全或不准确之处,那么它可以在该注册报告书提交后不迟于十天之内,派人通知或发出证实通知电,并在派人通知或发出这种电报通知之后十天之内给予听证机会……

此处将形容词 incomplete or inaccurate 转化成名词"不完全或不准确之处",并将名词 notice 和 sending 转化为动词"通知"和"发出……"。

8. …issue an order prior to the effective date of registration refusing to permit such statement to become effective until it has been amended in accordance with such order.

……要求根据这一命令进行修订后才能允许该报告书生效。

此处将双重否定结构 refuse…until 转化成肯定结构。

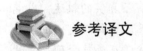 **参考译文**

证券注册和生效

第 6 节(a)根据以下所规定的条件,任何证券都可以以提交注册报告书的形式向委员会注册。报告书一式三份——至少其中一份应由每个发行人、其主要执行官员、主要财务官员、监理官员或主要会计官员、董事会大多数成员或行使类似职能的人(或,如果没有董事会或行使类似职能的人们,则由具有管理这一发行权力的委员会或人们的大多数)签字,在发行人是外国人或准州居民时,则由美国经正式授权的代表在上面签字——如果该注册报告书所涉及的证券是由外国政府或其政治机构发行的,则只需要该证券的包销商签字。在我们所说的注册报告书上签字时,所有这些人的签字应被认为是该人有这样签的权力而这样签上的,在这种权力被否认的情况发生时,举证责任应在否认这一情况的一方。不具有签署权力的签名将构成违反本篇罪。只有其中规定的证券是提及所要发行的证券时,注册报告书才会被认为有效。

……

（c）向委员会提交的注册报告书，或注册报告书的修正案应被视为在收到时发生，但所提交的注册报告书除非附有美国邮政汇票或银行所付支票以支付第（b）小节中规定的费用数额，否则不被视为发生。

（d）任何注册报告书中包括的或随报告书一起提交的内容和资料都必须根据委员会规定的有关规则使公众能够得到，并且，注册报告书的副本、影印本或其他都应以委员会规定的合理价格向每一个申请人提供。

……

第8节（a）除非此后另有规定，否则注册报告书的生效日应是注册报告书提交后的第二十天或由委员会决定的更早的日子，这是在以公众得到有关发行人信息的充分性、对其证券的性质将被注册的便利、其与发行人的资本结构以及证券持有人的权力的关系能被理解，以及对公众利益和保护投资者等方面给予应有的注意为条件的。如果任何对这种报告书的修正案是在该报告书生效日以前提交的，则该注册报告书应被视为是在该修正案提交时提交的；但若经过委员会同意，在注册报告书生效日前提交的修正案，或是根据委员会命令提交的，则可作为注册报告书的一部分对待。

（b）如果委员会认为注册报告书看上去在某些实质性内容上有不完全或不准确之处，在该注册报告书提交后不迟于十天之内，派人通知或发出证实通知电，并在派人通知或发出这种电报通知之后十天之内给予听证机会（在由委员会确定的时间）之后，委员会可在报告书生效日前发出命令，要求根据这一命令进行修订后才能允许该报告书生效。当该报告书被根据这一命令加以修订后，委员会应宣布该注册报告书在第（a）小节中规定的时间或在宣布日——以晚者为准——生效。

（c）修正案是在注册报告书生效日以后提交的情况下，如果委员会认为这一修正案，看上去在任何实质性内容上都没有不完善或不准确的地方，则该修正案应在委员会对公众利益和保护投资者方面给予适当注意后所决定的日子生效。

（d）不论何时，如果委员会认为注册报告书在有关实质性事实上有不真实的叙述，或漏报了规定应报的或使报告书不致被误解的所必要的任何重要事实，在派人通知或发出证实电通知后，且在派人通知或发出该电通知之后的十五天之内给予听证机会（在委员会确定的时间）后，委员会可发布终止命令中断该注册报告书的有效性。当该报告书被根据终止令加以修订，该委员会可以宣布并根据这一宣布，该终止令停止生效。

（e）据此，委员会被赋予在任何情况下可进行检查的权力，以决定是否根据第（d）小节发出终止令。在进行这种检查时，委员会或由委员会指定的任何官员将能接触，并可要求发行人、包销人或其他任何人提供书籍、报告，使这些人宣誓并作出证词，对这些人进行检查，在同检查相应的有关事情上，委员会可根据自己的决定要求提供展示发行人资产和负债情况的资产负债表或其损益计算书，或要求同时提供二者，它们需经委员会批准的一公共会计师，或注册会计师证明。如果发行人或包销人不予合作，或阻碍或拒绝允许进行这类检查，这种行为就是发布终止令的适当的理由。

（f）本节规定的任何应注意内容都应被发至或送达发行人。在外国政府或其政治机构为发行人的情况下，发至或送达包销人。当外国人或准州的人为发行人时，发至或送达在注册报告书中提到的其在美国被正当授权的代表。在每一种情况下，这些内容都应以电报通知形式发至在该注册报告书中提供的地址。

Passage Two
证券发行

第十条 公开发行证券,必须符合法律、行政法规规定的条件,并依法报经国务院证券监督管理机构或者国务院授权的部门核准或者审批;未经依法核准或者审批,任何单位和个人不得向社会公开发行证券。

第十一条 公开发行股票,必须依照公司法规定的条件,报经国务院证券监督管理机构核准。发行人必须向国务院证券监督管理机构提交公司法规定的申请文件和国务院证券监督管理机构规定的有关文件。

发行公司债券,必须依照公司法规定的条件,报经国务院授权的部门审批。发行人必须向国务院授权的部门提交公司法规定的申请文件和国务院授权的部门规定的有关文件。

第十二条 发行人依法申请公开发行证券所提交的申请文件的格式、报送方式,由依法负责核准或者审批的机构或者部门规定。

第十三条 发行人向国务院证券监督管理机构或者国务院授权的部门提交的证券发行申请文件,必须真实、准确、完整。

为证券发行出具有关文件的专业机构和人员,必须严格履行法定职责,保证其所出具文件的真实性、准确性和完整性。

第十四条 国务院证券监督管理机构设发行审核委员会,依法审核股票发行申请。

发行审核委员会由国务院证券监督管理机构的专业人员和所聘请的该机构外的有关专家组成,以投票方式对股票发行申请进行表决,提出审核意见。

发行审核委员会的具体组成办法、组成人员任期、工作程序由国务院证券监督管理机构制订,报国务院批准。

第十五条 国务院证券监督管理机构依照法定条件负责核准股票发行申请。核准程序应当公开,依法接受监督。

参与核准股票发行申请的人员,不得与发行申请单位有利害关系;不得接受发行申请单位的馈赠;不得持有所核准的发行申请的股票;不得私下与发行申请单位进行接触。

国务院授权的部门对公司债券发行申请的审批,参照前二款的规定执行。

第十六条 国务院证券监督管理机构或者国务院授权的部门应当自受理证券发行申请文件之日起三个月内作出决定;不予核准或者审批的,应当作出说明。

第十七条 证券发行申请经核准或者经审批,发行人应当依照法律、行政法规的规定,在证券公开发行前,公告公开发行募集文件,并将该文件置备于指定场所供公众查阅。

发行证券的信息依法公开前,任何知情人不得公开或者泄露该信息。

发行人不得在公告公开发行募集文件之前发行证券。

第十八条 国务院证券监督管理机构或者国务院授权的部门对已作出的核准或者审批证券发行的决定,发现不符合法律、行政法规规定的,应当予以撤销;尚未发行证券的,停止发行;已经发行的,证券持有人可以按照发行价并加算银行同期存款利息,要求发行人返还。

第十九条 股票依法发行后,发行人经营与收益的变化,由发行人自行负责;由此变化引致的投资风险,由投资者自行负责。

第二十条 上市公司发行新股,应当符合公司法有关发行新股的条件,可以向社会公开募集,也可以向原股东配售。

上市公司对发行股票所募资金,必须按招股说明书所列资金用途使用。改变招股说明书所列资金用途,必须经股东大会批准。擅自改变用途而未作纠正的,或者未经股东大会认可的,不得发行新股。

第二十一条 证券公司应当依照法律、行政法规的规定承销发行人向社会公开发行的证券。证券承销业务采取代销或者包销方式。

证券代销是指证券公司代发行人发售证券,在承销期结束时,将未售出的证券全部退还给发行人的承销方式。

证券包销是指证券公司将发行人的证券按照协议全部购入或者在承销期结束时将售后剩余证券全部自行购入的承销方式。

第二十二条 公开发行证券的发行人有权依法自主选择承销的证券公司。证券公司不得以不正当竞争手段招揽证券承销业务。

▶ 词汇提示

依法　in accordance with the law
国务院　the State Council
授权　authorize
公开发行　openly issue
发行股票　issue shares
公司法　the Company Law
规定　provision
证券监督管理机构　securities regulatory body
公司债券　company bonds
依照　abide by
规定　stipulate
机构　organ
申请文件　application documents
法定职责　legal duties
工作程序　work procedures
接受……　be subject to…
执行　implement
指定场所　designated places
募集　subscription
符合　in compliance with
撤销　annul
同期　for the corresponding period

上市公司　listed company
股东　stockholder
证券代销　commission underwriting
代表　on behalf of
不正当竞争手段　improper means of competition

要点解析

1. 公开发行证券，必须符合法律、行政法规规定的条件。

Before publicly issuing securities, one must fulfill the provisions of laws and administrative rules and regulations.

本句中把条件句翻译成了时间状语从句，明确了前后的关系，强调了符合这一条件的必要性。

2. 公开发行股票，必须依照公司法规定的条件，报经国务院证券监督管理机构核准。

Before publicly issuing shares, one must abide by the provisions of the Company Law, and report to and attain prior approval from the securities regulatory body under the State Council.

原句中没有主语，翻译时补足了主语 one 用来代指公开发行股票的单位或个人。prior approval 强调了这一机构的最高权威性，the securities regulatory body under the State Council, 用 under 一词明确说明了二者的从属关系。

3. 发行人必须向国务院授权的部门提交公司法规定的申请文件和国务院授权的部门规定的有关文件。

The applicant-issuer must submit to the relevant department authorized by the State Council, application documents as required by relevant provisions of the Company Law and other relevant documents as stipulated by the relevant department authorized by the State Council.

由于宾语较长，此处将宾语后置，避免头重脚轻。原句中"发行人"翻译成 applicant-issuer 使意义更为准确。

4. 发行人依法申请公开发行证券所提交的申请文件的格式、报送方式，由依法负责核准或者审批的机构或者部门规定。

The organ or department legally in charge of examining and approving the application of an applicant-issuer who applies to publicly issue securities according to law shall decide the formats of application documents and the modes for submitting them.

原句包含了被动关系，翻译为主动句，强调了提出这些规定的主语。

5. 参与核准股票发行申请的人员，不得与发行申请单位有利害关系。

Personnel who are involved in approving stock issue applications shall not have any interests in units applying for the issue.

"利害关系"在此处是指利益关系，翻译成 interests 恰到好处。

6. 不予核准或者审批的，应当作出说明。

The organizations or departments shall give an explanation for applications that are not approved or examined.

原句中文省略了主语，此处补充为上文提到的 organizations or departments。

7. 发行证券的信息依法公开前，任何知情人不得公开或者泄露该信息。

Before making public the information on the stock issue in accordance with the law, any person who has information on the issue shall not disclose such information.

知情人是证券信息的知情人，补足必要信息之后不会产生歧义，保证了翻译的准确性。

8. 上市公司对发行股票所募资金，必须按招股说明书所列资金用途使用。

A listed company shall utilize the capital it procures from stock issue in accordance with the uses explained in the public issue subscription notice.

 参考译文

Stock Issuance

Article 10. Before publicly issuing securities, one must fulfill the provisions of laws and administrative rules and regulations; report, in accordance with the law, to the securities regulatory body under the State Council, or to a relevant department authorized by the State Council; and attain its prior approval. Without attaining prior approval according to law, no unit or individual is allowed to openly issue securities to the public.

Article 11. Before publicly issuing shares, one must abide by the provisions of the Company Law, and report to and attain prior approval from the securities regulatory body under the State Council. The applicant-issuer must submit to the securities regulatory body under the State Council, application documents as required by relevant provisions of the Company Law and other relevant documents as stipulated by the securities regulatory body under the State Council.

Before issuing company bonds, one must abide by the provisions of the Company Law, and report to and attain prior approval from a relevant department authorized by the State Council. The applicant-issuer must submit to the relevant department authorized by the State Council, application documents as required by relevant provisions of the Company Law and other relevant documents as stipulated by the relevant department authorized by the State Council.

Article 12. The organ or department legally in charge of examining and approving the application of an applicant-issuer who applies to publicly issue securities according to law shall decide the formats of application documents and the modes for submitting them.

Article 13. When submitting application documents to the securities regulatory body under the State Council or to a relevant department authorized by the State Council for the approval to issue securities, the applicant-issuer must furnish truthful, accurate, and complete information.

The special organizations and personnel in charge of issuing relevant documents for securities issuance must strictly execute their legal duties, and ensure that the documents issued by them are truthful, accurate, and complete.

Article 14. The securities regulatory body under the State Council shall establish an issuance examination committee that will examine and approve, according to law, the applications for share issuance.

The issuance examination committee will consist of professionals from the securities regulatory body under the State Council and outside experts hired by the securities regulatory body under the State Council. They will decide by casting their votes on the applications for share issuance, and expressed views on their deliberations.

The securities regulatory body under the State Council shall formulate the specific provisions for establishing the issuance examination committee, and the appointment periods and work procedures for its personnel, and submit them to the State Council for its approval.

Article 15. The securities regulatory body under the State Council shall be responsible for approving stock issue applications in accordance with the law. The approval procedure shall be made public and subject to supervision in accordance with the law.

Personnel who are involved in approving stock issue applications shall not have any interests in units applying for the issue; shall not receive gifts from units applying for the issue; shall not hold stocks of the approve issue; and shall not have private contact with units applying for the stock issue.

The examination and approval of a company's application for bond issue by State Council-authorized departments shall be implemented in accordance with the stipulations of the previous two paragraphs.

Article 16. The securities regulatory body under the State Council or State Council-authorized departments shall make a decision within three months from the date of receipt of stock issue application papers. The organizations or departments shall give an explanation for applications that are not approved or examined.

Article 17. When a stock issue application is examined and approved, the stock issuer shall, in accordance with the stipulations of laws and administrative rules and regulations, issue a public subscription notice before the public issue of the stock, and place the notice in designated places for the public to read.

Before making public the information on the stock issue in accordance with the law, any person who has information on the issue shall not disclose such information.

The issuer shall not issue stocks before issuing a public subscription notice.

Article 18. When the securities regulatory body under the State Council or State Council-authorized departments discovers that the approval or decision to examine and approve a stock issue is not in compliance with the stipulations of laws and administrative rules and regulations, they shall annul the approval and decision. The stock issue shall be canceled if the issue has not commenced. For stocks already issued, stockholders shall ask the issuer to recall the issue price and the interest calculated on the price, using the bank deposit interest rate for the corresponding period.

Article 19. After the issue of stock in accordance with the laws, the issuer shall be responsible for changes in the operations and profits; and investors shall be responsible for investment risks arising from these changes.

Article 20. When a listed company issues new stocks, it shall comply with the conditions required by the Company Law on new stock issue. It may sell the new stocks to the public or to existing stockholders.

A listed company shall utilize the capital it procures from stock issue in accordance with the uses explained in the public issue subscription notice. Changes in the listed capital uses in the stock issue explanations shall be approved by the general shareholders' meeting. A company shall not issue new stocks if it makes unauthorized changes in the use of capital which are not corrected or which are not approved by the shareholders' meeting.

Article 21. A securities company shall, in accordance with the stipulations of laws and administrative rules and regulations, underwrite to sell the securities an issuer offers for public subscription. The underwriting business is operated on a commission or sole agency basis.

Commission underwriting refers to the method whereby a securities company undertakes to sell securities on behalf of the issuer and return all unsold securities to the issuer at the end of the underwriting period.

The sole agency method of underwriting refers to the method whereby a securities company acquires all securities of the issuer in accordance with the agreement, or acquires all unsold securities after the public offer at the end of the underwriting period.

Article 22. An issuer who publicly issues securities has the right to select an underwriting securities company. Securities companies shall not procure the underwriting business with improper means of competition.

Section II 技能拓展

翻译技巧

信用证英语的语言特点及翻译

信用证英语属专门用途英语（English for Specific Purposes，ESP），具有法律文本的一般特点：行文严谨、用词准确、规范、正式，专业性强。

一、信用证的词汇特征及翻译

1. 信用证常使用专业术语

信用证里大量使用专业术语，包括一些在函电里所使用的缩略语。外贸行业所使用的专门术语，不了解外贸业务的人很难准确地理解它的确切含义。例如：

bona fide holder 善意持有人 （议付行向受益人垫付资金、买入跟单汇票后，即成为汇票持有人，也就是善意持有人。）

neutral document 中性单据 （指不表现出口商名称的单据）

……

2. 某些多义词在信用证中的特殊含义

例如：All bank charges outside U.K. are for our principals' account, but must claimed at the time of presentation of documents.

在英国境外发生的所有银行费用，应由开证人负担，但必须在提交单据时索取。

这里的 principal 不是"首长"，"主要的"之意，而是指开证申请人。

再如：Drawee bank's charges and acceptance commission are for buyer's account.

付款行的费用和承兑费用由卖方负担。

acceptance 不是"接受"之意，而是"承兑"，即远期汇票的付款人明确表示同意按出票人的指示，于票据到期日付款给持票人的行为。

3. 介词短语的使用

信用证常使用简单的介词结构取代从句来表达复杂的含义，体现出这种文本简洁、正式的特点。翻译时可将从句结构表达出来。

against 一词在信用证中出现的频率很高，而其在信用证中的词义与在普通英语中完全不同。在普通英语中，against 是介词，可以表示"反对"，"碰撞"，"紧靠"等意思。但在信用证中，against 一词用来表示"凭……"，"以……"，它在信用证中的词义在一般的字典中并没有出现。如：

This credit is valid until November 20, 2003 in New York for payment available against the presentation of the following documents.

本信用证在 2003 年 11 月 20 日在纽约到期前，凭提交以下单据付款。

再举几个类似例子：

Upon presentation of the documents to us, we shall authorize your head office backing department by airmail to debit the proceeds to our foreign business department account.

一俟向我行提交单证，我行将用航空邮件授权你总行借记我行国外营业部账户。

On receipt of the required documents which comply with the terms of this credit, we will remit proceeds in accordance with your instructions.

当收到该证项下相符的单据时，我（开证行）将按贵行指令付保证金。

Documents must be negotiated in conformity with the credit terms.

与该证相符的单据须议付。

4. 古体词语使用较多

古体词语主要是 here, there 加上介词构成的复合词。例如：hereby=by means of（以此方式，特此），herein=in this document（此中，在此文件中），thereby=by that means（因此；在那方），therein=in that，in that particular（在那里；在那点上）……这些词语的使用可避免一些不必要的重复，同时可以使文体显得正式，庄重。

5. 分数、数字、日期表达的正确理解与翻译

1）分数

in duplicate 一式两份；in triplicate 一式三份；in quadruplicate 一式四份；in quintuplicate 一式五份；in sextuplicate 一式六份；in septuplicate 一式七份；in octuplicate 一式八份；in nonuplicate 一式九份；in decuplicate 一式十份

2）数字

1/3 original B/L must be sent to the opener by airmail.

三份正本提单中的一份必须通过航空件寄给开证人。

3）日期

① 如果装船日期为：在某月某日之后，和在某月某日之前，应使用 after 和 before。如：6月25日之后，7月10日之前装船。应译为：Shipment will be effected after the 25th of June and before the 10th of July. 在此，after 和 before 应理解为不包括所提到的日期。即6月25日和7月10日装船是错误的。

② 如果装船期为：到某月某日止，从某月某日，直到某月某日等词，用 to, from, until。使用这些词时，应理解为包括所提到的日期。如：Time of shipment: from 10th to 20th August. 10日和20日都包括在内。

③ 如果装船期规定为：最晚不迟于9月30日，一般表述为：Latest date of shipment: 30th September.

二、L/C 中长句的特点及翻译

信用证中多长句，这也是信用证作为法律文体的一种特点。长句中从句修饰成分较多，结构较复杂，大多是复合句，并很少使用标点符号。这种一气呵成，结构复杂的长句使信用证文体显得庄重严谨，以免双方产生误解和纠纷。在翻译时，必须正确理解句子主干与它的修饰成分，不能把连贯的意思拆开来译，否则会造成错误的理解。例如：

We hereby agree with the drawers, endorsers and bona-fide holders of the drafts drawn under and in compliance with the terms of this credit that such drafts shall be duly honored on due presentation and delivery of documents as herein specified.

凡根据本信用证并按其所列条款而开具的汇票向我行提示并交出本证规定的单据者，我行同意对其出票人、背书人及善意持有人履行付款义务。

分析：这是开证行在自由议付信用证中加列的保证文句。该句 agree with... of... 中，drawers, endorsers and bona-fide holders 是并列成分，为 agree with 的宾语；而 drafts drawn under and in compliance with the terms of this credit 为 of 的宾语，然后要分析清楚 that such drafts... 是 agree 的宾语从句，表述开证行履行付款义务的条件。

1. 省略系动词和助动词 "be"

1）省略系动词 be

例1：

a. Signed Commercial Invoice in three fold （商业发票一式三份）

b. Marine Insurance Policy in duplicate （海运保险单一式两份）

c. Packing list in five fold （装箱单一式五份）

例2：

a. Latest date of shipment 080523 （最迟装运期为2008年5月23日）

b. Latest date of shipment: FEB 28, 2008 （最迟装运期是2008年2月28日）

c. Shipment from Dalian to Hamburg （从大连运往汉堡或装运港是大连，目的港是汉堡）

分析：在对这些省略系动词的句子进行汉译时，首先要做到意义准确无误，然后考虑汉语行文的需要。如果需要的话，可以加上"是"，"为"，使行文更符合汉语习惯（见例2的汉译）；如果没有必要，则可不译（见例 1 的汉译）。

2）省略助动词 be

例 1：

a. Each document to be dated not later than B／L date. （所有单据的出单日期应不晚于提单日期。）

b. Documents to be presented 15 days after the date of shipment. （单据需在装运日后 15 天内交银行。）

c. All shipping documents to be sent direct to the opening office by registered airmail in two lots. （所有装运单据应以航空挂号信的形式分两次直接寄至开证行。）

d. Insurance to be effected by buyer. （保险由买方办理。）

例 2：

a. Invoice to show H. S. Code of Commodity Number of the Merchandise. （发票需显示商品的海关税则号。）

b. If Shipment in Container, Bill of Lading to evidence Container Number and Seal Number. （如果货物采用集装箱装运，提单应显示集装箱号和铅封号。）

例 3：

a. Partial shipment allowed. （分批装运允许。）

Transshipment prohibited. （转船不允许。）

b. Partial shipments: allowed. （分批装运允许。）

Transshipment: not allowed. （转船不允许。）

分析：例 1 和例 2 中的几个条款都是信用证中有关单据要求的实例，都省略了助动词 be。例 1 采用的是 be to be done（表示将来）的结构。其中 a 句规定了单据的出单日期，b 句规定了向银行交单的期限，c 句规定了向开证行寄单的办法，d 句则规定了保险由买方办理，暗含的意思是保险单由买方出具，卖方无须办理。例 2 采用的是 be to do 的结构，省略了助动词 be。其中 e 句规定了发票上需要额外显示的信息，属于信用证中的特殊要求，要照办。所有句子都省略了助动词 be，句式虽然简洁，但不会引起任何歧义。例 3 属于被动语态省去助动词 be，主要用在运输条款中。有关可否分批和转船的规定无非是"允许""不允许"和"禁止"三种情形。无论哪种情形，都习惯上省略助动词 be，言简意赅，清楚明了，翻译时可采用直译的方法。

2. 状语从句在 L/C 中的使用

在信用证中，需要阐明权利和义务时，必须要明确指出在什么情况下，什么时间和地点，以何种方式进行什么行动，因而会使用较多的时间、地点、方式和条件等状语。信用证中用来引导条件句的词语主要有：if；only if；in case of；provided；providing that 等。

英语中各种状语的位置非常灵活，可以位于句首，句末或句中。而汉语中则通常将表示假设的条件状语从句放在句首。一般情况下，在翻译信用证中的这类句子时，可以首先考虑将状语的位置移到句首，从而使句子的核心部分突出，而且使其结构简化。例如：

① Transshipment is allowed on condition that the entire voyage be covered by through B/L.

只有在整个运输途中都出示提货单的情况下才允许转船运输。

② This L/C will be duly honored only if the seller submits whole set of documents that all terms and requirements under L/C No. 45 673 have been complied with.

只有出口人提供与信用证 No. 45673 号项下相符的全套单据，本行才予以承付。

③ Unless a nominated bank is the confirming bank, the authorization to honor or negotiate does not impose any obligation on that nominated bank to honor or negotiate, except when expressly agreed to by that nominated bank and communicated to the beneficiary.

除非一家被指定银行是保兑行，对被指定银行进行兑付或议付的授权并不构成其必须兑付或议付的义务，被指定银行明确同意并照此通知受益人的情形除外。

④ If the bill of lading contains the indication "intended vessel" or similar qualification in relation to the name of the vessel, an on board notation indicating the date of shipment and the name of the actual vessel is required.

如果提单包含"预期船"字样或类似有关限定船只的词语时，装上具名船只必须由注明装运日期以及实际装运船只名称的装船批注来证实。

⑤ A transport document indicating that transshipment will or may take place is acceptable, even if the credit prohibits transshipment.

即使信用证禁止转运，银行也将接受注明转运将发生或可能发生的运输单据。

3. 长短句并列使用

信用证出于对篇幅和格式的需要，有时往往限制字数，尽量避免长句的使用。而限制长句使用的办法之一就是使用简单介词来缩短句子结构。例如：

① …Available with any bank by negotiation against the documents detailed herein and of your drafts at sight drawn on Bank of China.

（凭本信用证所列单据和开给中国银行的即期汇票可以在任何一家银行议付。）

此句用了六个介词，包含以下几层意思：

a. 本信用证的议付地点（with）——any bank （任何一家银行）
b. 本信用证的支付方式（by）——negotiation （议付）
c. 本信用证的付款条件（against, of）——documents and drafts（凭单据和汇票）
d. 本信用证的汇票期限（at）——sight （即期）
e. 本信用证的付款人（on）——Bank of China（中国银行）

事物都有两面性，但有时为了使表达更加清楚严密，信用证中也会出现比较长的句子。

② If a credit states that charges are for the account of the beneficiary and charges cannot be collected or deducted from proceeds, the issuing bank remains liable for payment of charges.

如果信用证规定费用由受益人负担，而该费用未能收取或从信用证款项中扣除，开证行依然承担支付此费用的责任。

③ We hereby engage with the drawers, endorsers and bona—fide holders of drafts drawn under and in compliance with the terms of the credit that such drafts shall be duly honored on due presentation and delivery of documents as specified if drawn and negotiated within the validity date of this credit.

凡根据本信用证开具与本信用证条款相符的汇票，并能按时提交本证规定的单据，我行保证对出票人、背书人和善意持有人承担付款责任，需在本证有效期内开具汇票并议付。

④ In reimbursement draw sight drafts in Pounds Sterling on Halifox Bank and forward them to our London Office, accompanied by your certificate that all terms of this letter of credit have been complied with.

偿付办法：由你方开出英镑即期汇票向哈里发银行支取。在寄送汇票给我伦敦办事处时，应随附你行证明，声明本证的全部条款已经履行。

4. 分词短语作定语

大多出现在信用证中对单据的一般要求和特殊要求中。一般要求直接出现在所需单据（Documents required）项下，而特殊要求则出现在特殊条款（additional conditions）项下。例如：

① 4 Signed invoices in the name of applicant certifying merchandise to be of China origin.

四份经签署的商业发票，以申请人为抬头，证明货物系中国原产。

② Copy of beneficiaries' telex to buyer quoting L/C number mentioning details of shipment.

受益人的电传副本一份，显示信用证号码，注明装运细节。

③ Beneficiaries' certificate certifying that one set of N/N shipping documents has been sent to buyer immediately after shipment has been made.

受益人证明一份，证明一套副本装运单据已经在装运后立即寄出。

④ Marine insurance policy in triplicate endorsed in blank with claim payable in Japan in the currency of the draft covering 110 percent of the invoice value including institute war clauses institute cargo clauses（all risks）institute SRCC clauses.

海运保险单一式三份，空白背书，按汇票的币别在日本进行索赔，按发票金额的110%投保，包括协会战争险、协会货物一切险和协会罢工暴动民变险。

⑤ Full set of clean" shipped on board" ocean bill of lading drawn to the order of Commercial Bank Zurich, showing beneficiary as shipper marked notify applicant and us bearing our L/C No. showing freight Prepaid. Name, address and telephone numbers of shipping agent must also appear on bill of lading.

全套清洁已装船海运提单，凭苏黎世商业银行指示，显示受益人为发货人，注明申请人和我行为被通知人，显示信用证号码，运费预付，以及船代理的名称、地址和电话号码。

5. 被动语态的使用

信用证要求突出动作的对象，而忽视动作的完成者，也就是说信用证的文体因素和语言环境要求强调客观事实，因而动词被动语态的出现率较高。例如：

① You are requested to advise the credit to the beneficiary without adding your confirmation.

请贵方将此证通知受益人，而无须对该信用证加具保兑。

② The number and the date of the credit and the name of our bank must be quoted on all drafts required.

请在所有汇票上注明该信用证号码、开证日期和我行名称。

③ All documents must be forwarded to us in one lot by special service courier.

请将所有单据以特快专递一次寄至我方。

分析：在对信用证中这类含有被动语态的句子进行汉译时，不宜使用汉语的"被"字句，因为这样会使汉语的行文不够流畅，如果上面的句子译成"你被要求将信用证……"和

"……被注明在所有汇票上"和"所有单据需……被寄至我行",译文欠通顺。正确的翻译方法是在汉语译文中不使用"被"字,而使用汉语的主动语态的形式。因为都是提出要求希望对方执行的句子,所以按照汉语的礼貌习惯,在所提的要求前加上"请"字,如"请通知""请注明"和"请寄至"使语气大大缓和,有利于和谐贸易关系的建立和任务的执行,从而促进国际贸易的开展。

 法律宝典

金融证券基础知识

证券的定义

证券是各类财产所有权或债权凭证的通称,是用来证明证券持有人有权依票面所载内容,取得相关权益的凭证。所以,证券的本质是一种交易契约或合同,该契约或合同赋予合同持有人根据该合同的规定,对合同规定的标的采取相应的行为,并获得相应的收益的权利。

证券的分类

(一)按其性质不同,证券可以分为有价证券和凭证证券两大类。

凭证证券则为无价证券,包括活期存款单、借据、收据等。

有价证券可以按不同的标准做不同的分类。按发行主体来划分可以分为政府证券、金融证券和公司证券。按上市与否,可以分为上市证券和非上市证券。

(二)按证券所载内容可以分为三类。

(1)货币证券,可以用来代替货币使用的有价证券商业信用工具,主要用于企业之间的商品交易、劳务报酬的支付和债权债务的清算等,常见的有期票、汇票、本票、支票等。

(2)资本证券,它是指把资本投入企业或把资本供给企业或国家的一种书面证明文件,资本证券主要包括股权证券(所有权证券)和债权证券,如各种股票和各种债券等。

(3)货物证券,是指对货物有提取权的证明,它证明证券持有人可以凭证券提取该证券上所列明的货物,常见的有栈单、运货证书、提货单等。

股票的定义

股票是股份公司(包括有限公司和无限公司)在筹集资本时向出资人发行的股份凭证。代表着其持有者(即股东)对股份公司的所有权。这种所有权是一种综合权利,如参加股东大会、投票表决、参与公司的重大决策、收取股息或分享红利等。同一类别的每一份股票所代表的公司所有权是相等的。每个股东所拥有的公司所有权份额的大小,取决于其持有的股票数量占公司总股本的比重。股票一般可以通过买卖方式有偿转让,股东能通过股票转让收回其投资,但不能要求公司返还其出资。股东与公司之间的关系不是债权债务关系。股东是公司的所有者,以其出资额为限对公司负有限责任,承担风险,分享收益。

术语积累

big/large-cap stock, mega-issue   大盘股
list   上市

bourse 证交所
corporate champion 龙头企业
Shanghai Exchange 上海证交所
pension fund 养老基金
mutual fund 共同基金
hedge mutual fund 对冲式共同基金
share 股票
valuation 股价
underwriter 保险商
government bond 政府债券
saving account 储蓄账户
equity market 股市
shareholder 股东
delist 摘牌
money-loser 亏损企业
inventory 存货
traded company, trading enterprise 上市公司
stakeholder 利益相关者
transparency 透明度
MSNBC: Microsoft national broadcast 微软全国广播公司
damage-control machinery 安全顾问
efficient market 有效市场
intellectual property 知识产权
opportunistic practice 投机行为
WorldCom 世通公司
bribery 行贿
entrepreneur 企业家
cook the book 做假账
regulatory system 监管体系
audit 审计
accounting firm 会计事务所
Great Depression 大萧条
portfolio 投资组合
money-market 短期资本市场
capital-market 长期资本市场
volatility 波动
diversification 多元化
commodity 期货
real estate 房地产

option 期权
call option 看涨期权
put option 看跌期权
merger 并购
arbitrage 套利
Securities & Exchange Commission 〈美〉证券交易委员会
dollar standard 美元本位制
flight 贬值
budget 预算
deficit 赤字
bad debt 坏账
output 产值
macroeconomic 宏观经济
fiscal stimulus 财政刺激
a store of value 保值
transaction currency 结算货币
forward exchange 期货交易
intervention currency 干预货币
Treasury bond 财政部公债
current-account 经常项目
pickup in rice 物价上涨
Federal Reserve 美联储
inflation 通货膨胀
deflation 通货紧缩
tighter credit 紧缩信贷
monetary policy 货币政策
awash in excess capacity 生产力过剩
foreign exchange 外汇
spot transaction 即期交易
forward transaction 远期交易
option forward transaction 择期交易
swap transaction 掉期交易
quote 报价
settlement and delivery 交割
buying rate 买入价
selling rate 卖出价
spread 差幅
contract 合同
at par 平价

premium 升水
discount 贴水
direct quotation method 直接报价法
indirect quotation method 间接报价法
dividend 股息
domestic currency 本币
floating rate 浮动利率
parent company 母公司
credit swap 互惠贷款
venture capital 风险资本
virtual value 虚拟价值
physical good 物质产品
abstract good 抽象产品
Patent & Trademark Office 专利与商标局
book value 账面价值
physical capital 实际资本
IPO: initial public offering 新股首发
job machine 就业市场
welfare capitalism 福利资本主义
collective market cap 市场资本总值
global corporation 跨国公司
transnational status 跨国优势
transfer price 转让价格
General Accounting Office 〈美〉会计总会
consolidation 兼并
leveraged 杠杆
acquiring company 收购公司
bad loan 呆账
chart of cash flow 现金流量表
clearly-established ownership 产权清晰
debt to equity 债转股
diversity of equities 股权多元化
economy of scale 规模经济
emerging economies 新兴经济
exchange-rate regime 汇率机制
fund and financing 筹资融资
global financial architecture 全球金融体系
go public 上市
growth spurt （经济的）急剧增长

have one's "two commas"　百万富翁
hedge against　套期保值
housing mortgage　住房按揭
holdings　控股，所持股份
holding company　控股公司
initial offerings　原始股
initial public offerings　首次公募
innovative business　创新企业
intellectual capital　智力资本
inter-bank lending　拆借
internet customer　网上客户
investment payoff period　投资回收期
joint-stock　参股
mall rat　爱逛商店的年轻人
means of production　生产要素
(the) medical cost social pool for major diseases　大病医疗费用社会统筹
mergers and acquisitions　并购
mobile-phone banking　移动电话银行业
moods　人气
net potato　网虫
non-store selling　直销
offering　新股
online-banking　网上银行业
online-finance　在线金融
online client　（银行的）网上客户
paper profit　账面收益
physical assets　有形资产
project fund system　项目资本金制度
pyramid sale　传销
recapitalize　资产重组
regional currency blocks　地区货币集团
regulate　调控
sell off　变现
share (stock) option　期权，股票认购权
smart card　智能卡
slash prices　杀价
spare capacity　闲置的生产能力
strong growth　强劲的增长势头
switch trade　转手贸易

take...public 上市
tap the idle assets 盘活存量资产
transaction （银行的）交易
transfer payment from the exchequer 财政转移支付

Section III 巩固练习

词汇与短语

1. registration statement
2. board of directors
3. underwriter
4. capital structure
5. amendment
6. postal money order
7. take effect
8. assets and liabilities
9. a balance sheet
10. certified accountant
11. 国务院
12. 发行股票
13. 公司法
14. 证券监督管理机构
15. 公司债券
16. 申请文件
17. 法定职责
18. 工作程序
19. 股东
20. 证券代销

句子与段落

1. 证券交易当事人依法买卖的证券，必须是依法发行并交付的证券。非依法发行的证券，不得买卖。
2. 依法发行的股票、公司债券及其他证券，法律对其转让期限有限制性规定的，在限定的期限内，不得买卖。
3. 经依法核准的上市交易的股票、公司债券及其他证券，应当在证券交易所挂牌交易。
4. 证券在证券交易所挂牌交易，应当采用公开的集中竞价交易方式。证券交易的集中竞价应当实行价格优先、时间优先的原则。
5. 证券交易当事人买卖的证券可以采用纸面形式或者国务院证券监督管理机构规定的其他形式。
6. If any accountant, engineer, or appraiser, or any person whose profession gives authority to a statement made by him, is named as having prepared or certified any part of the registration statement, or is named as having prepared or certified a report or valuation for use in connection with the registration statement, the written consent of such person shall be filed

with the registration statement.

7. If any such person is named as having prepared or certified a report or valuation (other than a public official document or statement) which is used in connection with the registration statement, but is not named as having prepared or certified such report or valuation for use in connection with the registration statement, the written consent of such person shall be filed with the registration statement unless the Commission dispenses with such filing as impracticable or as involving undue hardship on the person filing the registration statement.

8. Any such registration statement shall contain such other information, and be accompanied by such other documents, as the Commission may by rules or regulations require as being necessary or appropriate in the public interest or for the protection of investors.

9. It shall be unlawful for any person, directly or indirectly, to make use of any means or instruments of transportation or communication in interstate commerce or of the mails to offer to sell or offer to buy through the use or medium of any prospectus or otherwise any security, unless a registration statement has been filed as to such security, or while the registration statement is the subject of a refusal order or stop order or (prior to the effective date of the registration statement) any public proceeding or examination under section 8.

10. The registration statement, when relating to a security other than a security issued by a foreign government, or political subdivision thereof, shall contain the information, and be accompanied by the documents, specified in Schedule A, and when relating to a security issued by a foreign government, or political subdivision thereof, shall contain the information, and be accompanied by the documents, specified in Schedule B; except that the Commission may by rules or regulations provide that any such information or document need not be included in respect of any class of issuers or securities if it finds that the requirement of such information or document is inapplicable to such class and that disclosure fully adequate for the protection of investors is otherwise required to be included within the registration statement.

Unit Thirteen

Public Law
国际公法

Section I 译例研究

❱❱ *Passage One*
The Rio Declaration on Environment and Development

The United Nations Conference on Environment and Development,

Having met at Rio de Janeiro from 3 to 14 June 1992,

Reaffirming the Declaration of the United Nations Conference on the Human Environment, adopted at Stockholm on 16 June 1972, and seeking to build upon it,

With the goal of establishing a new and equitable global partnership through the creation of new levels of cooperation among States, key sectors of societies and people,

Working towards international agreements which respect the interests of all and protect the integrity of the global environmental and developmental system,

Recognizing the integral and interdependent nature of the Earth, our home,

Proclaims that:

Principle 1

Human beings are at the centre of concerns for sustainable development. They are entitled to a healthy and productive life in harmony with nature.

Principle 2

States have, in accordance with the Charter of the United Nations and the principles of international law, the sovereign right to exploit their own resources pursuant to their own environmental and developmental policies, and the responsibility to ensure that activities within their jurisdiction or control do not cause damage to the environment of other States or of areas beyond the limits of national jurisdiction.

Principle 3

The right to development must be fulfilled so as to equitably meet developmental and environmental needs of present and future generations.

Principle 4

In order to achieve sustainable development, environmental protection shall constitute an integral part of the development process and cannot be considered in isolation from it.

Principle 5

All States and all people shall cooperate in the essential task of eradicating poverty as an indispensable requirement for sustainable development, in order to decrease the disparities in standards of living and better meet the needs of the majority of the people of the world.

Principle 6

The special situation and needs of developing countries, particularly the least developed and those most environmentally vulnerable, shall be given special priority. International actions in the field of environment and development should also address the interests and needs of all countries.

Principle 7

States shall cooperate in a spirit of global partnership to conserve, protect and restore the health and integrity of the Earth's ecosystem. In view of the different contributions to global environmental degradation, States have common but differentiated responsibilities. The developed countries acknowledge the responsibility that they bear in the international pursuit of sustainable development in view of the pressures their societies place on the global environment and of the technologies and financial resources they command.

词汇提示

Declaration　*n.* 宣言
Rio de Janeiro　里约热内卢
reaffirm　*v.* 重申
Stockholm　斯德哥尔摩
equitable　*adj.* 公正的，合理的
integral　*adj.* 构成整体所必需的
interdependent　*adj.* 相互依赖的
proclaim　*v.* 宣布
be entitled to　有权利，应当
jurisdiction　*n.* 司法权
constitute　*v.* 构成
eradicate　*v.* 消除
indispensable　*adj.* 必不可少的

disparity   *n.* 差距
priority   *n.* 优先权
conserve   *v.* 保护

▶ 法律术语

The United Nations Conference on Environment and Development   联合国环境与发展会议
Declaration of the United Nations Conference on the Human Environment   联合国《人类环境宣言》
sustainable development   可持续发展
the Charter of the United Nations   《联合国宪章》
sovereign right   主权权利
standard of living   生活水平
developing country   发展中国家
environmental degradation   环境退化
developed countries   发达国家

▶ 要点解析

1. The Rio Declaration on Environment and Development
此标题由文件签订地点 Rio、文件类型 Declaration 和文件内容 on Environment and Development 组成，在翻译时宜将 on Environment and Development 提至中间，将 Declaration 移至最后，进行语序的调整，合理地处理中英文语言表达习惯上的差异。

2. With the goal of establishing a new and equitable global partnership through the creation of new levels of cooperation among States, key sectors of societies and people，…
介词短语 with the goal 在翻译成中文时，采用介词短语动词化的翻译方法，将其译成动词短语"怀着……的目标"，更符合目标语读者阅读习惯；此处介词短语 through the creation of new levels of cooperation among States, key sectors of societies and people 翻译时提至前面，把 the goal of establishing a new and equitable global partnership 移到后面，更能体现前因后果的逻辑关系。

3. Working towards international agreements which respect the interests of all and protect the integrity of the global environmental and developmental system，…
翻译时应调整词序，将 which 引导的非限制性定语从句放在其所修饰的名词前面。

4. Proclaims that 是宣言正文开始的常用标志，通常将其译为"兹宣告"。

5. in accordance with the Charter of the United Nations and the principles of international law 作为插入语，翻译成中文时应注意语序的调整。译为"根据《联合国宪章》和国际法原则"。

6. …shall be given special priority. International actions in the field of environment and development should also address the interests and needs of all countries.
句中短语 give special priority 根据上下文，可被译为"受到优先考虑"。

7. International actions in the field of environment and development should also address the interests and needs of all countries.

此处短语 address the interests and needs of all countries 中，address 作为动词来用，可根据语境译为"着眼于所有国家的利益和需要"。

8. In view of the different contributions to global environmental degradation,…

句中介词短语 in view of 译成中文时，经常动词化，通常译为"鉴于……"。

参考译文

里约环境与发展宣言

联合国环境与发展会议，

于1992年6月3日至14日在里约热内卢举行，

重申了1972年6月16日在斯德哥尔摩通过的联合国《人类环境宣言》，并试图在其基础上再推进一步，

怀着在各国、社会各个关键性阶层和人民之间开辟新的合作层面，从而建立一种新的、公平的全球伙伴关系的目标，

致力于达成既尊重所有各方利益，又保护全球环境与发展体系的国际协定，

认识到我们的家乡地球的整体性和相互依存性，

兹宣告：

原则1 人类处于普受关注的可持续发展问题的中心。他们应有权以与自然相和谐的方式享有健康而富有生产成果的生活的权利。

原则2 根据《联合国宪章》和国际法原则，各国拥有按照其本国的环境与发展政策开发本国自然资源的主权权利，并负有确保在其管辖范围内或在其控制下的活动不致损害其他国家或在各国管辖范围以外地区的环境的责任。

原则3 为了公平地满足今世后代在发展与环境方面的需要，求取发展的权利必须实现。

原则4 为了实现可持续的发展，环境保护工作应是发展进程整体的组成部分，不能脱离这一进程来考虑。

原则5 为了缩小世界上大多数人生活水平的差距，更好地满足他们的需要，所有国家和所有人都应在根除贫穷这一基本任务上进行合作，这是实现可持续发展的一项不可少的条件。

原则6 发展中国家、特别是最不发达国家和在环境方面最易受伤害的发展中国家的特殊情况和需要应受到优先考虑。环境与发展领域的国际行动也应当着眼于所有国家的利益和需要。

原则7 各国应本着全球伙伴精神，为保存、保护和恢复地球生态系统的健康和完整进行合作。鉴于导致全球环境退化的各种不同因素，各国负有共同的但是又有差别的责任。发达国家承认，鉴于他们的社会给全球环境带来的压力，以及他们所掌握的技术和财力资源，他们在追求可持续发展的国际努力中负有责任。

Passage Two
公民权利和政治权利国际公约

序　　言

本公约缔约各国，

考虑到，按照联合国宪章所宣布的原则，对人类家庭所有成员固有尊严及其平等和不移的权利的承认，乃是世界自由、正义与和平的基础，

确认这些权利是源于人身的固有尊严，

确认，按照世界人权宣言，只有在创造了使人人可以享有其公民和政治权利，正如享有其经济、社会和文化权利一样的条件情况下，才能实现自由人类享有公民及政治自由和免于恐惧和匮乏的自由的理想，

考虑到各国根据联合国宪章负有义务促进对人的权利和自由的普遍尊重和遵行，

认识到个人对其他个人和对他所属的社会负有义务，应为促进和遵行本公约所承认的权利而努力，

兹同意下述各条：

第一条

一、所有人民都有自决权。他们凭这种权利自由决定他们的政治地位，并自由谋求他们的经济、社会和文化的发展。

二、……

三、本公约缔约各国，包括那些负责管理非自治领土和托管领土的国家，应在符合联合国宪章规定的条件下，促进自决权的实现，并尊重这种权利。

第二条

一、本公约每一缔约国承担尊重和保证在其领土内和受其管辖的一切个人享有本公约所承认的权利，不分种族、肤色、性别、语言、宗教、政治或其他见解、国籍或社会出身、财产、出生或其他身份等任何区别。

二、……

第三条

本公约缔约各国承担保证男子和妇女在享有本公约所载一切公民和政治权利方面有平等的权利。

第四条

一、在社会紧急状态威胁到国家的生命并经正式宣布时，本公约缔约国得采取措施克减其在本公约下所承担的义务，但克减的程度以紧急情势所严格需要者为限，此等措施并不得与它根据国际法所负有的其他义务相矛盾，且不得包含纯粹基于种族、肤色、性别、语言、宗教或社会出身的理由的歧视。

……

第六条

一、人人有固有的生命权。这个权利应受法律保护。不得任意剥夺任何人的生命。

二、在未废除死刑的国家，判处死刑只能是作为对最严重的罪行的惩罚，判处应按照犯罪时有效并且不违反本公约规定和防止及惩治灭绝种族罪公约的法律。这种刑罚，非经合格法庭最后判决，不得执行。

……

第七条

任何人均不得加以酷刑或施以残忍的、不人道的或侮辱性的待遇或刑罚。特别是对任何人均不得未经其自由同意而施以医药或科学试验。

词汇提示

公约　covenant
序言　preamble
固有的　inherent
不可分割的　inalienable
遵守　observance
负有义务　having duties
努力　strive for
由于　by virtue of
与……一致　in conformity with
基于　on the ground of
遭受　subject to
任意地　arbitrarily
被剥夺　be deprived of
承担　undertake
克减　derogate
种族灭绝　genocide
侮辱人的　degrading
同意　consent

法律术语

缔约国　the States Parties
世界人权宣言　the Universal Declaration of Human Rights
政治自由　political freedom
经济，社会和文化权利　economic, social and cultural rights
公民和政治权利　civil and political rights
自决权　the right of self-determination
非自治领土　Non-Self-Governing Territories
托管领土　Trust Territories

生命权　right to life
死刑　death penalty
判处死刑　sentence of death
种族灭绝罪　the crime of genocide

要点解析

1. 本公约缔约各国
此处翻译时要注意符合目的语的表达习惯，可译为"The States Parties to the present Covenant"。

2. 联合国宪章所宣布的原则
英译时将"原则"提到前面，"将联合国所宣布的"译成非谓语从句来修饰它，译为"the principles proclaimed in the Charter of the United Nations"。

3. 只有在创造了使人人可以享有其公民和政治权利，正如享有其经济、社会和文化权利一样的条件情况下，才能实现自由人类享有公民及政治自由和免于恐惧和匮乏的自由的理想，……
此句是个条件句，其中"只有……才……"使用 only…if…句型。

4. 本公约每一缔约国承担尊重和保证在其领土内和受其管辖的一切个人享有本公约所承认的权利……
此句中的"受……"一般译为"subject to…"，如 subject to heat 和 subject to law 等。

5. 保证在其领土内和受其管辖的一切个人享有本公约所使用的权利
此句中译英时使用减译的策略，采用 ensure sb. sth. 结构而非 ensure sb. have sth.，应译为"ensure to all individuals within its territory and subject to its jurisdiction the rights recognized in the present Covenant"。

6. 采取措施克减……，但克减的程度……
翻译时可采用合译法将两句合成一句，译为"take measures derogating from their obligations under the present Covenant to the extent strictly required by the exigencies of the situation"。

7. 不得任意剥夺任何人的生命
此句是主动语态，可利用中英语态的转换，变主动为被动，译为"No one shall be arbitrarily deprived of his life"，使其更符合英语表达习惯。

8. 这种刑罚，非经合格法庭最后判决，不得执行。
句中的"非……，不得……"是双重否定形式，英译时可将其转换为肯定形式，译为："This penalty can only be carried out pursuant to a final judgment rendered by a competent court."

9. 任何人均不得加以酷刑或施以残忍的、不人道的或侮辱性的待遇或刑罚。
句中"任何人均不得"可译为"no one shall"。

 参考译文

International Covenant on Civil and Political Rights

Preamble

The States Parties to the present Covenant,

Considering that, in accordance with the principles proclaimed in the Charter of the United Nations, recognition of the inherent dignity and of the equal and inalienable rights of all members of the human family is the foundation of freedom, justice and peace in the world,

Recognizing that these rights derive from the inherent dignity of the human person,

Recognizing that, in accordance with the Universal Declaration of Human Rights, the ideal of free human beings enjoying civil and political freedom and freedom from fear and want can only be achieved if conditions are created whereby everyone may enjoy his civil and political rights, as well as his economic, social and cultural rights,

Considering the obligation of States under the Charter of the United Nations to promote universal respect for, and observance of, human rights and freedoms,

Realizing that the individual, having duties to other individuals and to the community to which he belongs, is under a responsibility to strive for the promotion and observance of the rights recognized in the present Covenant,

Agree upon the following articles:

Article 1

1. All peoples have the right of self-determination. By virtue of that right they freely determine their political status and freely pursue their economic, social and cultural development.

2. …

3. The States Parties to the present Covenant, including those having responsibility for the administration of Non-Self-Governing and Trust Territories, shall promote the realization of the right of self-determination, and shall respect that right, in conformity with the provisions of the Charter of the United Nations.

Article 2

1. Each State Party to the present Covenant undertakes to respect and to ensure to all individuals within its territory and subject to its jurisdiction the rights recognized in the present Covenant, without distinction of any kind, such as race, color, sex, language, religion, political or other opinion, national or social origin, property, birth or other status.

2. …

Article 3

The States Parties to the present Covenant undertake to ensure the equal right of men and women to the enjoyment of all civil and political rights set forth in the present Covenant.

Article 4

1. In time of public emergency which threatens the life of the nation and the existence of which is officially proclaimed, the States Parties to the present Covenant may take measures derogating from their obligations under the present Covenant to the extent strictly required by the exigencies of the situation, provided that such measures are not inconsistent with their other obligations under international law and do not involve discrimination solely on the ground of race, color, sex, language, religion or social origin.

…

Article 6

1. Every human being has the inherent right to life. This right shall be protected by law. No one shall be arbitrarily deprived of his life.

2. In countries which have not abolished the death penalty, sentence of death may be imposed only for the most serious crimes in accordance with the law in force at the time of the commission of the crime and not contrary to the provisions of the present Covenant and to the Convention on the Prevention and Punishment of the Crime of Genocide. This penalty can only be carried out pursuant to a final judgement rendered by a competent court.

…

Article 7

No one shall be subjected to torture or to cruel, inhuman or degrading treatment or punishment. In particular, no one shall be subjected without his free consent to medical or scientific experimentation.

Section II 技能拓展

翻译技巧

被动语态在法律英语中的运用及翻译

英语法律语言同其他社会方言一样，是人们根据社会文化环境和交际目的、交际对象等语用因素，在长期使用中形成的一种具有自身规律的语言功能的变体。语言的社会功能，使得法律英语拥有自己独特的风格与个性。它不仅有自己的词汇特点、句法特点、篇章特点，就连在动词使用的语气、语态与时态方面也与普通英语有所区别。其中，就包括了大量被动语态的运用。本文将探讨被动语态在法律英语中运用的原因、目的、功能，并提出翻译的具体方法、技巧和应当注意的问题。

一、法律英语被动语态运用的原因与功能

（一）由英语语言自身的特点决定

英语中被动语态的使用本身就比较普遍，这样的例子真是数不胜数。例如：

① The question will be discussed in the meeting.
② His reputation is tainted by his connection with the drug dealers.
③ A contract between an adult and a minor is said to be voidable.

只要留心观察，就会发现英语表达惯用被动语态。因为法律语言是法律文化的载体，所以英语的这一特点自然就反映到法律中去。

（二）由法律语言的准确性与客观性决定

法律语言必须准确而客观。而正是因为这个特点，才使其拥有了一系列的语言特征。如果在法律文件中过多地使用第一人称或第二人称，就容易让人造成一种主观臆断的印象，而无法体现法律的准确性与客观性。试比较以下例句①和②，③和④：

① All disputes arising from the performance of this Contract shall, through amicable negotiations, be settled by the Parties hereto.
② The parties hereto shall, through amicable negotiations, settle all disputes arising from this Contract.
③ Implied-in-law contracts are quasi-contracts, because the obligation is created by law in absence of agreement, to prevent unjust enrichment.
④ Implied-in-law contracts are quasi-contracts, because law creates the obligation to prevent unjust enrichment in absence of agreement.

细细体会和分析上面的两对例子，就会发现运用被动语态表达的例句①和③所传达的意思具有客观性，让人感觉冷峻，不带有主观色彩，并且没有加入人的主观臆断。正是因为这样，被动语态才能在法律英语中广泛地使用。

（三）隐藏和弱化法律主体

隐藏和弱化动作的行为者是被动结构最大的功能。在法律英语中，有时为了避免指出动作发出者或隐藏和弱化法律主体就会运用被动语态，以此来模糊对法律行为主体的认定。例如：

① This law is formulated to protect the legitimate rights and interests of commercial banks, depositors and other clients.
为了保护商业银行、存款人和其他客户的合法权益，制定本法。
② A mistake was made in the written opinion.
书面判决书中有一个错误。

出于各种目的，如保持法律英语的客观性、动作施事者很明显或者并不重要或者是为了委婉等，作者就会根据情况运用被动语态。

（四）突出施事者

当然，使用被动语态可以隐藏和弱化行为者，但在某些情况下也可以突出施事者。可以通过 by 短语把主动句当中的主语移至句末，这样，动作的执行者就位于信息焦点的位置，从而强调了句子谓语动词的执行者。因此，被动句也能够成为突出逻辑主语或行为施事的一种手段。例如：

The document on the major issues of the Company, including but not limited to, the management plan, the monthly report, quarterly report and annual report, shall be signed jointly by the General Manager and the Deputy General Manager, then the documents shall come into effect.

公司的重要文件，包括，但不限于管理计划、月度、季度及其年底报告，须经总经理和副总经理会签方为有效。

这句话运用被动句强调了公司的重要文件必须得由总经理和副总经理签字才有效的这个事实。以上可见，出于不同的原因和目的，被动语态广泛运用于法律英语中。那么，在翻译时如何处理这些被动语态呢？下面我们就来分别阐述。

二、法律英语汉译时被动语态的翻译

（一）译成被动句

1. 以"被动"对"被动"，即用中文的"被"字来翻译，并且保留句子中的主语

例如：

① All his property was disposed of in the judicial sale.

在司法拍卖中，他所有的财产都被处置了。

② Any event or circumstance beyond the control of the Parties to the Contract shall be deemed an event of Force Majeure.

双方如遭受无法控制的事件或情况应被视为不可抗力。

2. 译成中文里带"使""由""把"等字的被动句

例如：

① This Contract shall be written in Chinese version and in English version. The two languages shall be equally authentic.

本合同应由中文和英文写成，两种文字具有同等效力。

② The check was presented to the bank yesterday.

昨天已把支票交给了银行。

③ Until the debts in question are repaid, the property of the branch shall not be transferred outside of the territory of China.

未清偿债务之前，不得把分支机构的财产转移到中国境外。

3. 译成"为……所"的句型

例如：

A judge shall not be swayed by eloquent arguments.

法官不应为雄辩所左右。

（二）译成主动句

1. 译成汉语主动句型，但表示被动意味

① An order paper must be properly negotiated to return its negotiability after transfer.

转让后保留记名票据的流通性，票据就必须适当议付。

② No money shall be drawn from the treasury but in consequence of appropriations made by law; and a regular statement and account of the receipts and expenditures of all public money shall be published from time to time.

除了依照法律的规定拨款之外，不得自国库中提取任何款项；一切公款收支的报告和账目，应经常公布。

2. 主语移至谓语之后译为宾语

① Labor law and insurance law have been partially codified in the United States.

美国已经编纂了部分的劳动法和保险法。

② Copyright law has been enacted in our county.

我国已经颁布了版权法。

3. 译成带有表语的主动句

An endorsement on a check may be made in blank or special.

支票上的背书可以是空白的也可以是指明受益人的。

4. 原文有主动者时，可用主动者作为主语，译为主动句

例如：

① The board of directors shall keep minutes of resolutions on matters discussed at the meetings. The minutes are signed by the direct or present at the meeting and by the person who recorded the minutes.

董事会应当对所议事项的决定做出正式的会议记录，出席会议的董事和记录员在会议记录上签字。

② The Arbitration fee shall be borne by the losing party unless otherwise awarded by the Arbitration Commission.

败诉方应当承担仲裁费用，但仲裁委员会另有裁定的除外。

5. 含主语从句的被动句型译为主动句

以 it 作形式主语的句子，翻译时可转为主动形式。有时不加主语，有时可加上"有人""大家""我们"等不确定主语。例如：

① It is suggested that the board of meeting be put off till next Monday.

有人建议董事会推迟到下周一举行。

② If the dispute cannot be settled through negotiation, it is feared that the two counties might resort to force.

如果纠纷不能通过协商解决，人们担心两国可能会诉诸武力。

③ It must be pointed out that the adversary system tends to reduce litigation to a costly game, in which the lawyers become the principal players and the outcome will turn on their skill rather than on the true merit of the case.

有人指出抗辩制把诉讼变为一场费钱的游戏，律师成了主角，而结果则取决于他们的技巧而非案件本身的是非曲直。

（三）译成无主句

如果英语句子中没有出现主动者，在翻译成汉语时无法补充而且也没有必要补充，就可以把它译成无主句。例如：

① Unless this account is paid within next fifteen days, it will be necessary to take appropriate action.

除非在十五天之内把账还清，否则就有必要采取适当的行动。

② Partial shipments are allowed unless the credit specially states otherwise.

除非信用证另有特殊规定，否则不得分批装运。

三、英汉互译时应注意的问题

虽然被动语态在法律英语中被广泛地使用，但是，这并不意味着在把汉语被动句译成英

文时，就可以一味地滥用被动语态。在运用时还得视情况而定。以下情况可以考虑运用被动语态来翻译。

（一）强调动作的接受者

要使汉语句子引起读者对于动作接受者的注意，可以将其译为被动句。例如：

合同双方对本合同发生的任何争执应首先通过各方主管部门互相信赖的精神予以解决。如在 30 天内本合同双方不能解决时，双方可以推荐第三方予以调解。

Any disputes arising out of this Contract shall first be settled by the Parties hereto through consultation with their higher authorities in accordance with the spirit of mutual trust. Should such consultation fail to settle the dispute within thirty days of notification to such higher authorities, mediation may be concluded by a third party selected by the Parties hereto.

在这个例句中，原文虽然用了主动语态，但译文却用了被动语态，目的就是引起人们对动作接受者的注意。

（二）隐藏或弱化行为主体

1. 行为主体不言自明或者并不重要

例如：必须改善我们的工作。

译文 1：We must improve our work.

译文 2：Our wok must be improved.

在译文 2 中，行为主体不用说也是显而易见的，所以，在翻译时，可以用被动句来处理。

2. 出于某些目的故意隐藏行为主体

试比较下面的例子：

① A mistake was made in the written opinion. 在书面判决书中有一个错误。

② The judge made a mistake in the written opinion. 法官在书面判决书中犯了一个错。

以上两个例子可以看出使用被动句和使用主动句的区别。有时作者为了委婉，故意隐藏或弱化行为主体而采用被动句。

法律宝典

国际法基础知识

一、什么是国际法

国际法（International Law）指适用主权国家之间以及其他具有国际人格的实体之间的法律规则的总体。国际法又称国际公法，处理的是不同国家的国内法之间的差异。国际法与国内法截然不同，国内法是一个国家内部的法律，它调整在其管辖范围内的个人及其他法律实体的行为。

二、国际法的造法形式

《国际法院规约》第 38 条将国际法的主要造法方式即国际法规则形成的方式归结为三：条约、国际习惯法和为各国承认的一般法律原则。这已得到几乎是普遍一致的赞同。

条约和其他经一致同意的协议是具有法律拘束力的，国际法主体可以通过它们宣布、修改或发展现行的国际法。它们也可以通过条约将尚未组织起来的国际社会转变为联合的或凌驾于国家之上的全球性或区域性的国际社会。而国际习惯法实质上就是适用于尚未组织起来的国际社会的国际法，国际习惯法常常是以早期条约的某些条款为其渊源，这些条款后来就被承认为法规。但是也有个别的国际法规则是由世界列强的大致相同的实践发展而成的。为各国所承认的一般法律原则只有在国际习惯法或条约法没有相应的规则与之平衡的情况下才起作用，所以它的造法作用是辅助性的。这种原则必须是一般的法律原则，而不是作用范围有限的法律规则；它还必须得到有相当多的国家的承认。

三、国际法的基本原则

国际法的基本原则是：各国主权平等，互相尊重主权和领土完整，互不侵犯，互不干涉内政，平等互利，和平共处，和平解决国际争端，禁止以武力相威胁和使用武力，以及民族自决原则等。

四、国际法的特征

首先，国际法的主体主要是国家。而国内法的主体主要是自然人和法人。其次，国际法是国家以协议的方式来制定的。国内法则是由国家立法机关依一定程序来制定的。最后，国际法采取与国内法不同的强制方式。国际法主要是依靠有组织的国际强制机关加以维护，保证实施，而国内法的强制方式主要依靠国家的。

术语积累

adjudication　裁判
administration of justice　司法裁判
alienability　可让与性
capitulations　领事裁判权条约
civil jurisdiction　民事管辖权
collective recognition　集体承认
common law　普通法
de facto　事实上
defendant state　被告国
delictual responsibility　不法行为责任
denunciation　退约，废约
economic aid　经济援助
equitable treatment　公平待遇
exile government　流亡政府
force majeure　不可抗力
full powers　全权证书
host state　东道主
identical treatment　同等待遇
incorporation　并入，法人
inviolability　不可侵犯性
innocent passage　无害通过权

injunctive relief 强制性救济
insurrection 叛乱
international custom 国际习惯
internal affairs 内政
international territories 国际化领土
international transaction 国际交往
international wrong 国际不法行为
judicial decision 司法判决
judicial legislation 司法立法
land-locked sea 内陆海
laws of war 战争法规
mandatory state 委任统治国
marginal sea 边缘海
不歧视 non-discrimination
不可裁判性 non-justiciability
国籍 nationality
门户开放 open door
所有权 ownership
海盗行为 piracy
政治庇护 political asylum
规约 statute
后条约 subsequent treaty
非法使用 usurpation
单一国 unitary state
不当得利 unjust enrichment
单方行为 unilateral act
单方声明 unilateral declaration
托管领土 trust territory
托管国 trust state
领海 territory sea
领土主权 territorial sovereignty
发展权 right to development
食物权 right to food
和平权 right to peace
民族权 right of peoples
交往权 right of intercourse
条约的修订 revision of treaty
决议 resolution
限制解释 restrictive interpretation

剩余主权　residual sovereignty
国际法渊源　sources of international law
个别意见　separate opinion
定着渔业区　sedentary fishery
诉讼费用保证金　security for cost
联合国　the United Nations
国际法院　the International Court of Justice
国际租借　international lease
联合国国际法委员会　International Law Commission

Section III　巩固练习

词汇与短语

1. admission of alien
2. civil war
3. dependent state
4. encroachment
5. humanitarian intervention
6. high seas
7. international convention
8. international engagement
9. immunity
10. expatriation

11. 政治犯
12. 战争罪
13. 附庸地位
14. 既得权
15. 领水
16. 特别使团
17. 属地原则
18. 国家身份
19. 中止条约
20. 法律解释

句子与段落

1. Every State has the duty to refrain in its international relations from the threat or use of force against the territorial integrity or political independence of any State, or in any other manner inconsistent with the purposes of the United Nations.

2. Such a threat or use of force constitutes a violation of international law and the Charter of the United Nations and shall never be employed as a means of settling international issues.

3. Every State has the duty to refrain from the threat or use of force to violate the existing international boundaries of another State or as a means of solving international disputes, including territorial disputes and problems concerning frontiers of States.

4. The territory of a State shall not be the object of military occupation resulting from the use of force in contravention of the provisions of the Charter.
5. All States shall pursue in good faith negotiations for the early conclusion of a universal treaty on general and complete disarmament under effective international control and strive to adopt appropriate measures to reduce international tensions and strengthen confidence among States.
6. No State or group of States has the right to intervene, directly or indirectly, for any reason whatever, in the internal or external affairs of any other State.
7. Consequently, armed intervention and all other forms of interference or attempted threats against the personality of the State or against its political, economic and cultural elements are in violation of international law.
8. No State may use or encourage the use of economic political or any other type of measures to coerce another State in order to obtain from it the subordination of the exercise of its sovereign rights and to secure from it advantages of any kind.
9. No State shall organize, assist, foment, finance, incite or tolerate subversive, terrorist or armed activities directed towards the violent overthrow of the regime of another State, or interfere in civil strife in another State.
10. Each State Party to the present Covenant undertakes to take steps, individually and through international assistance and co-operation, especially economic and technical, to the maximum of its available resources, with a view to achieving progressively the full realization of the rights recognized in the present Covenant by all appropriate means, including particularly the adoption of legislative measures.
11. The States Parties to the present Covenant undertake to guarantee that the rights enunciated in the present Covenant will be exercised without discrimination of any kind as to race, color, sex, language, religion, political or other opinion, national or social origin, property, birth or other status.
12. Developing countries, with due regard to human rights and their national economy, may determine to what extent they would guarantee the economic rights recognized in the present Covenant to non-nationals.
13. The conduct of an organ placed at the disposal of a State by another State shall be considered an act of the former State under international law if the organ is acting in the exercise of elements of the governmental authority of the State at whose disposal it is placed.
14. The conduct of an organ of a State or of a person or entity empowered to exercise elements of the governmental authority shall be considered an act of the State under international law if the organ, person or entity acts in that capacity, even if it exceeds its authority or contravenes instructions.
15. The conduct of a person or group of persons shall be considered an act of a State under international law if the person or group of persons is in fact acting on the instructions of, or

under the direction or control of that State in carrying out the conduct.

16. The conduct of a person or group of persons shall be considered an act of a State under international law if the person or group of persons is in fact exercising elements of the governmental authority in the absence or default of the official authorities and in circumstances such as to call for the exercise of those elements of authority.

17. Every State has the duty to promote through joint and separate action universal respect for and observance of human rights and fundamental freedoms in accordance with the Charter.

18. The establishment of a sovereign and independent State, the free association or integration with an independent State or the emergence into any other political status freely determined by a people constitute modes of implementing the right of self-determination by that people.

19. Every State has the duty to refrain from any forcible action which deprives peoples referred to above in the elaboration of the present principle of their right to self-determination and freedom and independence.

20. In their actions against, and resistance to, such forcible action in pursuit of the exercise of their right to self-determination, such peoples are entitled to seek and to receive support in accordance with the purposes and principles of the Charter.

21. Principle 1　Man has the fundamental right to freedom, equality and adequate conditions of life, in an environment of a quality that permits a life of dignity and well-being, and he bears a solemn responsibility to protect and improve the environment for present and future generations. In this respect, policies promoting or perpetuating apartheid, racial segregation, discrimination, colonial and other forms of oppression and foreign domination stand condemned and must be eliminated.

    Principle 2　The natural resources of the earth, including the air, water, land, flora and fauna and especially representative samples of natural ecosystems, must be safeguarded for the benefit of present and future generations through careful planning or management, as appropriate.

    Principle 3　The capacity of the earth to produce vital renewable resources must be maintained and, wherever practicable, restored or improved.

    Principle 4　Man has a special responsibility to safeguard and wisely manage the heritage of wildlife and its habitat, which are now gravely imperiled by a combination of adverse factors. Nature conservation, including wildlife, must therefore receive importance in planning for economic development.

    Principle 5　The non-renewable resources of the earth must be employed in such a way as to guard against the danger of their future exhaustion and to ensure that benefits from such employment are shared by all mankind.

22. 为实现这一环境目标，将要求公民和团体以及企业和各级机关承担责任，大家平等地共同努力。各界人士和许多领域中的组织，凭他们有价值的品质和全部行动，将确定未来世界环境的格局。各地方政府和全国政府，将对在他们管辖范围内的大规模环境政策和行动，承担最大的责任。为筹措资金以支援发展中国家完成他们在这方面的责任，还需要进行国际合作。种类越来越多的环境问题，在范围上是地区性或全球性的，或者影响着共同的国际领域，将要求国与国之间广泛合作和国际组织采取行动以谋求共同的利益。

Unit Fourteen

Arbitration
仲　裁

Section I　译例研究

>> Passage One
Convention on the Recognition and Enforcement of Foreign Arbitral Awards

Article I

1. This Convention shall apply to the recognition and enforcement of arbitral awards made in the territory of a State other than the State where the recognition and enforcement of such awards are sought, and arising out of differences between persons, whether physical or legal. It shall also apply to arbitral awards not considered as domestic awards in the State where their recognition and enforcement are sought.

2. The term "arbitral awards" shall include not only awards made by arbitrators appointed for each case but also those made by permanent arbitral bodies to which the parties have submitted.

3. When signing, ratifying or acceding to this Convention, or notifying extension under article X hereof, any State may on the basis of reciprocity declare that it will apply the Convention to the recognition and enforcement of awards made only in the territory of another Contracting State. It may also declare that it will apply the Convention only to differences arising out of legal relationships, whether contractual or not, which are considered as commercial under the national law of the State making such declaration.

Article II

1. Each Contracting State shall recognize an agreement in writing under which the parties undertake to submit to arbitration all or any differences which have arisen or which may arise between

them in respect of a defined legal relationship, whether contractual or not, concerning a subject matter capable of settlement by arbitration.

2. The term "agreement in writing" shall include an arbitral clause in a contract or an arbitration agreement, signed by the parties or contained in an exchange of letters or telegrams.

3. The court of a Contracting State, when seized of an action in a matter in respect of which the parties have made an agreement within the meaning of this article, shall, at the request of one of the parties, refer the parties to arbitration, unless it finds that the said agreement is null and void, inoperative or incapable of being performed.

Article III

Each Contracting State shall recognize arbitral awards as binding and enforce them in accordance with the rules of procedure of the territory where the award is relied upon, under the conditions laid down in the following articles. There shall not be imposed substantially more onerous conditions or higher fees or charges on the recognition or enforcement of arbitral awards to which this Convention applies than are imposed on the recognition or enforcement of domestic arbitral awards.

Article IV

1. To obtain the recognition and enforcement mentioned in the preceding article, the party applying for recognition and enforcement shall, at the time of the application, supply:

(a) The duly authenticated original award or a duly certified copy thereof;

(b) The original agreement referred to in article II or a duly certified copy thereof.

2. If the said award or agreement is not made in an official language of the country in which the award is relied upon, the party applying for recognition and enforcement of the award shall produce a translation of these documents into such language. The translation shall be certified by an official or sworn translator or by a diplomatic or consular agent.

…

Article VI

If an application for the setting aside or suspension of the award has been made to a competent authority referred to in article V(1)(e), the authority before which the award is sought to be relied upon may, if it considers it proper, adjourn the decision on the enforcement of the award and may also, on the application of the party claiming enforcement of the award, order the other party to give suitable security.

词汇提示

enforcement   *n.* 执行
appoint   *v.* 委派
permanent   *adj.* 常设
parties   *n.* 当事人
ratify   *v.* 批准
accede to   加入
notify   *v.* 通知

hereof　*adv.* 于此
reciprocity　*n.* 互惠
submit　*v.* 提交
in respect of　关于
court　*n.* 法院
at the request of　应……要求
null and void　*adj.* 无效的
inoperative　*adj.* 失效的
incapable of being performed　不能实行
binding　*adj.* 有约束力的
onerous　*adj.* 困难，苛刻
preceding　*adj.* 前面的
authenticate　*v.* 鉴定
certify　*v.* 核准
adjourn　*v.* 延缓

▶ 法律术语

arbitrator　*n.* 仲裁员
arbitral awards　仲裁裁决
arbitral bodies　仲裁机关
contracting state　缔约国
national law　国内法
declaration　*n.* 声明
agreement in writing　书面协定
arbitral clause　仲裁条款
arbitration agreement　仲裁协议
exchange of letters or telegrams　互换函电
rules of procedure　程序规则
duly authenticated original award　原裁决之正本
duly copy　正式副本
give security　提供担保
set aside the award　撤销裁决
suspension of the award　中止裁决
consular agent　领事人员

▶ 要点解析

1. Convention on the Recognition and Enforcement of Foreign Arbitral Awards

标题中 recognition 和 enforcement 都是名词，翻译成中文时注意名词的动词化，可将其译为"承认及执行外国仲裁裁决公约"。

2. This Convention shall apply to the recognition and enforcement of arbitral awards made in the territory of a State other than the State where the recognition and enforcement of such awards are sought, and arising out of differences between persons, whether physical or legal.

此句是一个复杂的句子，应注意剖析句子主干部分，然后理清各成分的意思，确保对原文的正确理解。此句中主干部分是 This Convention shall apply to the recognition and enforcement of arbitral awards，而"made in …"和"arising out…"是并列关系，用来修饰名词 arbitral awards。

3. It may also declare that it will apply the Convention only to differences arising out of legal relationships, whether contractual or not, which are considered as commercial under the national law of the State making such declaration。

句中的插入语 whether contractual or not 翻译时注意将形容词 contractual 动词化，可译为"不论其为契约性质与否"，更加符合汉语表达习惯。

4. Each Contracting State shall recognize an agreement in writing under which the parties undertake to submit to arbitration all or any differences which have arisen or which may arise between them in respect of a defined legal relationship, whether contractual or not, concerning a subject matter capable of settlement by arbitration.

此句是一个长句，包括多个 which 引导的非限制性定语从句、插入语，以及非谓语从句，因此句子意思比较分散，翻译时应注意到中英文表达习惯上的差异，合理进行语序的调整，使译文符合读者阅读习惯，可译为："当事人以书面协定承允彼此间所发生或可能发生之一切或任何争议，如关涉可以仲裁解决事项之确定法律关系，不论为契约性质与否，应提交仲裁时，各缔约国应承认此项协定。"

5. The court of a Contracting State, when seized of an action in a matter in respect of which the parties have made an agreement within the meaning of this article…

句中的 when seized of an action，根据语境，可译为"受理诉讼"。

6. …at the request of one of the parties, refer the parties to arbitration, unless it finds that the said agreement is null and void, inoperative or incapable of being performed.

句中的 at the request of one of the parties 为介词短语，注意介词短语的动词性转化，可译为"应当事人一方之邀请"。

7. "the authority before which the award is sought to be relied upon…"可译为"受理援引裁决案件之机关"。

参考译文

承认及执行外国仲裁裁决公约

第一条

一、仲裁裁决，因自然人或法人间之争议而产生且在声请承认及执行地所在国以外之国家领土内作成者，其承认及执行适用本公约。本公约对于仲裁裁决经声请承认及执行地所在国认为非内国裁决者，亦适用之。

二、"仲裁裁决"一词不仅指专案选派之仲裁员所作裁决，亦指当事人提请仲裁之常设仲裁机关所作裁决。

三、任何国家得于签署、批准或加入本公约时，或于本公约第十条通知推广适用时，本着互惠原则声明该国适用本公约，以承认及执行在另一缔约国领土内作成之裁决为限。任何国家亦得声明，该国唯于争议起于法律关系，不论其为契约性质与否，而依提出声明国家之国内法认为系属商事关系者，始适用本公约。

第二条

一、当事人以书面协定承允彼此间所发生或可能发生之一切或任何争议，如关涉可以仲裁解决事项之确定法律关系，不论为契约性质与否，应提交仲裁时，各缔约国应承认此项协定。

二、称"书面协定"者，谓当事人所签订或在互换函电中所载明之契约仲裁条款或仲裁协定。

三、当事人就诉讼事项订有本条所称之协定者，缔约国法院受理诉讼时应依当事人一造之请求，命当事人提交仲裁，但前述协定经法院认定无效、失效或不能实行者不在此限。

第三条

各缔约国应承认仲裁裁决具有拘束力，并依援引裁决地之程序规则及下列各条所载条件执行之。承认或执行适用本公约之仲裁裁决时，不得较承认或执行国内仲裁裁决附加过苛之条件或征收过多之费用。

第四条

一、申请承认及执行前条，为取得前条所称之承认及执行的，应于申请时提具：

（甲）原裁决之正本或其正式副本，

（乙）第二条所称协定之原本或其正式副本。

二、倘前述裁决或协定所用文字非为援引裁决地所在国之正式文字，申请承认及执行裁决前条应备具各该文件之此项文字译本。译本应由公设或宣誓之翻译员或外交或领事人员认证之。

……

第六条

倘裁决已经向第五条第一项（戊）款所称之主管机关声请撤销或停止执行，受理援引裁决案件之机关得于其认为适当时延缓关于执行裁决之决定，并得依请求执行一造之声请，命他提供妥适之担保。

Passage Two
中华人民共和国仲裁法

第一条　为保证公正、及时地仲裁经济纠纷，保护当事人的合法权益，保障社会主义市场经济健康发展，制定本法。

第二条　平等主体的公民、法人和其他组织之间发生的合同纠纷和其他财产权益纠纷，可以仲裁。

第三条　下列纠纷不能仲裁：
（一）婚姻、收养、监护、扶养、继承纠纷；
（二）依法应当由行政机关处理的行政争议。

第四条　当事人采用仲裁方式解决纠纷，应当双方自愿，达成仲裁协议。没有仲裁协议，一方申请仲裁的，仲裁委员会不予受理。

第五条　当事人达成仲裁协议，一方向人民法院起诉的，人民法院不予受理，但仲裁协议无效的除外。

第六条　仲裁委员会应当由当事人协议选定。
仲裁不实行级别管辖和地域管辖。

第七条　仲裁应当根据事实，符合法律规定，公平合理地解决纠纷。

第八条　仲裁依法独立进行，不受行政机关、社会团体和个人的干涉。

第九条　仲裁实行一裁终局的制度。裁决做出后，当事人就同一纠纷再申请仲裁或者向人民法院起诉的，仲裁委员会或者人民法院不予受理。
裁决被人民法院依法裁定撤销或者不予执行的，当事人就该纠纷可以根据双方重新达成的仲裁协议申请仲裁，也可以向人民法院起诉。

第十条　仲裁委员会可以在直辖市和省、自治区人民政府所在地的市设立，也可以根据需要在其他设区的市设立，不按区划层层设立。
仲裁委员会由前款规定的市的人民政府组织有关部门和商会统一组建。
设立仲裁委员会，应当经省、自治区、直辖市的司法行政部门登记。

第十一条　仲裁委员会应当具备下列条件：
（一）有自己的名称、住所和章程；
（二）有必要的财产；
（三）有该委员会的组成人员；
（四）有聘任的仲裁员。
仲裁委员会的章程应当依照本法制定。

第十二条　仲裁委员会由主任一人、副主任二至四人和委员七至十一人组成。
仲裁委员会的主任、副主任和委员由法律、经济贸易专家和有实际工作经验的人员担任。仲裁委员会的组成人员中，法律、经济贸易专家不得少于三分之二。

第十三条　仲裁委员会应当从公道正派的人员中聘任仲裁员。
仲裁员应当符合下列条件之一：
（一）从事仲裁工作满八年的；
（二）从事律师工作满八年的；
（三）曾任审判员满八年的；
（四）从事法律研究、教学工作并具有高级职称的；
（五）具有法律知识、从事经济贸易等专业工作并具有高级职称或者具有同等专业水平的。
仲裁委员会按照不同专业设仲裁员名册。

词汇提示

监护　guardianship
抚养　child maintenance
继承　inheritance
行政机关　administrative organs
当事人　the party
自愿　voluntary
人民法院　people's court
无效　invalid
受理　accept an action
管辖　jurisdiction
撤销　cancel
不予执行　disallow
直辖市　municipality directly under the Central Government
自治区　autonomous region
章程　Articles of Association

法律术语

中华人民共和国仲裁法　Arbitration Law of the People's Republic of China
社会主义市场经济　socialist market economy
经济纠纷　economic disputes
合法权益　legitimate rights
仲裁协议　arbitration agreement
仲裁委员会　arbitration commission
一裁终局　single ruling system
司法行政部门　judicial administrative department
仲裁人　arbitrator
审判员　judge

要点解析

1. 中华人民共和国仲裁法

注意法律标题的英译，需将仲裁法 arbitration law 放在开头，译成"arbitration law of…"；另外要注意"中华人民共和国"要译出全称 the People's Republic of China，不可将其简单地译为 China。

2. 为保证公正、及时地仲裁经济纠纷，保护当事人的合法权益，保障社会主义市场经济健康发展,制定本法。

句中的"为保证……,保护……,保障……,制定本法"法律用语,通常译为"This Law is formulated for the purposes of …"。

3. 平等主体的公民、法人和其他组织之间发生的合同纠纷和其他财产权益纠纷,可以仲裁。

注意语序的适当调整,翻译时可将"合同纠纷和其他财产权益纠纷"放在前面,将定语"平等主体的公民、法人和其他组织之间发生的"进行后置,译为"Disputes over contracts and disputes over property rights and interests between citizens, legal persons and other organizations as equal subjects of law"。

4. 仲裁不实行级别管辖和地域管辖。

句中的级别管辖即按级别管辖,可译为"jurisdiction by level system"。

5. 仲裁依法独立进行,不受行政机关、社会团体和个人的干涉。

句中的"依法进行"是法律中经常出现的词语,可译为"be conducted in accordance with the law";"不受行政机关、社会团体和个人的干涉"可以译为"independent of any intervention by administrative organs, social organizations or individuals"。

6. 裁决做出后,当事人就同一纠纷再申请仲裁或者向人民法院起诉的,仲裁委员会或者人民法院不予受理。

此句翻译时注意理清句子意思,可分为两层含义:第一层含义即裁决做出后,仲裁委员会不予受理当事人就同一纠纷申请的仲裁,译为"The arbitration commission shall not accept any application for arbitration";第二层含义为裁决做出后,人民法院也不予受理当事人就同一纠纷所做的起诉申请,译为"nor shall a people's court accept any action submitted by the party in respect of the same dispute"。

7. "设立仲裁委员会"在英译时将其动词名词化,译为"the establishment of an arbitration commission",作为整个句子的主语。

8. "省、自治区、直辖市"是中国政治特有名词,译为"province, autonomous region and municipalities directly under the Central Government"。

9. 仲裁委员会应当从公道正派的人员中聘任仲裁员。

句中的"公道正派"即公平正直,可译为"fair and honest"。

参考译文

Arbitration Law of the People's Republic of China

Article 1. This Law is formulated for the purposes of ensuring that economic disputes shall be impartially and promptly arbitrated, protecting legitimate rights and interests of the relevant parties and guaranteeing the healthy development of the socialist market economy.

Article 2. Disputes over contracts and disputes over property rights and interests between citizens, legal persons and other organizations as equal subjects of law may be submitted to arbitration.

Article 3. The following disputes shall not be submitted to arbitration:

1. disputes over marriage, adoption, guardianship, child maintenance and inheritance;

2. administrative disputes falling within the jurisdiction of the relevant administrative organs according to law.

Article 4. The parties adopting arbitration for dispute settlement shall reach an arbitration agreement on a mutually voluntary basis. An arbitration commission shall not accept an application for arbitration submitted by one of the parties in the absence of an arbitration agreement.

Article 5. A people's court shall not accept an action initiated by one of the parties if the parties have concluded an arbitration agreement, unless the arbitration agreement is invalid.

Article 6. An arbitration commission shall be selected by the parties by agreement. The jurisdiction by level system and the district jurisdiction system shall not apply in arbitration.

Article 7. Disputes shall be fairly and reasonably settled by arbitration on the basis of facts and in accordance with the relevant provisions of law.

Article 8. Arbitration shall be conducted in accordance with the law, independent of any intervention by administrative organs, social organizations or individuals.

Article 9. The single ruling system shall be applied in arbitration. The arbitration commission shall not accept any application for arbitration, nor shall a people's court accept any action submitted by the party in respect of the same dispute after an arbitration award has already been given in relation to that matter. If the arbitration award is canceled or its enforcement has been disallowed by a people's court in accordance with the law, the parties may, in accordance with a new arbitration agreement between them in respect of the dispute, re-apply for arbitration or initiate legal proceedings with the people's court.

Article 10. Arbitration commissions may be established in the municipalities directly under the Central Government, in the municipalities where the people's governments of provinces and autonomous regions are located or, if necessary, in other cities divided into districts. Arbitration commissions shall not be established at each level of the administrative divisions. The people's governments of the municipalities and cities specified in the above paragraph shall organize the relevant departments and the Chamber of Commerce for the formation of an arbitration commission. The establishment of an arbitration commission shall be registered with the judicial administrative department of the relevant province, autonomous region or municipalities directly under the Central Government.

Article 11. An arbitration commission shall fulfil the following conditions:

1. it must have its own name, domicile and Articles of Association;
2. it must possess the necessary property;
3. it must have its own members; and
4. it must have arbitrators for appointment.

The articles of association of the an arbitration commission shall be formulated in accordance with this Law.

Article 12. An arbitration commission shall comprise a chairman, two to four vice-chairmen and seven to eleven members. The chairman, vice-chairmen and members of an arbitration commission must be persons specialized in law, economics and trade and persons who have actual working experience. The number of specialists in law, economics and trade shall not be less than two-thirds of the members of an arbitration association.

Article 13. The arbitration commission shall appoint fair and honest person as its arbitrators. Arbitrators must fulfil one of the following conditions:

1. they have been engaged in arbitration work for at least eight years;
2. they have worked as a lawyer for at least eight years;
3. they have been a judge for at least eight years;
4. they are engaged in legal research or legal teaching and in senior positions; and
5. they have legal knowledge and are engaged in professional work relating to economics and trade, and in senior positions or of the equivalent professional level. The arbitration commission shall establish a list of arbitrators according to different professionals.

Section II 技能拓展

翻译技巧

论法律专业术语的特殊性及其英译技巧

一、法律专业术语的特殊性

1. 内涵上的特定性

法律专业术语内涵上的特定性主要表现在两个方面。一是每个专业术语基本上对应于一个特定的法律概念，因此，翻译时不能随意用其他词语来代替。例如：汉语法律专业术语"原告"在英语中就只能够译为 plaintiff 而不能译为其他。但是"原告"一词在北京外国语大学英语系《汉英词典》编写组编的《汉英词典》（修订版缩印本）中却有 plaintiff 和 prosecutor 两个译义。这是值得商榷的。因为 prosecutor 代表的是国家和社会的整体利益，他们行使国家的公诉权来指控犯罪，更多是在刑事诉讼的意义上来使用的，因此，西南交通大学学报（社会科学版）第 8 卷 prosecutor 被翻译为中文时，应是"公诉人"，而不应是"原告"。同理，在汉语中"过失"这个法律专业术语只能翻译为 negligence，而不能够翻译为 mistake。二是某个术语即使在本国语言中属多义词，但是该词一旦作为法律专业术语出现，它在含义上就须是特指，也就是说它只能保留一个义项。例如："管辖"一词在汉语中就有管理、统辖两个词义。在第二个词义中该词又有对人员的统辖和对事务、区域、案件等的统辖之分。与此相应，在英语中，"管辖"一词的含义有 have jurisdiction over 和 administer 两个意思。在此，显然"管辖"就法律意义而言，只能够取其 have jurisdiction over (a) case (s) 或者 jurisdiction over a person 之意而不能用其他的词义。

2. 词性的变异性

法律专业术语词性上的变异性是指有些术语在通常意义上的使用与在法律层次上的使用

意义有所不同，其词性也可能发生变化。如"不作为"这个词，在汉语中使用时，常常是用作动词词组，在句子中充当谓语；而当其作为法律语言使用时，就不再是动词词组，而是具有动词功能的法律名词，在句中常常充当主语和宾语。比如我们可以说，渎职罪"在客观方面的表现形式，大多数是作为，少数也可以是不作为"。在这里"不作为"显然是用作系动词"是"的宾语。英语中也存在这种现象，比如 not proven 就是由动词 prove 转化而来的过去分词形式，其中 not 是副词，proven 是过去分词，作为一个固定的结构，它们具有形容词的功能，意思是"未证实的"。可是当我们从法律英语的角度来观察，这个词组显然又被名词化了，它可以在句中作为主语和宾语来使用，此时其含义是"证据不足"。例如，在"Another difference is that in Scottish Criminal Law a third verdict of 'not proven' is possible intermediate between guilty. It is equivalent to an acquittal."一句中，not proven 显然是用作 of 的宾语。

3. 时际特征和地域特征

法律庄严神圣而不可朝令夕改，因此法律及其语言载体的发展较为缓慢。但是即便如此，随着时代的变迁，总会有一些新的词汇涌现在法律语言中，并渐渐地演化为专门的法律术语。据称，《现代汉语词典》第 6 版经过修订已经收录了相当一批法律新词，但这些被收录的法律词汇仅仅是近年来出现的法律专门术语中的小部分。而有些法律词汇诸如"探视权""离婚损害赔偿"等，虽然早已出现在众多的法律法规和法律文件之中，由于"时差"的原因，却尚未被收录在词典中。这种情况在一定程度上反映了法律英语的时际特征。当这些新词没有被收录于我国的法律词典中，而且也不见诸国外的法律词典和法规中的时候，其翻译的难度是可想而知的。

4. 词语的类义性

类义词是指意义同属某一类别的词，归于同一义类的词则分别表示同一属概念之内的若干种概念。英汉法律专业术语存在大量的类义词，这是其又一大特点。在我国刑法中一共有10 个类罪名，如危害国家安全罪、危害公共安全罪、破坏社会主义市场经济秩序罪等，这些类罪名都是一个个的属概念。在这些类罪名之下又包括了若干具有该类性质的具体罪名。比如，危害国家安全罪之下就有背叛国家罪、分裂国家罪、武装叛乱罪、颠覆国家政权罪、投敌叛变罪、间谍罪等 14 种危害国家安全的罪名。这些具体罪名就是类罪名之下的种概念。由于现实中的犯罪都是具体的，因此，类罪名不能成为定罪得以引用的根据，即不能根据类罪名定罪。同理，如果我们在翻译中将具体罪名译为类罪名，就会抹杀类罪名之下各个具体罪名之间的区别，外国读者就会难以理解我们定罪量刑的根据。

二、法律专业术语英译方面的问题和原因

我们在法律文本翻译方面存在不少的问题。法律专业术语在一些译本中的不准确译法，引起了一些专家和学者的质疑。

1. 英译时违反法律术语内涵上的特定性

英译时译者将汉语文本中的同一法律概念用多个不同的英语法律术语来表述。例如《中华人民共和国著作权法》英文译本将对著作权的"侵犯"，时而译成 prejudice（如第 12 条），时而又译成 infringe（如第 48 条）。但是，根据多本英文词典的词义和例句来看，infringe 所强调的是对权利的侵犯，而 prejudice 则多指的是对人、物和利益的侵犯。1978 年牛津大学出版社出版的《现代高级英汉双解辞典》第 549 页上关于 infringe 词条的用法举例是"infringe a rule (an oath, copyright, patent)"。从该词条的用法来看，infringe 一词主要是与知识产权意义上的"权利"搭配。而从该词典第 826 页上关于 prejudice 一词的用法举例来看，prejudice 一词则是指对于"any existing right or claim"的侵害。由此可以看出，infringe 在意义上针对性更强，主要是指对知识产权意义上的"权利"的侵害，prejudice 则有"泛指"的意义，它是指对人、物和任何意义上的权益的侵犯。显然二者在词义上是有区别的。如果我们不加区别地使用，就不严谨和准确。

2. 望文生义

国务院法制办公室和法规译审和外事司联合编写、1998 年出版的《中华人民共和国法律法规汉英对照词语手册》将"物证"翻译成 material evidence。此种译法中，"物证"的"物"恰好对应了英文中 material；而"物证"中的"证"又与 evidence 相配。这种译法貌似正确，但实际上其表达的意思却与所要表达的意思相距甚远。根据 BLACK'S LAW DICTIONARY 第七版对 material evidence 的解释，该词实际上是指"evidence having some logical connection with the consequential facts or the issues"，其意为"与案件的事实或结果存在逻辑关系的证据"，它既可能是言词证据也可能是实物证据。

3. 词不达意

与翻译中的望文生义极为类似的另一种翻译错误是词不达意。译者在法律术语的英译过程中，用一个在形式上较为相像或相似的英语法律专业术语来翻译母语中的法律术语，但是译文的意思却相去甚远。比如，有的译者用 the third party 来翻译中文法律术语里的"第三者"。其实 the third party 是"第三人"，而非"第三者"之意。第三人是指民事诉讼中在原、被告之外的，认为本案的审理结果与自己有利害关系，因此自行申请或由法院追加进入原、被告之间已在进行的诉讼中的当事人。而"第三者"在中文里则是指介入、干扰和破坏别人合法婚姻的人，既可能是男性，也可能是女性；既可能是已婚的，也可能是未婚的。

4. 译文不准确

这类问题指法律术语的翻译虽然基本正确，但是却不够准确。例如，原来的《中华人民共和国中外合资经营企业法》第五条规定外国合营者"如果有意以落后技术和设备进行欺骗，造成损失，应赔偿损失"。当时的英文译本却把该条译为："If the foreign joint venturer causes losses by deception through the intentional use of backward technology and equipment, it shall pay compensation for the losses."此种译文，译者没有仔细推敲"损失"在数量上的含义，没有管它是一项损失还是多项损失，就统统将其译为复数，这种译法显然是十分草率的。因为，如果有不法外商故意使用落后的技术设备进行欺诈，而他们给中外合资经营企业造成的这项损失仅仅是单数的 loss，即"一项损失"，那么"外国合营者"就可能钻法律译文的漏洞，主张他们仅仅造成了 loss（一项损失），而非该法译文中的 losses（两项或两项以上的损失）而拒绝赔偿。

三、法律专业术语的英译技巧

法律术语的翻译不仅要进行语言的转换，而且要涉及法律思维、法律理念的变化、协调和衔接。不同法律制度下的法律概念所具有的差异性在翻译中几乎难以避免。因此，法律术语的翻译不仅要求语言的语词间要基本对应，而且还要力求做到译出的法律术语与原文本的法律术语在法律功能（legal function）上基本对等。这是法律术语的庄严性和规范性使然。因此，法律专业术语的翻译要特别遵循"忠实"（faithfulness）、"准确"（exactness）和"统一"（consistency）的原则。

1. 准确理解原文中法律术语的意义

法律专业术语的作用在于以简洁的词或词组来陈述一项内容复杂的或含义广泛的法律概念或法则。由于要译出的法律术语的内在意义通常要比其外在形式复杂得多，因此在翻译时我们不能单就字面意义去直译，或望文生义，一定要准确理解原法律术语的意义，否则就无法将原术语的真正含义准确、完整地表达出来。

2. 尽量使用与本国法律原词相对等或最相类似的法律专业术语

就法律意义与法律后果而言，法律术语在英语和汉语中都各有其规定性，不可随意更改其形式。要达到法律意义和法律后果上的对等，就必须要在目标文本中尽量寻求与本国法律原词对等或最相类似的语词，只有这样，才能避免引起歧义。

3. 无对等词的翻译时，应强调神似

由于法律制度和历史文化的差异，我国法律中许多术语和规范在英语中根本就不存在，就是说二者之间在翻译上没有对等性。比如，中文中的"第三者"翻译成英语可能是"情人""情夫""情妇"或"婚外的恋人"之类的词语。但这些词在英语中并无褒贬色彩，有的词如"情人"甚至还近于褒义。但是在我国汉民族的语言习惯中这类词却往往使人与"奸夫淫妇"产生联想。与此相关，还有一个词叫"插足"。"第三者"的"插足"显然有抢夺、甚至霸占他人配偶之义。就是说，"第三者"不仅仅是要在别人的家庭中伸进一条腿，而且要把本属于别人的婚姻家庭据为己有。就此而言，英语中的 put one's foot in 和 participate 及 take part in 等词均不足以准确表达其意。在此情况下，较为可行的办法是在正确理解原词内涵的基础上，再在翻译上赋予其感情色彩。由于"第三者插足"所造成的后果是破坏、扰乱了别人的合法婚姻家庭关系，所以，我们认为用 step in 这一短语来翻译"插足"这个词较为妥当。因为 step in 本身就有 participate（加入）和 intervene（干扰）的双重含义。另外该词作为动词也恰到好处地表达了"伸腿"的动作。

4. 切忌不要以偏概全，也不能"笼而统之"

以偏概全和"笼而统之"都不能揭示事物的本质特征。法律翻译的庄严性和严谨性要求概念的翻译必须精准，法理必须通顺，因此以偏概全和"笼而统之"是法律翻译的大忌。尤其在涉及罪名翻译的时候，我们绝不能以类罪名来取代具体罪名。因为，只有具体罪名才能表明相应犯罪的本质特征，也才能对其正确地科以刑罚。只有做到了以上几点，法律专业术语的翻译才能取得较理想的效果。

法律宝典

仲裁基础知识

一、仲裁的含义

仲裁一般是当事人根据他们之间订立的仲裁协议，自愿将其争议提交由非官方身份的仲裁员组成的仲裁庭进行裁判，并受该裁判约束的一种制度。仲裁活动和法院的审判活动一样，关乎当事人的实体权益，是解决民事争议的方式之一。仲裁裁决是终局性的，对双方都有约束力，双方必须执行。仲裁协议有两种形式：一种是在争议发生之前订立的，它通常作为合同中的一项仲裁条款出现；另一种是在争议之后订立的，它是把已经发生的争议提交给仲裁的协议。这两种形式的仲裁协议，其法律效力是相同的。

二、仲裁的分类

根据所处理的纠纷是否具有涉外因素，仲裁可分国内仲裁和涉外仲裁。前者是该国当事人之间为解决没有涉外因素的国内民商事纠纷的仲裁；后者是处理涉及外国或外法域的民商事务争议的仲裁。

根据是否存在常设的专门仲裁机构，仲裁可以分为临时仲裁和机构仲裁。临时仲裁是当事人根据仲裁协议，将他们之间的争议交给临时组成的仲裁庭而非常设性仲裁机构时进行审理并作出裁决意见书的仲裁。机构仲裁是当事人根据其仲裁协议，将他们之间的纠纷提交给某一常设性仲裁机构所进行的仲裁。

根据仲裁裁决的依据不同，仲裁可分为依法仲裁和友好仲裁。依法仲裁是指仲裁庭依据一定的法律规定对纠纷进行裁决。友好仲裁则是指依当事人的授权，依据它所认为的公平的标准作出对当事有约束力的裁决。

三、仲裁法的含义

仲裁法即调整仲裁关系的法律。它是规定仲裁的范围和基本原则、仲裁机构的地位及设立、仲裁员、仲裁庭的组成和仲裁程序的进行、仲裁参与人和仲裁机构或仲裁员在仲裁程序中的权利与义务、仲裁裁决的效力等内容及调整由此而引起的其他仲裁关系的法律规范的总称。

仲裁法有广义和狭义之分。狭义的仲裁法，仅指以仲裁法为名称的单行法或者仲裁法典，如《中华人民共和国仲裁法》；广义的仲裁法除指单行法和仲裁法典外，还包括所有涉及仲裁制度的法律规范，比如民事诉讼法和合同法中关于仲裁的规定以及行政法规、规章中的有关内容。

▶ 术语积累

special stipulations 特别规定
general principle 一般原则
stateless persons 无国籍人
foreign civil case 涉外民事案件
notarial acts 公证行为
foreign affairs arbitration agency 涉外仲裁机构
reach a written agreement 达成书面协议
the award made by an arbitration agency 仲裁机构的裁决
final ruling 终极裁决
arbitration award 仲裁裁决
arbitration procedure 仲裁程序
arbitration agreement 仲裁协议
arbitration notice 仲裁通知
foreign nationals 外国公民
preservative measures in litigation 诉讼保全

note of acceptance　承诺书
withdrawal of a recognition　承认的撤回
foreign affairs lawyer office　涉外律师事务所
counsel fee　律师费
submit the dispute to the arbitration agency　将纠纷提交至仲裁机构仲裁
shall not bring the suit in a people's court　不得向人民法院起诉
may bring the suit in a people's court　可以向人民法院起诉
economic dispute arises between foreign enterprises or organizations　外国企业、组织间的纠纷
the person against whom such action is directed　被申请人
a party of Chinese nationality　中国籍的当事人
foreign legal person　外国法人
the country where the party resides　当事人所在国
judicial assistance agreement　司法协助协议
the copy of the bill of complaint　诉讼副本
当事人　the parties
原告　the plaintiff
被告　the defendant
提供证据　provide evidence
申请执行　file an appeal
委托代理人　entrusted agent
委托关系　clientage
委托人　client
书证　documentary evidence
证人证言　testimony of witness
陈词　allegation
鉴定结论　expert conclusions
证明人　authenticator
证明书　testimonial letter
有效证明书　certificate of validity
公证证明　certification by notary
案由　the cause of action
诉讼请求　the claims
裁定　order
书面裁定　a written order
原判　the original judgement
驳回上诉　reject the appeal
维持原判　sustain the original judgement
重审　retrial
复查案件　reexamine the case

申诉书   petition for revision
涉外案件   cases involving foreign interests
地域管辖   territorial jurisdiction
基层人民法院   the basic people's courts
高级人民法院   the higher people's courts
最高人民法院   the Supreme People's Court

Section III   巩固练习

 词汇与短语

1. attorney at law
2. foreign trade arbitration
3. arbitrator
4. arbitration clause
5. arbitration court
6. notary office
7. foreign immunity
8. dispute concerning foreign affairs or nationals
9. upon the application of a party
10. foreign jurisdiction
11. 诉讼参加人
12. 诉讼权利能力
13. 进行辩论
14. 请求调解
15. 委托事项和委托权限
16. 审判人员
17. 适用的法律
18. 口头裁定
19. 中级人民法院
20. 申请执行的期限

 句子与段落

1. An arbitration agreement shall include the arbitration clauses provided in the contract and any other written form of agreement concluded before or after the disputes providing for submission to arbitration.
2. Arbitration commissions are independent of administrative organs and there are no subordinate relations with any administrative organs nor between the different arbitration commissions.
3. If the arbitration matters or the arbitration commission are not agreed upon by the parties in the arbitration agreement, or, if the relevant provisions are not clear, the parties may supplement the agreement.
4. An arbitration agreement shall exist independently. Any changes to, rescission, termination or invalidity of the contract shall not affect the validity of the arbitration agreement.

5. An arbitration tribunal has the right to rule on the validity of a contract.
6. The applicant may abandon or alter his arbitration claim.
7. The respondent may accept the arbitration claim or object to it. It has a right to make a counterclaim.
8. A party may apply for property preservation if, as the result of an act of the other party or for some other reasons, it appears that an award may be impossible or difficult to enforce.
9. If one of the parties applies for property preservation, the arbitration commission shall submit to a people's court the application of the party in accordance with the relevant provisions of the Civil Procedure Law.
10. The parties and their legal representatives may appoint lawyers or engage agents to handle matters relating to the arbitration.
11. An arbitration tribunal may comprise three arbitrators or one arbitrator. If an arbitration tribunal comprises three arbitrators, a presiding arbitrator shall be appointed.
12. If the parties fail, within the time limit prescribed by the Arbitration Rules, to select the form of the constitution of the arbitration tribunal or fail to select the arbitrators, the arbitrators shall be appointed by the chairman of the arbitration commission.
13. After the arbitration tribunal is constituted, the arbitration commission shall notify the parties in writing of the composition of the arbitration tribunal.
14. If the parties agree to have one arbitrator to form an arbitration tribunal, the arbitrator shall be selected jointly by the parties or be nominated by the chairman of the arbitration commission in accordance with a joint mandate given by the parties.
15. The people's court shall rule to cancel the award if it holds that the award is contrary to the social and public interests.
16. If a party applies for cancellation of an award, an application shall be submitted within 6 months after receipt of the award.
17. After the submission of an arbitration application, the parties may settle the dispute among themselves through conciliation. If a conciliation agreement has been reached, the parties may apply to the arbitration tribunal for an award based on the conciliation agreement. Then may also withdraw the arbitration application.
18. If the parties fall back on their words after the conclusion of a conciliation agreement and the withdrawal of the arbitration application, application may be made for arbitration in accordance with the arbitration agreement.
19. Before giving an award, an arbitration tribunal may first attempt to conciliate. If the parties apply for conciliation voluntarily, the arbitration tribunal shall conciliate. If conciliation is unsuccessful, an award shall be made promptly.
20. When a settlement agreement is reached by conciliation, the arbitration tribunal shall prepare the conciliation statement or the award on the basis of the results of the settlement agreement. A conciliation statement shall have the same legal force as that of an award.
21. Article 62 The parties shall execute an arbitration award. If one party fails to execute the

award, the other party may apply to a people's court for enforcement in accordance with the relevant provisions of the Civil Procedure Law, and the court shall enforce the award.

Article 63 A people's court shall, after examination and verification by its collegiate bench, rule not to enforce an award if the party against whom an application for enforcement is made provides evidence proving that the award involves one of the circumstances prescribed in Clause 2, Article 217 of the Civil procedure Law.

Article 64   If one party applies for enforcement of an award while the other party applies for cancellation of the award, the people's court receiving such application shall rule to suspend enforcement of the award.

If a people's court rules to cancel an award, it shall rule to terminate enforcement. If the people's court overrules the application for cancellation of an award, it shall rule to resume enforcement.

22. 仲裁员有下列情形之一的，必须回避，当事人也有权提出回避申请：
（一）是本案当事人或者当事人、代理人的近亲属；
（二）与本案有利害关系；
（三）与本案当事人、代理人有其他关系，可能影响公正仲裁的；
（四）私自会见当事人、代理人，或者接受当事人、代理人请客送礼的。

Unit Fifteen

The World Trade Organization
世界贸易组织

Section I 译例研究

>> Passage One
Marrakesh Agreement Establishing the World Trade Organization

Recognizing that their relations in the field of trade and economic endeavour should be conducted with a view to raising standards of living, ensuring full employment and a large and steadily growing volume of real income and effective demand, and expanding the production of and trade in goods and services, while allowing for the optimal use of the world's resources in accordance with the objective of sustainable development, seeking both to protect and preserve the environment and to enhance the means for doing so in a manner consistent with their respective needs and concerns at different levels of economic development,

Recognizing further that there is need for positive efforts designed to ensure that developing countries, and especially the least developed among them, secure a share in the growth in international trade commensurate with the needs of their economic development,

Being desirous of contributing to these objectives by entering into reciprocal and mutually advantageous arrangements directed to the substantial reduction of tariffs and other barriers to trade and to the elimination of discriminatory treatment in international trade relations,

Resolved, therefore, to develop an integrated, more viable and durable multilateral trading system encompassing the General Agreement on Tariffs and Trade, the results of past trade liberalization efforts, and all of the results of the Uruguay Round of Multilateral Trade

Unit Fifteen The World Trade Organization 世界贸易组织

Negotiations,

Determined to preserve the basic principles and to further the objectives underlying this multilateral trading system,

Agree as follows:

Article I   Establishment of the Organization

The World Trade Organization (hereinafter referred to as "the WTO") is hereby established.

Article II   Scope of the WTO

1. The WTO shall provide the common institutional framework for the conduct of trade relations among its Members in matters related to the agreements and associated legal instruments included in the Annexes to this Agreement.

…

Article III   Functions of the WTO

1. The WTO shall facilitate the implementation, administration and operation, and further the objectives, of this Agreement and of the Multilateral Trade Agreements, and shall also provide the framework for the implementation, administration and operation of the Plurilateral Trade Agreements.

2. The WTO shall provide the forum for negotiations among its Members concerning their multilateral trade relations in matters dealt with under the agreements in the Annexes to this Agreement. The WTO may also provide a forum for further negotiations among its Members concerning their multilateral trade relations, and a framework for the implementation of the results of such negotiations, as may be decided by the Ministerial Conference.

3. The WTO shall administer the Understanding on Rules and Procedures Governing the Settlement of Disputes (hereinafter referred to as the "Dispute Settlement Understanding" or "DSU") in Annex 2 to this Agreement.

4. The WTO shall administer the Trade Policy Review Mechanism provided for in Annex 3 to this Agreement. With a view to achieving greater coherence in global economic policy-making, the WTO shall cooperate, as appropriate, with the International Monetary Fund and with the International Bank for Reconstruction and Development and its affiliated agencies.

▶ 词汇提示

with a view to   为了，旨在
Marrakesh   马拉喀什
optimal   *adj.* 充分的，最优的
respective   *adj.* 各自的
consistent   *adj.* 符合的
commensurate   *adj.* 相当的，相等的
be desirous of   期望
reciprocal   *adj.* 互惠的

mutually　*adj.* 互相的
advantageous　*adj.* 有利的
viable　*adj.* 有活力的
durable　*adj.* 持久的
facilitate　*v.* 促进
affiliated　*adj.* 附属的

法律术语

full employment　充分就业
real income　实际收入
effective demand　有效需求
reduction of tariffs　削减关税
barriers to trade　贸易壁垒
discriminatory treatment　歧视待遇
multilateral trading system　多边贸易体制
trade liberalization　贸易自由化
institutional framework　体制框架
Plurilateral Trade Agreements　多边贸易协议
multilateral trade relations　多边贸易关系
Settlement of Disputes　争端解决
Trade Policy Review Mechanism　贸易政策评审机制
economic policy-making　经济决策
International Monetary Fund　国际货币基金组织
International Bank for Reconstruction and Development　国际复兴开发银行

要点解析

1. Marrakesh Agreement Establishing the World Trade Organization
马拉喀什建立世界贸易组织协定

2. ... seeking both to protect and preserve the environment and to enhance the means for doing so in a manner consistent with their respective needs and concerns at different levels of economic development,...

句中的"in a manner consistent with..."根据下文，可译为"以符合……的方式"。此句较长，raising, ensuring, expanding, allowing for, protect, preserve, enhance 可译为"提高……，保证……，扩大……，允许……，加强……"并列成分。

3. there is a need for positive efforts...
该句译成中文时可将名词短语 need for positive efforts 动词化，译为"有必要作出积极的努力"。

4. Being desirous of contributing to these objectives by entering into reciprocal and mutually advantageous arrangements directed to the substantial reduction of tariffs and other barriers to trade and to the elimination of discriminatory treatment in international trade relations, …

此句是一个长句，翻译时应注意适当调整语序，将"by entering into…"和"directed to…"提到前面，将"contributing to…"放到后面，更符合汉语表达习惯。

5. The World Trade Organization (hereinafter referred to as "the WTO") is hereby established.

句中的 hereinafter 和 hereby 是法律和商务文件的常用语，体现了此类文件的庄重性，可译为"以下"，"特此"。

6. The WTO shall provide the common institutional framework for the conduct of trade relations among its Members in matters related to the agreements and associated legal instruments included in the Annexes to this Agreement.

句中的 provide institutional framework 可以译为"提供机制框架"。

7. … as may be decided by the Ministerial Conference.

句中的 as may be decided by the Ministerial Conference 翻译时可提到全句的开头，译为"如果部长会议作出决定"。

8. … the WTO shall cooperate, as appropriate, with the International Monetary Fund and with the International Bank for Reconstruction and Development and its affiliated agencies.

句中的"cooperate, as appropriate" 即 cooperate appropriately，译为"适当的合作"。

 参考译文

马拉喀什建立世界贸易组织协定

承认其贸易和经济关系的发展，应旨在提高生活水平，保证充分就业和大幅度稳步提高实际收入和有效需求，扩大货物与服务的生产和贸易，为持续发展之目的扩大对世界资源的充分利用，保护和维护环境，并以符合不同经济发展水平下各自需要的方式，加强采取各种相应的措施；

进一步承认有必要作出积极的努力，以确保发展中国家，尤其是最不发达国家，在国际贸易增长中获得与其经济发展相适应的份额；

期望通过达成互惠互利的安排，切实降低关税和其他贸易壁垒，在国际贸易关系中消除歧视待遇，为实现上述目标做出贡献；

从而决心建立一个完整的、更有活力的和持久的多边贸易体系，以包括关税与贸易总协定、以往贸易自由化努力的成果和乌拉圭回合多边贸易谈判的所有成果；

决心保持该多边贸易体制的基本原则和加强体制的目标；

协议如下：

第一条　组织的建立

建立世界贸易组织（以下简称世贸组织）。

第二条　世贸组织的范围

1. 世贸组织应为其成员之间与本协议各附件中的协议及其法律文件有关的贸易关系，提供共同的体制框架。

……

第三条 世贸组织的职能

1. 世贸组织应促进本协议和多边贸易协议的执行、管理、运作，以及进一步实现各协议的目标，并对诸边贸易协议的执行、管理和运作提供框架。

2. 世贸组织应为各成员处理与本协议各附件有关的多边贸易关系提供谈判场所。如果部长会议作出决定，世贸组织还可为各成员的多边贸易关系的进一步谈判提供场所，并为执行该谈判的结果提供框架。

3. 世贸组织应管理实施本协议附件二有关争端解决的规则与程序的谅解（以下简称"争端解决谅解"）。

4. 世贸组织管理实施附件三的贸易政策评审机制，世贸组织应和国际货币基金组织与国际复兴开发银行及其附属机构进行适当的合作，以更好地协调制定全球经济政策。

Passage Two
中华人民共和国加入议定书

序 言

世界贸易组织（"WTO"），按照部长级会议根据《马拉喀什建立世界贸易组织协定》（"《WTO协定》"）第12条所作出的批准，与中华人民共和国（"中国"），

忆及中国是《1947年关税与贸易总协定》的创始缔约方，

注意到中国是《乌拉圭回合多边贸易谈判结果最后文件》的签署方，

注意到载于WT/ACC/CHN49号文件的《中国加入工作组报告书》（"工作组报告书"），

考虑到关于中国WTO成员资格的谈判结果，

协议如下：

第一部分 总则

第一条 总体情况

1. 自加入时起，中国根据《WTO协定》第12条加入该协定，并由此成为WTO成员。

2. 中国所加入的《WTO协定》应为经在加入之日前已生效的法律文件所更正、修正或修改的《WTO协定》。本议定书，包括工作组报告书第342段所指的承诺，应成为《WTO协定》的组成部分。

3. 除本议定书另有规定外，中国应履行《WTO协定》所附各多边贸易协定中的、应在自该协定生效之日起开始的一段时间内履行的义务，如同中国在该协定生效之日已接受该协定。

4. 中国可维持与《服务贸易总协定》（"GATS"）第2条第1款规定不一致的措施，只要此措施已记录在本议定书所附《第2条豁免清单》中，并符合GATS《关于第2条豁免的附件》中的条件。

第二条 贸易制度的实施

Unit Fifteen　The World Trade Organization　世界贸易组织

(A) 统一实施

1.《WTO 协定》和本协定书的规定应适用于中国的全部关税领土，包括边境贸易地区、民族自治地方、经济特区、沿海开放城市、经济技术开发区以及其他在关税、国内税和法规方面已建立特殊制度的地区（统称为"特殊经济区"）。

……

第三条　非歧视

除本议定书另有规定外，在下列方面给予外国个人、企业和外商投资企业的待遇不得低于给予其他个人和企业的待遇。

……

第四条　特殊贸易安排

自加入时起，中国应取消与第三国和单独关税区之间的、与《WTO 协定》不符的所有特殊贸易安排，包括易货贸易安排，或使其符合《WTO 协定》。

第五条　贸易权

……

第六条　国营贸易

1. 中国应保证国营贸易企业的进口购买程序完全透明，并符合《WTO 协定》，且应避免采取任何措施对国营贸易企业购买或销售货物的数量、价值或原产国施加影响或指导，但依照《WTO 协定》进行的除外。

2. 作为根据 GATT1994 和《关于解释 1994 年关税与贸易总协定第 17 条的谅解》所作通知的一部分，中国还应提供有关其国营贸易企业出口货物定价机制的全部信息。

第七条　非关税措施

1. 中国应执行附件 3 包含的非关税措施取消时间表。在附件 3 中所列期限内，对该附件中所列措施提供的保护在规模、范围或期限方面不得增加或扩大，且不得实施任何新的措施，除非符合《WTO 协定》的规定。

……

▶ 词汇提示

序言　preamble
根据　accord to
忆及　recall
签署方　signatory
考虑到　having regard to
谈判　negotiation
成员资格　membership
由此　thereby
更正　rectify
修改　modify
附件　annex

统一实施　uniform administration
规定　provision
不符　not in conformity with
透明　transparent
通知　notification
机制　mechanism
执行　implement
取消　elimination

法律术语

议定书　Protocol
部长级会议　Ministerial Conference
马拉喀什协定　Marrakesh Agreement
缔约方　contracting party
关税与贸易总协定　General Agreement on Tariffs and Trade
乌拉圭回合多边贸易谈判　Uruguay Round of Multilateral Trade Negotiations
义务　obligations
服务贸易总协定　General Agreement on Trade in Services ("GATS")
豁免　exemptions
关税领土　customs territory
少数民族自治区　minority autonomous areas
经济特区　Special Economic Zones
经济技术开发区　economic and technical development zones
关税　Tariffs
易货贸易　barter trade
国营贸易　State Trading

要点解析

1. 中华人民共和国加入议定书

翻译标题时应注意中英标题的不同，将"议定书"前置，将"中华人民共和国加入"按英文标题习惯译成介词短语后置，可译为"Protocol on the Accession of the People's Republic of China"。

2. 《1947年关税与贸易总协定》的创始缔约方

和标题一样，在英译时要进行次序的调整，应将中心词"创始缔约方"放在最前面，将缔约的文件名称放在后面，译为"an original contracting party to the General Agreement on Tariffs and Trade 1947"。

3. 注意到中国是《乌拉圭回合多边贸易谈判结果最后文件》的签署方

句中的"注意到"在文中可译为英语短语"taking note of …"。

4. "协议如下"为经济和法律合同文书的常用语,通常被译为 Agree as follows。

5. "此处生效"一般英语文书中可被译为 come into effect 等,但在法律或经贸文件中经常被译为 enter into force。

6. "中国加入的《WTO 协定》"译为"The WTO Agreement to which China accedes"作为句子的主语,将"经在加入之日前已生效的法律文件所更正、修正或修改的《WTO 协定》"译为"the WTO Agreement as rectified, amended or otherwise modified by such legal instruments as may have entered into force before the date of accession"作表语。

7. 《WTO 协定》和本协定书的规定应适用于中国的全部关税领土

句中的"应"因为出现在法律文书中,是具有法律效力的。不能将其按字面意思译成 should 或 ought to,准确的翻译应为 shall。

8. 在下列方面给予外国个人、企业和外商投资企业的待遇不得低于给予其他个人和企业的待遇。

句中的"在以下几个方面"通常可译为"in respect of…"。

参考译文

Protocol on the Accession of the People's Republic of China

Preamble

The World Trade Organization ("WTO"), pursuant to the approval of the Ministerial Conference of the WTO accorded under Article XII of the Marrakesh Agreement Establishing the World Trade Organization ("WTO Agreement"), and the People's Republic of China ("China"),

Recalling that China was an original contracting party to the General Agreement on Tariffs and Trade 1947,

Taking note that China is a signatory to the Final Act Embodying the Results of the Uruguay Round of Multilateral Trade Negotiations,

Taking note of the Report of the Working Party on the Accession of China in document WT/ACC/CHN/49 ("Working Party Report"),

Having regard to the results of the negotiations concerning China's membership in the WTO,

Agree as follows:

Part I General Provisions

Article 1. General

1. Upon accession, China accedes to the WTO Agreement pursuant to Article XII of that Agreement and thereby becomes a Member of the WTO.

2. The WTO Agreement to which China accedes shall be the WTO Agreement as rectified, amended or otherwise modified by such legal instruments as may have entered into force before the date of accession. This Protocol, which shall include the commitments referred to in paragraph 342

of the Working Party Report, shall be an integral part of the WTO Agreement.

3. Except as otherwise provided for in this Protocol, those in the Multilateral Trade Agreements annexed to the WTO Agreement that are to be implemented over a period of time starting with entry into force of that Agreement shall be implemented by China as if it had accepted that Agreement on the date of its entry into force.

4. China may maintain a measure inconsistent with paragraph 1 of Article II of the General Agreement on Trade in Services ("GATS") provided that such a measure is recorded in the List of Article II Exemptions annexed to this Protocol and meets the conditions of the Annex to the GATS on Article II Exemptions.

Article 2. Administration of the Trade Regime

(A) Uniform Administration

1. The provisions of the WTO Agreement and this Protocol shall apply to the entire customs territory of China, including border trade regions and minority autonomous areas, Special Economic Zones, open coastal cities, economic and technical development zones and other areas where special regimes for tariffs, taxes and regulations are established (collectively referred to as "special economic areas").

…

Article 3. Non-discrimination

Except as otherwise provided for in this Protocol, foreign individuals and enterprises and foreign-funded enterprises shall be accorded treatment no less favourable than that accorded to other individuals and enterprises in respect of.

…

Article 4. Special Trade Arrangements

Upon accession, China shall eliminate or bring into conformity with the WTO Agreement all special trade arrangements, including barter trade arrangements, with third countries and separate customs territories, which are not in conformity with the WTO Agreement.

Article 5. Right to Trade

…

Article 6. State Trading

1. China shall ensure that import purchasing procedures of state trading enterprises are fully transparent, and in compliance with the WTO Agreement, and shall refrain from taking any measure to influence or direct state trading enterprises as to the quantity, value, or country of origin of goods purchased or sold, except in accordance with the WTO Agreement.

2. As part of China's notification under the GATT 1994 and the Understanding on the Interpretation of Article XVII of the GATT 1994, China shall also provide full information on the pricing mechanisms of its state trading enterprises for exported goods.

Article 7. Non-Tariff Measures

1. China shall implement the schedule for phased elimination of the measures contained in Annex 3. During the periods specified in Annex 3, the protection afforded by the measures listed in that Annex shall not be increased or expanded in size, scope or duration, nor shall any new measures

be applied, unless in conformity with the provisions of the WTO Agreement.

...

Section II　技能拓展

 翻译技巧

法律文本翻译中模糊词语的处理

既然模糊性是人类自然语言的一种基本属性，模糊词语在法律文本语言中普遍存在，那么在翻译中对模糊信息的处理就极为重要。针对模糊表达不同的语义、语用功能，译者可以根据具体情况，灵活处理。具体说来，可以有以下几种处理方法：

1. 直译

直译即用一种语言的模糊语去翻译另一种语言中的模糊语，从而保留模糊信息。例如：

① We the People of the United States, in order to form a more perfect Union, establish Justice, insure domestic Tranquility, provide for the common defense, promote the general Welfare, and secure the Blessings of Liberty to ourselves and our Posterity, do ordain and establish this Constitution for the United States of America.

我们合众国人民，为了形成一个更完善的联邦，建立正义，保障国内安定，提供共同的防御，促进普遍的福利，并将自由的恩赐被及我们子孙后代，特制定与创立这部美利坚合众国宪法。

英语中的 perfect、common、general 三个模糊词语，分别译成"完善的""共同的""普遍的"。

② 合同无效或者被撤销后，因该合同取得的财产，应当予以返还；不能返还或者没有必要返还的，应当折价补偿。（《中华人民共和国合同法》第五十八条）

After a contract becomes invalid or is rescinded, any property obtained under the contract shall be returned. If it is impossible or unnecessary to return the property, compensation shall be made at an estimated price. (Article 58, Contract Law of the People's Republic of China)

③ 拘役的缓刑考验期限为原判刑期以上一年以下，但是不能少于二个月。（《中华人民共和国刑法》第七十三条）

The probation period for suspension of criminal detention shall be not less than the term originally decided but not more than one year, however, it may not be less than two months. (Article 73, Criminal Law of the People's Republic of China)

汉语中的"不能""没有必要""少于"和英语中的 impossible、unnecessary、less than 可谓是模糊对模糊。

④ 特种设备发生事故，事故发生单位应当迅速采取有效措施，组织抢救，防止事故扩大，减少人员伤亡和财产损失，并按照国家有关规定，及时、如实地向……等有关部门报告。

In case of any accident of special equipmen, the unit where the accident happens shall take immediate and effective measures and organize the rescue to prevent the accident from spreading and to reduce the casualties and property losses. It shall also make a prompt and truthful report to…

原文采用模糊词语 immediate、effective、prompt 对无法定量的情况进行限制，概括地规范了法律主体应该施行的法律行为，从而体现了立法的科学性。如果把模糊词语改成确定性的词语，就可能使法律失去公正性。

⑤ The registered capital shall generally be represented in Renminbi, or may be in a foreign currency agreed upon by the parties to the joint ventures.

合营企业的注册资本一般以人民币表示，也可以用合营各方约定的外币表示。

这里的 generally 和 may 都表达的是模糊的概念，可分别译成"一般"和"可以"。

2. 意译：化模糊为精确

对于某些模糊表达，直译的效果不如意译，可根据原文的精神实质，将模糊信息翻译成相对的精确语言。例如：

① The seller are allowed to load 5% more or less and the price shall be calculated according to the unit price.

卖方可溢短装 5%，价格仍按上述单价计算。

句中模糊词语 more or less 没有直译为"多装或少装"，而是意译为专业术语"溢短装"。

② The parties shall observe the principle of good faith in exercising their rights and fulfilling the obligations.

当事人行使权利、履行义务应当遵循诚实信用原则。

句中模糊词语 good faith 翻译成汉语成语"诚实信用"。

③ The production and business operating plans of an equity jointventure shall be submitted to the competent authorities for record and shall be implemented through economic contract.

合营企业生产经营计划，应报主管部门备案，并通过经济合同方式执行。

原文中的 competent 常用的意思是"有能力的、能胜任的"，这儿根据上下文采用变通译法翻译为"主管"，符合了汉语的表达习惯。

3. 补充

根据原文的精神实质，在译成目的语时，进行适当的添加模糊词语，使之通顺，更易于理解和符合目的语法律语言的文体特征。例如：

① 签约双方的任何一方，由于台风、地震和双方同意的不可抗力事故而影响合同的执行时，则延迟执行合同的期限应相当于事故所影响的时间。

If either party is prevented from executing the contract by such causes of Force Majeure as typhoon, earthquake or other events agreed upon by both parties, the time for the execution of the contract shall be extended by a period to the effect of those causes.

台风、地震都是不可抗力，所以"和"译为 or，并且添加了 other 进一步表明了原文中的逻辑关系。

② A proposal for concluding a contract addressed to one or more specific persons constitutes an offer if it is sufficiently definite and indicates the intention of the offer or to be bound in case of acceptance.

（向一个或一个以上特定的人提出的订立合同的建议，如果十分确定并且表明要约人在得到接受时承受约束的意旨即构成要约。）

原文中没有"十分"，在翻译时增译表示模糊概念的数量词"十分"。

③ But for many, the fact that poor people are able to support themselves almost as well without government aid as they did with it is in itself a huge victory.

但对许多人来说，穷人能够不靠政府救济养活自己，而且生活得几乎和过去依靠政府救济时生活得一样好，这件事本身就是一个巨大的胜利。

原文中 many 本身就是一个表达模糊的数词，在翻译时如果把它对译成"许多"，读者会觉得译者交代得不够彻底。因此，在此处增加"人"这样会使整个结构变得清楚、明朗。另外在处理 as they did with it 结构时有必要将 they、it 等表示模糊概念的代词用汉语的实词表现出来以减少理解和表达上的歧义。

④ A proposal for concluding a contract addressed to one or more specific persons constitutes an offer if it is sufficiently definite and indicates the intention of the offer to be bound in case of acceptance.

涉及一方或多方的协议提案，只有当此意思表示的内容具体明确，并说明要约人受该意思表示的约束和受要约人承诺后，才能成为要约。

法律意义中"要约"涉及要约人和受要约人双方。该意思表示经受要约人承诺后，要约人就受该意思表示的约束。而原文中并没表明要约涉及的双方，意义较模糊。因此对短语 the intention of the offer to be bound 的翻译此处应添加"要约人受该意思表示的约束"，而介词短语 in case of acceptance 应翻译为"和受要约人承诺"，使其符合法律条文的意义。

4. 省略

对于一些在原文中并不具有实际意义的或者是为了不留漏洞、起防患于未然作用的模糊表达，在翻译中可以省略。例如下句中的 with respect to 和 the objectives of：

① The parties undertake to act in good faith with respect to each other's rights under this contract and to adapt all reasonable measures to ensure the realizations of the objectives of this contract.

双方将公平地对待相互所享有的合同赋予的权利，并采取一切合理的措施保证本合同的实施。

同样，下句中的 if any 也没有翻译出来。

② We as the Seller reserve the right to lodge a claim for direct losses sustained, if any.

作为卖方，我们有权对遭受的直接损失提出索赔。

③ Mr. Justice Douglas rejected the death penalty because it was administered in such a way as to discriminate against unpopular minorities.

道格拉斯法官先生反对这种执行死刑的方式。因为它会导致对一些"不受欢迎的"少数群体的歧视。

原文中的 in such a way 并没有指出死刑执行的具体方法，因而是一个模糊概念。如果照字面译出，势必不符合译文的语法习惯。在此使用省略法，使其更符合中文的表达习惯。

5. 具体情况，灵活处理

俗话说："翻译无定法，全在译者的匠心。"由于英汉两种语言属于不同的语系，存在差异，有时可以在不影响理解的基础上，灵活处理。例如上文提到的模糊化精确，反之，也可以精确化模糊。例如：

① It's two and two makes four that the parties shall, pursuant to law, have the right to enter into a contract on their own free will, and no unit or person may unlawfully interfere.

很明显，当事人依法享有自愿订立合同的权利，任何单位和个人不得非法干预。

two and two makes four 是确切词语，这里译作模糊词语"很明显"。

法律语言中有些模糊词语，翻译时为了达到"通顺"的标准，可以重新释义。例如：

② This section sets out the scope of the installations covered by these specifications as well as specially required supplies and service, but without excluding other necessary components and services not mentioned.

本节提出了本规范中包括的设备范围以及特别要求的供货和服务，但还应该包括尚未提到的其他必要的部件和服务。

without excluding 重新释义为"还应该包括"。

③ The state constitution provides that it is lawful for the citizens to carry guns. In recent years hundreds and hundreds of innocent people have died of this and one need not look for a lesson.

该州宪法规定，公民携带枪支是合法的，正因为如此，近年来有成千上万的无辜的人惨遭枪击身亡，教训历历在目。

原文中的 hundreds and hundreds of 的基本意思是"几百""几千"，这里译成"成千上万"更符合原文的夸张程度。

 法律宝典

世界贸易组织基础知识

一、什么是世界贸易组织

世界贸易组织（World Trade Organization），是一个全球性的贸易组织。于1994年4月15日由马拉喀什市举行的关贸总协定乌拉圭回合部长会议决定成立，以取代成立于1947年的关贸总协定（GATT）。1995年1月1日正式开始运作，该组织负责管理世界经济和贸易秩序，总部设在瑞士日内瓦莱蒙湖畔。1996年1月1日，它正式取代关贸总协定临时机构。与关贸总协定相比，世贸组织涵盖货物贸易、服务贸易及知识产权贸易，而关贸总协定只适用于商品货物贸易。

二、世界贸易组织的宗旨和原则

世贸组织的宗旨是：提高生活水平，保证充分就业和大幅度、稳步提高实际收入和有效需求；扩大货物和服务的生产与贸易；坚持走可持续发展之路，各成员方应促进对世界资源的最优利用、保护和维护环境，并以符合不同经济发展水平下各成员需要的方式，加强采取

Unit Fifteen The World Trade Organization 世界贸易组织

各种相应的措施；积极努力确保发展中国家，尤其是最不发达国家在国际贸易增长中获得与其经济发展水平相适应的份额和利益；建立一体化的多边贸易体制。

世界贸易组织的目标是建立一个完整的，包括货物、服务、与贸易有关的投资及知识产权等内容的，更具活力、更持久的多边贸易体系，使之可以包括关贸总协定贸易自由化的成果和乌拉圭回合多边贸易谈判的所有成果。

三、中国的 入世

1995年7月11日，世贸组织总理事会会议决定接纳中国为该组织的观察员国。2001年12月11日，中国正式加入世界贸易组织，成为其第143个成员。至此，中国自1986年申请重返关贸总协定以来，为复关和加入世界贸易组织已进行了长达15年的努力。

中国的"入世"有利于参与国际经济合作和国际分工，促进经济发展；有利于扩大出口和利用外资，并在平等条件下参与国际竞争；有利于促进技术进步、产业升级和经济结构调整，进一步完善社会主义市场经济体制；有利于改革开放、社会主义市场经济的发展和人民生活水平的提高；也有利于直接参与21世纪国际贸易规则的决策过程，摆脱别人制定规则而中国被动接受的不利状况，从而维护合法权益。但是，随着市场的进一步扩大，关税的大幅度减让，外国产品、服务和投资有可能更多地进入中国市场，中国国内一些产品、企业和产业也将面临更加激烈的竞争。

▶ 术语积累

antidumping measure　反倾销措施
additional non-tariff barrier　附加非关税壁垒
adjustment of charges　根据现存配额调整税收
adverse balance of payments　国际收支逆差
aggregate demand　总需求
aggregate imports　进口总额
British preference countries　英联邦特惠国
breach of customs regulations　违反海关规定
border price　边境免税价格
border protection　边境保护
border tax　边境征税
capital transactions　资本交易
capital yield　资本收益
cash deposit　保证金
North American Free Trade Area　北美自由贸易区
ceiling bindings　上限约束
fair competition　公平竞争，公平交易
General Agreement on Tariffs and Trade　关税及贸易总协定
General Council　总理事会，总评议会
import licensing　进口许可

import penetration　进口渗透
Initial Negotiating Rights　最初谈判权
Intellectual property rights　知识产权
labor relation　劳资关系
Most-Favoured-Nation Treatment　最惠国待遇
multilateral trade　多边贸易
National Treatment　国民待遇
quota　配额，限额
steering committee　筹划指导委员会
secretariat　秘书处，书记处，秘书（书记，部长等）的职位
trade barrier　贸易壁垒
tariff barriers　关税壁垒
tariff concession　关税优惠
tariff agreement　关税协定
target market　目标市场
争端解决机构　dispute settlement body
东盟自由贸易区　ASEAN Free Trade Area
中美洲共同市场　central American common market
国际收支　balance of international payments/ balance of payment
反补贴税　countervailing duty
出口补贴　export subsidy
生产补贴　production subsidy
市场准入　market access
海关完税价值　customs value
风险管理/评估　risk management/ assessment
实行国民待遇　grant the national treatment to
瓶颈制约　"bottleneck" restrictions
非洲、加勒比和太平洋国家集团　African, Caribbean and Pacific Group
粮食安全　food security
免费搭车者（享受其他国家最惠国待遇而不进行相应减让的国家）　free-rider
政府采购　government procurement
灰色区域措施　grey area measures
WTO最不发达国家高级别会议　WTO "High-level" Meeting for LDCs
商品名称及编码协调制度　Harmonized Commodity and Coding System
专门的营销机构　market boards
自然人　natural person
利益的丧失和减损　nullification and impairment
专家组　panel
诸边协议　plurilateral agreement

自然人流动　presence of natural person
消费膨胀　inflated consumption
慢性萧条　chronic depression
进口环节税　import linkage tax
全球配额　global quota
基础税率　base tariff level
既定日程　"built-in" agenda
规避　circumvention
国际清算　international settlement
垃圾融资　junk financing

Section III　巩固练习

词汇与短语

1. advance payment
2. Trade Policy Review Mechanism
3. a prudent monetary policy
4. competition mechanism
5. comparative advantage
6. fair competition
7. economic returns
8. per capita GDP
9. proprietary intellectual property rights
10. regional protectionism
11. 全球经济一体化
12. 风险资金
13. 国民经济
14. 国有企业
15. 合法经营
16. 三资企业
17. 外商直接投资
18. 外向型经济
19. 市场经济
20. 广交会

句子与段落

1. Import and export prohibitions and restrictions, and licensing requirements affecting imports and exports shall only be imposed and enforced by the national authorities or by sub-national authorities with authorization from the national authorities.

2. China shall allow prices for traded goods and services in every sector to be determined by market forces, and multi-tier pricing practices for such goods and services shall be eliminated.

3. Foreign individuals and enterprises and foreign-funded enterprises shall, upon accession, be accorded treatment no less favourable than that accorded to other individuals and enterprises

in respect of the provision of border tax adjustments.

4. In critical circumstances, where delay would cause damage which it would be difficult to repair, the WTO Member so affected may take a provisional safeguard measure pursuant to a preliminary determination that imports have caused or threatened to cause market disruption.

5. China shall publish in the official journal the list of goods and services subject to state pricing and changes thereto.

6. There shall be a Ministerial Conference composed of representatives of all the Members, which shall meet at least once every two years.

7. In the intervals between meetings of the Ministerial Conference, its functions shall be conducted by the General Council.

8. The General Council shall convene as appropriate to discharge the responsibilities of the Dispute Settlement Body provided for in the Dispute Settlement Understanding.

9. The Dispute Settlement Body may have its own chairman and shall establish such rules of procedure as it deems necessary for the fulfillment of those responsibilities.

10. The General Council shall convene as appropriate to discharge the responsibilities of the Trade Policy Review Body provided for in the TPRM.

11. The Trade Policy Review Body may have its own chairman and shall establish such rules of procedure as it deems necessary for the fulfillment of those responsibilities.

12. The General Council shall make appropriate arrangements for effective cooperation with other intergovernmental organizations that have responsibilities related to those of the WTO.

13. The Director-General shall appoint the members of the staff of the Secretariat and determine their duties and conditions of service in accordance with regulations adopted by the Ministerial Conference.

14. The General Council shall adopt the financial regulations and the annual budget estimate by a two-thirds majority comprising more than half of the Members of the WTO.

15. The WTO shall have legal personality, and shall be accorded by each of its Members such legal capacity as may be necessary for the exercise of its functions.

16. The WTO shall be accorded by each of its Members such privileges and immunities as are necessary for the exercise of its functions.

17. The officials of the WTO and the representatives of the Members shall similarly be accorded by each of its Members such privileges and immunities as are necessary for the independent exercise of their functions in connection with the WTO.

18. The WTO shall continue the practice of decision-making by consensus followed under GATT 1947.

19. At meetings of the Ministerial Conference and the General Council, each Member of the WTO shall have one vote.

20. In exceptional circumstances, the Ministerial Conference may decide to waive an obligation imposed on a Member by this Agreement or any of the Multilateral Trade

Agreements.

21. Market disruption shall exist whenever imports of an article, like or directly competitive with an article produced by the domestic industry, are increasing rapidly, either absolutely or relatively, so as to be a significant cause of material injury, or threat of material injury to the domestic industry. In determining if market disruption exists, the affected WTO Member shall consider objective factors, including the volume of imports, the effect of imports on prices for like or directly competitive articles, and the effect of such imports on the domestic industry producing like or directly competitive products.

22. 中国承诺只执行已公布的，且其他 WTO 成员、个人和企业可容易获得的有关或影响货物贸易、服务贸易、TRIPS 或外汇管制的法律、法规及其他措施。此外，在所有有关或影响货物贸易、服务贸易、TRIPS 或外汇管制的法律、法规及其他措施实施或执行前，应请求，中国应使 WTO 成员可获得此类措施。在紧急情况下，应使法律、法规及其他措施最迟在实施或执行之时可获得。

Keys

Unit one

词汇与短语

1. 陈述，阐明
2. 优先于
3. 准立法的
4. 列举
5. 立法行为
6. 依照的，依据的
7. 实体的
8. 实施，履行
9. 司法的，法律的
10. 权利法案
11. Common Law
12. civil law
13. stare decisis
14. equity
15. supreme court
16. case law
17. subordinate to
18. private law
19. legal science
20. precedent

句子与段落

1. Laws are sometimes referred to as substantive or procedural.
2. Substantive law defines rights, and procedural law establishes the procedures by which rights are protected and enforced.
3. This concept of decided cases as a source of law is often referred to as the common law system, which must be contrasted with the civil law system developed in continental Europe.
4. The civil law countries have codified their law so that the main source of law in those countries is to be found in the statutes rather than in the cases.
5. Law is not simply a set of rules of conduct. It is also a means to impose responsibility and to enforce social justice.
6. 税法很符合法律是上级对下级的命令这一定义。
7. 一般来说公法影响到公众，私法则处理有秩序的社会中个人间的关系。
8. 可以根据法律的渊源把法律分成宪法、国会立法、司法判决和行政法规。
9. 在美国，已经判决的案子也是法的一个渊源，这与欧洲大陆不同。后者法律的主要渊源是成文法条。
10. 在现代西方世界三种主要的法律传统中，罗马—日耳曼法系历史最悠久，影响最深远，分布范围最为广泛。
11. In the United States, common law has been the predominant influence. Since most of the colonists were of English origin, they naturally followed the laws and customs of their mother

country. But in Louisiana, and to some extent Texas and California, the civil law has influenced the legal systems, because these states were founded by the French and Spanish. However, much of the law in every state of the United States is statutory, and statutes are becoming incresingly important. Case law, or common law, remains an important source of law because of the extreme difficulty in reducing all law to writing in advance of an issue being raised.

12. Treaties entered into by the United States are also considered the supreme law of the land pursuant to the U.S. Constitution, as are federal laws. In the case of a conflict between a treaty and a federal statute, the one that is later in time or more specific will typically control. Treaties to which the United States are a party may be found in the U.S. Treaties Service, the Statutes at Large, the Treaties and other International Acts Series issued by the State Department, as well as the United Nations Treaty Series.

13. Federal administrative bodies issue rules and regulations of a quasi-legislative character; valid federal regulations have the force of law and preempt state laws and rules. Rules and regulations may be issued only under statutory authority granted by Congress. The President also has broad powers to issue executive orders. An executive order is a directive from the President to other officials in the executive branch.

14. The United States is a common law country. Every U.S. state has a legal system based on the common law, except Louisiana (which relies on the French civil code). Common law has no statutory basis; judges establish common law by applying previous decisions (precedents) to present cases. Although typically affected by statutory authority, broad areas of the law, most notably relating to property, contracts, and torts are traditionally part of the common law.

15. Reported decisions of the U.S. Supreme Court and of most of the state appellate courts can be found in the official reporter of the respective courts. Those decided from at least 1887 to date can also be found in the National Reporter System, a system of unofficial reporters. Decisions of lower state courts are not published officially, but can usually be found in unofficial reports.

16. 美国法院体系是政府联邦体系的组成部分，它以两级结构为特点，包括州法院和联邦法院。每个州都有自己的法院体系，由民事和形式初审法院组成，有时还包括上诉法院和州最高法院。

17. 英国法最初主要是以撒克逊习惯法为基础的氏族部落法组成的。当时的部落会议就是审判机关。而后，相继出现了地方法庭、百家村法庭和市民法庭来解决纠纷。法律主要是依靠十户联保制度加以实施。

18. 诺曼征服之后，在当时同时行使立法、行政、司法三大职能的君主法庭的支持下，国王建立了一个强有力的中央集权政府。所谓"常设巡回制"，即国王派出御前会议成员，去往全国各郡，进行巡回检查、征收赋税和审判案件的制度。这一制度适用后，即产生了普通法。各地习惯法中行之有效的规定被采纳适用，而摒弃其中的恶法，在此过程中，逐渐形成了通行于全国的普通法。

19. "普通法"和"制定法"用来表示普通法法系社会的一般法律渊源。普通法表现在法院的判决中，制定法则以立法制定为基础。美国的普通法虽然源于英国人民的习俗和惯例，但在当今的美国，"普通法"一般指由法院判决形成的判例法。

20. 制定法一般指由立法机构正式通过的法律。在美国，立法机构包括美国国会、州立法机关和地方市议会或市政委员会。行政法规和规章一般也划为制定法。最后，市政机构的法规，尽管有时被特别称为"法令"，也是制定法的一种。

Unit Two

词汇与短语

1. prohibit
2. infringe
3. obligation
4. legitimate
5. procession
6. demonstration
7. civil rights
8. state organ
9. public organization
10. in accordance with

11. 规定的
12. 归属于
13. 选举令
14. 弹劾
15. 法定人数
16. 行使权力
17. 休会
18. 有权
19. 应……的请求
20. 达到

句子与段落

1. Citizens of the People's Republic of China have the right as well as the duty to work.
2. The state expands facilities for the rest and recuperation of the working people and prescribes working hours and vacations for workers and staff.
3. The state protects the rights and interests of women, applies the principle of equal pay for equal work to men and women alike and trains and selects cadres from among women.
4. Maltreatment of old people, women and children is prohibited.
5. It is the sacred duty of every citizen of the People's Republic of China to defend the motherland and resist aggression.
6. 本宪法所规定的立法权，全属合众国的国会，国会由一个参议院和一个众议院组成。
7. 合众国副总统应为参议院议长，除非在投票票数相等时，议长无投票权。
8. 国会应至少每年集会一次，开会日期应为十二月的第一个星期一，除非他们通过法律来指定另一个日期。
9. 参众两院得各自规定本院的议事规则，处罚本院扰乱秩序的议员，并且得以三分之二同意，开除本院的议员。
10. 在国会开会期间，任一议院未得别院同意，不得休会三日以上，亦不得迁往非两院开会的其他地点。
11. All citizens of the People's Republic of China who have reached the age of 18 have the right to vote and stand for election, regardless of nationality, race, sex, occupation, family background, religious belief, education, property status, or length of residence, except persons deprived of

political rights according to law.

12. The freedom and privacy of correspondence of citizens of the People's Republic of China are protected by law. No organization or individual may, on any ground, infringe upon the freedom and privacy of citizens' correspondence except in cases where, to meet the needs of state security or of investigation into criminal offences, public security or procuratorial organs are permitted to censor correspondence in accordance with procedures prescribed by law.

13. Work is the glorious duty of every able-bodied citizen. All working people in state enterprises and in urban and rural economic collectives should perform their tasks with an attitude consonant with their status as masters of the country. The state promotes socialist labour emulation, and commends and rewards model and advanced workers. The state encourages citizens to take part in voluntary labour. The state provides necessary vocational training to citizens before they are employed.

14. Citizens of the People's Republic of China have the right to material assistance from the state and society when they are old, ill or disabled. The state develops the social insurance, social relief and medical and health services that are required to enable citizens to enjoy this right. The state and society ensure the livelihood of disabled members of the armed forces, provide pensions to the families of martyrs and give preferential treatment to the families of military personnel.

15. Citizens of the People's Republic of China have the freedom to engage in scientific research, literary and artistic creation and other cultural pursuits. The state encourages and assists creative endeavours conducive to the interests of the people made by citizens engaged in education, science, technology, literature, art and other cultural work.

16. 我们美利坚合众国的人民，为了组织一个更完善的联邦，树立正义，保障国内的安宁，建立共同的国防，增进全民福利和确保我们自己及我们后代能安享自由带来的幸福，乃为美利坚合众国制定和确立这一部宪法。

17. 凡年龄未满二十五岁，或取得合众国公民资格未满七年，或于某州当选而并非该州居民者，均不得任众议员。

18. 所有弹劾案，只有参议院有权审理。在开庭审理弹劾案时，参议员们均应宣誓或誓愿。如受审者为合众国总统，则应由最高法院首席大法官担任主席；在未得出席参议员的三分之二同意时，任何人不得被判有罪。

19. 弹劾案的判决，不得超过免职及取消其担任合众国政府任何有荣誉、有责任或有俸给的职位之资格；但被判处者仍须服从另据法律所作之控诉、审讯、判决及惩罚。

20. 参议员与众议员得因其服务而获报酬，报酬的多寡由法律定之，并由合众国国库支付。两院议员除犯叛国罪、重罪以及扰乱治安罪外，在出席各该院会议及往返各该院途中，有不受逮捕之特权；两院议员在议院内所发表之演说及辩论，在其他场合不受质询。参议员或众议员不得在其当选任期内担任合众国政府任何新添设的职位，或在其任期内支取因新职位而增添的俸给；在合众国政府供职的人，不得在其任职期间担任国会议员。

Unit Three

词汇与短语

1. practitioner
2. the Bar
3. interrogation
4. norm
5. barrister
6. solicitor
7. argue cases in court
8. the case at bar
9. learned treatises on law
10. permanent disbarment of lawyers
11. 控告，起诉
12. 陪审团
13. 法官席；法院；法庭
14. 委托人
15. 律师事务所
16. 聆讯
17. 专职法律顾问
18. 诉讼
19. 司法部长
20. 检察官

句子与段落

1. 对法律职业的管理主要是各州需要考虑的问题，每个州对其执业准入都有自己的要求。
2. 关于联邦法院执业的准入规则，各法院在这方面的规定不尽一致，但是一般来讲，那些有资格在州最高法院执业的人在办完一些小手续后便可能被获准在联邦法院执业。
3. 执业律师可以在其委托人的公司董事会担任董事，经商或者积极参与公众事务，这已十分普遍。
4. 美国律师的执业领域不仅包括出庭辩护，而且包括提供法律咨询及起草法律文书。
5. 政府部门中的律师业得到了相应的发展，20 名律师中的 2 名律师现在是联邦、州、县、镇政府的雇员，这里面不包括法官。
6. 在我们职业传统中，律师无疑最钟爱担任公共事务的领导。
7. 英国历史上形成的出庭律师和事务律师的区别没有在美国扎根，也就是说在美国，（律师）这一职业没有区分为一些律师是享有特殊的或排他的权利而出庭辩护的，另一些律师是专长于起草法律文书的。
8. 随着公司的成长、企业的复杂化，由政府规章所引起的大量问题使得这样的企业非常迫切地希望在他们雇用的人中有受过法律培训的员工，这些人同时对企业的特定问题与情况非常熟悉。
9. Trial lawyers represent their clients in litigation. Office practice lawyers prepare documents, advise business and settle estates.
10. Lawyers give advice not only on legal matters, but also on other matters such as business decisions and family affairs.
11. Lawyers should seek to avoid litigation by negotiating for compromise.
12. Office lawyers' advocacy for their clients is not directed at the judge or the jury.
13. When a lawyer is defending an unpopular cause, he must know that he is also defending the system of law.
14. Through the development of local, state, and national bar associations, the promulgation of ethics

codes, disciplinary rules and procedures, and the definition and tightening of the entrance requirements to law schools, the legal profession was able to control the supply of lawyers and limit access and entry into the profession.

15. Since the younger generation of lawyers will not ascend to positions of power for another decade or two, given the strongly gerontocratic character of professional governance, the divergence of interests, styles, and demography between rulers and ruled is likely to generate considerable tension".

16. The present influx of women into the profession has not necessarily resulted in women gaining access to "power positions" such as senior partnerships, tenured professorial positions, important judgeships, and upper level government jobs.

17. Out of 400 law firms invited, only two participated in the hearings. Some of the explanations offered for this lack of response included the inconvenience of timing of the hearings and the belief that since the firms employed few or no minorities, they had little to contribute.

18. To be a successful lawyer, a clever brain and a silver tongue are very important. Especially in the first half of the nineteenth century, the most famous lawyers were those known as great orators. By modern standards, they seem flowery and overblown. But in those days before radio and television appeared speeches of lawyers were more like a show, which were also the key to a lawyer's reputation. With his oratory, he could catch his potential clients.

Unit Four

词汇与短语

1. 行政行为；机关行为
2. 行政单位
3. （美）明确列举的权力
4. 标准程序
5. 正式（非正式）裁决
6. 行政法官
7. 日常行政活动
8. 成文法
9. 案例法
10. 合理依据
11. notice-and-comment procedure
12. judicial review
13. judicial department
14. delegation doctrine
15. administrative discretion
16. administrative procedural law
17. judicial action
18. congressional committee
19. adjudicatory hearing
20. substantive law

句子与段落

1. 目前，行政法学者注意到，不仅传统法治观点已经不足以应对现代国家在处理合法及合法性问题时的需要，而且行政法议题也直接且不可避免地涉及宪法和政治理论问题。
2. 对这些更广泛领域的挑战其反应是积极的，富有启发性的，尽管这些挑战也许还处于成长期，但是行政法已经展现出在其关注的重要问题和主题范围方面日益成熟的迹象。
3. 大量的司法审查是关于自然正义的本质和范围的，这实际上意味着听证的原则和反歧视原则。美国的正当程序原则，结合其他司法管辖区制定的其他类似原则，增加了程序公正的利益。

4. 问责的另一个途径是可以在特殊机关的创建过程中找到的，尤其是这样或者那样的特别法庭。特别法庭现在是行政领域中的一个熟知特色，其范围是相当大的。
5. 问责的方法则超越了参与的概念。其中一个方法来自于美国成立以来被广泛接受的"认真研究学说"。简而言之，"认真研究学说"要求行政法决定应当严格审查，以确保它们是最合理的使用。
6. In one sense, administrative law refers to the body of law legislative, administrative and adjudicative—by which the programmers of welfare and regulation are created and maintained. Law in this sense is simply the instrument by which the goals of welfare and order are achieved; it consists of the laws, practices and institutions through which legislative objectives are attained.
7. However, the study of particular areas of law and administration soon leads to wider concerns. Is each area of regulation distinct and discrete, or is it possible to identify general patterns into which each can be fitted? Are there values and principles which lie at the foundation of all areas of administration and which can be generalized into a coherent legal framework?
8. In that sense, administrative law is concerned with questions about how different administrative tasks should be carried out, about the suitability of different kinds of institutions for different tasks, and about the general nature of administration and regulation.
9. Indeed, the central question in the development of the subject, both in practice and in theory, has been how to extend the rule of law to provide a set of values appropriate to the modern state.
10. 有时法治思想和理念能够挑起社会变革，但是这种变革往往是有一定滞后性的。行政法恰恰适应这一总体格局。20世纪伟大的社会和经济转型最近才开始反映在行政法领域。福利国家的兴起以及社会和经济活动的监督意味着20世纪中后期政府的大幅度扩张。新型而广泛的立法程序蓬勃发展，新型行政主体不断涌现，人们的生活受到了更多的制约和规制。在本世纪（20世纪）即将结束的时候，行政法在探寻法律原则和价值观念、思想和制度的过程中将继续发展和成熟，最终必将在法治的框架内建立起"行政国家"。

Unit Five

词汇与短语

1. 约束力
2. 司法一致性
3. 口头辩论
4. 遵守先例
5. 自然法
6. 民法法系
7. 民法通则
8. 长官法
9. 《罗马民法大全》
10. 市民法
11. capacity for civil rights
12. civil conduct
13. civil juristicacts
14. case law
15. the Law of Nations
16. judge-made law
17. unwritten law
18. lex regia
19. criminal procedure
20. appellate court

句子与段落

1. 法典第三条界定了习惯的概念：习惯是长期的、不断重复的惯行，习惯通常被认为已经具有法律效力。但是，法典第三条明确规定，习惯不得废除立法或与立法相冲突。
2. 因此，路易斯安那州法官并不通过判决制定法律，法典赋予他们解释法律的职责，其解释必须尽可能地与立法机关制定、通过的法典内容一致或尽可能与公认的习惯相一致。
3. 民法的第二种含义指调整私人之间纠纷的法律规范的总称，区别于以侵犯公共利益的犯罪行为为规制对象的刑法。也就是说，此种意义上的民法，与刑法构成相对应的关系。
4. 民法（法系）是区别于普通法系的法律制度或法律体系，它起源于古罗马查士丁尼皇帝主持编纂的《罗马民法大全》。普通法系诉讼的结果取决于先前判例的裁决。
5. 例如，欧洲的法官在争议案件中，经常积极地介入对案件事实问题的认定，而很少使用陪审团，路易斯安那州的法官更像其普通法州的同行，是中立的、消极的事实发现者和裁决者，而把最终的裁决交给陪审团。
6. Louisiana judges, unlike their common-law counterparts, are not bound by judicial precedent. Common-law judges adhere to the doctrine of stare decisis, which mandates that the outcome of a lawsuit be governed by previous decisions in similar cases.
7. Since a jury award could be overturned on appeal, the plaintiff with a strong case may wish to file in a common-law state. On the other hand, if the plaintiff is uncertain of success at the trial level, the possibility of broader review on appeal may make Louisiana the better choice.
8. The Louisiana Civil Code, enacted in 1870 and still largely in force, clarifies and simplifies the earlier laws. The 1870 code is written in English, signaling a shift toward a partial Americanization of Louisiana's legal culture. To this day, Louisiana enjoys the distinction of being the only state in the United States to have a civil law system rather that a common-law system.
9. Civil law systems, which trace their roots to ancient Rome, are governed by doctrines developed and compiled by legal scholars. Legislators and administrators in civil law countries use these doctrines to fashion a code by which all legal controversies are decided.
10. One meaning of civil law refers to a legal system prevalent in Europe that is based on written codes. Civil law in this sense is contrasted with the common-law system used in England and most of the United States, which relies on prior case law to resolve disputes rather than written codes.
11. 在美国，"民法"（civil law）一词有两种含义。民法第一种含义指流行于欧洲的、建立在成文法典基础上的法律制度，这种意义上的民法区别于英国和美国大多数州所采用的普通法法律制度。普通法系根据判例法而不是成文法典解决法律纠纷。民法的第二种含义指调整私人之间纠纷的法律规范的总称，区别于以侵犯公共利益的犯罪行为为规制对象的刑法。也就是说，此种意义上的民法，与刑法构成相对应的关系。
12. Civil law systems differ from common-law systems in another important way: in a common-law jurisdiction, appellate courts, in most instances, may review only findings of law. However, civil law appellate courts may review findings of fact as well as findings of law. This allows Louisiana appellate courts to declare a jury's decisions erroneous, impose its own findings of fact, and

possibly even reduce a damage award. This is a significant consideration for a plaintiff who has a choice of whether to file suit in Louisiana or in another state (to bring suit in a particular state and the lawsuit).

Unit Six

词汇与短语

1. 死罪
2. 法定罪行；法定犯
3. 未成年犯罪
4. 未成年辩护
5. 可宽恕的杀人
6. 暴力性重罪
7. 严重过失
8. 有罪杀人
9. 犯罪要素（件）
10. 单行法规（律）
11. justifiable homicide
12. criminal code
13. death penalty
14. non-fatal robberies
15. adulterous conduct
16. criminal sanction
17. first degree murder
18. heavy penalty
19. statutory offense
20. pleas of guilty

句子与段落

1. 当这样一个法则，即对某个社会成员的危害就是对整个社会的危害取代了报私仇的习俗后，犯罪的概念才出现。这样，对过错者采取行动的权力，理所当然地属于作为人民的代表——政府。
2. 刑罚最早是由罚金、伤害身体的处罚（众所周知的肉体刑）或者死刑组成。肉体刑的最主要形式有鞭笞、烙印和断肢。到后来出现了另一种由社会决定的刑罚——流放。
3. 实际上，监禁在18世纪晚些时候已经开始了，但早期的监禁只是用于监禁悬而未决案件中的犯人或扣押游民。
4. 这个论断已经成为研究刑法的学者一直关心的问题，他们写了许多著作，论述刑罚使用中的两个基本问题："什么是刑罚的合法目的？"和"什么是适用刑罚的道德依据？"
5. 即使在现代社会中，当决定对同类采用强制性刑罚措施时，大部分刑罚措施中所具有的严厉性特点，也强调了社会所面临的对此争议的重要意义。
6. In the United States today, imprisonment, probation and parole are the primary forms of punishment for all but most petty crimes (where fines remain especially significant).
7. Capital punishment, as we shall see, has been abolished altogether in several states and is available in all others only for a single type of crime (homicide). Corporal punishment also has been abolished. Under certain circumstances, however, solitary confinement is still permitted, although not viewed as a dominant form of punishment.
8. Although the concept of a criminal offense is well established today, this was not always the case. The recognition of a class of illegal acts known as crimes was a product of a gradual historical development. Society made several crucial determinations in accepting the concept of crime, some

of which are still being reexamined today.

9. Originally, the acts we now view as crimes were torts; in other words, all wrongs were originally considered to be private wrongs. In the early history of the law, the state (in those days represented by the king) did not concern itself with punishing wrongs except those directed against the state, such as treason.

10. It is important that at this stage merely to be aware of the general nature of the punishments used in the past and today. The nature of the various punishments imposed clearly reflects our consistent treatment of crimes as serious, wrongful acts.

11. 就像在19世纪初，监狱是刑罚学的首要发展一样，缓刑和假释的应用也是20世纪初刑罚学的首要发展。缓刑和假释都包括将犯人放置于社会中监控起来，而不是投入监狱。在缓刑的情况下，罪犯不用先入狱，而是将其在受到监控情况下放置于社会。在假释的情况下，犯人必须先经过一段时间的监禁后，再放出来并监控起来。在这两个过程中，如果犯人违反监控的规定，将被监禁起来执行剩余的刑期。

12. At the time the American colonies broke away from England, over 200 different felonies were recognized under English law, and each of the felonies was subject to capital punishment. Many of the felonies of that period, though capital offenses, were offenses we today would classify a no more than misdemeanors. Eighty percent of the executions were for property offenses, and some involved only petty theft. Executions were public affairs, attended by huge crowds, and often carried out as cruelly as possible. As might be expected, considerable dissatisfaction existed, both in this country and in England, with the heavy use of capital punishment. Courts and judges managed in various ways to avoid the imposition of the death sentence.

Unit Seven

词汇与短语
1. 不当履行
2. 禁止反言
3. 不可抗力
4. 选择权合同
5. 实盘；不可撤销要约
6. 允诺的不容否定
7. 公平原则
8. 诚实信用原则
9. 合同标的
10. 合同义务
11. general terms and conditions
12. provisional order
13. purchase contract
14. purchase order
15. draft a contract
16. null and void
17. standard terms
18. fraud or coercion
19. obligee
20. obligor

句子与段落
1. 承诺是受要约人按照要约人规定的条件对要约人提出的要约做出同意的意思表示。

2. 有失公平的合同和基于误解签订的合同都是无效合同的范例。
3. 家庭性质的协议发生在同一家庭成员之间，而社会性质的协议发生在朋友或熟人之间。
4. 除生活必需品合同、受益性服务合同之外，未成年人签订的合同可能属于可撤销合同。
5. 一个人如果出于对文件性质的误解而在一份书面文件上签了名，那么他将有权抗辩，否认订立合同。
6. 要约最实质的特点是要约的制作者在没有更进一步的协议时，只要其条件被接受，必须受约束。
7. The most important rule with regard to an acceptance is that it must correspond with the offer.
8. The rule that there can be no acceptance by "silence" does not mean that it is always necessary to communicate words of acceptance to the offeror.
9. A third function of form is to protect the weaker party to the transaction by giving him a written statement of its terms.
10. The document would be "void for the purpose of creating a legal estate" but it would be a perfectly valid agreement for a lease which could be enforced by the tenant.
11. Customary terms are best regarded as incorporated on grounds of convenience, irrespective of the intention of the parties.
12. The parole evidence rule only applies to evidence of statements made before or at the time of the execution of the written contract.

Unit Eight

词汇与短语

1. 遗嘱信托
2. 生前信托
3. 通过诉讼才能占有的动产
4. 实际占有的动产
5. 无追索权
6. 所有人；业主
7. 租借；租赁协议
8. 租地权
9. 消极地役权
10. 不豁免财产
11. joint tenancy
12. life estate
13. future interest
14. time share interest
15. mortgagee
16. mortmain
17. residuum
18. privity of estate
19. security deposit
20. severalty

句子与段落

1. 根据地产持续期间的不同，地产可分为两大类：完全保有地产权和租赁地产。
2. 现代法律中财产有两个基本类型：不动产与动产。
3. 我们决定某物属附属物的主要意义是，此后它将被视为土地的一部分，除不动产的所有人，一般不允许把它移走。
4. 适合性原则常被用于涉及工厂、农场、制造厂或工业设施的场合。

5. 可期待的地产有两类，依当事人行为设立的，称残余权；依法律设定的，称复归权。
6. 终生地产是一项可终生保有但不能继承的地产权。
7. A reversion is a future estate created by operation of law to take effect.
8. A remainder is the remnant of the whole estate disposed of after a preceding part of the same has been given away.
9. A life estate normally terminates upon the death of the life tenant or of the person on whose life the estate depends.
10. A reversioner has neither actual nor constructive possession nor the right to either, but only an estate in expectancy.
11. The essence of a remainder is that it is to arise immediately on the determination of the particular estate by lapse of time or other determinant event, and not in abridgment of it.
12. At common law, the right of re-entry is not alienable, assignable, or devisable.

Unit Nine

词汇与短语
1. 标准产品商标
2. 防范性商标
3. 共同所有权
4. 可申请取得版权的
5. 版税
6. 禁令
7. 侵犯商标之诉
8. 三维标记
9. 对等原则（互惠原则）
10. 侵权；（对著作权、专利权、商标权等的）侵犯
11. antitrust laws
12. patent pooling
13. certification mark
14. a registered trademark
15. a goods trademark
16. a service trademark
17. a collective trademark
18. a certification trademark
19. a well-known trademark
20. a related companies trademark

句子与段落
1. 知识产权法是有关无形财产如版权、注册的外观设计、商标、专利的法律权利的法律。
2. 版权是一种权利，它禁止第三方未经授权对某人已在书中、音乐作品中、绘画中、电影胶片中表述的思想，以有形方式进行复制。
3. 商标可使货物和服务的提供人把他们的货物与其他的货物和服务区别开来。
4. 专利法给予发明人独占的、排他的权利去使用其发明或授权他人使用其发明。
5. 一个基本原则是：版权法不保护"思想"，只保护"思想的表现形式"。
6. 商标是特定产品的标记。
7. 注册时效一般为7年。
8. A mark used in respect of goods and services that is substantially identical with or deceptively similar to a registered trade mark will be an infringement.
9. The rationale of the patent system is that it provides protection for novel inventions.
10. The invention must involve an element of novelty and have some practical use.

11. A petty patent will be granted initially for a twelve month term.
12. The term of a standard patent is sixteen years from the date of lodgment of the date of the patent provided necessary renewal fees are paid.
13. Copyright may not be perpetuated by periodic redrafting of the design documents upon which a product is based.
14. A graphic work includes any painting, drawing, diagram, map, chart or plan, and any engraving, etching, lithograph, woodcut or similar work.

Unit Ten

词汇与短语

1. 伪证
2. 抵押
3. 遗嘱中有的
4. 亡故的
5. 胁迫
6. 受托人
7. 无效的
8. 取消
9. 继任人
10. 条款
11. means of production
12. illegitimate children
13. natural parents
14. statutory agent
15. partition the estate
16. cultural object
17. hereditary
18. legacy-support agreement
19. proximity of blood
20. statutory successor

句子与段落

1. A citizen may, by making a will, donate his personal property to the state or a collective, or bequeath it to persons other than the statutory successors.
2. The right to inheritance or legacy of a competent person shall be exercised on his behalf by his statutory agent. The right to inheritance or legacy of a person with limited capacity shall be exercised on his behalf by his statutory agent or by such person himself after obtaining the consent of his statutory agent.
3. Questions pertaining to succession should be dealt with through consultation by and among the successors in the spirit of mutual understanding and mutual accommodation, as well as of amity and unity. The time and mode for partitioning the estate and the shares shall be decided by the successors through consultation. If no agreement is reached through consultation, they may apply to a People's Mediation Committee for mediation or institute legal proceedings in a people's court.
4. Where there are obligations attached to testamentary succession or legacy, the successor or legatee shall perform them. Those who fail to perform the obligations without proper reasons may, upon request by a relevant organization or individual, entail nullification of his right to inheritance by a people's court.
5. Wills made by persons with no capacity or with limited capacity shall be void. Wills shall manifest the genuine intention of the testators; those made under duress or as a result of fraud shall be void. Forged wills shall be void. Where a will has been tampered with, the affected parts of it shall be void.
6. 此遗嘱代表了我处置全部财产的意愿，并且我愿意放弃我死亡时的财产处置权。

7. 委托管理的全部财产的保有、管理和分配都将根据规章执行，不能视为单独的依遗嘱建立的信托基金。
8. 我授权委托管理人按信托基金条款分割、管理、保有和分配信托基金，如上述条款同修订和重新表述的信托宣言一样适用同样范围和同等方式。修订和重新表述的信托宣言在此全文表述，但并没有规定可以进行任何的后续修改。
9. 本遗嘱所涉遗产之外的遗产税，除了构成基金财产的部分，应由上述财产获得者支付。
10. 他随后当着我们的面签名，当时我们所有人都在场。而我们应他的请求，当着他的面也签下我们的名字，作为遗嘱的见证人。

Unit Eleven

词汇与短语

1. 中国税制
2. 国际税收
3. 风险投资分析
4. 预算会计
5. 成本会计
6. 国际私法
7. 诉讼法学
8. 知识产权学
9. 刑法学
10. 律师实务
11. Arbitration Law
12. Financial Law
13. International Commercial Law
14. Basic Accountancy
15. Financial Accountancy
16. Taxation Management
17. Management Theory
18. Corporation Law
19. Contracts Law
20. Taxation Law

句子与段落

1. 专利权是政府对一项新发明授予的独立性权利，以给予发明鼓励和奖励。
2. 规定必须使用注册商标的商品，未经核准注册的，不得在市场销售。
3. 法院应原告申请签发禁令，制止被告侵犯版权。
4. 未经版权所有人的许可复制受版权法律保护的资料是违法的。
5. 条款规定双方当事人之间的任何争端应提交仲裁而非进行诉讼。
6. "Property ownership" means the owner's rights to lawfully possess, utilize, profit from and dispose of his property.
7. Property ownership shall not be obtained in violation of the law. Unless the law stipulates otherwise or the parties concerned have agreed on other arrangements, the ownership of property obtained by contract or by other lawful means shall be transferred simultaneously with the property itself.
8. Property may be owned jointly by two or more citizens or legal persons. There shall be two kinds of joint ownership, namely co-ownership by shares and common ownership. Each of the co-owners by shares shall enjoy the rights and assume the obligations respecting the joint property in proportion to his share. Each of the common owners shall enjoy the rights and assume the obligations respecting the joint property. Each co-owner by shares shall have the right to withdraw

his own share of the joint property or transfer its ownership. However, when he offers to sell his share, the other co-owners shall have a right of pre-emption if all other conditions are equal.

9. Enterprises under ownership by the whole people shall lawfully enjoy the rights of management over property that the state has authorized them to manage and operate, and the rights shall be protected by law.

10. The following income is exempted from, or reduced of, the income tax:
    1) profits earned by a foreign investor from an enterprise with foreign investment are exempted from the income tax;
    2) interest income from loans lent to the Chinese Government and state banks of China by international financial organizations is exempted from the income tax;
    3) interest income from loans lent to state banks of China by foreign banks at preferential interest rates is exempted from the income tax; and
    4) on the royalty received from the supply of proprietary technologies for scientific research, energy resources exploration, development of the communications industry, agricultural, forestry and animal husbandry production, and the development of important technologies, the income tax may be charged at the reduced rate of 10 percent upon approval by the competent department of the State Council for taxation, and if the technology supplied is advanced or the terms are preferential, the income tax may be exempted from.

    Where, apart from those provided by this Article, it is necessary to grant preferential treatment of income tax reduction or exemption for the profits, interests, rental, royalty and other income, the State Council shall make regulations thereon.

Unit Twelve

词汇与短语

1. 注册报告书
2. 董事会
3. 包销商
4. 资本结构
5. 修正案
6. 邮政汇票
7. 生效
8. 资产和负债情况
9. 损益计算书
10. 注册会计师
11. the State Council
12. issue shares
13. the Company Law
14. securities regulatory body
15. company bonds
16. application documents
17. legal duties
18. work procedures
19. stockholder
20. commission underwriting

句子与段落

1. Securities bought or sold by parties to securities transactions in accordance with the law must be issued and delivered in accordance with the law. Illegally issued securities should not be sold or bought.
2. Stocks, corporate bonds or other securities issued in accordance with the law, whose transfer term

us specified by law, may not be bought or sold within the limited term.
3. Stocks, corporate bonds or other securities approved for listing on stock markets in accordance with the law shall be quoted on stock exchanges.
4. Securities quoted on stock exchanges shall be openly transacted at the centralized competitive price. The principle of giving priority to price and time shall be practiced in applying the centralized competitive price to security transactions.
5. Types of securities bought or sold by parties to security transactions may be paper type or other types prescribed by the Securities Supervision and Administration Department of the State Council.
6. 如果任何会计师、工程师、鉴定人或那些职业赋予他权力可这样做的人因准备或核实注册报告书的一部分，或是因准备或核实与注册报告书有关的一份报告或评价书被列入名单，必须有该人的一个书面同意字据与注册报告书一起提交存档。
7. 如果任何这类人准备了或核实了一个与注册报告书有关的一份报告或评价书（而不是公开的、官方的文件或声明），并且已被采用，但此人却没有被列入名单之列，那么此人的书面同意字据也须和注册报告书一起提交存档。
8. 如果这样做不切实际或对提交注册报告书的人造成极大的麻烦，委员会将免除这种规定。委员会如果认为在公众利益或保护投资方面是必要的，或合适的话，可通过条例或规则要求注册报告书中包括其他内容，并附带其他文件。
9. 任何人直接或间接从事下述活动是非法的：在州际贸易中利用任何交通或通信手段或工具，或邮寄手段或工具；通过利用任何媒介或说明书或其他任何证券出售报价或买入报价，除非该证券的注册报告书已提交；或当该注册报告书被拒绝或撤销（在注册报告中生效日前），可根据第 8 节该注册报告书处于公开程序或审查之中时。
10. 有关非外国政府或非外国政府的政治机构发行证券的注册报告书须包括和附带表 A 所指定的内容和文件；有关外国政府及其政治机构发行证券的注册报告书须包括和附带表 B 所指定的内容和文件，但如果委员会发现要求提供这种内容和文件不适用于某一类证券，或是发现如果在注册报告书中不提供这种内容和文件，就已对投资者提供足够的保护时，委员会可通过条例或规则规定有关这类发行人或证券的注册报告书不必包括或附带这种内容或文件。

Unit Thirteen

词汇与短语

1. 外国人的准许入境
2. 内战
3. 附属国
4. 侵占
5. 人道主义干涉
6. 公海
7. 国际公约
8. 国际约定
9. 豁免
10. 流放国外
11. political offence
12. war crime
13. vassalage
14. vested rights
15. territorial waters
16. special missions
17. territorial principle
18. statehood
19. suspension of treaty
20. statutory interpretation

句子与段落

1. 每一国皆有义务在其国际关系上避免以侵害任何国家领土完整或政治独立之目的，或以与联合国宗旨不符之任何其他方式使用威胁或武力。
2. 此种使用威胁或武力构成违反国际法及联合国宪章之行为，永远不应用为解决国际争端之方法。
3. 每一国皆有义务避免使用威胁或武力以侵犯他国现有之国际疆界，或以此作为方法，解决国际争端，包括领土争端及国际疆界问题在内。
4. 国家领土不得作为违背宪章规定使用武力所造成之军事占领之对象。
5. 所有国家皆应一秉诚意从事谈判，俾早日缔结在有效国际管制下普遍及彻底裁军之世界条约，并努力采取缓和国际紧张局势及加强国际信心之适当措施。
6. 任何国家或国家集团均无权以任何理由直接或间接干涉任何其他国家之内政或外交事务。
7. 因此，武装干涉及对国家人格或其政治、经济及文化要素之一切其他形式之干预或试图威胁，均系违反国际法。
8. 任何国家均不得使用或鼓励使用经济、政治或任何他种措施强迫另一国家，以取得该国主权权利行使上之屈从，并自该国获取任何种类之利益。
9. 任何国家均不得组织、协助、煽动、资助、鼓动或允许目的在于以暴力推翻另一国政权之颠覆、恐怖或武装活动，或干预另一国之内政。
10. 每一缔约国家承担尽最大能力，单独采取步骤或经由国际援助和合作，特别是经济和技术方面的援助和合作，采取步骤，用一切适当方法，尤其包括用立法方法，逐渐达到本公约中所承认的权利的充分实现。
11. 本公约缔约各国承担保证：本公约所宣布的权利应予普遍行使，不得有如种族、肤色、性别、语言、宗教、政治或其他见解、国籍或社会出身、财产、出生或其他身份等任何区分。
12. 发展中国家在适当顾到人权及它们的民族经济的情况下，得决定它们对非本国国民的享受本公约中所承认的经济权利，给予什么程度的保证。
13. 由另一国交由一国支配的机关，若为行使支配该机关的国家权力要素而行事，其行为依国际法应视为支配该机关的国家的行为。
14. 国家机关或经授权行使政府权力要素的个人或实体，若以此种资格行事，即使逾越权限或违背指示，其行为仍应视为国际法所指的国家行为。
15. 如果一人或一群人实际上是在按照国家的指示或在其指挥或控制下行事，其行为应视为国际法所指的一国的行为。
16. 如果一人或一群人在正式当局不存在或缺席和在需要行使上述权力要素的情况下实际上正在行使政府权力要素，其行为应视为国际法所指的一国的行为。
17. 每一国均有义务依照宪章以共同及个别行动，促进对于人权与基本自由之普遍尊重与遵行。
18. 一个民族自由决定建立自主独立国家，与某一独立国家自由结合或合并，或采取任何其他政治地位，均属该民族实施自决权之方式。
19. 每一国均有义务避免对上文阐释本原则时所指之民族采取剥夺其自决、自由及独立权利之任何强制行动。
20. 此等民族在采取行动反对并抵抗此种强制行动以求行使其自决权时，有权依照宪章宗旨及原则请求并接受援助。

21.
- 准则一　人类有权在有尊严和福利的生活环境中，享有自由、平等和充足生活条件的基本权利，并且负有保护和改善这一代和将来世世代代的环境的庄严责任。在这方面，促进或维护种族隔离、种族分离与歧视、殖民主义和其他形式的压迫及外国统治的政策，应该受到谴责和必须消除。
- 准则二　为了这一代和将来世世代代的利益，地球上的自然资源，包括空气、水、土地、植物和动物，特别是自然生态中具有代表性的标本，必须通过周密计划或适当管理加以保护。
- 准则三　地球生产非常重要的再生资源的能力必须得到保持，而且在实际可能的情况下加以恢复或改善。
- 准则四　人类负有特殊的责任保护和妥善管理由于各种不利的因素而现在受到严重危害的野生生物后嗣及其产地。因此，在计划发展经济时必须注意保护自然界，其中包括野生生物。
- 准则五　在使用地球上不能再生的资源时，必须防范将来把它们耗尽的危险，并且必须确保整个人类能够分享从这样的使用中获得的好处。

22. To achieve this environmental goal will demand the acceptance of responsibility by citizens and communities and by enterprises and institutions at every level, all sharing equitably in common efforts. Individuals in all walks of life as well as organizations in many fields, by their values and the sum of their actions, will shape the world environment of the future. Local and national governments will bear the greatest burden for large-scale environmental policy and action within their jurisdictions. International cooperation is also needed in order to raise resources to support the developing countries in carrying out their responsibilities in this field. A growing class of environmental problems, because they are regional or global in extent or because they affect the common international realm, will require extensive cooperation among nations and action by international organizations in the common interest.

Unit Fourteen

词汇与短语

1. 律师
2. 外贸仲裁
3. 仲裁员
4. 仲裁条款
5. 仲裁法庭
6. 公证处
7. 外国人的豁免权
8. 涉外纠纷
9. 根据当事人的申请
10. 外国管辖权
11. participants in proceedings
12. the capacity for litigation rights
13. engage in debate
14. request conciliation
15. the matter and limits of authority entrusted
16. the judicial personnel
17. the law applied
18. an order issued orally
19. the intermediate people's courts
20. the time limit for applying for execution

句子与段落

1. 仲裁协议包括合同中订立的仲裁条款和以其他书面方式在纠纷发生前或者纠纷发生后达成的请求仲裁的协议。
2. 仲裁委员会独立于行政机关,与行政机关没有隶属关系。仲裁委员会之间也没有隶属关系。
3. 仲裁协议对仲裁事项或者仲裁委员会没有约定或者约定不明确的,当事人可以补充协议。
4. 仲裁协议独立存在,合同的变更、解除、终止或者无效,不影响仲裁协议的效力。
5. 仲裁庭有权确认合同的效力。
6. 申请人可以放弃或者变更仲裁请求。
7. 被申请人可以承认或者反驳仲裁请求,有权提出反请求。
8. 一方当事人因另一方当事人的行为或者其他原因,可能使裁决不能执行或者难以执行的,可以申请财产保全。
9. 当事人申请财产保全的,仲裁委员会应当将当事人的申请依照民事诉讼法的有关规定提交人民法院。
10. 当事人、法定代理人可以委托律师和其他代理人进行仲裁活动。
11. 仲裁庭可以由三名仲裁员或者一名仲裁员组成。由三名仲裁员组成的,设首席仲裁员。
12. 当事人没有在仲裁规则规定的期限内约定仲裁庭的组成方式或者选定仲裁员的,由仲裁委员会主任指定。
13. 仲裁庭组成后,仲裁委员会应当将仲裁庭的组成情况书面通知当事人。
14. 当事人约定由一名仲裁员成立仲裁庭的,应当由当事人共同选定或者共同委托仲裁委员会主任指定仲裁员。
15. 人民法院认定该裁决违背社会公共利益的,应当裁定撤销。
16. 当事人申请撤销裁决的,应当自收到裁决书之日起六个月内提出。
17. 当事人申请仲裁后,可以自行和解。达成和解协议的,可以请求仲裁庭根据和解协议作出裁决书,也可以撤回仲裁申请。
18. 当事人达成和解协议,撤回仲裁申请后反悔的,可以根据仲裁协议申请仲裁。
19. 仲裁庭在作出裁决前,可以先行调解。当事人自愿调解的,仲裁庭应当调解。调解不成的,应当及时作出裁决。
20. 调解达成协议的,仲裁庭应当制作调解书或者根据协议的结果制作裁决书。调解书与裁决书具有同等法律效力。
21. 第六十二条　当事人应当履行裁决。一方当事人不履行的,另一方当事人可以依照民事诉讼法的有关规定向人民法院申请执行。受申请的人民法院应当执行。

    第六十三条　被申请人提出证据证明裁决有民事诉讼法第二百一十七条第二款规定的情形之一的,经人民法院组成合议庭审查核实,裁定不予执行。

    第六十四条　一方当事人申请执行裁决,另一方当事人申请撤销裁决的,人民法院应当裁定中止执行。人民法院裁定撤销裁决的,应当裁定终结执行。撤销裁决的申请被裁定驳回的,人民法院应当裁定恢复执行。
22. In any of the following circumstances, an arbitrator must withdraw from the arbitration, and the parties shall have the right to apply for his withdrawal if he:

    1. is a party or a close relative of a party or of a party's representative;

2. is related in the case;
3. has some other relationship with a party to the case or with a party's agent which could possibly affect the impartiality of the arbitration;
4. meets a party or his agent in private, accepts an invitation for dinner by a party or his representative or accepts gifts presented by any of them.

Unit Fifteen

单词与短语
1. 提前偿还
2. 贸易政策审议机制
3. 稳健的货币政策
4. 竞争机制
5. 相对优势
6. 公平竞争
7. 经济回报
8. 人均国内生产总值
9. 自主知识产权
10. 地方保护主义
11. the integration of global economy
12. venture capital
13. the national economy
14. state-owned enterprise
15. lawful business operations
16. Sino-foreign joint ventures
17. foreign direct investment
18. outward-looking economy
19. market economy
20. Guangzhou Fair

句子与段落
1. 进出口禁止和限制以及影响进出口的许可程序要求只能由国家主管机关或由国家主管机关授权的地方各级主管机关实行和执行。
2. 中国应允许每一部门交易的货物和服务的价格由市场力量决定，且应取消对此类货物和服务的多重定价做法。
3. 在进行边境税的调整方面，对于外国个人、企业和外商投资企业，自加入时起应被给予不低于给予其他个人和企业的待遇。
4. 在迟延会造成难以补救损害的紧急情况下，受影响的 WTO 成员可根据一项有关进口产品已经造成或威胁造成市场扰乱的初步认定，采取临时保障措施。
5. 中国应在官方刊物上公布实行国家定价的货物和服务的清单及其变更情况。
6. 部长会议应当包括所有成员的代表，它应至少每 2 年召开一次会议。
7. 在部长会议休会期间，总理事会应当执行部长会议的各项职能。
8. 总理事会应在适当时间召开会议，以行使争端解决谅解所规定的争端解决机构的职责。
9. 争端解决机构应有自己的主席，并建立它认为必要的程序规则以行使其职责。
10. 总理事会应在适当时间召开会议，以行使贸易政策审议机制所规定的贸易政策审议机构的职责。
11. 贸易政策审议机构应有自己的主席，并建立它认为必要的程序规则以行使其职责。
12. 总理事会应就与世贸组织职责有关的各政府间组织的有效合作作出适当安排。
13. 总干事应任命秘书处的职员，并根据部长会议通过的规则确定他们的责任和任职条件。
14. 理事人采用的财务规则和年度预算应当由世贸组织过半数以上的成员以 2/3 的多数表决通过。

15. 世贸组织具有法人资格，各成员应赋予世贸组织享有执行其职责所需要的法律资格。
16. 世贸组织各成员赋予世贸组织为履行其职责所需要的特权和豁免。
17. 世贸组织各成员应同样给予世贸组织官员和各成员代表在其独立行使世贸组织有关职责时必要的特权和豁免权。
18. 世贸组织应当继续遵循《1947年关贸总协定》奉行的由一致意见作出决定的实践。
19. 在部长会议和总理事会上，世贸组织的每一成员有一票投票权。
20. 在例外情况下，部长会议可以决定豁免某成员方根据本协议和其他多边贸易协议所承担的某项义务。
21. 市场扰乱应在下列情况下存在：一项产品的进口快速增长，无论是绝对增长还是相对增长，从而构成对生产同类产品或直接竞争产品的国内产业造成实质损害或实质损害威胁的一个重要原因。在认定是否存在市场扰乱时，受影响的WTO成员应考虑客观因素，包括进口量、进口产品对同类产品或直接竞争产品价格的影响以及此类进口产品对生产同类产品或直接竞争产品的国内产业的影响。
22. China undertakes that only those laws, regulations and other measures pertaining to or affecting trade in goods, services, TRIPS or the control of foreign exchange that are published and readily available to other WTO Members, individuals and enterprises, shall be enforced. In addition, China shall make available to WTO Members, upon request, all laws, regulations and other measures pertaining to or affecting trade in goods, services, TRIPS or the control of foreign exchange before such measures are implemented or enforced. In emergency situations, laws, regulations and other measures shall be made available at the latest when they are implemented or enforced.

References
参考文献

[1] 陈忠诚. 法律英语阅读. 综合法律. 北京：法律出版社，2003.
[2] 陈忠诚. 法律与英语阅读. 民法. 北京：法律出版社，2003.
[3] 董梅，赵玉闪，陈劲帆. 法律英语中模糊词语及其翻译. 出国与就业（就业版），2011（10）.
[4] 董世忠，赵建. 法律英语. 上海：复旦大学出版社，1997.
[5] 董晓波. 法律文本翻译. 北京：对外经济贸易大学出版社，2011.
[6] 董晓波. 商务英语翻译. 北京：对外经济贸易大学出版社，2011.
[7] 董晓波. 法律专业英语教程：美国法律与法律制度. 北京：北京交通大学出版社，2011.
[8] 董晓波. 法律英语综合教程. 上海：复旦大学出版社，2009.
[9] 郭义贵. 法律英语. 北京：北京大学出版社，2004.
[10] 浩瀚. 法律英语900句. 北京：中国书籍出版社，2001.
[11] 何家弘. 法律英语世界：第1辑. 北京：法律出版社，1998.
[12] 何家弘. 法律英语. 2版. 北京：法律出版社，2004.
[13] 贺筠. 论法律专业术语的特殊性及其英译技巧. 西南交通大学学报（社会科学版），2007（3）.
[14] 黄进，宋连斌，徐前权. 仲裁法学. 北京：中国政法大学出版社，1997.
[15] 蒋浩. 中国加入世界贸易组织法律文件. 北京：法律出版社，2001.
[16] 李斐南，黄瑶. 现代法律英语. 广州：中山大学出版社，1997.
[17] 李斐南. 法律英语实务：中外法律文书编译. 广州：中山大学出版社，2005.
[18] 李克武. 合同法要论. 湖北：华中师范大学出版社，2006.
[19] 李丽. 法律英语词汇的特点及其翻译. 中国科技翻译，2005，18（3）.
[20] 梁慧星，龙翼飞，陈华彬. 中国财产法. 北京：法律出版社，1998.
[21] 刘海东，苏湘辉. 遗产继承法律通. 北京：法律出版社，2005.
[22] 刘艺工，屈文生. 法律英语. 北京：机械工业出版社，2003.
[23] 刘颖，吕国民. 国际法资料选编：中英文对照. 北京：中信出版社，2004.
[24] 陆效龙. 世界贸易组织文件汇编：多变贸易谈判乌拉圭回合各项成果的最终文件. 北京：中国经济出版社，1995.
[25] 马雯. 被动语态在法律英语中的运用及翻译. 安庆师范学院学报，2008（4）.
[26] 孙希光. 世界贸易：走向未来的贸易. 北京：对外经贸出版社，1996.
[27] 陶博，龚柏华. 法律英语：中英双语法律文书制作. 上海：复旦大学出版社，2004.

[28] 王晨. 法律专业英语. 哈尔滨：哈尔滨工业大学出版社，2010.
[29] 王承继. 商法. 上海：上海人民出版社，2002.
[30] 王江雨. 美国统一商法典信用证篇. 北京：中国法制出版社，2000.
[31] 王金玲. 英汉对照：法律英语导读：上下册. 北京：西苑出版社，1999.
[32] 魏焕华，洪小梅. 汉英汉英民事诉讼分类法律词语三用手册. 北京：商务印书馆，1999.
[33] 吴玲娣. 新编法律英语术语. 北京：法律出版社，2000.
[34] 杨丹. 论汉语法律文献中主题句的英译. 甘肃林业职业技术学院学报，2006（8）.
[35] 杨俊峰. 法律英语综合教程. 北京：清华大学出版社，2005.
[36] 姚骏华. 美国证券法. 北京：中国民主法制出版社，2006.
[37] 叶琳. 证券法教程. 北京：法律出版社，2005.
[38] 叶兴国. 世界贸易组织术语汇编. 上海：上海外语教育出版社，2001.
[39] 余冰清. 中华人民共和国仲裁法：英汉对照. 北京：外文出版社，2000.
[40] 张平华，刘耀东. 继承法原理. 北京：中国法制出版社，2009.
[41] 赵惠. 英语贸易合同汉译技巧的探讨. 考试周刊，2007（44）.
[42] 赵雁丽. 法律英语教程：上册. 西安：西安交通大学出版社，2003.
[43] 周建明. 财产的继承与分割. 南京：南京出版社，2001.
[44] 周明哲. 中英文对照法律类编. 北京：中国法制出版社，2002.
[45] 中华人民共和国国家知识产权局. 中华人民共和国知识产权法律法规选编. 北京：知识产权出版局，2003.
[46] 中华人民共和国证券法. 北京：外文出版社，2011.
[47] 中华人民共和国民法通则：英汉对照. 北京：外文出版社，1999.
[48] 迈克尔·杰克逊遗嘱全文曝光：中英文对照版［EB/OL］. http://ent.ifeng.com/special/stay/maikeerjiekexun/xinwen/200907/0702_7094_1230619.shtml.
[49] 中华人民共和国继承法中英对照［EB/OL］. http://wenku.baidu.com/view/c7cfcde8b8f67c1cfad6b820.html.
[50] http://baike.baidu.com/view/16428.html.
[51] http://baike.baidu.com/view/27332.html.
[52] http://baike.baidu.com/view/3929.htm.
[53] http://zh.wikipedia.org/wiki/%E5%AE%AA%E6%B3%95.
[54] http://zh.wikipedia.org/wiki/%E7%9F%A5%E8%AF%86%E4%BA%A7%E6%9D%83.
[55] http://lvshi.sz.bendibao.com/news/201078/220135_3.shtml.